7⁰⁰

FELIX MENDELSSOHN
AND HIS TIMES

Felix Mendelssohn Bartholdy

FELIX MEN
AND HIS

FELIX MENDELSSOHN
AND HIS TIMES

HEINRICH EDUARD JACOB

TRANSLATED FROM THE GERMAN BY
RICHARD AND CLARA WINSTON

PRENTICE-HALL, INC.

ENGLEWOOD CLIFFS, N. J.

Prentice-Hall International, Inc.
(London, Tokyo, Sydney, Paris)

Prentice-Hall of Canada, Ltd.

Prentice-Hall de Mexico, S. A.

CONTENTS

ILLUSTRATIONS

PREFACE

His name was Felix—and giving him this name was perhaps the only way his parents ever wronged him. Had they known he was to be a creative person, they would never have dared to call him "Felix"— "happy". Up to the time of Mendelssohn no genius could ever have pretended to such a name. Was Beethoven happy, when the world turned dumb as far as he was concerned, when the gods avenged themselves upon him by taking away his hearing? Was Schumann happy, who on the contrary heard too much, who fled the clamour of his inner voices until he could escape them no longer, and threw himself into the Rhine? Schubert, unknown and heavily burdened—was he happy? Or was Mozart, who died in poverty at the age of thirty-five? Hugo Wolf, who fell a prey to madness? Weber, whose life was exhausted by consumption before he reached forty? Chopin, who also died young of the same disease?

None of these great musicians was a happy man. Only one was: Mendelssohn. His life was sheltered, carefully guarded. He enjoyed fame, the whirl and flattery of artistic tours of a kind normally reserved for virtuosi, not composers. Other composers had to beg their way back and forth to Paris and London. Not he. For him ships were waiting, railroad trains, letters of recommendation. He had money that he had not had to earn, money that was his as the heir of a family fortune. Here was a genius who was nevertheless a rich man. Of course he knew life's small vexations as we all know them. He had his struggles with orchestras and impresarios. There was the dissatisfaction with himself that affects all men of great gifts. There was the fatigue of talent. But he was not oppressed by the terrible burdens that other composers had to bear, the cruel daily struggle for food and shelter. In this respect he was blessed; from boyhood on he could devote himself entirely to his art. And even his death was kind and smiling, although it came too early. At the age of thirty-eight, scarcely ravaged by life, almost without visible signs of illness, he passed away, to be mourned by an amazed world.

Felix, then? *Felicissimus!* He did not even have to breast that misunderstanding, that failure to win recognition, which embittered the lives of other composers. When Chopin was asked, in Paris, about Robert Schumann's music, he had the effrontery to say: "That is no music."

Schumann, in turn, did not understand Wagner. And when Johannes Brahms heard that people were playing "that charlatan Liszt" at "decent concerts", he used bad language. But all of these, however much they failed to recognize the worth of their contemporaries, revered Mendelssohn. Envy and incomprehension were not to be *his* lot.

But that was so only during his lifetime. For the posthumous fate of this German composer has been quite the reverse of that of any other genius. None of the other masters, despite their struggles, would have bartered their sufferings for such a fate. Not that Felix Mendelssohn was to endure that "oblivion" which has so often been the destiny of great artists. Heinrich Schütz and the sons of Bach are forgotten, and we do not protest. Or if we do, our protest is directed against Fashion, which looks on with indifference while the music of some master dies from neglect. But in Mendelssohn's case, neglect was not a fruit of time and change. A political dictatorship of racial fanatics struck his life's work from the tablets of German art.

That happened in 1933—when so many other things happened. And yet it was not so sudden, not so astonishing; ugly whispers, nasty gossip, had been directed against his work and his name for many decades before. Shots had been fired at him out of the darkness. The greatness of this composer did not fit into the scheme of certain ideologues. If only he had been more of a minor figure. The racialists found poets, painters, sculptors, even other musicians, easier to discredit than Mendelssohn whose work and influence had struck root so deeply in the German people's spirit. It was not easy to persuade the Germans, when they gathered in their leisure hours, that they must no longer sing:

> *Wer hat dich, du schöner Wald,*
> *aufgebaut so hoch da droben?*
> *Wohl den Meister will ich loben*
> *so lang noch mein 'Stimm' erschallt.*
> (Lofty woods, who dared to raise you
> High upon the mountain's side?
> While my strength and voice abide,
> Master Builder, I shall praise you.)

For a full hundred years the German people had found their sorrows, their joys, their landscape and their lyric impulse reflected in Mendelssohn's songs: "Es ist bestimmt in Gottes Rat, dass man vom Liebsten, was man hat, muss scheiden." "O Täler weit, o Höhen, o schöner grüner Wald, du meiner Lust und Wehen andächt'ger Aufenthalt..." These were the matins of the German soul, these were the songs the people

loved. "Wem Gott will rechte Gunst erweisen . . ." "Durch schwankende
Wipfel schiesst goldner Strahl . . ." "Ein Schifflein ziehet leise . . ." "Es
fiel ein Reif in der Frühlingsnacht . . ." Was the singing of such songs to
be illegal? But there was a way to save the situation; all that was needed
was deception; the songs could stand, if the name of the composer were
suppressed. That was easy to do—such things are easy in a dictatorship.
And the masses accepted the trick as they accepted so much else. As long
as the dictatorship did not demand vast sacrifices of lives and physical
comforts, they were not going to get excited over what happened to art
and artists. Only a few persons shook their heads when the statue of
Mendelssohn which stood in front of the Gewandhaus in Leipzig was
knocked off its pediment.

What was a Jewish composer?

And then the reign of terror collapsed. Old values reappeared. Was
the work of Mendelssohn among them? The master's 150th birthday
answered that question affirmatively. During the dark years of the dictatorship books and musical scores bearing the name of Felix Mendelssohn
were systematically wiped out. They were not so soon made available—
the barbarians had been only too thorough in their work, and reprinting
is a slow and costly affair. But in the concert hall and over the radio it did
prove possible to restore a great composer to his nation. To that extent,
Mendelssohn is no longer under shrouds. This book aims to be a part of
the process of rehabilitation; it aims to reinstate Mendelssohn in the place
where he belongs—in the middle of the nineteenth century, and standing
between Schumann and Brahms, who would be inconceivable without
him.

It is necessary to say a few words about the technical intentions of this
book. As the author has already shown in two earlier books on Haydn
and Mozart, it is impossible—and perhaps ridiculous—to present the life
and works of a great composer separately. For both together constitute
the man. Life and works merge. To force each into separate sections
would be like writing a book on Napoleon in two parts: "His private
life" and "His campaigns". Furthermore, the character of the times is
absolutely germane to the life of every great man. The times include his
great contemporaries; the times include the past and foreshadow the
future. Mozart is more than the rococo—but at the same time we cannot
conceive him apart from the limits, customs and oddities of that era.
Mendelssohn *is* "Biedermeier"—but a Biedermeier which has cast off
any trace of provincialism. Mendelssohn is even, in a sense, a child of the
English victory at Waterloo; a child of Early Victorianism.

Then again, he who would write on musical matters must be a musician. But every musical example and every technical analysis must—if it is to come to life—be illuminated in terms of its psychological causation. Why did the master write it that way and not some other way? Unless musical examples are treated in this manner, they become foreign bodies within a biography.

And finally, this book is no *Vita* of Mendelssohn—at least not in the sense that the master's life and work are narrated in their chronological order. In the case of this artist who was "old in childhood and young in maturity" it seemed advisable to violate chronology upon occasion, to leap backward and forward, in order to do justice to his inner nature.

Not every composer lends himself to such a procedure. But for Felix Mendelssohn, who was "complete" in almost every one of his phases—never merely old or young—we think that it is the right approach.

HEINRICH EDUARD JACOB

New York and Zurich, 1958

BOOK ONE

PREPARATION

With the tremendous tumult that he bears within himself he begins to reach out symbolically for the tremendous tumult of the outer world.

—HUGO VON HOFMANNSTHAL

FOUR CHORDS AND A SUMMER NIGHT

1826. Berlin was a great city, a populous but constricted city. "A city without lungs", an art historian called it.[1] You did not find open country until you had gone some distance outside the gates. The houses had no gardens in which men, women and children could take their ease after the day's duties were done.

The houses crowded one upon the other. Their tenants were army officers, officials of the growing Prussian bureaucracy, small tradesmen. Berlin had none of those ancient cathedrals with wide open squares before them such as the towns of West and South Germany boasted.[2] It lacked the bridges which gave character to Paris—for the Spree was no Seine—and fed its populace without benefit of the big colourful markets of Paris, where summer vegetables were heaped artistically. No, that was not the style of Berlin. Rather, one might say that there was a Dutch quality to many parts of Berlin, especially when a faint smell of fish wafted into the streets from the sluggish canals. . . . In Amsterdam, though, people could go for a walk by the water, for the quays along the *grachten* were wide. In Berlin the houses came down too close to the water's edge.[3] The buildings were small and seemed to gasp for air—especially on summer nights, when the heat was oppressive.

Only in a few places did the unbroken line of buildings yield to openness. Number 3 Leipziger Strasse was surrounded by a magnificent park-like garden which in summer was a paradise of cool green. It belonged to Abraham Mendelssohn, banker and Berlin alderman. He had bought the property from the von der Reck family and transformed the rather neglected mansion, really a small palace, into one of the most delightful dwellings in the city.[4] The house was hard to heat in winter. But in summer the eighteenth-century residence with its big rooms, harmonious lines, graceful wings, and attached orangery (big enough for theatrical performances and concerts for hundreds of guests), became a dream-like, airy place. The family who lived in such surroundings was greatly to be envied, though they did not keep this beauty wholly for themselves. A

---

[1] K. Scheffler: *Berlin, ein Stadtschicksal*. Berlin, 1910.
[2] Wilhelm Hausenstein: *Europäische Hauptstädte*. Munich, 1954.
[3] G. Hasenberger: *Holländisch-Berlin*. Berlin, 1859
[4] H. Mackowsky: *Häuser und Menschen im alten Berlin*. Berlin, 1923.

special apartment was reserved for Ludwig Robert, brother of that extra-ordinary woman Rahel Levin, and he would come to spend some weeks there every summer—a beloved guest. And Alexander von Humboldt had set up a laboratory and observatory in the garden. He was busy much of the time making magnetic observations.[5]

On 25th August 1826 the Mendelssohns were entertaining an old friend, Johann Franz Encke, director of the Berlin Observatory. The family had listened to his learned discourses all through dinner. He was currently occupied with studies of the temperature of space and of stars.[6] Young Felix Mendelssohn, who ordinarily was wholly absorbed in music, had followed his talk with deepest interest. Afterwards Felix had gone into the garden—how red and twinkling the stars were on this summer night!—and had sat down at the table where he did his composing.

August. The blossoms of the lofty lilac hedges had faded months ago. But other scents had taken their place: from the linden-trees and the wild grapes, and from the clematis that wreathed the walls of the house. What a mixture! Perfumes could dance and whirl when they were stirred by a night wind. A faint breeze and then another had just sported with the fragrances of the flowers. Now a third and a fourth ripple of wind followed the other two.

Young Mendelssohn raised his head and listened. Four breezes, four strange chords. He had written them weeks ago, but had never been entirely sure of them.

He would never have set them down if Fanny, his elder sister—who was a first-rate musician herself—had not approved that idiosyncratic and bold succession of chords. They had also been approved by Adolf Bern-hard Marx, who was his teacher and, though ten years older than Felix, also a friend. Marx had said: "A new music begins here."[7]

What were all those flickering lights out there in the garden? Those

[5] H. Klencke: *Alexander von Humboldts Reisen, Leben und Wissen.* Leipzig, 1882.

[6] C. Bruhns: *Johann Franz Encke, sein Leben und Wirken.* Leipzig, 1869.

[7] L. Leven: *Mendelssohn als Lyriker.* Krefeld, 1927.

were fire-flies darting at one another, circling around one another. Suddenly one dashed away. But already the others had darted after it and caught it again within their circles of light.[8] And the boy, sitting at his table, set these strange effects of light to music, captured them in delicate, extraordinarily swift rhythms:

Today the boy, who normally was never satisfied with his work, was convinced that these bars were right. And many years later he confessed to an English friend, the composer William Sterndale Bennett: "That night I encountered Shakespeare in the garden!"[9]

The work he was finishing that night was, of course, the overture to *A Midsummer Night's Dream*—and remarkably graphic music it was. If it had not been graphic it would not have been Shakespearian. For Shakespeare's language was never "mood"; it had the quality of magic realism, an exactitude suffused in allegoric grandeur. Shakespeare was "the most perfect poet who ever lived". That had been well dinned into Felix and his two sisters by his excellent tutor, Karl Wilhelm Ludwig Heyse. (Herr Heyse himself was no poet, but his son, Paul Heyse, was destined to be one.) The great English poet's plays were read in German in the Mendelssohn household.[10] For Fanny, Felix and Rebecca were not so very brilliant in their English lessons. But the Mendelssohn family also had a splendid reason for reading Shakespeare in German. They took an almost proprietary pride in the translations. Who, after all, had made the plays accessible to the Germans? Who but August Wilhelm Schlegel, the great man who was the brother-in-law of Aunt Dorothea of Vienna as well as Friedrich Schlegel's brother.[11] True, there was a certain amount of bad blood among the Schlegels; some of them had been hardly on speaking terms

[8] G. Barre: *Mendelssohns Naturgefühl*. Berlin, 1882.

[9] R. Lüders-Gross: *Shakespeare und seine Komponisten*. Hamburg, no date.

[10] P. Heyse: *Jugenderinnerungen und Bekenntnisse*. Berlin, 1900.

[11] M. Susman: *Frauen der Romantik*. Jena, 1929.

with one another for years. But nevertheless the Mendelssohn family was proud of A. W. Schlegel's translation. Herder, Eschenburg and many others had tried to translate Shakespeare. But how lame and wooden their versions were. August Wilhelm Schlegel alone had contrived to present a Shakespeare that the Romantic age could understand. He had made Shakespeare into a contemporary.

And what industry! Felix stood up, strolled about a bit, had a few spoons of the sherbet, and sat down again, deeply agitated. He vowed to be as industrious as August Wilhelm Schlegel, who had tried twelve different translations of such a simple passage as, "Thy life hath had some snatch of honour in it":

> *Dein Leben hat von Ehrgefühl gezeugt.*
> *Dein Leben zeugte stets von Ehrgefühl.*
> *Dein Leben hat gezeigt, du hältst auf Ehre.*

Twelve versions, before he was satisfied.[12] Felix Mendelssohn resolved to imitate such perfectionism, to change and delete again and again, until his measures were absolutely right. An artist must not let himself cut corners.

Twelve times? No, a passage must be re-examined twenty-four times. There was that splendid E major theme which still needed tightening:

And first, once again, there must come those four breezes in mystifying iteration: the two flutes in E, the B flat clarinets; in the third measure two bassoons in A; in the fourth measure all the winds together, including oboes and horns pianissimo, fading away and never quite fading out, in a long-drawn-out fermata....

Peals of laughter from the adjoining wing. Rebecca and Fanny were entertaining their own set of friends. A few boys' voices were among the group. It would be terrible if they should come out to say good-bye, and disturb him at this moment. He would have to blow out the light and steal away to his room. Anything but exchange of greetings now. It was

[12] B. von Brentano: *August Wilhelm Schlegel*. Stuttgart, 1944.

not that Felix did not care for girls. Only he disliked the way they dominated the lives of boys; he shied away from the dull, aching longings they brought in their train. Very soon now Berlin University, and Hegel's lectures there, would be of far more moment to him than women, those thieves of time.

Because love was something he had not yet experienced, and was still indifferent to, there were whole sections in *A Midsummer Night's Dream* which he did not understand. Puck and Glow-worm appealed to him. But not the pangs and infidelities of the bewitched couples. It would have taken a Mozart to compose music for all that: the misery of love, the wrath of love, the humiliation of love. Mozart had wept for women; he had dedicated his *Così fan tutte*, to the beloved and hated fair sex, and had used this opera of cynical infidelity to make mock of those who mocked him.[13] Mendelssohn would never weep over women. He would never mock women either, and therefore would also never descend to hell in crashing chords like Mozart's Don Giovanni.

Tonight he was working out the scherzo section of his overture to *A Midsummer Night's Dream*. A scherzo! His friend A. B. Marx had recently warned him against making his music too "scurrying". The thing to bear in mind, in music for a play, was to show character, Marx had said.[14] Wasn't a scherzo exactly the way to do it? To use music for humorous effects—that was the trick! Often, in walking about Berlin, he would set the names of people and firms to music, and laugh himself sick.[15] He would hum the names under his breath. Even such admirable people as his teacher, A. B. Marx, were wonderful material for musical jokes. Marx always wore his trousers too short, and his shoes were of a size that people in Berlin called "tugboats". Adolf Bernhard Marx: what a name! He knew just how to render that in music: he would use heavy, flat-footed trochees in descending fourths and fifths, followed by the second-chord, G-A. But that didn't sound like Marx, rather like Mrx. The clank would be all right.

Weren't most people funny? Actually, they all were funny. Old Haydn, whom people turned up their noses at nowadays, had known that. What poor judgment people had, incidentally. Haydn had seen human beings as comic animals, and had given to animals human comicality.[16] All that

[13] H. E. Jacob: *Mozart oder Geist, Musik und Schicksal*. Frankfurt am Main, 1956.

[14] A. B. Marx. *Erinnerungen aus meinem Leben*. Berlin, 1865.

[15] F. Schulz: *Der Tonwitz*. Leipzig, no date.

[16] H. E. Jacob: *Joseph Haydn, His Art, Times and Glory*. New York, 1950.

roaring and tramping, for instance, and the marvellous animal passages in *The Creation....* thinking of this, the young composer wrote the donkey's cry into his Scherzo: Heehaw, heehaw. He wrote it twice, where before he had had it only once:

Not only the artisans whom Shakespeare had used for comic characters. Berlin artisans were funny too, with their cheeky manner.[17] He liked them, though, and he loved Berlin better than any other city. He loved living here, and having this big house and garden.

If artisans were funny, how much funnier were those who called themselves their betters. Heinrich Heine, for example, so self-important with his poems and "North Sea Sketches". He would stand in a snobbish Byronesque pose waiting for a compliment, and if no one made him any, he would sulk. One evening Heine had been at the house and people started talking about Jean Paul. "What does Jean Paul amount to? He's never seen the sea," Heine remarked with elaborate casualness. But Fanny, with her tart tongue, put him in his place: "Of course, he doesn't have an uncle to pay travelling expenses for him."[18]

The more important people were, the more they tended to slip into absurdity. For example, a frequent guest of his father's, Rahel von Varnhagen, formerly Rahel Levin. An unattractive, almost ugly woman, but people hung on her every word. But the funniest thing was the way her own husband worshipped her. Whenever people burst into laughter or cries of assent after Rahel had spoken, Varnhagen would run over and ask: "What did she say?" Felix did not quite like a certain air of pretentiousness that surrounded the couple. He really could not stand intellectual women; he didn't like the way they seemed always to be sitting on a pedestal and delivering themselves of oracles. In days to come he would feel the same distaste for that famous woman Bettina von Arnim, although he would always respect her.[19] Varnhagen, though, was a good fellow, basically. While other tutors looked out for the chance to make good marriages (Professor Heyse would make such a marriage, too), this

[17] P. Dahlke: *Handwerkerhumor und Vormärz.* Berlin, 1912.
[18] E. Devrient: *Meine Erinnerungen an Felix Mendelssohn Bartholdy.* Leipzig, 1872.
[19] Ibid.

impoverished young man had taken a poor Jewess to wife. And certainly Rahel was not beautiful.[20]

On second thoughts, people were not funny at all. As the young man considered the matter, his inner scales tipped in the opposite direction. "The very fact of being human makes men worth our reverence," Moses Mendelssohn, his wonderful grandfather, had said.[21] Then were all men worthy of reverence? Certainly it was difficult to feel that all the time, but Goethe and Lessing had both said the same. Reverence! Reverence for father and mother. That came easily. He felt he should kneel down every day and thank God for such parents. For his father upon whom God had showered such success. For his musical mother who had learned of the *Well-tempered Clavier* from one of the sons of Bach.[22]

Reverence. Reverence for music, too. But in North Germany there was little in that line which could command Felix Mendelssohn's respect, not to speak of reverence. And in Paris, where he had already been, the situation was no better, would not be any better—even though his father might think differently. His father never could entirely throw off his worship for French taste. What an idea, to have asked Cherubini: "Do you think my son is talented?" And then to listen to shallow compliments, coupled with a few crude allusions to the wealth of the Mendelssohns.[23]

Felix could not stand the Parisians. But it would be different if he lived in Vienna and could see the gods walking the streets, gods whom most people incomprehensibly took for ordinary men. Mozart and Haydn were dead, of course—but Beethoven, the Thunderer, still lived. As the boy's mind lingered on this, he did not know that today, as he was writing Finis under the score of his overture, Beethoven had little more than a year to live. He would never see a line of Mendelssohn's music—and that would be just as well. Felix trembled when he thought of the possibility. It was just about two years since his father had wanted to send a quartet by Felix to Vienna, for Beethoven's opinion. Terrified and furious, and finally tearful, Felix had begged him not to. It would have been sacrilege —for the present he was still a dilettante.[24]

[20] R. Varnhagen: *Ein Buch des Andenkens für ihre Freunde*. Berlin, 1834.
[21] O. Zarek: *Moses Mendelssohn, ein jüdisches Schicksal in Deutschland*. Amsterdam, 1936.
[22] S. Hensel: *Die Familie Mendelssohn 1729–1847*. Berlin, 1879.
[23] G. Confalonieri: *Il Romanzo di Luigi Cherubini*. Milan, 1948.
[24] F. Garnett: "Great Musicians of Yesterday." *Musical Times*. London, 1892.

But he had seen one great composer, and his whole being had been receptive to this great man's personality. That had also been a few years ago: after a performance of *Der Freischütz* his father had sent his carriage to the Opera House to fetch the celebrated Carl Maria von Weber. Weber had entered and waited for young Mendelssohn to come along. But Felix was absolutely panic-stricken at the prospect of riding in the carriage with the great composer—perhaps Weber would even deign to address him! Instead of getting in, the boy ran all the way home and arrived in time to open the carriage door for the master.[25]

But now Weber was dead, had died under such terrible circumstances that Felix could not think of it without anguish. Weak, consumptive, he had nevertheless journeyed to London to make some money for his wife and children. Ah, what a man he had been! That emaciated, friendly face with its long, straight nose. Felix would be happy to have some memento of him, if only the glasses that he had worn while conducting. ...He had gone to London to rehearse his *Oberon*. Felix shuddered to think that this last work of Weber's had been the story of Oberon. Wieland's, not Shakespeare's Oberon—but still a ghostly music woven of water and air, with elfin horns.

When, two months ago, the news had come that Weber was dead in London, Felix had asked Ludwig Berger whether it was still possible, still permissible, to write some music on the same theme, as a sort of tribute to Weber. And Berger, the piano virtuoso, had replied: "You may. You are already beyond him."[26]

Recollections of Weber's music came pouring into his mind. What better way to do homage to the master than by quotation? He chose a few unimportant measures, those rising and rocking measures (their effect is almost of a timid waltz) from Weber's "Song of the Sea Maiden":

But with deepest reverence he constructed the grand Finale of his overture out of it:

[25] Ibid.
[26] K. Gaede: *Alte und neue Klaviermeister*. Leipzig, no date.

And now it sounded quite different. Gentle. Echoing. Expansive. Unforgettable. Had not these notes already haunted him when he wrote the fortissimo of the wedding theme? But now the measures truly belonged to him, belonged wholly. For a legitimate quotation which we borrow from another must also be transformed into an idea of our own. What a vast space is occupied by these measures, in which Shakespeare's verses are caught:

> First, rehearse this song by rote:
> To each word a warbling note,
> Hand in hand, with fairy grace,
> Will we sing, and bless this place....
> With this field-dew consecrate,
> Every fairy take his gait;
> And each several chamber bless,
> Through this palace, with sweet peace:
> Ever shall in safety rest,
> And the owner of it blest.

Gracious stillness. Vibrations of earnestness.... Only then did Felix conclude the overture pianissimo with the four chords with which he had begun it. Everything had dissolved into air.

Now he stood up, reeling slightly. The candles in the orangery had burned down. It was the 26th August 1826. By now it was two o'clock in the morning, and only a few hours before sunrise. He had a vision of his bed, and as he placed his palm against his smarting eyes he almost fell asleep on his way to his bedroom.

GRANDFATHER MOSES MENDELSSOHN

All those who knew Mendelssohn in his young days agree in one observation: his "ready fatigability", as they called it. He could not see a sofa or a couch without stretching out on it.[1] The time of day did not matter. But once he was lying in a horizontal position, his languor disappeared. Thus stretched out, he could talk with friends for hours, would joke, would even compose while lying down. This trait was all the stranger because Mendelssohn was not at all a weakly young man.

[1] F. Hiller: *Felix Mendelssohn-Bartholdy*. Cologne, 1874.

In his boyhood, in fact, he had been as sprightly as a young billy-goat. Ferdinand Hiller first met him on a street in Frankfurt when Felix, then thirteen, sprang with one great leap to the shoulders of a man walking ahead of him—Aloys, the piano virtuoso—and insisted on being carried along. Felix was afraid of nothing and no one. His parents had put emphasis on the physical training of their young prodigy. Felix had a gymnastics tutor—something not at all customary at the time—who was a pupil of Friedrich Ludwig Jahn, the founder of gymnastics in Germany. In addition he was a good swimmer and an enthusiastic dancer; at the frequent family dances his sisters' girl friends flew in and out of his arms.[2] He "danced like a cultivated gale", Rahel Varnhagen said of him—with her love for paradoxical formulations.

And yet there were these frequent bouts of tiredness, this craving for rest. Was something within this youth of sixteen aware of the long and weary way his family had travelled in three-quarters of a century? Felix Mendelssohn, the Berliner, was the grandson of Moses Mendelssohn who had turned up in Berlin more than eighty years before, a helpless, hunchbacked child from Dessau. His real name had been Moses Dessau, or son of Mendel of Dessau.

What was little Moses Dessau doing, tramping the roads, when actually he was forbidden by law to do so? (He carried no permit with him.) He was on his way to visit his Talmud teacher, the famous David Hirschel Fränkel, who had been called to Berlin to serve as chief rabbi of the Jewish community in that city. Otto Zarek[3] relates how the family in Dessau managed to equip the little wayfarer with a ducat in gold and a torn old coat. The boy travelled on foot. Covered with dust, emaciated from hunger, he reached the gates of Berlin at last. But the guards by the western gates scornfully refused to admit the boy. He had to tramp on farther round the Prussian capital. For Jews could ask admission only at the Rosenthaler Gate. "Admission?" Zarek continues his account:

A painful interrogation. The guard began the examination—that dialogue straight out of a comedy between a swaggering soldier and a timorous Jewish boy.

The guard: "Name?"

The boy only guesses the meaning of the question; he does not know German, except for a single word that he is saving. He stammers: "Moses."

[2] K. Bauer: *Aus meinem Bühnenleben*. Weimar, 1871.
[3] Otto Zarek: *Moses Mendelssohn, ein jüdisches Schicksal in Deutschland*. Amsterdam, 1936.

Abraham Mendelssohn, Felix Mendelssohn's father. Drawing by Wilhelm Hensel, circa 1829. Property of the Mendelssohn family. (*Photo Handke, Bad Berneck*)

Leah Mendelssohn, Felix Mendelssohn's mother. Drawing by Wilhelm Hensel. (*Historia-Photo, Berlin*)

Moses Mendelssohn, Felix Mendelssohn's grandfather. Red chalk drawing by Daniel Chodo-
wiecki. (*Historia-Photo, Berlin*)

Felix Mendelssohn aged thirteen. Drawing by
Wilhelm Hensel. (*National Galerie, Berlin*)

The mustachioed soldier smiles condescendingly: "Where from?"

"Dessau."

The guard notes down the answer. "To see whom?"

The boy raises his head. The question is repeated, and this time he thinks he understands. He gives the name: "Rabbi Fränkel."

"What for?"

Moses trembles. How meekly he stands, a hunchbacked gnome before a huge Fafnir in the uniform of a Prussian grenadier. Now is the time for it, for that word, that single German word which he was taught at home. *Lernen* is the magic word— to learn. The boy almost sounds it out; he can scarcely make the foreign language pass his lips.

"To learn!" he repeats. Then the guard lets him pass. He knows this type of Talmud pupil, the kind who gather in swarms around the rabbi. But he shakes his head in astonishment at this specimen, this poor, ragged, hunchbacked, abysmally ugly fourteen-year-old with the large, dark, intelligent eyes.

In the records of the watch that October day of the year 1743 the following entry appears: "Today there passed through the Rosenthaler Gate six oxen, seven swine, one Jew."

To learn, to learn. We may imagine the word echoing in the mind of Moses' grandson as he considered his future. Nothing quite so glorious as music, of course. But still, were there not many other worthwhile things with which a young man might occupy himself? Perhaps he would study law, become a *doctor juris*. He could study under the famous founder of legal history, Professor Eduard Gans,* whose name and whose peculiar waddle were a joke in Berlin—but whose keen intelligence could not be laughed at. Or on the other hand he might study classical literature under Professor Böckh. Felix Mendelssohn had already begun working on a translation for his tutor, Karl Wilhelm Heyse; he was doing *The Woman of Andros*, a comedy by Terence, in the original metres. (Heyse would publish it with notes that very year—the "youthful author" remaining anonymous.)

Or should he not instead study history—to which he felt particularly drawn, Universal history as it was called nowadays—Herder and Schiller had popularized the term. To do that, he would have to study for years —and read, about all that had happened in Egypt, Assyria and distant

* *Gans* = goose.

India. (India, land of the *Mahabharata*, which the learned Franz Bopp had just discovered.) Then study the Crusades, Elizabethan England and France during the Revolution. A single life was not enough for all that had to be covered. "I need seven lives!" Goethe, whom he worshipped, had once said. If he had felt that, an ordinary mortal would not manage with twenty-one lives.

His Grandfather Moses had never taken an interest in history.[4] And that had been wise of him. For had he looked more deeply into Antiquity, the Middle Ages and Modern Times, he would probably have lost courage, would never have dared to venture on something so radically new as his own life, which flagrantly overstepped the boundaries of all that a Jew dared to be, in that time and place. A short time after his arrival in Berlin Moses began to learn German, to abandon the strict rites of his co-religionists, and to answer the indignant question, "Aren't you a Jew any more?" with an intransigent: "*I am a man!*" The word humanism had been around for a long time. But it was something altogether novel for a member of the Berlin Jewish community to become an adherent of humanism. In earlier times such a step would have ended with the *cherem*, the thunder of anathema.

But soon books by Moses were appearing which roused his contemporaries to amazement. The foreigner had learned German, philosophical German, with fantastic speed, and he now joined in discussion of the questions that were stirring the intellectuals of Germany. He met Gotthold Ephraim Lessing—and the encounter was fraught with consequences. Stimulated by Lessing, Moses wrote his *Philosophical Dialogues* in imitation of Plato. As a pupil and follower of Leibnitz he defended Leibnitz's system against the attacks of that great mocker, Voltaire, who had drawn a parody of Leibnitz in his *Candide or The Best of all Possible Worlds*.[5] *Letters on the Feelings* and other works on aesthetics followed. And finally there came in 1767 his most famous work, *Phaedo, or On the Immortality of the Soul*.[6]

To Lessing, Moses Mendelssohn was more than an interesting fellow-thinker. Moses was a living symbol in the fight against intolerance which had engaged the best minds for centuries. This cause was a tradition in Lessing's family. His grandfather Theophilus, Mayor of Kamenz, had shocked his contemporaries with an essay *On the Universal Tolerance of*

[4] F. Muncker: "Moses Mendelssohn". *Allgemeine Deutsche Biographie*.
[5] M. Kayserling: *Moses Mendelssohn, sein Leben und seine Werke*. Leipzig, 1862.
[6] G. B. Mendelssohn: *Moses Mendelssohns gesammelte Schriften*. Leipzig, 1843-45.

all Religions. He had defended this thesis before the faculty of Leipzig University. The word *tolerance* took on a new meaning. The grandson took up the battle-cry.[7] But he was motivated not so much by his grandfather's example as by his own emotions, for he had come to love and understand the Jew, Moses Mendelssohn. But for his acquaintance with Moses, he would never have known of the exceptional laws, the extortion, the humiliations inflicted upon this people. For instance if a Jew died owing money to any Christian, he was not permitted burial until the heirs or the Jewish community had settled the debts. The Jews paid body-taxes. They were forbidden to travel. And there was the oath for Jews, that archaic, ridiculous special oath which Jews were required to swear in court: "May I be consumed by the fire that burned Sodom and Gomorrah, and by all curses that are written in the Torah; and may God never come to my aid who created the leaves and grass and all things, if I tell a falsehood here. May all the ten plagues of Egypt be sent down upon me. May my house and my goods, my wife and all my children be punished with sulphur and brimstone. . . ." The Christian swore simply: "So help me God." But the Jew, who in popular belief had always been vengeful and cruel, had to bind himself by stronger oaths. It was a strange, blood-chilling formula, but ludicrous also when it rang out under the low grey skies of Leipzig, Frankfurt or Berlin.

For even in Berlin it was so. Frederick the Great plumed himself on being a freethinker, but he still oppressed the Jews as harshly as a bigoted petty prince or the town council of some middling municipality. Were not the Jews magicians? Making money from money was considered a wicked business, something bordering on sorcery. For this reason the court bankers and the masters of the coinage for lords great and small were mostly Jews—in Germany and elsewhere. Wherever a bankruptcy, a debasement of the coinage or an inflation took place, it was blamed not on the excesses, the wars, the amorous escapades or the mania for expensive building of the ruling caste. No, it was always the fault of the Jews.[8] Harsh levies were made on them. Occasionally when popular indignation ran high, Jews were killed, or forced to emigrate, only to begin again elsewhere their unpopular but necessary business of dealing in money.

A man like Frederick the Great certainly did not believe in sorcery. Nevertheless he found the Jews hateful. Perhaps the reason was that the philosopher of Sans-Souci was by nature a despiser of mankind. Why should he except the Jews—the most contemptible of all—from his general

[7] E. Schmidt: *Lessing.* Berlin, 1899.
[8] O. Zarek: op. cit.

contempt? Moreover, the King, who had been schooled by Voltaire, put
great emphasis on *esprit*. For the most part, the Jews were deficient in
this quality and did not cultivate it. Those who must battle for the bare
minimum of life are hardly in a position to display *esprit*. The Jews
seemed to be dried-up reckoners, good for nothing but underwriting the
porcelain factories, the Prussian silk industry and other branches of the
economy—by being forced to purchase the products. For that very reason
there was an element of self-hatred in the hatred that Frederick the Great
bestowed upon Prussian Jewry.[9] For he loved to philosophize and his
soaring intellect did not like being checked by everyday economic coer-
cions and political necessities, in other words, by money. To him the Jews
were the very symbols of money. And who was this Moses Mendelssohn?
True, he represented the quality the King respected—*esprit*—but he could
not be admitted to the Academy because of his origins.

But a fig for the precious Academy. Neither Maupertuis nor Kant was
the famous writer of the day; Mendelssohn was far more popular. His
books appeared in large editions, and sometimes had a portrait of the
author for a frontispiece. Studying this copper engraving, people came to
the conclusion that this Jew was far from ugly. Johann Kaspar Lavater
actually pronounced him handsome.[10] He praised the splendid arch of
his forehead (which was to be inherited by Felix Mendelssohn) and the
beautiful structure of his eye-sockets. "In the depths of these eyes lies a
Socratic soul."

Lavater went on to speak of Moses Mendelssohn's social charm. "If he
is really ugly, it is the ugliness of Aesop, the ancient Greek fabulist.
Genial and candid in converse, he is nimble of tongue, though his speech
will be suddenly checked in its course by a bond imposed by nature" (in
addition to his hump and weakly constitution, Moses also stammered). It
is significant that in the very decade in which Winckelmann was to
publicize the classical ideal of beauty and stress the quality of symmetry,
so unsymmetrical a head as that of Moses Mendelssohn should none the
less have been found appealing.

Moses Mendelssohn was a cripple—but perhaps that was a grace. Had
not Maimonides in the twelfth century observed: "The philosophers
teach that the strength of youth is inimical to most ethical virtues and that
the knowledge which leads to love of God cannot develop in youth
because of the fire of the bodily humours".[11] If that were so, then young

[9] K. Brunner: *Der Judenhass und das Denken*. Berlin, 1922.
[10] J. G. Lavater: *Physiognomische Fragmente*. Leipzig, 1773–78.
[11] O. Goldberg: *Maimonides, Kritik der Jüdischen Glaubenslehre*.
Vienna, 1935.

Moses Mendelssohn was defended from physical temptations; he was born for the intellectual life.[12]

Although his books were widely read, Moses Mendelssohn was still poor. There were, of course, respectable posts like that of librarian, which offered security to men of letters. Lessing held such a post. But there were no such sinecures for a Jew. A co-religionist, the silk dealer Bernhard, engaged Moses as a tutor for his children. One day the book-keeper of the firm fell ill. Bernhard asked Moses to take over his duties. Mendelssohn was a precise thinker; precise thinking is valuable in business. The temporary book-keeper made a few practical suggestions to his employer, and got on well with the silkworkers; he, the educated man, treated them without condescension. How would he like to be permanent book-keeper? Bernhard scarcely dared to make the proposal. But amazingly enough, Moses accepted the post. He had come to see poverty as the greatest enemy of his intellectual endeavours.

"Henceforth", Otto Zarek narrates, "he went to his office every morning at eight o'clock and was not able to leave it until late evening. Yet he worked smiling; he had chosen this duty and now he was meeting it. Yet sometimes he was overwhelmed by the longing for freedom. As the years went by, he more and more felt the hardship of the long hours in the dark office. Lessing understood his complaint: 'Oh, business matters! What a burden. They crush me to the ground and consume the strength of my best years. Like a donkey I creep through my span of life with loaded back, and worst of all, self-love tells me that perhaps Nature created me to be a parade-mount. What is to be done, my dear friend? Let us commiserate with one another and be content....' "[13]

In the end, Moses outlived his friend by four years. Lessing never recovered from the shock of losing his beloved wife in childbed. His mind became deranged. He had fits of maniacal laughter; the handwriting of his manuscripts became unrecognizable, the strokes of the letters strange and wildly slanting. In December 1780 Lessing wrote to his lifelong friend Mendelssohn: "Ah, my dear friend, the play is over!" But by the time he died on 15th February 1781 he had made his greatest contribution to literature and his greatest gift to his contemporaries. This was his play, *Nathan the Wise*.

Moses Mendelssohn *was* Nathan. Until Lessing met Mendelssohn he had had no conception of "what art it took to live as a Jew".[14] Nathan, the sage and diplomat at an Oriental court—Nathan, the only one to

[12] O. Zarek: op. cit.   [13] O. Zarek: op. cit.
[14] H. York-Steiner: *Die Kunst als Jude zu leben*. Vienna, 1928.

survive the massacre of his family—was a master of the art of "balancing", was expert at "preventing atrocities", as a prominent Jew had to be. The core of this revolutionary play was the Parable of the Three Rings, which was not Lessing's own. It came from a story by Boccaccio. Four centuries before the Age of Reason this great Italian interceded for the equality of the three great religions of civilization.[15] And when Nathan on the stage began his tale:

> Long years ago a man lived in the East
> Who owned a priceless ring passed on to him
> From a beloved hand. The stone was an
> Opal that sparkled with a hundred hues
> And had the secret force to make its wearer
> Pleasing to the eyes of God and man. . . .

the world held its breath. The heir of the magic ring had two facsimiles made, in order not to put any of his sons at a disadvantage. There was no telling the three rings apart. In making his point—that the claim of each great religion to sole validity was a monstrous deception—Lessing revolutionized the age, and made possible the humanism of Goethe and Schiller and of German classicism in the nineteenth century.

Moses Mendelssohn may some day be forgotten, but his portrait in Lessing's *Nathan the Wise* will remain, forever enjoining future generations:

> Neither of us
> Has chosen for himself his people.
> Are we our people? What then is a people?
> Are Jew and Christian rather Jew and Christian
> Than men?

This was the proud and difficult patrimony of Felix Mendelssohn— Felix, scion of a happier age.

LOYALTIES, LOYALTIES

The crippled philosopher had not remained a celibate. He married and was the father of eight children, two of whom died in their infancy. The other six, however, survived him (he died in 1786), and carried on the

[15] H. Hauvette: *Boccace, Étude biographique et littéraire.* Paris, 1914.

Mendelssohn tradition. There were three sons, three daughters—some of them celebrated and none of them unimportant.[1]

Berthold Auerbach has related[2] the story of Moses Mendelssohn's courtship. The anecdote is both touching and credible. The young lady in question was Fromet Gugenheim, daughter of a Hamburg merchant. She had worshipped the witty and learned Mendelssohn, whom she knew, however, only through his writings. Finally Moses accepted her invitation to visit the Gugenheim family. He was much struck by the girl, but he was well aware that his own appearance must be a shock to her. He asked her father what had been Fromet's impression of him.

"Well, reverend Rabbi," Herr Gugenheim replied, "I don't know whether I ought to tell you. You are a philosopher, a wise man. I know you won't blame the child, but she was frightened when she saw you. . . ."

"Because of my hump? Ah, I expected it. But before I leave I'd like to bid your daughter good-bye."

Then he went in to see Fromet, who was sewing. They talked quietly and pleasantly with one another, but the girl did not look up from her work. Moses brought up the old proverb, Marriages are made in heaven. Then he smilingly enlarged upon the subject. "Yes, at the birth of a child the word is cried out in heaven: This man will receive that woman. Now when I was born my wife's name was cried out to me, but at the same time the message came: Unfortunately she will be a hunchback. Then I said: Dear God, a girl who is misshapen will have a hard and bitter time of it; a girl ought to be beautiful. Dear God, give *me* the hump and let the girl grow up tall and straight."

As soon as Moses had spoken these words Fromet Gugenheim threw her arms around his neck. She gladly became his wife, and their marriage was a most happy one.

Ernst Wolff, a biographer of Felix Mendelssohn, has remarked concerning this little tale that "in its peculiar mixture of Oriental beauty and resigned philosophy" it would be worthy of *Nathan the Wise*.[3] And in truth Lessing's parable of the ring with its image of a solemn legacy had a very special meaning in the history of the Mendelssohn family.

The principal heiress of the family intellect was Dorothea Mendelssohn, later Dorothea Veit and still later the wife of Friedrich Schlegel. In Dorothea, however, her father's patient gentleness had been transformed into a passionate and combative vein. She did a good deal to keep the

---

[1] S. Hensel: *Die Familie Mendelssohn 1729–1847*. Berlin, 1879.
[2] B. Auerbach: *Zur guten Stunde*. Stuttgart, 1872.
[3] E. Wolff: *Felix Mendelssohn-Bartholdy*. Berlin, 1909.

spirit of Romanticism militant—and also aggravated the strife between the Schlegel brothers. For August Wilhelm Schlegel, the elegant gentleman and surpassingly sensitive interpreter of the poetry of other nations, was very different in character from Friedrich, the profounder, more erring, more mystical brother. Ricarda Huch, who rediscovered German Romanticism for the twentieth century, did Dorothea an injustice.[4] As so many others have done, she fell under the spell of the personality of Karoline Schlegel, the sister-in-law and enemy of Dorothea Schlegel. Karoline's charm remains all the stronger because she died young. It is too easy to side with her against her adversary Dorothea. We must look to Haym for a fairer description of Felix Mendelssohn's strange and brilliant aunt.[5]

"She was capable of the utmost devotion, the most self-sacrificing loyalty. This she demonstrated through harsh tribulations in her relationship with Friedrich, her selfish, demanding, anything but genial husband. A strong spirit dwelt in that frail body, above all strong in not fighting back, enduring, renouncing. It was her pride to devote her whole life to that of her beloved husband." She interposed herself as interpreter and explainer between Friedrich Schlegel and the theologian Schleiermacher, who had the ungrateful task of defending Friedrich's most immoral book, *Lucinde*. Schleiermacher's task was indeed not easy, for it was a book about free love. Dorothea had her acid moments; then, as Haym recounts, she looked more ugly than usual "wrinkling her nose and protruding her lips; anger did not become her". But wrath was followed by humility; she felt that all Friedrich's failures might be her own fault. Or again she would shake her head—true daughter of Moses Mendelssohn—over the eccentricities of the Romantic school. Friedrich was a professional Catholic artist and an excellent satirist. Dorothea had no objection to that, but "she became really fond of him only when he began to prove his worth as a competent citizen in a genuine State". And to cry shame upon this philistine desire within herself, she suddenly wrote a novel, *Florentin*, which was marked by flashes of genius and a deep uncertainty about the rules of German grammar.

Dorothea Mendelssohn was successively Jewess, Protestant and Catholic —and we may be sure that she adhered to each of the religions in turn with conviction. That is, she believed, with Lessing, that one civilized religion was just as valid as any of the others. It was in the same spirit that her brother Abraham, Felix Mendelssohn's father, had his children

---

[4] Ricarda Huch: *Die Blütezeit der Romantik*. Leipzig, 1905.
[5] R. Haym: *Die Romantische Schule*. Berlin, 1870.

baptized (this was done when Fanny was eleven and Felix seven years old—on 21st March 1816). The father himself did not become a Christian until six years later. He was really interested only in the ethical message of the new religion. Inwardly, he rejected all faith in the revelations of the Old and the New Testaments.[6]

Here is the letter he wrote to his daughter Fanny, on the occasion of her confirmation in 1820. It tells us a great deal of the nature of his own beliefs:

> Does God exist? What is God? Is a part of our selves eternal and does it live on after the other part is gone? And if so, where? And how?—I do not know the answers to any of these questions and have therefore never taught you anything concerning them. But I do know that there exists in me and in you and in all men an eternal tendency to everything that is good, true and right, and that a conscience exists which admonishes us and guides us when we depart from the good. I know this, believe in it, and live in this belief; it is my religion. I could not teach it to you and no one can learn it; everyone has it who does not deliberately and knowingly renounce it. And you would not do so; I can be sure of that from the example of your mother, that noblest and worthiest of mothers—who is religion in human form. You grew up under her protection. Your mother was and is—and my heart tells me will long continue to be—the providence and guiding star for all of us. If you look upon her and consider the good that she has shown you, and if your heart fills and your eyes overflow with gratitude, with love and with reverence for her—then you feel God and are being devout.
>
> This is all that I can tell you about religion, all that I know. The form in which your religious instructor has conveyed it to you is historical, and like all the creations of mankind is change-able. Several thousand years ago the Jewish form was the dominant one, then the pagan, now it is the Christian. We, your mother and I, were born in Judaism and raised in it by our parents, and without having had to change this form we have followed the God in ourselves and our own consciences. We have raised you and your brothers and sisters in Christianity because it is the form of religion accepted by most civilized men and con-tains nothing that might lead you away from the good; on the contrary, much that guides you toward love, toward obedience,

[6] S. Hensel: op. cit.

toward tolerance and toward resignation—even if only in the example of the Author of the religion, an example recognized by so few and followed by even fewer.

Some may say that this is not much of a statement. Are these reasons enough to become an apostate? The dominant tone seems to be, merely, resignation. And yet the gesture was a more forceful one than it appeared to be. For Moses Mendelssohn had *not* had his children baptized. He had given a sharp answer to Lavater when the Swiss pastor suggested that "since he was already no longer a Jew, he might at least become a Christian". And the best people in Germany felt that he was right in standing by his Jewish identity. But after the so-called Wars of Liberation, Abraham Mendelssohn did have his children baptized. In so doing, he was setting aside his Jewish identity for a German one, and that was an act of some importance. We can sense in it the impetus, the well-nigh mystical impetus, felt by the entire German nation, after the victory over Napoleon. The great pagan in Paris, whom many called the Antichrist himself, had been sufficient of a threat to unite disparate nations. Now everything that was still "disunited" in those nations had to be swept away: foreign philosophies, foreign religions. People had become simultaneously "German and devout"; the Romantic Age had begun. It seemed that only Christians could really experience Romanticism. And so Abraham Mendelssohn broke down the partition wall between his children and his contemporaries, and had them baptized.

The whole subject of Napoleon was a perplexing one. Actually there was not a Jew in the world who did not have cause to be grateful to the conqueror. Heinrich Heine made him his hero, and dedicated a book to Napoleon. For Napoleon had vigorously repressed an anti-Jewish movement in Alsace. He had taught the French that Jews were something else besides usurers and bloodsuckers. In 1808 he had instituted civil equality between Jews and Christians.[7]

Abraham Mendelssohn, too, had once been a Francophile Jew. When he had been serving his apprenticeship in 1803 in the Paris banking house of Fould, he had been much impressed by the magnificent sureness of Napoleon's conduct of government. How wisely the First Consul—later the Emperor—dealt with the problems of property and law. What a wonderful creation was the Code Civil. The excesses of revolution had been overcome—there remained the equality of citizens and religions. Lessing's appeal for tolerance in his *Nathan the Wise* had remained only paper in Germany; in Paris it had become reality. France under Napoleon

[7] S. Dubnow: *Weltgeschichte des Jüdischen Volkes*. Berlin, 1925–29.

was a land of enlightenment and Abraham Mendelssohn did not want to return to a land where his forefathers had been kept in virtual slavery.

And yet he did return. For personal reasons; there was no logic about it. Because his mother lived in Hamburg. And because his heart's choice, the young heiress Leah Salomon, did not want to marry an underling. Abraham had once written proudly to his equally Francophile sister, Henriette Mendelssohn (who stayed in Paris teaching in the household of General Sebastiani): *Je préférais manger de pain sec à Paris*. But now he and his brother started a banking house in commerce-minded Hamburg. This brother was Joseph Mendelssohn who had also inherited a good share of his father's commercial talent, but who was more interested in other matters. He was the *littérateur* of the family, poetic, apt at languages, secretly smiled at, but also admired. Abraham Mendelssohn soon became sole director of the Hamburg bank, and proved to have a great gift for finance. In a comfortable country home in the vicinity of Hamburg (a home that already hinted of future luxury in Berlin) his three children were born: Fanny on 15th November 1805; Felix on 3rd February 1809; and Rebecca on 11th April 1811. Paul, often jokingly called "Lazy" by his father, did not appear on the scene until 1813.

The family now had its feet solidly planted on the soil of the Free Hanseatic City of Hamburg. They spoke German, but in almost every sentence they uttered a word or two of French slipped in. "The evening of my arrival", Leah wrote to her sister-in-law Henriette, "I allowed myself the pleasure of opening my Paris chest and putting on my two gala robes. Heavenly! But only useful for attending the Emperor Napoleon's *cour*. The most wonderful, richest, shiningest, silkiest, gracefullest chamois Peking velvet dress, and the most delicate *façonné* pink mixed with white, divinely trimmed and cut. My husband was beside himself with *enthusiasme*. . . ."[8] But now the Mendelssohn family shared the experience of all other citizens of Hamburg. They became acquainted with the conduct of the French outside France. They learned of tyrannical oppression, monstrous extortions, which began soon after the Treaty of Tilsit, after the unlucky war against Napoleon which ended with the defeat of Prussia in 1806.

Hamburg's situation was unique. Hamburg lived by its shipping. Napoleon's Continental Blockade was the ruin of this shipping trade. His Imperial Majesty's decree, issued on 21st November 1806, forbade all trade in English goods, confiscated all warehouses in which such goods were stored, and declared every ship transporting contraband English

---

[8] S. Hensel: op. cit.

goods a legitimate prize. Those who had lived by commerce were impoverished overnight—and they were a good half of the citizenry of
Hamburg. Thus, it became a patriotic duty for the Germans to evade
Napoleon's decree. Inland cities, Leipzig in particular, would pay any
price for English cloth; so-called colonial goods—spices, coffee, tea, sugar
and tobacco from overseas—were in even greater demand.

The result was that Hamburg turned into a gigantic smugglers' camp.
High and low took part in running the blockade. Skinny folk who had
tramped to Altona in the early morning—in those days Altona, across the
Elbe from Hamburg, was a city belonging to the Danes—would return
fat at night, their bodies wound around with skeins of English yarn, or
swathed in cottons. The French customs officials could not understand
why so many peole were dying in Altona and had to be buried in Hamburg—until they discovered that the coffins were filled with bags of coffee.[9]

For the common man, all this was mostly a sport, an adventure. But
if you owned a bank as did the Mendelssohn brothers, you could go much
further. The rich Hamburgers equipped ships flying neutral flags to carry
on wholesale trade with England. This was possible, of course, only if
French officialdom was corruptible. And it was. Marshal Mortier, the
governor of the Hanseatic cities, had his price. He even had a financial
interest in the re-shipment of English coal to Frankfurt, Leipzig and
Berlin. Rumours of these activities came to Napoleon's ears, and he
removed Mortier. His place was taken by Marshal Brune who proved
to be, as the Emperor later said, "an intrepid robber". He and his accom-
plices, Consul La Chevardière and City Commandant Lallemand, received
400,000 francs from the Hamburgers, who in return were allowed to mock
the imperial decree. Brune had the inventories falsified; overnight only
Danish imports were stored in Hamburg.[10]

Brune was followed by Bernadotte, Bernadotte by Marshal Davout, the
dread warrior, victor of Eckmühl and Auerstädt.[11] Historians' judgments
waver concerning him. According to some, his loyalty to Napoleon was
extreme and he mercilessly expelled from Hamburg those merchants who
were known to be blockade-breakers and smugglers.[12] Other historians,
however, suggest he wanted to take over the business of smuggling for

[9] W. Vogel: *Die Hansestädte und die Kontinentalsperre*. Munich and
Leipzig, 1913.
[10] C. Mönckeberg: *Hamburg unter dem Drucke der Franzosen
1806–14*. Hamburg, 1864
[11] Th. v. Haupt: *Hamburg und der Marschall Davout. Aufruf an die
Gerechtigkeit*. 1814.
[12] P. Frh. v. Holtzhausen: *Davout in Hamburg*. Mülheim/Ruhr, 1892.

himself alone.[13] Whatever his motives, among the blockade-breakers who were in grave danger and had to steal out of Hamburg under cover of darkness was the Mendelssohn family. Abraham, Leah and their three small children fled. They arrived in Berlin not as impoverished refugees, however, but as loyal Germans who had staked their fortune in the struggle against Napoleon.

For there could be no doubts about the political loyalties of Abraham Mendelssohn. When Frederick William III's famous proclamation, "To my People" appeared, and the war against Napoleon broke out, Abraham Mendelssohn provided equipment for volunteers. That same year of 1813, while the balance swayed between the defeat at Dresden and the victory of Leipzig, an army hospital was established in Prague with money supplied by Mendelssohn and others such as Rahel Varnhargen, who temporarily abandoned her intellectual pursuits for patriotic duties and worked eighteen hours a day nursing the wounded.[14] After the victory Mendelssohn, honoured as the benefactor of his fellow-citizens, was elected to the Municipal Council of Berlin.

In civil life he had come far. But how did this affect his religion? He had given the matter thought for many years. Abraham was not impulsive like his sister Dorothea. A cautious man, he pondered the problem deeply: in what direction ought he to guide his beloved children? He had long ago ceased being a believing Jew. But was that a reason for becoming a Christian? An unending war of pros and cons broke out in his soul. The final impetus to change was given to him by his wife's brother, who discarded the name of Salomon and called himself Bartholdy.[15] Probably Abraham asked his reasons and his brother-in-law Bartholdy responded: "You say you owe it to the memory of your father—do you think you have done anything evil by giving your children the religion which you consider the better one *for them*? Rather it is an act of homage which you and I and all of us owe to Moses Mendelssohn's efforts in the interests of true Enlightenment; and he would have acted as you do for your children, perhaps as I do for myself. A man can remain loyal to an oppressed, persecuted religion; he can impose it upon his children as a candidature for a lifelong martyrdom—*as long as he thinks that it alone will bring salvation*. But as soon as he no longer believes that, it is barbarism to do anything of the kind."

Again we may think: a practical decision—but scarcely idealistic. As a

[13] De Bloqueville: *Le Maréchal Davout, Prince d'Eckmühl.* Paris, 1883.
[14] R. Varnhagen: *Ein Buch des Andenkens für ihre Freunde.* Berlin, 1834.
[15] S. Hensel: op. cit.

matter of fact, ideals and prudence are inextricably intermingled in such
a view. We have no call to look for fervent religious experience in a man
born in the eigtheenth century and raised under the auspices of *ratio*. It
was reserved for Felix Mendelssohn's generation, for those born in the nineteenth century, to experience such spiritual awakenings, which transformed
the "inner Saul into a Paul".

There was a distant relative of the Mendelssohns in Göttingen, son of
the merchant Emanuel Mendel. He studied Plato devotedly, and one day
felt a lightning-flash in his soul when Schleiermacher cried out to him:
"Do you not think that Plato's doctrine of the pure word is expressed
even more purely in the Gospel of Saint John?"[16] From that moment on
Mendel became a Christian, calling himself Neander, the new man.
This August Neander eventually developed into a formidable Protestant
scholar, the greatest theologian of his time. He despised rationalism, but
he also opposed orthodoxy because of its intolerance toward intellectual
progress. Neander preached a Christ who was "a supernatural principle
in historical epiphany". In this formula the words historical and supernatural neatly balanced each other.... Another famous Jewish convert
was Eduard Gans, who brought into his new religion his forefathers'
passion for Talmudic legalisms. Baptized in 1825, he applied Hegel's
dialectic to jurisprudence. His *Das Erbrecht in weltgeschichtlicher
Entwicklung* was the first book on comparative legal history.[17] A third
convert, Professor Friedrich Julius Stahl, showed how far Jewish intellectuality in Christian garb could go. In politics he ardently advocated the
principle of legitimacy; in religion he preached unswerving faith in
Revelation. Stahl assailed the lingering remnants of the French Revolution's belief in popular sovereignty and the Rousseauian Social Contract.
He attacked the religious philosopher Schleiermacher (a product of the
eighteenth century!), who seemed to him too liberal in ecclesiastical
affairs. Stahl was the real founder of the Conservative Party of Prussia. In
speeches and pamphlets (*The Monarchist Principle, Against the French
Imperial Crown*) he showed the legitimists how much stronger they really
were than all the democrats and revolutionaries of Forty-eight.... Thus
he laid the intellectual foundations for Bismarck's Empire.[18]

Here were three men of ancient Jewish traditions who had entered the
Christian world; three men who had taken different directions within it.
Who would dare to question their idealistic motives? But then there were

[16] I. L. Jacobi: *Erinnerungen an August Neander*. Berlin, 1882.
[17] P. Marheineke: *Rede am Grabe des Professors Gans*. Berlin, 1839.
[18] F. Julius Stahl: *Die Revolution und die konstitutionelle Monarchie*.
Berlin, 1849.

the host of others born in Judaism who also went over to Christianity: the lawyers, doctors, scientists, thinkers and politicians, painters, actors, musicians. Were all of them idealists when they adopted the new religion? If we ask this question, we must remember how many avenues would have been closed to these Jews if they had not been baptized.

With what right, we may ask, was baptism *demanded* of the Jews? Were not German Protestants, Catholics and Jews theoretically equal in the possession of civil rights? Many people thought Heinrich Heine was insulting both his old and his new religion when he described his baptism as a "ticket of admission into European culture". It was a tactless remark —but it expressed perfectly the reality of conditions in Germany.

Would not a keen observer like Municipal Councillor Mendelssohn be struck by how little loyalty some Christians displayed? Many Jewish volunteers had joined the Prussian army. Sons of Berlin families, the Franz Hausschildts, Moritz Itzigs and Ephraim Wolfs, shed their blood on the battlefield of Lützen. Their reward was a farce called *Unser Verkehr* ("Our Associates"), mocking the customs of the Jews, which appeared on the boards in the capital.[19] The author was a Breslau eye-doctor, Karl Sessa. His comedy attacked the law which made Jews Prussian citizens. The better part of the Berlin public cried out indignantly against the actors who had lent their services to such a piece of slander. In one scene the comedian Wurm made fun of the Old Testament dietary laws and of the Jews' abhorrence of pork; he was pulled off the stage and given a beating.

Nevertheless, the farce made some impression upon the rabble. Berliners asked each other whether Jewish volunteers had the right to wear the Iron Cross. Ought they not rather attach a large coin to their caps—money being their chief concern?[20] On the other hand there were honourable preachers, like Johann Gottfried Zunkel of Weimar, who took a different view. While giving the consecrated wafer to volunteer soldiers in church Zunkel caught sight of the unbaptized son of the "court Jew" Elkan, also a member of the company. He started, but then placed his hand on the communicant's head: "And may you, my son, be blessed by the God of your fathers Abraham, Isaac and Jacob."[21]

[19] K. A. Varnhagen von Ense: *Denkwürdigkeiten des eigenen Lebens*. Berlin, 1922–23.

[20] I. Assing: *Briefe von Stägemann an Varnhagen*. Leipzig, 1865.

[21] K. Khun: *Aus dem alten Weimar, Skizzen und Erinnerungen*. Wiesbaden, 1905.

NOW LISTEN, ALL OF YOU

Toward the end of October in the year 1821 a roomy travelling coach stood before the Mendelssohn home. Professor Zelter, one of Felix's music teachers, was waiting in it. The destination was Weimar—Weimar and His Excellency Privy Councillor Johann Wolfgang von Goethe, Minister of State, with whom Zelter entertained friendly relations. Solemn and deeply moved, Abraham and Leah Mendelssohn went with their son to the carriage. The father once more gave him superfluous advice about sitting properly at table and behaving like a grown-up. Then the door of the coach closed, and the parents stood looking after the departing vehicle.

This was no ordinary visit that twelve-year-old Felix Mendelssohn was making. A veritable Goethe cult was practised in the Mendelssohn household. Nor was that something to be taken for granted at the beginning of the 1820's. Goethe was then a little read and rather unpopular author. His *Werther*, his *Götz von Berlichingen*, were forgotten.[1] Goethe perennially offended the German nation by ignoring the emotion of the moment. If patriotism was expected of him, he insisted on being cosmopolitan. If Christianity was expected of him, he displayed his pagan side. He drew back from the realm that everybody was excitedly rediscovering, the Middle Ages, and seemed still to prefer classical antiquity. Yet—as the Mendelssohns clearly saw—whatever he did was not done out of contrariness. Goethe did not oppose his own times because he longed for a different age, but because he was timeless. If the reactionaries looked to him, they were mistaken; he was not supporting them when he spoke out against the Wartburg festivals, the excesses of the student associations, and democratic tumult.* What good could come out of the streets? Both Revolution and Reaction belonged to "time", and both therefore were

[1] J. P. Eckermann: *Gespräche mit Goethe in den letzten Jahren seines Lebens*. Leipzig, 1939.

* On 18th October 1817 some 500 German students met at the Wartburg, the castle above the town of Eisenach, to celebrate the 300th anniversary of the Reformation. These students, for the first time, raised the black, red and gold flag as a symbol of their patriotic devotion to the cause of a united Germany. They organized an all-German *Burschenschaft* to replace the multitude of student associations. Because of its radicalism and fanatical patriotism, the *Burschenschaft* was soon dissolved by the authorities of the various German states.—Translators' note.

The pavilion in the garden of the Mendelssohn home, No. 3 Leipziger Strasse, Berlin. Pen drawing by Felix Mendelssohn. (*Photo Handke, Bad Berneck*)

Karl Friedrich Zelter. Chalk drawing by J. J. Schmeller, 1826.
(*Photo Nationale Forschungsstätten, Weimar*)

evil.[2] He himself was timeless as the granite to which he paid tribute in a wonderful essay as "being itself". Nowadays, however, Goethe made public pronouncements infrequently. When polemical or partisan poems were expected of him, he knew how to hold his peace. He was occupied with geology and with that theory of colour which (as his opponents constantly commented) interested no one at all.

And now the boy Mendelssohn was on his way to this granite rock, this timeless judge. How would he fare there? He could not guess that his visit was destined to produce an upheaval not only in his own mind, but also among the friends of art in the small town of Weimar.

Johann Christian Lobe, musician of the Weimar court orchestra, was frequently called to the home of the Minister of State, Goethe, to play in quartets there. During that first week of November in the year 1821 he observed—and remembered for the rest of his life—that: "Three music-stands stood ready for us by the side of the open piano. On the piano lay a roll of music notebooks. One notebook was entitled, *Studies in Double Counterpoint*; another, *Fugues*; a third, *Canons*. Then came *Quartets for Piano, Violin, Viola and 'Cello*. On all the notebooks, which were titled in a firm, graceful hand, was the name of the composer: Felix Mendelssohn-Bartholdy."[3]

While the musicians were taking their places, Lobe relates, a tall man entered "whom one might have taken, because of his stiff military bearing, for a former sergeant. It was Zelter. 'I have come beforehand, gentlemen, to ask a favour of you. You are going to meet a twelve-year-old boy, my pupil. His ability as a pianist will astonish you, and his talent for composition will in all probability astonish you still more. Now the boy has a peculiar character. The fawning of amateurs does not affect him; but he listens eagerly to the opinions of musicians and takes everything at face value, for the young sprout is naturally too inexperienced to distinguish between well-meant encouragement and merited appreciation. Therefore, gentlemen, if you are prompted to sing his praises, which I both hope and fear, please do so moderato, without too much noisy instrumentation, and in C major, the most colourless of the keys. Hitherto I've preserved him from vanity and overestimation of himself, those damnable enemies of all artistic progress.' "

After this strange warning Felix "came prancing in, a thriving, perfectly beautiful boy of decidedly southern type, slender and agile. Thick

[2] F. Soret: *Zehn Jahre bei Goethe, 1822–33, Erinnerungen*. Leipzig, 1920.
[3] J. C. Lobe in *Der Gartenlaube*, Christmas issue, 1866.

black curly hair flowed down to the nape of his neck; spirit and animation sparkled in his eyes". Goethe entered immediately after him, reverently greeted by all; his demeanour was sober and composd, as if he had likewise been warned by Zelter. He listened with obvious eagerness, but his only comment on various movements was, "Good!" or, "Bravo!"—while his face took on a deeper and deeper flush.

"When the last movement was over, Felix jumped off his bench and looked around at each of us in turn, a question in his eyes. No doubt he now wanted to hear something about his work. But Goethe, apparently still under the spell of Zelter's warning, contented himself with saying: 'The faces of these gentlemen plainly declare that your production has pleased them. Now go down into the garden, where you are awaited, and cool off, for you look as if you were on fire.' "[4]

As soon as Felix had left the room, the tempo and the tone of the conversation changed completely. Zelter and Goethe no longer concealed their enthusiasm. Prodigy was not a term in good favour—but "What this little man is capable of in improvisation and sight-reading is simply prodigious. I would not have thought it possible as such an age" Goethe said.

"And yet," Zelter replied, "you heard little Mozart play in Frankfurt. That must have been in 1763."

"Just so," Goethe agreed.

Such comments naturally gratified Zelter. Some remarks were made about the imitativeness of children, in the light of which the productions of young persons often became less impressive. It was necessary to distinguish between inspiration and skill, Zelter said. Goethe shook his head and remarked rather sharply that he knew perfectly well how to distinguish. He looked at the string players, who had so far stayed out of the discussion. Now they fell in with Goethe's tone and opined that Felix Mendelssohn "was producing more independent ideas than Mozart at the same age, for the latter had turned out nothing but adroit imitations of his models. From this it seemed likely that in this boy the world had been blessed with a second Mozart; it seemed all the more certain since the child radiated health and since all the outer circumstances of his life were so favourable to him...."

"Let us hope so!" Goethe said.

Lobe thus substantiates Goethe's comparison of Mendelssohn and young Mozart—not the most accurate comparison, for Mendelssohn's genius was for epic and lyric forms, while (not to mention other vast differences) Mozart was a dramatic composer.

[4] J. C. Lobe: loc. cit.

This meeting between Goethe and young Mendelssohn was not the first. The previous occasion has been preserved for history in the chronicle of another eyewitness. The man in question was Ludwig Rellstab, a trained musician and somewhat redoubtable critic, who was invited to be present.[5] He already knew Felix from Berlin, having attended the Mendelssohn Sunday concerts, and could therefore have scarcely been surprised at the way the young man acquitted himself in Weimar. He had heard Felix when he was barely ten play Hummel's very difficult B-flat minor Concerto at sight, and perform Johann Sebastian Bach's *Well-Tempered Clavier* by heart.[6]

According to Rellstab, the meeting took place as follows. He was talking with Zelter on the upper storey of Goethe's house (Ottilie von Goethe was present) when Felix Mendelssohn timidly entered. "He probably thought Goethe himself was there, but Goethe was still in his room and had not come out to greet us. . . . No attention was paid to the boy, since the others were still unacquainted with his extraordinary gifts. I presume that in addition to Zelter I was the only one who knew of them. It was one of Zelter's principles to take no notice of him at all, and so his gifted pupil must have felt rather uncomfortable during these first minutes. However, his numbness quickly vanished, and he soon put himself on a cheery footing with the younger ladies. The boy was so lively that these gay relations soon went a little too far, and without his having showed anything of his musical talent, he became the darling of them all."

It seems that Goethe did not put in an appearance for the rest of the afternoon. He only emerged in the evening—for he had invited a sizeable company to a musical *soirée*. While everybody rose in silence, Goethe greeted his intimate friend Zelter with particular amiability. Zelter in Berlin always dressed in a rather careless, democratic fashion. But here, because Goethe was a cabinet minister and various official personages such as Knebel, Froriep and Duchess Anna Amalia's ladies-in-waiting were present, he had donned old-fashioned breeches, silk stockings, and black patent-leather pumps with silver spangles, such as were worn before the French Revolution. The contrast between this get-up and his manner of speaking provided Rellstab with a good deal of amusement.

Goethe now glanced at Felix and gave proof of his psychological acumen: "My friend Zelter has brought me his little pupil. He is going to give us a sample of his musical gifts; but I am told he is also extraordinarily talented in every other respect. You are no doubt acquainted

[5] L. Rellstab: *Aus meinem Leben*. Berlin, 1862.
[6] O. Bie: *Das Klavier und seine Meister*. Munich, 1898.

with the doctrine of temperaments; every person contains all four within himself, but the mixtures are in varying proportions. In the case of this boy I would guess that he possesses the minimum possible amount of phlegm and a maximum of its opposite."[7]

How did Goethe know? Had he already heard of the incident which had occurred that afternoon when Felix had taken a bellows from the fireplace and used it to blow apart the carefully curled coiffure of a Weimar lady-in-waiting? . . . Joking was second nature to him.

But earnestness was first nature, and that came to the fore now. Goethe opened the Streicher grand piano which Rochlitz had obtained for him. The candles were placed. Felix Mendelssohn was to play. He asked Zelter: "What should I play?"

"Well, whatever you can!" Zelter replied with a rather supercilious air. "Something that's not too hard for you, at any rate."

Rellstab thought this remark unwise. "Since there was no possible piece that Felix could not easily have mastered, it seemed an uncalled-for slur on his abilities." After some discussion back and forth it was finally decided that he would improvise, and he asked his teacher for a theme which he could vary. Now Zelter committed the almost incredible faux pas of suggesting the rococo ditty, "Ich träumte einst von Hannchen".

"I don't know the song," Felix said.

"Then I'll play it for you."

Zelter sat down at the piano and with his stiff hands (he had several paralysed fingers) played a very simple song in G Major, dominated by a movement of triplets. "Felix", Rellstab continues his account "first repeated the song, and without reflection—taking the triplet figure *unisono* in both hands, brought his fingers into the track of the main figure, so to speak. . . . But then he plunged without more ado into the wildest allegro. The gentle melody was transformed into a surging figure which he took first in the bass, then in the soprano voice, developing it with lovely contrasts—in short, created a torrential fantasia that poured out like liquid fire —Hummel's manner of dealing with such tasks must have been most in his mind. The whole company was thunderstruck; the boy's small hands worked into the masses of tone, mastered the most difficult combinations; the passages rumbled and dropped like so many pearls, flew by in ethereal whispers; a stream of harmonies flowed forth; surprising contrapuntal phrases were built up among them—only the banal melody was rather neglected and scarcely had a voice in this brilliant parliament of musical tones."[8]

[7] L. Rellstab: op. cit.   [8] L. Rellstab: op. cit.

Rellstab and all the others noticed Felix's remarkable instinct for brevity, even in the stress of improvisation. He did not play one minute longer than he should have. Then, in the enraptured silence, Professor Zelter boomed out condescendingly: "Well, well, you must have been imagining gnomes or dragons. That was a wild ride!" In reality, of course, Zelter was immoderately proud of the boy's *début*. But to Rellstab's vexation—a vexation shared by Felix's famous piano teacher, Ludwig Berger, the old pedagogue treated perfection as something to be taken for granted. Meanwhile Goethe stood up and hugged the boy "in whose childlike features happiness, pride and embarrassment were limned. Goethe took his head between his hands and gave him rough kindly caresses, saying: 'But you will not get away with that alone. You must play more for us before we acknowledge you fully.'"

Goethe, as was well known, was very fond of the Bach fugues.[9] Felix was now asked to play one of these. He played it completely unprepared, and with perfect sureness. But: "Why did you leave out the trill?" Zelter asked, frowning. "Because it cannot be played." "I see, I see," Zelter mused in a faintly ironical tone. "Because *you* cannot play it?" "Professor," Felix replied modestly, but with distinct self-assurance, "I do not think anyone can play it. Perhaps it should not be there."

This mixture of artistic insight, modesty and self-assurance delighted the company, who applauded loudly. Goethe asked for a minuet. Felix, who grasped his meaning at once, said: "There is only one," and played the minuet from *Don Giovanni*. Goethe wanted the overture to the opera; the young pianist flatly refused, saying that it was no task for the piano. But the overture to *Figaro* was a different matter; he could play that. And now, Rellstab continues, "he began to play it with a lightness, sureness, roundness and clarity such as I have never heard since. At the same time he reproduced the orchestral effects so excellently, so transparently, and by little touches in the instrumentation produced so cunningly the illusion of accompanying voices, that the effect was utterly enchanting and I might almost say that it gave me more pleasure than any orchestral performance ever did."

Goethe became more and more enlivened. Now he could not have enough of joking with and teasing the boy: "So far you have only played pieces you knew; now let us hear whether you can play something you don't know. I'll fetch something and try you."

Therefore he went out. To fill in the pause, Rellstab asked the boy for a Rondo by Cramer, which Ludwig Berger was very fond of and usually

[9] F. Smend: *Goethes Verhältnis zu Bach*. Berlin, 1954.

worked up with his pupils.[10] "Yes," Felix Mendelssohn exclaimed, "Herr Berger plays that beautifully." At Rellstab's request he began on it, but only tentatively. At one point he struck a false note. Rellstab asked him as he faltered: "Shouldn't it be C-sharp here?" "Yes," Felix said, tossing his head. "C or C-sharp—it can be either!" He did not want to admit that his finger had slipped—but several years later he laughingly mentioned the incident to Rellstab.[11]

Goethe returned to the room carrying music. "Do you think you can play this?"

For Felix, there was no mistaking the clearly inscribed notes in tiny handwriting. A Mozart manuscript! Felix glowed. "An inexpressible feeling of enthusiasm and joy, of admiration and premonition, seized us all," Rellstab relates. The aged Goethe and Mozart, buried these thirty years— here was a greeting from Mozart, via the hand of Goethe, to young Felix Mendelssohn. Felix played with perfect assurance. It was an Adagio, not very difficult, though with a great many demisemiquavers. Well, Goethe laughed, Mozart's scores were well known to be cleanly written. "But what is this here? Take care!"

With that, he placed another sheet on the rack. "It certainly looked very strange. It was hard to say whether these were musical notes or a sheet of lined paper that had been sprayed with ink and then rubbed over. Felix Mendelssohn gave a laugh of surprise. 'What kind of writing is this? How can I read it?'"

"Guess who wrote it?"

"Zelter had come to the piano and looked over Felix's shoulder. 'Why, that was certainly written by Beethoven. You can see it a mile away. He always writes as if he were using a broomstick and afterwards had rubbed his sleeve over the page....'

"In spite of Zelter's sarcasms, Felix suddenly became very grave. A holy awe appeared upon his countenance. He gazed fixedly at the manuscript, and a glow passed over his face as a sublime idea slowly emerged out of the chaos of smudged notes and words scribbled among them. But all this lasted only a second. 'You see!' Goethe cried challengingly. 'I told you so. You will be stuck. Now try, show us what you can do.'"

Felix attacked the song. It took remarkable prescience to determine what had been left, out of ten or twenty deleted passages, and to establish the connections. Rellstab, who stood at the piano, studied the sheet of music in amazement and tried to hum some of the passages, but failed.

[10] K. Gaede: *Alte und neue Klaviermeister*. Leipzig, no date.
[11] L. Rellstab: op. cit.

Mendelssohn alone, it seemed, was able to take in the whole page at one glance. When he attacked the song for the second time, he played the voice part as well, and at one point interrupted himself to exclaim: "That is pure Beethoven—I would have recognized him from that bit alone."

With that Goethe was content—and from then on all Weimar was eager to hear the young piano virtuoso. How modest Felix nevertheless remained is revealed by the fact that, a few days later, attending a party given by the Grand Duchess, he wept when he was asked to play after Johann Nepomuk Hummel, the friend of Haydn and Beethoven.

The letters he wrote from Weimar remained the pride of the Mendelssohn family for decades.[12] Letters from a twelve-year-old boy, they still read with wonderful freshness. And they give us a different version of his first meeting with Goethe:

Weimar, 6 November 1821

...Now listen all of you! Today is Tuesday. Sunday the sun of Weimar, Goethe, arrived. In the morning we went to church, where half of Handel's 100th psalm was given. The organ is big, and yet weak; the Maria organ is much more powerful, although small. This one has 50 registers, 44 voices and 1 times 32 feet. Afterwards I wrote you the little letter of the 4th, and went to the "Elephant", where I drew Lucas Cranach's house. After two hours Professor Zelter came: "Goethe is here, the old gentleman is here!" At once we rushed down the steps into Goethe's house. He was in the garden and was just coming around a hedge. Isn't that strange, father dear? He is very friendly, but I think all pictures of him are not good likenesses. We then looked at his very interesting collection of fossils, which his son had arranged, and kept saying: "Hm, hm, I'm very pleased"; afterwards I walked for half an hour in the garden with him and Professor Zelter. Then we went to table. You would not think him seventy-three, but in his fifties. After dinner Fräulein Ulrike, the sister of Frau Ottilie, asked him for a kiss, and I did likewise. Every morning I receive a kiss from the author of *Faust* and *Werther*, and every afternoon two kisses from my father and friend Goethe. Think of it!! In the afternoon I play for Goethe for more than two hours; part of the time I improvised....

And four days later he continued:

Last time I was with him I played him the G minor sonata,

<hr/>

[12] S. Hensel: *Die Familie Mendelssohn 1729–1847*. Berlin, 1879.

which he liked very much. . . . I am playing much more here than I do at home, rarely less than four hours, at times six and even eight hours. Every afternoon Goethe opens the Streicher piano, saying: "I haven't heard you at all today; give me a little noise," and then he will sit down beside me and when I am finished I ask for a kiss or take one. You cannot imagine his kindness and friendliness, nor the wealth of minerals, busts, copper-engravings, small statues and big drawings that the Pole Star of poets owns. I don't find his stature imposing; he is not much taller than father. But his bearing, his speech, his name are imposing. He has a tremendously resonant voice, and he can shout like ten thousand warriors. His hair is not yet white, his walk is firm, his talk gentle. Tuesday Professor Zelter wanted to take us to Jena and from there straight on to Leipzig; Saturday evening Adele Schopenhauer was with us, and contrary to his habit Goethe also stayed the whole evening. The talk turned to our departure, and Adele decided that we must all go and throw ourselves at Professor Zelter's feet and beg for a few additional days. He was haled into the room, and now Goethe unleashed his voice of thunder, scolded Professor Zelter for wanting to take us along to that dull old town, ordered him to be still and to obey without contradicting, to leave us here, to go to Jena alone and come back, and overcame him so completely that he will do as Goethe says. After this triumph Goethe was beset on all sides; his mouth and hands were kissed, and those who could not reach him to kiss him caressed him and kissed his shoulders; if he had not been at home I think we would have accompanied him to his house as the Roman people did Cicero after the first Catiline oration. Incidentally, Fräulein Ulrike had thrown her arms around his neck too, and since he is paying her court (she is very pretty), all this together had a most excellent effect. . . .

Observations of a twelve-year-old boy. Not at all overwhelmed by the aura of the great man, he describes it all with the delicate humour of a Jean Paul. But the observations are sharp and unerring. Adele Schopenhauer, for example: the portrait of her drawn by Felix agrees astonishingly with the picture of her that emerges from her later autobiography, *Leben einer Einsamen*.[13] And that voice of thunder—like something out of the Old Testament or Handel. Goethe, ordinarily soft-spoken, knew how to enforce respect if he so wished—as he had done that time in the

---

[13] Adele Schopenhauer: *Leben einer Einsamen*. Leipzig, 1921.

Weimar Theatre when a stupid audience laughed at a play by Ludwig Tieck and he had boomed down into the pit: "No laughter!"[14]

As for the kisses that Goethe daily gave the "Jew-boy", the anti-Semite Houston Stewart Chamberlain, the well-known English renegade and son-in-law of Richard Wagner, takes Goethe to task for having so contaminated himself.[15]

A WORD ABOUT ZELTER

Who was this man who for decades took charge of the "ministry of music" in Goethe's house? He was Karl Friedrich Zelter, a Berliner whom the Bavarian Riethmüller called "that loutish bear from the north" —not without secret admiration.[1]

Born the son of a mason, Karl Friedrich had risen rapidly out of his class. He had intended to be an architect until he was called to succeed Fasch as director of the Berlin *Singakademie*. To Zelter, Haydn's music was supreme. His enthusiasm for the choruses of *The Creation* and *The Seasons* was boundless—as is evident in the letter he wrote in March 1804 to Haydn in Vienna to persuade the old man, who could no longer travel, to come to Berlin.[2]

On the whole the secret of Zelter's charm lay in his manner of blunt rudeness. It was a rather artificial rudeness, which he employed more or less on principle. He took pleasure in making his pupils tremble, reducing the girls to tears, and then making up for it by a show of rough kindliness. His witticisms were famous. In mind and character Zelter was "an original". But he also went to some trouble to keep up his reputation for eccentricity. There is, for example, the case of those famous five hundred letters Zelter wrote to Goethe, whose rough-hewn quality so delighted the great man. The fact is that Zelter prepared preliminary drafts of these letters, and in copying them out edited them skilfully to add to the impression of spontaneous vigour.[3]

Goethe was uncommonly fond of him. Among the many people with whom he exchanged letters, he prized Zelter next to Schiller. The contrast

[14] Ph. Stine: *Goethe als Theaterleiter*. Berlin, 1905.
[15] H. Stewart Chamberlain: *Goethe*. Munich, 1912.
[1] B. Riethmüller: *Monacensia*. Munich, no date.
[2] H. E. Jacob: *Joseph Haydn: His Art, Times and Glory*. New York, 1950.
[3] L. Geiger: *Briefwechsel zwischen Goethe und Zelter*. Leipzig, 1902.

of their natures was one factor. Goethe was the son of a Frankfurt patrician, later ennobled; Zelter was a petty bourgeois of proletarian origin
who, with a touching craving for education, aimed all his aspirations
toward the world of Goethe, and quickly found his way into it. Had his
show of roughness been genuine, he would never have succeeded, for he
would have scarcely been able to navigate through all the subtleties of
that world. As early as June 1798, when his acquaintance with Zelter
was still new, Goethe wrote to August Wilhelm Schlegel: "Zelter's talk
is as robust as a mason's, but his feelings are sensitive and musical." It
was Zelter's sensitivity that moved Goethe. When Zelter's wife died, the
bereaved husband wrote a short memorial to her in which he included a
description of her singing: "The tones flowed gently and freely the
moment she opened her mouth. . . . Through three and a half octaves my
wife's scale was like a precious string of polished diamonds, merging the
one into the other and at the same time separate; from which there proceeded a cantilena that was no surprise, but that delighted me afresh
more and more, the more I heard it."[4] This could have been written only
by a man whose display of roughness was merely a protective shell for a
deep vulnerability.

The friendship with Goethe began after Zelter had set to music a few
poems which Goethe had contributed to Schiller's *Musenalmanach*.[5] Two
years after Schiller's death, in 1807, Zelter—operating from distant Berlin
—arranged the famous Thursday concerts in Goethe's house. This meant
that many hours each week were devoted to music, which would have
been merely a burden for an unmusical person. But it is really time to
put aside the myth that Goethe was unmusical. In his youth he had
learned the clavier and 'cello, and he could read a score intelligently even
when no instrument was at hand. We should not overestimate his con-
versance with music, however; it was a matter of course in the eighteenth
century, a normal part of a gentleman's education. The locus of Goethe's
problem with music lay elsewhere. He feared music, feared to be over-
powered by it. He had once made his Werther die of overpowering love;
now, in his old age, he did not want to become a "romantic fool for
music". Led by Zelter's firm hand, there was little likelihood that he
ever would.

Goethe's interest in acoustics was far from incidental. Even before he
had made the acquaintance of Zelter he had written to the well-known
musician Johann Friedrich Reichardt that what was wanted was a

[4] K. F. Zelter: *Selbstdarstellung*, selected by Willi Reich. Zürich, 1955.
[5] H. J. Moser: *Goethe und die Musik*. Leipzig, 1949.

modern theory of sound—as a counterpart to his theory of colour. "Let us", he suggested, "attack acoustics together. These great subjects must be explored by several persons simultaneously if science is to advance." Nothing came of this suggestion, but that was Reichardt's rather than Goethe's fault. Reichardt preferred to compose settings of Goethe's poems (he issued them in three volumes), rather than plunge into a study of the physics of sound. Goethe remained convinced, however, that the phenomena of sound obeyed fixed laws, that in the realm of tone there existed something corresponding to the rainbow in colour. He spoke of tonal prisms, and had a fruitful dispute with Zelter over the nature of the triad and the distinction between major and minor.[6]

A number of writers had insinuated that Zelter abused his power over Goethe to keep the master away from other composers who might have put Zelter's own compositions into the shade. Perhaps he did. In the case of Mozart, at any rate, he did not succeed; perhaps he had been on the scene too short a time. As director of the Weimar Theatre, Goethe showed remarkable boldness in putting on all the major operas of Mozart from 1791 (the year of Mozart's death) to 1798. They were all performed in German. Even the librettos of the operas interested him, so that he began to work on a continuation of *The Magic Flute* until Schiller suggested to him that such an enterprise was pointless with Mozart dead.[7]

Zelter's own position on Mozart, whose genius he did not deny, was not free of human resentments. With his Prussian, puritanical nature, he was outraged by the ease with which Mozart had composed. He took no account of the profound passion underlying that ease, and misunderstood Mozart's eroticism. A full thirty years after Mozart's death he was still nursing these charges. In a letter to Goethe he took occasion to say that wanton wiles and "much time spent with women" had carried off Mozart at so early an age. A wilder mis-statement could scarcely be conceived.[8]

But there is no doubt that Zelter must be blamed for Goethe's lack of understanding for the two greatest composers of his old age: Franz Schubert and Ludwig van Beethoven. In the case of Schubert, of course, the misunderstanding was more or less inevitable. Not only Zelter, but all the other musicians of the Goethe circle would have considered Schubert's songs revolutionary—had they even known them. Schubert's compositions infringed upon the "primacy of poetry". Goethe's poems were stanzaic

[6] H. J. Moser: op. cit.
[7] R. Benz: *Die Welt der Dichter und die Musik*. Düsseldorf, 1949.
[8] L. Geiger: op. cit.

in structure. Schubert, and Beethoven in part, ignored this fact. They conceived the poem as a plot and composed dramatic, forward-moving music to the stanzas. Goethe would have none of this. Not perceiving that this bold musical approach impressed his poem upon the listener even more strongly, he feared that his texts would drown in the music. A melody, he insisted, should be strictly neutral so that it would fit all stanzas.

Zelter shared this view, although for reasons other than Goethe's— since he himself was, after all, a musician and not a poet. He once cleverly defended his theory in a lengthy letter to Loewe, the ballad master. "I am", he wrote (the letter is undated but was written some time around 1824), "not in favour of through-composing stanzaic poems." A melody, he went on to say, ought to be of such a nature that it could be heard with pleasure several times. In through-composition, on the other hand, the melody became stuck to the text. "Words are dead; the tongue casts them off; in tone alone dwells the life of the song." Curious words, these. Zelter seemed to be saying that to "through-compose" a poem was to make music subservient to every turn of phrase in the text. On the contrary, he felt, a stanzaic melody ought to be sufficiently dominant to adjust gracefully but imperiously to the poet's language. On this score Zelter rejected Loewe's through-composed ballads.[9]

To our modern sensibility, just the opposite is correct. Music only serves the text properly if each of its subsidiary voices, each of the accompanying figures, illuminates the poem polyphonically. When Zelter wrote condescendingly to Loewe, "I like to let the accompaniment proceed so that if necessary the melody may stand *without* it," the good old man was simply making it only too clear that he was not Schubert's contemporary.

Can we imagine Schubert's "Erlkönig" without Schubert's accompaniment?[10] Without that galloping figure:

Could the onrushing G minor, which fills the whole poem with action, possibly be omitted? The music gives us, more graphically than any

[9] H. J. Moser: op. cit.
[10] F. Günther: *Schuberts Lied*. Stuttgart, 1928.

words, the horse and rider; they brush by us and already have become an echo.

Yet Goethe did not hear that. He did not even open the package of music sent him from Vienna on 17th April 1816 by Josef von Spaun, accompanied by a letter recommending "a nineteen-year-old composer named Franz Schubert".[11] Movingly, Spaun's letter spoke of the young man's talent. Among the songs included in the package were "Gretchen am Spinnrad", "Erlkönig", "Heidenröslein", "Erster Verlust", "Wanderers Nachtlied", "Rastlose Liebe". Poor Schubert? Poorer Goethe, who was never to know the miracles that had been performed with his own poems, never to know Gretchen's lullaby of death. For when she spins, "Meine Ruh ist hin, mein Herz ist schwer", the accompaniment ceases to be a musical figure; it becomes phantasmal reality.

Goethe did actually hear Schubert's "Erlkönig"—long after Schubert's death, performed by the dramatic singer Wilhelmine Schröder-Devrient;[12] he was more impressed by her magnificent singing than by the strange composition. On the other hand he praised Corona Schröter's altogether inconsequential setting of the same poem. Corona Schröter, whom he had once sketched sleeping, the charming lady of Weimar and the darling of her friends. She set the "Erlkönig" to music for a social occasion and sang it at night on the bank of the Ilm river.[13] Everyone was entranced. The social occasion was the performance of Goethe's singspiel, Die Fischerin; the ballad of the Earl King had no real business there, but was used as a prelude to the singspiel, for which the entire court of Weimar had assembled. To Goethe, man of the eighteenth century that he was, singing songs was a matter of sociability. Mozart, too, had had the same feeling. Zelter certainly had it. These men loved rounds as they loved games of forfeits and good-natured teasing. They knew nothing of the boundless loneliness out of which Beethoven and Schubert had created their songs. We shall have a good deal more to say later on about Felix Mendelssohn's reasons for combining, in the choral productions of his great decade, the Schubert and the Zelter veins: loneliness and sociability ("Wer hat dich, du schöner Wald . . .").

There had been a good many attempts to wean Goethe away from the musical influence of Zelter. Johann Christian Lobe—the man who accompanied young Mendelssohn—had made one such gallant effort in 1820.

[11] F. Hug: Franz Schubert: Leben und Werk eines Frühvollendeten. Frankfurt am Main, 1958.
[12] E. Genast: Aus Weimars klassischer und nachklassischer Zeit. Stuttgart, 1904.
[13] H. J. Moser: op. cit.

In his masterly *Goethe and Beethoven*, Romain Rolland has given a detailed account of this scene at Weimar, deriving his facts from Lobe's own account.[14]

Lobe tried to make Goethe aware of the antiquated quality of Zelter's compositions. Zelter, Lobe pointed out, always placed accent, rhythm and melody so that they accorded with the words, but his figuration was outmoded. Modern composers, he argued, have given the accompaniment "the dignity of an auxiliary expression of the sentiment". If Goethe were to listen to the bass and middle voices of Zelter's songs, the melody being eliminated, he would find a singular lack of any movement sympathetic to the emotion of the poem. Zelter's accompaniments were always purely mechanical. In a song by Mozart, Weber or Beethoven, on the other hand, the life and stirring of the emotion in question was frequently felt even without the melody, when the accompaniment was played independently. . . . It was to be hoped that music would ultimately reach the point at which every subsidiary voice made a contribution, no matter how small, to the expression of the feeling.

"Goethe", Romain Rolland writes, "listened silent and attentively, with bowed head. Then he went to the piano, opened it and said: 'Give me an example. If your deductions are correct, you should be able to prove them.'"

Thereupon Johann Christian Lobe played a song of Zelter's, melody and accompaniment separately. He then followed with one of Beethoven's —one of the songs of Klärchen from *Egmont*:

> Die Trommel gerühret!
> Das Pfeifchen gespielt!
> Mein Liebster gewaffnet
> Dem Haufen befiehlt,
> Die Lanze hoch führet,
> Die Leute regieret.

But either because Lobe did not play well enough or Goethe at this moment remembered the feelings of gratitude he had toward loyal old Zelter—whatever the reason, he shook his head and remained silent for a while. Then he declared that theoretically what the advocates of novelty wanted was all very interesting. The proposition that every voice ought to have something to say on its own sounded very well indeed. But it was still open to question whether this rule really applied to every musical work of art. There were after all weaknesses and unrealities in art which

[14] Romain Rolland: *Goethe and Beethoven*. New York, 1931.

had to be retained; otherwise one approached too close to nature and that would produce a clash that would destroy everything.... In a significant dialogue "On Truth and Verisimilitude" he had as early as 1797 advanced the difficult proposition: "What is true to art and true to nature are completely different matters." And as late as 1820 he wrote in a letter to Zelter: "To paint sounds by sounds, to thunder, to trumpet, to plash, to slap, is detestable."[15]

And this pillar of conservatism, this Zelter whose influence over Goethe was so enormous, brought Mendelssohn into his house only a year after Lobe's protest. Well trained, a good pupil, the boy for the present put on an excellent sham of being a conservative himself, though a few years later he was to ascend the peaks of Romanticism with his *Overture to A Midsummer Night's Dream*. Zelter sinned against Schubert (though he hardly knew his name) and against Beethoven, whom he did not understand. But he partially atoned for all this by his gift of Mendelssohn to Goethe in 1821, and of Goethe to Mendelssohn.

As yet Felix was still a child—so much a child, with a childlike love of toys and novelties that Adele Schopenhauer cut out for his amusement the silhouette of a musical scale, with a winged hobby-horse riding over it. Below this Goethe wrote the following piece of album verse:

> When hobby horses gallop over
> The lines and spaces of the score,
> You'll boldly ride through music's clover
> And lighten many a heart that's sore
> As you have done with youthful charms;
> We all of us wish you back in our arms.[16]

It was no pious wish. The "precious boy" came back to visit many times. Soon he was no longer a boy, but a young man and a master. The name Felix, crops up again and again in the correspondence between the two old men—as if he were a grandson. Again and again Goethe asked after him, and never tired of hearing news about him from Zelter. Abraham, Leah and Fanny paid visits to Goethe's house in Weimar— and his mother Leah had the strange experience of hearing Goethe, now nearing eighty, declare: "He is my David—and I am Saul...."

[15] H. J. Moser: op. cit.
[16] Johann Wolfgang von Goethe: *Gedichte*. Volständige Ausgabe, Stuttgart, 1949.

REVIEWS AND CONDESCENSIONS

When Felix's first compositions appeared in print, the critics found themselves confronted by a curious task. He was Zelter's favourite pupil, and Zelter was a commanding figure in Berlin musical life. Thus the old man would have been offended if the F minor Quartet (opus 2) dedicated to him had been received unfavourably. Nevertheless the critics found—and they were not entirely wrong—that Mendelssohn's amazing control of form was accompanied by a certain poverty of ideas (as is frequently the case with children). But "these are defects which will fall away of their own accord once this talented composer has achieved greater intellectual freedom." This F minor piano quartet had been preceded by another in C minor (opus 1), dedicated to Prince Radziwill, which was more vigorous and independent in invention and in the development of the thematic material. A concluding motif like this one:

would not have disgraced the later Mendelssohn.[1]

As a rule gifted children have experienced nothing but their own diligence and their ambition to please grown-ups. But that was not the case with opus 4, the F minor Violin Sonata, which Felix wrote for his dear friend Eduard Rietz, the young violinist who was to die of consumption soon afterwards. Here the critics made a bad mistake. Instead of greeting the sonata with an enthusiastic Aye, they adopted an air of benevolent condescension toward it, and administered the kind of praise that young people cannot bear. A certain Lukas van Leyden—or rather, a man who was hiding behind this pseudonym—undertook to analyse the sonata as an expert theorist. With patently phony fatherliness he began—we take the liberty of condensing somewhat:[2]

> "Two fine young men come along and want to play us some music, and an old man like myself is supposed to review it. Ah, I'd sooner fiddle along with them. But that is not even necessary,

[1] E. Wolff: *Felix Mendelssohn-Bartholdy*. Berlin, 1909.
[2] *Berliner Allgemeine Musikalische Zeitung*. Berlin, 1825.

for one of the friends, young Herr Rietz, is supposed to be a first-rate fiddler—in the good old style, with a fondness for a big, full bow and a firm, juicy tone. . . . And the other, Mendelssohn, is a fine fellow in his own right, too. I recently saw part of a symphony of his, a fugal movement on a good subject—and the inevitable wind instruments follow along in imitation with another theme.

"——But the present sonata particularly pleased me. One of the best things about it is that young Herr Mendelssohn did not call it *grande Sonate* or *grande Sonate pathétique et mélancholique* as is the unfortunate habit nowadays. Because people will insist on having everything big, big. . . .

"The sonata is composed in F minor—young composers are much disposed toward the minor—I would wager that young Herr Mendelssohn has already written a good many other things in the minor. The violin begins improvising away, and would have climbed right up out of sight, as so often happens, if there were no ground bass. But just at the right time the friend at the piano intervenes, suggesting that without a sound theme the thing probably won't work out too well. So the composer remembers the fiddler and from the piano plays his friend a regular violin theme, fine and delicate and full of *élan*:

I understand, young gentlemen: if one of you is longing for G flat major, the other soon leads him off to the parallel key A flat major. But still I must shake my head over the shift to G flat. If you boys like such makeshifts, don't be so shifty about it. If a person's heart is swelling so that he'd like to jump out of his skin, he doesn't creep like a thief around the corner. . . . But now take a look at your music sheet:

The fiddle hops in one spot, the right hand at the piano reaches out as though it had burned its fingers, and the left does not dare even to approach—and to top it off, ritenuto! ... And then, my dear Herr Mendelssohn, what kind of transition is that between your main and secondary themes! The main theme concludes in the first measure of the fifth staff, and now the bass stumbles, like a sleepy servant, some eight measures behind his master. It would no doubt have been better to continue the figure with a bigger motion down below. Not to mention better improvements. That kind of thing carries its own punishment; for behold, in the working out and transition to the reprise this fine stumbler of a bass comes rushing up twice more."

From this point on, van Leyden no longer bothered to maintain even a semblance of amiability. Lingering on a fermata in E flat; newfangled emotional cloudiness. Sometimes the piece was almost in Haydn's manner; but what was the meaning of floating off this way into B flat major? "At the finale, however, the young gentlemen make up for it all and turn out something both good and correct before they part with a handshake." With a similar handshake and the gruff pronouncement, "Those who cannot take criticism are not worthy of praise", the pseudonymous Lukas also takes his leave.

No ambitious young artist could endure such condescension. In his later life—apart from his unfortunate attempt at opera, *The Wedding of Camacho*—Mendelssohn was to undergo little unfavourable criticism. Everything he wrote, whether orchestral or chamber music, *lied* or oratorio, was received by his contemporaries with overwhelming approbation. Neither Haydn, Mozart nor Beethoven ever basked in such sunlight. Nor were they particularly touchy if they were not understood. Mozart, in fact, rather enjoyed adverse criticism, and would sling gutter expressions at his detractors.

But Felix Mendelssohn was touchy, although he concealed his hurt feelings behind humour. He even made up a few verses on the subject, which he gave to his mother for her birthday on 15th March 1826:

> If the composer's tone is grave,
>> He puts us all to sleep;
> If the composer's tone is gay,
>> He isn't one bit deep.
>
> If the composer's tune is long,
>> Pity the mangy cur;

> If the composer's tune is short,
>   Why then it doesn't stir.
>
> If the composer's line is clear,
>   Plainly he's a fool;
> If the composer is obscure
>   Send him back to school.
>
> No matter how he turns his phrase,
>   Nobody's content;
> Therefore the composer must
>   Follow his own bent.

And this was the plaint of a composer who was soon to be the most spoiled of all. What would Schubert have said—then at the age of twenty-nine and with only two more years to live? He was not even attacked by the critics; he was too unknown, was composing only for his friends, the Spauns, Schobers, Sayrhofers and Schwinds. In the same issue of the Berlin musical journal which treated Mendelssohn's sonata for Rietz with such insulting condescension, an inspired correspondent from Vienna wrote:

"The young composer Schubert goes on indefatigably writing songs; his first productions, especially the 'Erlenkönig' [sic!] have won an audience which, however, seems to be gradually diminishing [!]. A Mass by him has also been published by Diabelli. His ballads are more successful. The most sought-after and saleable wares in Vienna, however, continue to be the favourite songs from the musical farces of the suburban theatres."[3]

A C MINOR SYMPHONY

Lucas van Leyden had chided Felix for the "frowns" and fake Beethovenizing of his music. Was he altogether in the wrong? Youth does have this love of the tragic. This is understandable simply in terms of contrast: a young person protected from every raw wind that blows thinks it would be perfectly splendid to be Beethoven and spend his life in some gloomy C minor. Felix had never seen Beethoven, but he knew of

[3] Ibid.

his tribulations. Here was a man of immeasurable greatness—like Prometheus who had brought the gift of fire to mankind, Beethoven had given
his age a new music. And like Prometheus, who was so cruelly punished
for his temerity, Beethoven was punished by loss of hearing.

Young Mendelssohn fired a Beethoven salvo of violins in the first
Allegro of his C minor Symphony—a symphony remarkable in many
ways, though it had nothing Beethovenian about it.

Its first performance took place in the Mendelssohn concert hall. His
friend Marx, who as usual occupied the corner seat of the first row, sat
with crossed legs and listened attentively. He jotted down the notes of the
initial theme. The work was still unprinted and he did not have the score;
therefore, with a certain cautiousness, he put a small question mark above
the third measure.

And he wrote the following commentary: "A searing fire pours out of
this first Allegro—and in the second subject the wind instruments strain
toward this wild blaze like a band of imploring virgins in rippling veils.

Oboes, clarinets, flutes. . . ." Imploring virgins—rippling veils! How rightly Marx had guessed. For Felix had actually become entangled in Beethoven's *Coriolanus* here, in the tragic strife between wrath and gentleness which fills Beethoven's overture. Felix had never experienced that conflict, but he had participated in it through Beethoven's music—and how he longed to be Beethoven!

Mendelssohn was never to know Richard Wagner's interpretation of the *Coriolanus* overture. And he would only have smiled at Wagner's dictum that *every* one of Beethoven's tone-paintings depicted the struggle of man and woman. But he would have had to agree with Wagner's conclusion that "gentleness overwhelms savagery", that the hero Coriolanus "with a terrible and violent hand stabs like a sword, straight into his own heart, all the power which he had hitherto devoted to the destruction of his native land, in order that peace and reconciliation may prevail". That had scarcely been the conception of the author, Heinrich von Collin. But —Wagner concludes his essay—that was how Beethoven drew his musical portrait of Coriolanus.[1]

But *Coriolanus* was not the only influence on Felix in his C minor Symphony. There are also traces of Beethoven's *Waldstein Sonata* which though written twenty years before was still so alien to most people. But young Mendelssohn understood that it was no attempt to destroy the old sonata form, but to expand all the proportions of that form.[2] People had complained that this sonata was "much too long"—so long, in fact, that Beethoven was compelled to remove the F major Andante. But Felix Mendelssohn knew better. He was mad about the figuration and the luxuriant cadenzas. He had also all but memorized the strange opening. As yet he did not dare to draw the necessary conclusion for himself: to eliminate the usual broad and brilliantly resounding tonic chord and instead—as he was later to do—to "toss wanton tonal chains wildly about". "The cadenza will have to show me what key I am really writing in."

Marx, sitting there taking his notes, found the Finale too spendthrift with its orchestral tutti and mighty thunder of drums. What next? The second movement, the Adagio, dissolved in the middle into "soft, almost insipid melodies". What had become of Beethoven? Didn't this smack of Mozart, not the tragic but the too-charming Mozart whom the new musicians, the followers of Beethoven, were beginning to find unbearable? The flute here was much too weak—this was no place for cantilena.

---

[1] R. Wagner: *Gesammelte Schriften und Dichtungen*. Leipzig, 1907.
[2] A. Wheelock Thayer: *Ludwig van Beethovens Leben*. Leipzig, 1911.

But then Marx breathed a sigh of relief, for the Scherzo came rushing in with its "wild whimsy", gradually to be "tempered to yearning sadness by an overwhelmingly beautiful trio". And suddenly Beethoven was back, in the energetic presto finale which brought the symphony to an animated end.

It was the symphony of a fifteen-year-old boy who "did not want to be Mendelssohn because he did not know what that was". But he would soon know.

THE OCTET

"Jesting is only for those who are grave and deep." This saying of Nietzsche's applies to Mendelssohn. Teasing was in fact an essential outlet for him. Since Mozart's childhood, no young man's head had been so crammed with music: the Piano Sonata in G minor which he played to Goethe (which later appeared in his posthumous works as opus 105); another in D major; another for piano and clarinet; the *Characteristic Pieces* (opus 7) dedicated to his teacher, Ludwig Berger; the Piano Quartet in B flat minor, whose dedication was accepted by Goethe and which was published as opus 3; the F sharp minor Capriccio, opus 5; the remarkable D major Sextet (piano, violin, two violas, 'cello and double bass), which Felix himself did not much care for and which was published only after his death as opus 110. In addition he was producing compositions for the church, such as a five-voiced *Kyrie eleison* and a *Magnificat* for choir and orchestra. Also: the String Quintet in A major (opus 18) *singspiele* for family use—these latter by no means casually sketched out, but written with sufficient polish so that they might be given in public if occasion arose. It was a great deal—in fact it was too much. For a while Felix compensated for this excessive creative activity by a very healthy craving for sleep. He was capable of falling asleep while standing or talking. When that faculty disappeared—much later in life—his health would be seriously endangered.

But in the main his chief relaxation was through "nonsense"—dressing up, playing pranks with his friends and sisters. They would put on masks and convert midsummer to carnival time; they would rush through the garden or climb recklessly out on the roof at night, meowing like tomcats, to hand fruit in at the window of a lady with a Polish name.[1] Or a rather blasé Felix would condescend to be worshipped by the friends of his little

---

[1] A. B. Marx: *Erinnerungen aus meinem Leben*. Berlin, 1865.

sister Rebecca, by Doris Zelter and clever little Therese Schlesinger.[2] Sometimes, too, Bernhard Klein, the young musician from Cologne, whom old Zelter could not bear, would join the party. But then, who could bear Zelter? Certainly Marx could not—he spoke acidly of Zelter's claims upon Felix. "Zelter saw the fish swimming—and now he actually imagines that he taught him to swim."[3]

Along with Marx, the Heydemann brothers, and his best friend, Klingemann, who was later to enter upon a diplomatic career, Felix founded a "garden newspaper". An old table, ten sheets of paper, ink and pens, were all the equipment needed. Every member of the household who passed by was waylaid and forced to contribute a comment, a charade, a poem, a quip, or a sentiment from the depths of his soul. All this stuff was read in succession, and the more preposterous it was, the more the editors roared with laughter. (The practice was continued for months; in winter, when there was no lingering in the garden, a "snow and tea newspaper" was substituted.) The grown-ups put up with the levy: Henrik Steffens, the Norwegian historian of Romanticism,[4] whose mental state was such that he always ran a slight fever, made his contribution to the newspaper. Town Councillor Mendelssohn did likewise—was it here that he first inscribed his famous *bon mot*: "In the past I was my father's son and now I am my son's father"? Master Zelter in person, the rising young historian Droysen, and no less a personage than Alexander Humboldt all obliged with inscriptions for the amusement of the young.[5]

But the young were not always so giddy-minded. They had serious discussions, as for example when they spoke of Jean Paul Richter, the polar opposite of Goethe, and went so far as to say that Jean Paul was sometimes more modern and more absolute than the circumspect Olympian of Weimar. The most radical of the group was Rebecca Mendelssohn—"a plump girl, a dear child, so pretty, so good, every pound an angel", Heinrich Heine wrote of her. In passionate accents she would recite from the final pages of Jean Paul's *Die Flegeljahre* ("The Awkward Age"): "Then I saw out there—I do not know whether it was near or far—the *true land* spread out before me in a twilit sheen. . . . Tiny green-and-gold clouds dropped warm rain over the land, and liquid light overflowed and dripped down from the chalices of roses and lilies."[6] And she would exclaim: "Don't tell me Goethe could have written that!"

[2] Th. Schlesinger-Devrient: *Jugenderinnerungen*. Stuttgart, 1905.
[3] E. Wolff: *Felix Mendelssohn-Bartholdy*. Berlin, 1909.
[4] R. Huch: *Die Blütezeit der Romantik*. Leipzig, 1905.
[5] A. B. Marx: op. cit.
[6] Jean Paul Richter: *Flegeljahre*. Stuttgart, 1957.

This sort of talk made Felix uneasy. But before he could protest, the conversation had turned away from Jean Paul and come around to Beethoven. Everyone had the greatest reverence for Beethoven, as was only right, yet was it not strange that someone should say (it was Horn, the doctor) that music must stop when Jovian Beethoven died? How could anyone say such a thing? Music would never die—and great as Beethoven was, you had to ask yourself whether it was not time for his "self-righteous accents" and his penetrating "characteristic music" to be replaced by music in gentler moods. . . . At which point Marx flared up, for it was he who had propagated the idea—in a recent article—that the death of Beethoven would mean the death of music. The rest of the company tried to placate him. It was better to draw him out on the subject of painting in music,[7] which was a pet idea of his. "Must music always be sculptural?" Marx had written. "Must there always be motifs? Do not the shifts in tonal colours suffice? The blue Meander that has just been drawn by a flute is turned green, blackish green, by a gentle French horn. Can't you hear that?" Everyone found that approach intriguing. But Felix Mendelssohn did not like to have the subject talked to death. He hated conversation about the arts; he felt there was something unchaste about it.[8]

Composing was a responsible kind of work. It was far more difficult than writing, as singing was more difficult than talking. Dissonances among words were never noticed; they hardly mattered. There were no pitches among words, no high and low; they ran along on a level. But music was entirely different. If a piece of music was false it infected adjacent ideas, it made the whole world deaf and blind. It was not good for musicians to talk about music. Arguments and verbal battles were all right for the writer, the *homo literatus*, but not for the composer, who must guide himself entirely by his ear.

And so Felix listened. But suddenly a smile played over his features. He had noticed that there were eight persons in the garden: his close friend Rietz, the Heydemanns,[9] Fanny and Therese, Klingemann, and Kielmann, the confidential clerk of Schickler's bank and an ardent 'cellist who always asked the Mendelssohns whether he might bring his wife with him. The wife always turned out to be his 'cello. . . .[10] And as Felix looked at the lively group, he realized that for a good hour he had really

---

[7] A. B. Marx: *Maigruss an die Kunstphilosophen*. Berlin, 1828.

[8] E. Wolff: op. cit.

[9] O. Dambach: *Gedächtnisrede auf Ludwig Ed. Heydemann*. Berlin, 1874.

[10] G. Parthey: *Jugenderinnerungen*. Berlin, 1871.

been working on his Octet. Eight persons, eight voices. And no flutes and horns this time. Eight string-instruments could no doubt be made to yield a blue-green Meander. E flat major. Four violins, two violas, two 'cellos. . . . Still, it was not to be merely a string quartet multiplied by two. Every instrument would have its individual part, and would contribute to a meaningful dialectic. It would be music of an ethereal sort that rose high above intellectuality.

The architecture of the piece was glorious, free, bold, expansive; there was nothing crowded and crooked about it. And everything was in balance. The Octet is purest, truest Mendelssohn and perhaps this was the first time that he found himself. There is not a single note in it which is vague and indeterminate. On the other hand nothing is overdetermined or obdurate; no part gets into a rut as sometimes happened with the sonatas and symphonies of the classicists, who often carried a good thing too far, developing developments and varying variations. Mendelssohn was a classicist too. But his classicism of form was coupled with subjective romanticism and that was something utterly new. It was a new kind of music when, above the billowing inner parts, the first violin climbs "like to the lark at break of day arising":

A second introduces the second subject:

They join. Then, unisono, fortissimo, the semiquaver passages roar along: all eight instruments carry the first subject away. The second movement, lyrical and somewhat like a folk song, is a meditative Andante. Underneath this apparent simplicity, however, there is a surreptitious polyphony which the composer cleverly conceals; it is as though he wanted to let his listeners hear nothing but colours. It was a trick which no one before him had mastered but Carl Maria von Weber in that passage which begins in the tenth measure of the *Freischütz* overture. But

Weber used his thematic material in an entirely different way. It would have exceeded his powers to make an "allegro leggierissimo" the heart of a fantasy. Yet this is the *tour de force* which the young composer of the Octet carried off so brilliantly. Here is music as fey as the words with which Goethe concluded his Walpurgis Night scene in the First Part of *Faust*:

> Scudding clouds and misty meads
>> Are tinged by light of day.
> Gusts in the leaves and wind in the reeds
>> And all is blown away.

"It is a complete success," Fanny exulted.[11] "I was the only one he told what he had in mind. The whole piece is played staccato and pianissimo, with shivering tremolandos and light, brilliant flashes of inverted mordents. Everything is new, strange and yet so familiar, so intimate; one feels so close to the world of spirits, lifted so lightly into the air; one is tempted to take a broomstick in hand, the better to follow the light-hearted company. At the end the first violin flutters upward, light as a feather—and all is blown away."

Here was the keen insight of a loving sister. She herself was a talented composer—though this gift of hers remained a private one. Her parents did not think that it became a girl to put her talents on display. Mendelssohn incorporated some of his sister's compositions into his own works.

All is blown away. But a Scherzo cannot conclude a work. Hence a racing polyphonic Presto formed the Finale of the Octet. Mysterious in the true Mendelssohn spirit—with that dreamy depth which is also found in *A Midsummer Night's Dream*, in the *Hebrides* overture, and in the masterpieces of his maturity. The main subject of the Scherzo returns again as an airy pianissimo, only to be scared away by the rough final motifs.

It is truly an amazing work. The Capriccio, the "goose-pimply whisking", was a mode he created for himself. In that sphere no one could teach him anything: neither Mozart, who is light but not as light as air, nor Weber, whose lightness is also a good deal heartier. It is not to be found in Bach, and certainly not in Beethoven, the wrathful Zeus, the mighty god with his "self-righteous accents". . . . The Octet was the overture to the *Overture to A Midsummer Night's Dream* which Felix was to write a year later. "Both works have earned immortality," Max Bruch said in 1900, "but to me the Octet will always remain the greater miracle."

[11] S. Hensel: *Die Familie Mendelssohn 1729–1847*. Berlin, 1879.

THE WEDDING OF CAMACHO

With the completion of these two works, the Octet and the *Midsummer Night's Dream* overture, the adept had become a master. Zelter could no longer play the role of teacher, though Felix continued to look to him for ideas about counterpoint. We may well see the influence of Zelter in Felix's antiquarian interest in older German music. But Zelter did not contribute to the romantic works, to the Octet and *A Midsummer Night's Dream*. For works such as these the influences of Adolf Bernhard Marx, Bernhard Klein and Ludwig Berger were of far greater importance.[1]

The overture to *A Midsummer Night's Dream* was originally composed as a piano piece for four hands, to be played by Fanny and Felix together; the composer later arranged it for orchestra. It was given its first performance in Stettin by Karl Loewe. Loewe, a distinguished musician and composer of *lieder*, performed the work on 20th February 1827 with a sumptuous orchestra containing twelve first violins. At that same concert Mendelssohn and Loewe played a double concerto for two pianos and Weber's grand F minor free concerto. Then Felix took part as a violinist in the performance of Beethoven's D minor Symphony. This was the first time he had appeared in public and he acquitted himself brilliantly.

For some months Felix had been working on a comic opera whose libretto was based on *The Wedding of Camacho* by Cervantes. Probably his friend Klingemann was responsible for the libretto. But the unfortunate book may have been written by someone else, who afterwards was in no hurry to admit his authorship.

It need not have been "unfortunate". Ever since Ludwig Tieck had translated *Don Quixote*—an accomplishment that contemporaries equated with the Schlegel translation of Shakespeare[2]—Cervantes had been the talk of the salons in Berlin. Felix Mendelssohn's tutor, Heyse, had probably introduced him to the masterpiece.[3] There is also little doubt that he was acquainted with both Tieck's and August Wilhelm Schlegel's opinion of *Don Quixote*: that poetry and parody were not at all contradictory; that it was quite wrong to consider Cervantes only as fore-

---

[1] K. Gaede: *Alte und neue Klaviermeister*. Leipzig, no date.
[2] F. W. Gubitz: *Berühmte Schriftsteller der Deutschen*. Berlin, 1854.
[3] K. W. F. Solger: *Vorlesungen über Ästhetik*. Leipzig, 1829.

shadowing the spirit of Enlightenment and as merely poking fun at the
falsity of the Romances of chivalry. Rather, Schlegel argued, *Don Quixote*
taken as a whole was an altogether romantic work.[4] "Even in minutiae,
romantic wit is evident in the plays on words, in the humour of the language, in the linking of two realms of language and meaning. Plays on
words serve ... just as do the significant playing with motives and situations, to illuminate identities in a flash, to reveal the unity of all existing
things in the cosmos, to allude to its eternal consonance. ... Wit is the
lightning which illuminates every passage in the great whole, even if only
for a moment—and therefore every witticism is sublime because it is a
reminder of the supernal."[5] Later Eichendorff was to go still further: it
did not matter, he wrote, that the contemporaries of Cervantes thought
Don Quixote's character laughable or that they, watching the clash
between insanity and reality, sided with the latter. Don Quixote, Eichendorff said, was in fact the true Romantic, "waging war on philistinism".[6]
With all this in the air, therefore, it was not so strange that young
Mendelssohn should have hit on the Spanish subject.

But still it was a bold fling. The problem was whether operatic music
could master irony. There was a single precedent, and that was Mozart's
Figaro, where the instruments of the orchestra make fun of the singer or,
on the other hand, the pantomime and tone of the singer cancel out
what the orchestra is saying. And these effects are achieved within an
atmosphere of such perfect beauty and keen characterization that it has
never been surpassed.[7]

Mendelssohn had already written a number of unpretentious operettas,
really *singspiele*, which had been performed before groups of friends in
the garden room. But *The Wedding of Camacho* was meant for the
public, though possibly not for an opera house, within whose vast dimensions this opera buffa might have been a bit lost. But it could be given in
a theatre. Since everybody who counted in Berlin in those days frequented
the home of the Mendelssohns, it was easy to arrange matters with Count
Brühl, supervisor of the Royal Theatre.

Brühl was a typical aristocrat. His idea of the best way to please the
court was to pay the closest attention to the historical accuracy of his
costuming. "He would never have forgiven himself", Marx writes, "for

    [4] A. W. Schlegel: *Sämtliche Werke*. Leipzig, 1846–47.
    [5] F. H. Mautner: *"Das Wortspiel und seine Bedeutung." Vierjahrs-
schrift*, 1931.
    [6] W. Brüggemann: *Cervantes und sein Don Quijote in Kunst-
anschauung und Dichtung der deutschen Romantik*. Münster, 1956.
    [7] E. Lert: *Mozart auf dem Theater*. Leipzig, 1913.

using a costume of the thirteenth century where what was wanted was a twelfth- or fourteenth-century costume."[8] Count Brühl could take a Schiller drama and mount it brilliantly. On the other hand he had not the faintest understanding of the so-called "modern stage-direction" which Goethe had instituted in Weimar. Brühl's productions always remained "court theatre"—but they satisfied the Berliner's love for spectacle. In a Brühl performance of Schiller's *Maid of Orleans* the coronation procession, with its array of princes, knights, dignitaries, attendants, children, maidens and soldiers, lasted for a full half-hour and became the heart of the drama. Someone like Brühl, then, would see nothing wrong with *The Wedding of Camacho*—though he might regret that the staging could not be made opulent enough.

There was one more important man who had to be won over: Gasparo Spontini. King Frederick William III of Prussia, a passionate lover of opera, had lured Spontini from Paris, had awarded him the Prussian *Ordre pour le mérite*, and appointed him director of operas with the further promise that he would have the decisive voice in the acceptance of new operas. He and Brühl were supposed to work together, neither being subordinate to the other. Spontini could scarcely make up for the defects of Brühl as director. His talents were musical rather than theatrical: he was one of the outstanding operatic composers of the time, surpassed only by his famous countrymen Cherubini and Rossini.

Spontini had many enemies. They ridiculed his almost womanish vanity, his moss-green frock-coat covered with decorations, his graceful attitudes, and his way of waving his lorgnette. The nationalistic faction made fun of the jumble of French, Italian and German in which he addressed the orchestra during rehearsals: "Meine Erren! Il faut remarquer, dass il forte doit être. . . ." It was up to the long-suffering concertmaster, Möser, to translate this gibberish—but the musicians had no quarrel with their conductor. For Spontini was a first-rate musician.[9]

The banker Abraham Mendelssohn was not among Spontini's enemies. Abraham was no professional musician, of course; but he had excellent eyes and ears, and a good grounding in music from his days in Paris. He held to the opinion that "there will never again be a greater composer of operas than Gluck". On the other hand he well understood that the time for psychological drama was past. The stock in trade of opera had changed. Nowadays it had to reflect splendour, Empire; it had to offer spectacular effects.

[8] A. B. Marx: *Erinnerungen aus meinem Leben*. Berlin, 1865.
[9] Ibid.

Abraham Mendelssohn had attentively followed Spontini's career. He remembered the opera *La Vestale* which had made such a tremendous hit in Paris in 1807, and on the strength of which Spontini had been appointed musical director to the Empress Josephine. We, of course, would find the plot of *La Vestale* somewhat stiff and absurd: Licinius, a young Roman, is in love with Julia, daughter of an aedile. But when he returns home from a campaign he finds that his sweetheart has become a vestal virgin, a guardian of the Sacred Fire. He seeks her out in the temple. They renew their love, but the Sacred Fire goes out because of this blasphemy. Licinius rushes off to secure the help of his faithful followers and liberate Julia from the temple. Before he returns, their misdemeanour is discovered. Julia is cursed and condemned to be buried alive. Licinius and his troops attempt to rescue her. There is a scene of general tumult. In the midst of it a flash of lightning strikes the torn veil that the erring vestal has left upon the altar. The veil catches fire, relighting the Sacred Flame. Thus the gods absolved Julia, and the Roman people gave her to Licinius as his wife.

Why should an opera of this sort have had such an overwhelming success? Evidently its Roman setting made it particularly timely, for France was in the throes of a Roman revival. Thus Spontini became the man of the hour, and the darling of Napoleon. But only two years later Spontini fell into disgrace. Oskar Fleischer has told the story in his essay, "Napoleon Bonapartes Musikpolitik".[10] Napoleon took the view that music was an implement of government and decreed that composers should write to order. Cherubini, the republican, refused to do so. Spontini, on the other hand, was willing to comply. Napoleon was preparing for his campaign in Spain and ordered Spontini to write an opera on a Spanish subject—with the object of whipping up feeling among the French. Napoleon even suggested the subject: *Ferdinand Cortez*. But the idea backfired. So magnificent was the music that the war-weary Parisians stood up and cheered the Spaniards on the stage. . . . Time and again the same embarrassing ovation took place. The opera house had become a nest of treason. Spontini was relieved of his post and barely escaped more serious punishment.[11]

Four years after Napoleon's defeat at Waterloo, Spontini composed a new opera, *Olympia*, in which he outdid himself in exotic effects. There was even a live elephant which appeared on the stage. It was on the basis

---

[10] *Zeitschrift der internationale Musikgesellschaft*. Leipzig, 1901–2.
[11] H. E. Jacob: *Joseph Haydn. His Art, Times and Glory*. New York, 1950.

of this fabulous success that the King of Prussia sent for Chevalier Spontini.

Spontini, however, may well have regretted the charge he had made. In 1821, only a year after his arrival at the Prussian court, the success of Weber's *Freischütz* became the occasion for an anti-Spontini demonstration.[12] A rain of leaflets descended from the upper galleries, containing doggerel verses ridiculing the new director. The king continued to support him, but the Romantics had made him the symbol of what they hated most. A new inwardness, and a new bourgeois temper as well, were on the rise. Once more opera was required to deal with human emotions. Politics and empty spectacle no longer satisfied popular taste.

The Romantics wanted none of Spontini, and he wanted none of Romanticism. As for Mendelssohn—it was natural for Spontini to be wary of him. A young man whom everyone made such a fuss over—was he not pro-Weber into the bargain? Spontini sent for the score—though he was very busy. He read it, smiled a little at its confusions and far-fetchedness, and soon put it aside. The Mendelssohn family seethed with impatience. Finally word came from the office of Count Brühl that the great man, Spontini, would not oppose a performance. But he would also do nothing to favour it. So the matter dragged on for over a year, until, quite unexpectedly, the opera was scheduled for rehearsal and the day set for the première.

At the last moment Felix almost withdrew his opera. Spontini had sent for him and condescendingly criticized the score. The interview took place in the theatre director's office; the great man waved his hand in a grand gesture at the dome of the French church outside the window, and said: "Mon ami, il vous faut des idées grandes, grandes comme cette coupole-là...." The comparison between architecture and music, which Spontini was making, was nothing new to Felix. Novalis and Friedrich Schlegel had already spoken of architecture as "frozen music". But that did not make Spontini's cavillings any more valid.

Nevertheless, with uncharacteristic timidity Felix was impressed by Spontini's words and had forebodings about his opera—which for the very reason that it was a comic opera was not likely to be understood by Spontini. And yet it was not a bad piece of work. Felix had laboured long and carefully over the three hundred and seventy-one pages of the score. There was a wealth of music and forms in the opera, there were rapid alternations of arias and ensembles, and the whole thing kept moving

[12] M. M. von Weber: *Carl Maria von Weber, ein Lebensbild*. Berlin, 1850.

at a brisk pace. Tinged in buffo colours, it reminded one a little of Mozart.

The libretto also dealt with—shades of *Figaro!*—a hampered marriage. A farmer named Carrasco is about to marry his daughter to the rich land-owner Camacho. But the young peasant girl Quiteria loves Basilio, a poor student. In order to hold up the marriage Basilio pretends suicide; he drives his dagger into his side and falls, apparently streaming blood, to the ground. A priest is fetched; but Basilio refuses to confess until Quiteria is wed to him—after all, he is on the point of death. The knight errant, Don Quixote, who is among the wedding guests, supports the student's plea; he points out to the landowner that he can marry Quiteria as a widow the next day. Everybody thinks this is a splendid plan. The priest marries Quiteria and the dying man—but at once Basilio springs to his feet; the blood was not blood, the suicide no suicide; he is unharmed and the happy husband.

What part did Don Quixote play in this affair? His presence really seems irrelevant. In the novel, perhaps, an incident of this sort might have some place, and throw some light on Quixote's character. But in the play, he really seems an arbitrary figure. Still, once this flaw was admitted, the music might well amaze the listener by its brilliant delineation of situations. Sentiment alternates with comedy. There are many graceful duets, choruses and trios. A monologue like Basilio's allegro aria, "Noch tröstet mich das Vorgefühl":

> I still have hope to win my suit,
>   By courage gain the bride,
> For on my sword and on my lute
>   I've ne'er in vain relied—

would have been perfectly at home in Weber's *Euryanthe*. Certainly that is true for the continuation of the same song, meditatively delicate, ritenuto and pianissimo:

> She's true to me, loves me alone,
>   Why should I then repine?
> Quiteria will be my own,
>   Her heart is mine, is mine.

Because he is poor, Basilio must gain his end by trickery. Not that the opera contains any hint of the social problems which underlie the story of Figaro. Rather there is a kinship with Eichendorff's light-hearted world:

Robert and Clara Schumann. (*Photo Ullstein, Berlin*)

Fanny and Rebecca, Felix Mendelssohn's sisters. Drawing by Wilhelm Hensel. (*Historia-Photo, Berlin*)

Oh students and soldiers are merry and gay,
Oh poets and soldiers will love when they may.
They sing and they roam and they fight for love's greeting
While others stay home for their selling and cheating.
But once they have found them a sweetheart to wed,
The world all around them counts less than their bed.

Not only is that a rather pretty lyric; it also contains the freshness of tone of a much later Mendelssohn. It is not a verse which could have been written by Klingemann, or by him exclusively; probably Karl Wilhelm Heyse and Hofrat Lichtenstein had had a hand in the libretto—we detect their type of humour here and there—as for example when someone addresses Don Quixote: "Idle Sir Nought, I meant to say Noble Sir Knight...." Or when Sancho Panza sings:

Shiver all with awe and fright
At the name's omnipotence!
Hark, he comes, the noble knight
Of the woeful countenance.

Mendelssohn was especially successful with Sancho Panza. The orchestra rollicks along as it accompanies his recitatives; Rossini could scarcely have done better. Male choruses support one another in neat oppositions. Felix had learned well from Zelter how to construct a firm choral passage.

As the story goes on, the plot thickens—to such a point that it is impossible to summarize it. The whole story takes a rather terrifying turn in an act played in a pitch-dark forest with everyone running about in wild confusion. Don Quixote suffers an attack of genuine madness: he mistakes the bride, Quiteria, for the maiden of his heart, Dulcinea del Toboso, and confounds Basilio with the fearful giant Montesinos. Felix succeeded in pouring some of the liquid fire of *A Midsummer Night's Dream* music, half frightful and half ludicrous, over this scene. But as a whole it remains disturbing because the audience does not know whether to laugh or be afraid. It is a great relief when the wedding finally takes place. A chorus of male and female cooks praise the eatables:

Now all hands are gaily whirring, joyfully the fires stirring,
Mixing, mingling wedding fires, crackling roasts and lovers' passion.
Brisk and juicy, onions sizzle, spice and dripping gaily frizzle,
Salt and nutmeg, oil and pepper, love a roast in their own fashion.

The orchestra smacks its lips along with Sancho Panza, as he invites everybody to eat and drink and be of good cheer. There is a festive march

A page of score of *The Wedding of Camacho*. Property of the
International Felix Mendelssohn Society.

in C major, and ballet music that is the best thing in the opera. Mendelssohn was again emulating *Figaro*. As at Susanna's wedding, there is a fandango and a Spanish bolero.[13]

[13] A. Einstein: *Mozart*. Zürich, 1950.

Everybody who counted in Berlin had come for the première. The applause after the first act was very hearty. Applause from the best families—as Felix sensed. Through a hole in the curtain he saw many familiar faces. A large part of the audience were friends of the Mendelssohn household. There in the third row of the orchestra sat Henriette Herz, wife of the Hofrat, more than sixty years old, but still beautiful.[14] Grey curls fell around her lifted, expectant face. She was a Sephardic Jew and had been Henriette de Lemos before she married Hofrat Herz, friend of Immanuel Kant. In her intellectual salon Felix's Aunt Dorothea had met Friedrich Schlegel, and Varnhagen had met his Rahel. Henriette had lost her money long ago, and subsisted by giving language lessons. She had a lively correspondence with Wilhelm von Humboldt, who wrote to her in German using the Hebrew alphabet. Were any of the Humboldts here, Felix wondered? He hoped not. It was bad enough to see that Henriette was accompanied by her close friend the theologian Schleiermacher.[15] Years ago he had converted this beautiful, lonely woman to Protestantism. It was a safe guess that Schleiermacher did not often attend the theatre, though this curiously taciturn and somewhat deformed man was a frequent guest at the Mendelssohn musicales. Felix felt a little ashamed at having the eminent preacher listening to this opera, which the young composer was already rejecting in his heart. A person like Schleiermacher should be given oratorios and similar sacred music, not comic opera.

Felix grew increasingly nervous. After the second act the applause was rather lame. Abraham Mendelssohn also had his enemies. A murmuring began in the stalls and galleries; people began asking[16] whether it would not have been wiser to have kept this rather half-baked opera for the Mendelssohn family circle. Felix, unhappy and vacillating, went over to the side of his opponents, and fled the house before the final curtain fell. The singers took their bows in his place—after the wedding scene and the banquet the applause had perceptibly increased.

Next day Blume, who was singing Don Quixote, fell ill. His illness lasted for weeks, and all performances of the opera were cancelled. Thus it was put on only once and then vanished completely from the repertory.

[14] I. Fürst: *Henriette Herz, ihr Leben und ihre Erinnerungen*. Berlin, 1850.

[15] *Schleiermacher und seine Lieben, nach Originalbriefen*. Magdeburg, 1910.

[16] G. Schünemann: "Mendelssohns Jugendopern." *Zeitschrift für Musik*, 5. Jahrg., 1923.

BOOK TWO

MUSIC OF YESTERDAY, MUSIC OF TOMORROW

The eternal blessing and benefaction
of music, its miraculous reciprocity
with the thirsting, craving ear—that
the third note accords with the first,
and the fifth likewise, and the *nota
sensibilis* rises like a fulfilled hope,
that dissonance plays the part of
deliberate spite or arrogant pride;
and the wonder of legato and in-
version that mercifully transforms
even the second, bringing it home to
the bosom of concordance. . . . And
the fugue and counterpoint, and the
canon a due, a tre, and so on—a
whole celestial structure, one part
interlocking with the other, built up
without mortar and sustained by
God's hand.

—FRANZ GRILLPARZER:
The Poor Minstrel

Mendelssohn's reaction to this failure was characteristic. A Mozart or a Wagner would have just begun to fight. Felix knew, at the bottom of his heart, that he was not a dramatist, that his forte was epic and lyric. He could be dramatic only within the frame of epic-lyric composition: in the symphonic tone-painting. In epic and lyric composition he was to become the most successful composer of his age. But he renounced any attempt to become a second Meyerbeer—a field in which he was foredoomed to failure. His father was somewhat disappointed by this; remembering as he did the glamour of the Paris opera house, the example of Gluck and the career of Spontini. Why should not his son also win these laurels?

But Felix Mendelssohn knew better. With the failure of *Camacho*, he began that curious game of hide-and-seek which was to continue to his dying day, a good twenty years. He was not hunting for the right opera, as he pretended to his friends—who considered him a second Mozart, to whom the operatic form was natural. On the contrary, he was terrified of opera. As soon as a libretto loomed on the horizon, Mendelssohn made himself scarce. And if a libretto were thrust under his nose, he demurred and cavilled until the author and his friends gave up in despair and somebody else set it to music.

There was one person he did not deceive. At some time, apparently, he told his father that he did not feel any inward vocation for dramatic music. His father upbraided him. In 1834, after another libretto had been submitted and found wanting, Abraham Mendelssohn wrote to Felix, "To my mind ... you do not have sufficient creative experience to know for certain that your distaste for it is an inward one, founded upon your talent and character. Except for Beethoven I know of no dramatic composer who did not write a large number of completely forgotten operas before he seized upon the right point at the right time and made a place for himself. You have made *only one single public attempt*, which was partially handicapped by the libretto and which in reality neither succeeded nor failed. Later you carped too much about the texts—did not find the right man, perhaps did not really look for him. I cannot help but think that more active searching and less rigorous demands would have surely led you to the goal...."[1]

[1] F. Mendelssohn-Bartholdy: *Briefe aus den Jahren 1830–47*. Leipzig, 1861.

Felix ran away from opera. But of course there was another stratum within himself in which he dreamed of stage success and grieved over his inability to achieve it. In 1834 he read a bad play by Kotzebue, based on a story in verse by Wieland, and spent months trying to construct a scenario which would improve on the original. It was *The Story of Pervonte*, and took place in a fantastic southern Italy that was purely the product of Wieland's imagination, among fairies and Shakespearian louts. The peasant lad Pervonte is an incurable lazybones who spends whole days stretched out on the hearth, sucking his fingers. When his mother bears down on him and orders him to get to work, he complains that his back hurts. By the favour of fairies Pervonte is transformed into a dapper young knight, and captures the heart of a princess. But in the end the transformed Pervonte grows weary of the grand life in which he has anything he wishes for. His last wish to the fairies is that everything may be as it was before; the princess is left high and dry, and Pervonte creeps happily back to his mother's hut.

An enigmatic tale. But Felix himself was a fairy prince. And with one part of his ego this level-headed, intelligent, knowledgeable young man believed in fairies and was forever hoping for their favour.

"The fairy-tale", Otto Gruppe has said, "lulls the will to sleep. It saves man from effort. It promises the individual the aid of the universe through the operations of sheer grace."[2] We must not forget that although fairy-tale and saga meet in folklore, they are radically different in their conceptions of the active and the passive hero. A saga hero may experience fairy-tale situations; Siegfried, for example, is endowed with the power to understand the voices of the birds. But that does not make him a typical fairy-tale hero. Siegfried is a man of active will, as Wagner himself was. But Felix Mendelssohn, aristocratic dreamer that he was, did not find happiness in the exercise of his will. As far as he was concerned, the gifts of life must be laid before him in his study.

Like most of the Romantics, Felix regarded fairy-tales as an age-old patrimony of the nation. He was right about that—except that we now know that there are not nearly as many national fairy-tales as the Romantics fancied. Fairy-tales are common property; they have only taken on their national colour in the centuries since they were brought from India, thousands of years ago. From the *Panchatantra* numberless currents of fable flowed westward and northward. There is a deep significance in the fact that the source of fairy-tale should have been in the passive culture of India. These tales of fortune and misfortune, of goblins' treasures

---

[2] O. Gruppe: *Zur Psychologie des Märchens*. Berlin, no date.

and witches' curses are, in their basic philosophy, more oriental than European. Virtue is always identified with the character who passively endures injustice and hardship.

Felix finished sketching the scenario of *Pervonte, or The Luck of the Lazy*, and sent it to Klingemann for polishing. Klingemann plunged into the work and produced a charming first act, full of whimsical dialogues and clever jests. He drew certain humorous parallels between Pervonte's somnolent habits and certain characteristics of Felix. In this first act we are cast into a world like that of Humperdinck.[3] For example, there is a monologue in the woods:

> Plenty of trees here. But chop wood? How dull and tiring.
> "Don't sit down," Mother said. I don't dare fall asleep or I'll get nothing to eat at home. I'd better sing myself awake. (*He yawns.*)
>
>> If all the stones were ducats
>> And the sea were full of fish,
>> I'd gather both in buckets
>> And never need to wish.
>
>> If all the squabs came ready grilled,
>> I surely would not be so lazy.
>> My belly would be easily filled
>> And I'd be happy as a daisy.
>
> Lazy? If a fellow is peaceful and stays nicely at home, they call him lazy. They don't understand. Ah, when I lie out-stretched and close my eyes, it's like being in paradise. I see beautiful things and think of all the old tales of bewitched castles and enchanted princesses and tables that set themselves. I'd like a table like that, covered with eats and drink. Hm, yes, drink? There must be a spring near here. Oh, wonder of wonders, there's the spring with one, two, three—three ladies lying fast asleep. Ladies with shining yellow crowns. They don't have to gather wood. And *so* beautiful. I'll wake them—no, it's awful to be waked. I won't wake them. . . .

Thus Klingemann poked gentle fun at his talented friend. And letters flew back and forth between Düsseldorf and London. But then progress on the libretto slowed down. The correspondence continued. But nothing

---

[3] *F. Mendelssohn-Bartholdys Briefwechsel mit Legationsrat Karl Klingemann.* Essen, 1909.

more was heard of the plan; it vanished completely from the letters. And that was just as well. Mendelssohn's scenario was clever and poetic, but *Pervonte* would never have made an opera. With its slight dimensions, it was good only for a concert overture, perhaps a comic overture like the overture to Victor Hugo's *Ruy Blas*. Had he ever gone ahead with that, Felix would have produced a masterpiece—and we are the poorer for not having it.

Wieland himself had not invented the fairy-tale motif of "the luck of the lazy". He had borrowed the theme from the famous collection *Il Pentamerone*, by Gianbattista Basile.[4] The conception that laziness makes people strange and may even drive them mad haunts the Grimm Brothers' story, *Lazy Trina*—at the end Trina no longer knows whether she is still herself. The theme crops up, in another form, in the fairy-tale of the division of the kingdom, in which only the laziest man can be king.[5] As the gigantic catalogue of his works proves, Felix Mendelssohn was anything but lazy. But he was committed to the principle that inspiration comes in sleep, for this was indeed the case with him. His friends used to remark laughingly that he had to be stood on his head before he really woke up.

Felix's game of hide-and-seek with opera became difficult when he found himself involved with a man who had some literary gifts, a man like Eduard Devrient, for example. Klingemann was only a dilettante, but Devrient, who was an actor and singer as well as writer, was an artist of parts, an individual of talent and originality.[6] He would not be put off by a smiling, "I'm afraid you haven't quite carried this off, my friend!" or, "This just isn't the thing for me." Devrient had known Felix for many years, and was perhaps his dearest friend next to Klingemann. To Devrient, Felix wrote with every token of impatience (but the impatience was never quite real when an opera was under discussion) on 13th July 1831: "Give me the right opera and I'll have it composed in a few months." Felix was writing from Milan, and perhaps the atmosphere of that opera city encouraged him to rashness. Nevertheless, he added prudently: "But unless a libretto really fires me, I will not even begin to set it."

The question was, did he want to find such a libretto? Perhaps he made his friends and his ambitious sisters believe it. But Karl von Holtei,

[4] J. Meyer-Brunn: *Das Glück des Faulen*. Leipzig, no date.

[5] F. Panzer: *Einleitung zu den Kinder-und Hausmärchen der Brüder Grimm*. Wiesbaden, 1957.

[6] E. Devrient: *Meine Erinnerungen an Felix Mendelssohn-Bartholdy*. Leipzig, 1872.

with whom he negotiated for a while, commented: "Mendelssohn will never find an opera subject that satisfies him; he is much too clever to do so."[7] On 26th April 1845—two and a half years before his death—Felix wrote to Devrient asking him to provide at least "the subject and the crudest scenario of an opera". But Devrient had already tried and failed. The composer had already rejected two librettos by his friend. One was *Olint and Sophronia*. The other was *Hans Heiling*, and in turning this one down, Felix made it clear once and for all that he was not the man for opera.

For here was a really significant subject, which moreover lent itself to effective dramatic treatment. Eduard Devrient had found the Bohemian legend of Hans Heiling in a story of Theodor Körner entitled *The Oaks of Karlsbad*. Hans Heiling, son of the Queen of the spirit world, falls in love with Anna, a mortal. But at a country fair, Anna meets Konrad who wins her affections from Hans. She is still drawn to Hans, however, and on her wedding day, a fight breaks out between the rivals. The spirits of the earth come to his aid. But before a battle can begin, their Queen intervenes, and calls her son back to his own people. Men must remain among men and spirits among spirits.

Mendelssohn rejected this libretto on the strange grounds that it reminded him too much of *Der Freischütz*. Devrient then sent the text anonymously to the composer Heinrich Marschner, who had two recent operas to his credit. These were *The Vampire* (after a neo-Greek legend he had found in Byron), full of magnificent spooky music, and *The Templar and the Jewess*, based on Scott's *Ivanhoe*. It is an interesting point that Mendelssohn had lived in Walter Scott's house in 1829,[8] and yet the charged atmosphere did not move him to write dramatic opera. His sojourn in the land of Scott yielded, instead, epic works like the "Hebrides" overture and the "Scottish" Symphony. But Heinrich Marschner, who had hardly ever set foot outside Germany, was attracted by the exotic material of the great romancer. The *Templar* must have been an extraordinary piece of work, for Wagner praised it for its "volcanic passion" and "enormous originality of feelings"—and Wagner did not find it easy to recognize the merits of contemporaries. Not only did Wagner study and assimilate Marschner's powerful mood-music and atmosphere of demonic despair, but actual plot motifs made their way from *The Templar and the Jewess* to *Lohengrin*.[9]

[7] E. Wolff: *Felix Mendelssohn-Bartholdy*. Berlin, 1909.
[8] S. Hensel: *Die Familie Mendelssohn 1729–1847*. Berlin, 1879.
[9] H. Gaartz: *Marschner als Opernkomponist*. Munich, 1913.

Marschner's third successful opera, then, was this very *Hans Heiling* which Mendelssohn had disdained. Hans Pfitzner, who in 1924 edited a new edition of *Hans Heiling* and restored it to the modern repertory (along with the two other Marschner operas) commented on "authenticity of these works". It is not just that "the horror, the melancholy, the jollity, are artistically realized in them; rather, the man who wrote them carouses with his drinkers and shudders at his own ghosts".[10]

This acute comment casts light upon the real reason why Felix Mendelssohn would not make use of the Heiling story—for Mendelssohn was very well aware of his own virtues and limitations. Of course he was an admirer of Weber, hardly less so than Marschner and Wagner. But what could he do with a ghostly theme? He could not continue Weber, could not conceive a second Wolf's Gorge scene, replete with shivers and instrumentation that made the spine tingle. He was a grandson of the Enlightenment; the sources of his mental life went back not only to Moses Mendelssohn, but also to Immanuel Kant, who had firmly rejected the "claims of the supernatural". Both Kant and Moses Mendelssohn had probably studied the famous Dutch preacher Balthasar Bekker's polemical book, *De betoverde wereld* ("The World Bewitched")—which had demonstrated to the men of the eighteenth century the "harmfulness of belief in spirits" and the results thereof.[11] And although Felix might not be fully aware of it, he was committed to the temper of the Enlightenment. Of course Felix was an emotional confederate of Clemens Brentano, and a lover of fairy-tales; but he liked them jocular and with a touch of irony.[12] He was not a man for legends. For one must believe in a legend to appreciate it.

The second quality in Marschner's music which Pfitzner held up for praise was the composer's gusto in the drinking scenes. Here, too, Felix would have had to bow out. He liked Rhenish wine well enough—if he had not been able to do justice to a good wine, he would not have been considered a real man in Düsseldorf, where he spent a good many years. But, aristocrat that he was, he had only horror for a life spent in drinking. "Der Trunk—ein Leben!" he once said contemptuously of Christian Dietrich Grabbe, the dramatist—paraphrasing the title of a famous play by Grillparzer, *Der Traum ein Leben*. He could not stand drunkards; even genius inspired by alcohol shocked his sensibilities. He was a great admirer of Ludwig Devrient, the leading Shakespearian actor of the day.

---

[10] H. Pfitzner: *Gesammelte Schriften 1926–29.*
[11] B. Bekker: *De betoverde wereld*. Amsterdam, 1691–93.
[12] O. Gruppe: op. cit.

But one day friends took him to Lutter and Wegner's smoky taproom where Ludwig Devrient—a man with a tiny, almost feminine mouth, black, curly hair, searing eyes, and a large, thin nose, was wont to come for relaxation. When in his cups, Devrient became a different person—powerful and blustering. On this occasion Devrient went into "a roaring counterpoint of Falstaff, Shylock and Lear, embracing a barrel and then stretching out on a table like a corpse". The scene was too much for Mendelssohn. He barely stopped himself from being sick, and made his escape into the open air.[13]

When Marschner's *Hans Heiling* was published, Mendelssohn was loud in his praises of it. Can we imagine how Mozart or Wagner would have reacted in a similar situation? These demonically jealous men, these temperamental geniuses, would never have forgiven themselves for having let a subject like this slip through their fingers. They would have vented their disappointment by tearing apart their rival's work—for opera was their very life.[14]

But it was easy for Mendelssohn to be gracious about someone else's triumph. Was this because he himself was no dramatist? He was at any rate no writer of operas. "Gentle soul" that he was, he could nevertheless encompass passion, devotion, wildness—but this, of course, was in the framework of the oratorio. For him, the home of strong feeling was the Biblical world, with its contrasts between barren desert and green oasis, wrath and humility. This was a sphere Mendelssohn could understand and out of it he created his *Paul* and *Elijah*. Behind these works stood the heritage of Bach and, still more, the spirit of Handel.

BACH AND THE ROMANTICS

On 25th December 1815 Rahel Varnhagen made the following entry in her journal: "Tonight I dreamed that I heard so beautiful a prelude from on high, or wherever it was that it came from—no matter, I could see nothing—that I had to fall to my knees; I wept, prayed and cried out again and again: 'Didn't I say so, music is God, *true* music'—by that I meant harmonies and not melodies—'is God!' The music became more

[13] Julius Bab: *Die Devrients*. Berlin, 1932.
[14] H. E. Jacob: *Mozart oder Geist, Musik und Schicksal*. Frankfurt am Main, 1956.

and more beautiful; I prayed, wept and cried out more and more. All that, the whole of being, became bright and more distinct within my breast as though illuminated by a glow—nothing actually shaped in the forms of thought. My heart cracked from weeping happily, and I awoke."[1]

Now Rahel was not a person with musical background. The fact that absolute divinity could nevertheless appear to her in the form of some supernal music (music that was harmony without melody), represented something new. This acoustic vision of God "as though illuminated by a glow—nothing actually shaped in the forms of thought", would have horrified the German classicists between Lessing and Schiller. It was thoroughly in keeping with the Romantic ideal.

Its significance is enhanced by the fact that it was also a *dream*—in other words, a "nocturnal message of reality",[2] as Gotthilf Heinrich von Schubert defined the dream. Rahel spoke of a prelude, and that meant that she was speaking of Bach—though a Romantic Bach who would have been suspect to the older generation, even to Zelter. We do not know how these lines of Rahel affected Felix Mendelssohn when they were published some twenty-one years later—he was not particularly sympathetic to Rahel's effusions—but he would certainly have assented to this particular kind of Bachian experience.

Zelter regarded the art of Bach as largely—though not exclusively— "grammar". Not that Zelter disdained grammar. When twelve-year-old Felix wrote on 3rd June 1821: "I am now toiling over an organ fugue which will see the light within the next few days," he was displaying the proper pride of a diligent boy anxious to turn out a perfect piece.[3] Members of his own generation like Schumann and Chopin would have protested against this business of a composer's effort. But—and in this Zelter was right—the science of the fugue *was* grammar: the theme in the tonic key, called the *dux* or leader, and the second voice at an interval of a fifth the *comes* or companion—these two, their answering one another, teasing, chasing, threatening, hurtling through narrow passages—all that was the "contentless content" of a fugue. The fugue was really nothing but technique;[4] but once you mastered this technique, nothing bad could happen to you any longer, even if you did not write fugally. Felix knew

[1] R. Varnhagen: *Ein Buch des Andenkens für ihre Freunde*. Berlin, 1834.
[2] R. Huch: *Die Blütezeit der Romantik*. Leipzig, 1905.
[3] S. Hensel: *Die Familie Mendelssohn 1729–1847*. Berlin, 1879.
[4] R. Stephan: *Das Fischer Lexikon der Musik*. Frankfurt am Main, 1957.

that Bach had written the most magnificent of fugues: concertante and permutation fugues, mirror and crab fugues, in which the theme turned upside down or ran backwards: double fugues, triple fugues, quadruple fugues. These were mathematical projections, only to be grasped by calculation.[5] Haydn had hated them, and Mozart had loved them only from the musical feeling that a composer *must* be able to manipulate every form. Christoph Michelmann in his book, *Die Melodie nach ihrem Wesen* (Danzig, 1755), had ruled that the composer must master the learned style but make it as cantabile as possible.[6] But the Romantics were not looking for this "cantabile compromise". They were seeking—and this was very strange—the altogether unfree style of the strict Bach. Only they were seeking him for romantic reasons.

The historical Bach had, of course, been entirely unromantic. He began composing at a time in which the Leibnitzian doctrine of "monads" dominated German baroque philosophy. Wilibald Gurlitt[7] has pointed out that Bach's entire opus was really "theodicy" in the Leibnitzian sense, a proof of the existence of God. According to monad doctrine the entire tangible world is composed of innumerable little molecules which are indivisible substance. Everything in the world is an aggregate of flowing groups of monads. There is only a single force that holds these numberless monads in fluid equilibrium: the grace of God. This grace is the source of the principle of construction which God established for the universe in the beginning: "pre-established harmony". Bach believed that music, too, was "pre-established divine order". Where it deviated from theology, it became, to his mind, "diabolical noise".

What bond could the Romantics have with a Bach who held such beliefs? The Romantic character, as Ricarda Huch has described it, swayed like a reed in the wind.[8] It was the creation of two historical worlds which were inherently contradictory. On the one hand Romanticism had been rendered possible only by the French Revolution and the liberation of the individual. On the other hand, in 1815 Romanticism set itself unequivocally on the side of pre-Revolutionary conditions; it opted for feudalism and the rule of princes. In an attempt to heal their inner split, the Romantics identified themselves with the Middle Ages, which they conceived as "the most stable of all ages". When Uhland discovered

---

[5] H. E. Jacob: *Joseph Haydn: His Art, Times and Glory.* New York, 1950.

[6] R. Steglich: *Über die kantable Art der Musik Johann Sebastian Bachs.* Zürich, 1957.

[7] W. Gurlitt: *Johann Sebastian Bach.* 1947.

[8] R. Huch: op. cit.

the Minnesingers, when Friedrich Heinrich von der Hagen published the original text of the *Nibelungenlied*, when Lachmann[9] and a dozen others began exploring the field of Germanic philology, when Arnim and Brentano awoke the German folk song from its enchanted sleep by the publication of their famous anthology, *Des Knaben Wunderhorn*—one of their most powerful motivations was their distrust of the "vacillating ego" and their desire to find something solid to lean on.

But what had Bach to do with these feelings—Bach who was not old but only outmoded; Bach, the bewigged baroque philistine from Saxony? Why were the Romantics suddenly talking about Bach in the same tone as Boisserée used for the Cologne cathedral and the medieval painters?[10] In doing so they were being altogether unhistorical, were they not? But strangely enough, it turned out that they were historical after all, that Romantic masters, like Mendelssohn who chose to overlook Bach's wig, had come to a historically more correct appreciation of Bach than would have been the case if they had noticed that his date of death was only 1750. They recognized him as timeless. But if they had to associate him with any particular time, that time would be the Middle Ages. As Albert Schweitzer has brilliantly and clairvoyantly expressed it, Bach was the Middle Ages, was their crowning glory and their summation. "Bach is a terminus. Nothing comes out of him; everything only leads up to him."[11]

The Romantics were avantgardists. They marched in the front rank. But that by no means implied that they were marching in the direction of "progress". The most militant composition of the eighteen-thirties was Robert Schumann's *March of the Davidsbund against the Philistines*. (The *Davidsbund* or Brotherhood of David was a society that existed only in Schumann's imagination.) And a comedy by Eichendorff was entitled *War against the Philistines*. One of the banners of this private army bore the name Bach. Schumann could not have been blamed had he failed to recognize the great composer hidden behind Bach's substantial wig and scholar's garb. But he did recognize Bach for what he was, perhaps by the help of Mendelssohn, perhaps by his own intuition.

Nevertheless the alliance remains strange. For Romanticism is subjectivism, the enthronement of the individual personality. But Bach was the most objective of all artists. He strove for anonymity, like the breed of men from whom he was descended: organists, town pipers, teachers and

---

[9] K. Lachmann: *Über die ursprüngliche Gestalt der Geschichte von der Nibelungen Not.* Berlin, 1816.

[10] S. Boisserée: *Denkmale der Baukunst am Niederrhein.* Munich, 1833.

[11] A. Schweitzer: *Johann Sebastian Bach.* Leipzig, 1947.

cantors. Those men were selfless servants of music. The Romantics shook their heads over Haydn, the wheelwright's son; the traces of the artisan in his approach to music struck them as philistine.[12] Why did they not shake their heads over Bach and *his* artisan's approach?

They did not do so because the work of Bach was of such massive proportions, because one single man had left such an astounding legacy. With their philosophy of the importance of the individual, they could not but be impressed. Then again, there was the fact that Bach had never attempted to simplify his creative tasks. Did not every artist try for striking effects? But Bach seemed not to have cared for them at all. He seemed to have given little thought to whether or not he was understood. Hans Joachim Moser has compared pages of scores by Bach and Handel. In Bach, he notes, "the very look of the page is usually a swarm of black notes, whereas in Handel the score as a rule appears white and transparent."[13] If Bach had been Handel, he would have written the prelude of his first sonata for solo violin "clearly, simply and perspicuously, plainly and rationally organized by the more frequent bar lines". It would have looked, Moser says, approximately as follows:

But Bach wrote it in a way which was far more difficult to read:

[12] H. E. Jacob: op. cit.
[13] H. J. Moser: *Johann Sebastian Bach*. Frankfurt am Main, 1957.

To play the latter a "gigantic breath from bar line to bar line is needed, and a fantastic freedom in performance".[14] Handel's manner of writing was essentially in the spirit of Renaissance and classicism; Bach's was Gothic-baroque. Not Holbein and Rubens, rather Rembrandt and Dürer. A silent Saint Jerome watching a lion. One who never leaves his study and who remains outside the ken of men. Bach wrote only for himself— and God.

Because this was so, because his contemporaries never looked upon Bach as a composer, but only as a peerless organist, the Bach cult of the Romantics represented the righting of an injustice. Romanticism "entered the lists for Bach like knight-errant for a lady", Charles Gounod put it. The metaphor is not completely apt. For, if truth were told, the situation was quite reversed. The Romantics may have thought that they were doing something for Bach. In fact, Bach immeasurably rewarded, repaid a thousandfold, the homage that the youth of 1830 paid him.

What he gave them was the security of faith—something that those young people who converted so easily back and forth between religions were desperately longing for. Life in God, God's life in us. Immortality and the remission of sin—all this coursed through their hearts; this was what the name of Bach meant to them. And Bach's certainty of faith was altogether unpolemical and undogmatic. It could be sensed in every bar of his music. (That this was historically incorrect is another matter entirely; Bach was in fact a militant Protestant,[15] a follower of Luther. The religious feuds of the time extended into the field of music, and Lutheran music was sharply ranged not only against Catholic music, but also against that of the other Reformed Churches and the Pietists. Bach's chorales and cantatas were part of this movement.) Nevertheless the Romantics were right when they saw Bach unhistorically. They saw him as nonsectarian because they thought he was above the battle. They considered him to be Christianity itself, and his music as God-sent.

Bach's chorales were like cathedrals, and inspired something of the same awe. For all their architectonic rigour, they were also fantasies with free development of the themes. "Komm, Gott Schöpfer, Heiliger Geist!", "Wenn wir in höchsten Nöten sind"—such works as these achieved something miraculous. Here was an entirely new type of music through which, as Albert Schweitzer has said, "The outlines of the old forms appear only as if glimmering through a fine mist."[16] Felix

---

[14] Ibid.
[15] A. Cherbuliez: *Johann Sebastian Bach*. Frankfurt am Main, 1957.
[16] A. Schweitzer: op. cit.

Mendelssohn was so moved by the richness of imagery in the chorale, "Schmücke dich, o liebe Seele", that he said to Schumann: *"If life had taken hope and faith from me, this single chorus would restore all."*[17]

Because Bach was "perfect religion" to the Romantics, he was also perfect art. That equation, once made, has been repeated ever since. When the Belgian composer E. Tinel recommended that the Catholic Church turn to the arch-Protestant Bach, for ideas on how to improve their singing, he justified it with the remark that "Bach is not a musician at all, but music itself". Oskar Loerke writing his fine study of Bach in 1925, coined an aphorism which might have issued from the lips of Friedrich Schlegel:[18] "To Bach Heaven was a continent, as America was to Columbus."[19] Even in Bach's secular compositions the religious element was present—as Hans von Bülow recognized when he said that Bach's *Well-Tempered Clavier* was like the 'Old Testament' alongside the 'New Testament' of Beethoven's piano sonatas. Bülow would scarcely have chosen such a figure of speech had not the Romantics already created this conception of Bach.

In so doing, they saved him from oblivion. In his own age Bach was left lying apart like some huge block of marble that would not fit in anywhere. The style of life practised by the Dresden court, the social elegance of the Late Baroque period, was not expressed by Bach—or so his contemporaries felt. He did not understand them, they felt, and retaliated with contempt. Music should be "worldly". "The ultimate aim of music is that it pleases the ear," said Johann Adolf Scheibe, an opponent of Bach.[20] Johann Mattheson and Friedrich Wilhelm Marpurg maintained that the whole duty of the "modern" composer was to provide "affect and ratio", emotion and reason. Johann Sebastian Bach's great son, Karl Philipp Emanuel—the Hamburg Bach—filled these requirements far better than his father, who had never thought of music in these terms. For Johann Sebastian had shared the creed of Luther: "After theology I give the highest place and greatest honour to music."[21]

Goethe, too, with his bias for rationality, had some difficulty fathoming Bach. But once the revelation had come to him, he clung to it ever after. Writing to Zelter on 9th June 1827, he declared that Bach was an artist of

[17] R. Schumann: *Gesammelte Schriften über Musik und Musiker*. Leipzig, 1891.
[18] F. Deibel: *Friedrich Schlegels Fragmente und Ideen*. Munich, 1905.
[19] O. Loerke: *Johann Sebastian Bach*. Frankfurt am Main, 1950.
[20] J. A. Scheibe: *Kritischer Musicus*. Leipzig, 1745.
[21] A. Prüfer: *Sebastian Bach und die Tonkunst des 19. Jahrhunderts*. Leipzig, 1902.

the highest sort. "Taking into account all the things that might weigh against him, this Leipzig cantor is a phenomenon of God: lucid, but ultimately not susceptible to elucidation." Goethe's official composer, Kapellmeister Reichardt—Zelter's rival—had a different opinion: "If Bach had possessed the sublime sense of truth and the deep feeling for expression that was Handel's, he would have been far greater than Handel; but as it is, he is only more industrious and more learned in his art."[22] And half a century later Nietzsche was to say: "In Bach there lingers too much crude Christianity, crude Germanism, crude scholasticism."[23]

THE RESURRECTED ST. MATTHEW PASSION

Zelter had the greatest admiration for Bach as an absolute musician. Nevertheless he was extremely sceptical of the usefulness of Bach's choral works, as far as their actual performance went. As director of the Singakademie Zelter knew the problems of the concert hall. One could not ask Enlightened Berliners to rave over such texts as, "O Eternity, Thou word of thunder!" or, "You will weep and wail!" The Bach cantatas and chorales might do for a small circle—but their appeal was very specialized.

Felix Mendelssohn did not agree. As a Romantic he was deeply affected by Bach's texts, whose pathos struck deep chords of feeling in him. He was moved by the way in which the master (though opera was so alien to him) strove for "minor realism" in his motets, cantatas and passions. As Felix Mendelssohn saw, Bach's technique was in some sense like the medieval sculptors'. How conscientiously Bach tried to capture all the nuances of his subject! If the word "sea" occurred anywhere in his baroque texts, even when used figuratively in some such phrase as "sea of suffering", the violins promptly began describing waves. Zelter the rationalist no doubt found it naïve when, at the passage where the crown of thorns is set upon the head of Christ, the notes became sharp and pointed as thorns, and the scourging was expressed in the orchestra by jagged, lashing beats. But Felix Mendelssohn's generation was in love

[22] G. Herz: *Johann Sebastian Bach im Zeitalter des Rationalismus und der Frühromantik*. Würzburg, 1935.

[23] F. Nietzsche: *Menschliches, Allzumenschliches*, Gesamt-Ausgabe. Leipzig, 1903–12.

with the Middle Ages, and found a special charm in this "unmodern", wood-carver's type of music.

There was another aspect to the question. Not only was Bach a wood-carver who patiently whittled out expressive figures. He was also something of a painter, a triptych-maker of the type of Matthias Grünewald. He painted supernatural landscapes, bathed in light not of this world. This again was not according to the taste of eighteenth-century men. But Felix Mendelssohn could reconstruct these panoramas, for Ludwig Berger and Bernhard Klein had taught him to "hear colours".[1]

Mendelssohn was also struck by the unique way Bach handled musical keys. He could make C major sound radiant and jubilant, but he could also give it a disagreeable turn, when it suited his dramatic purpose. C minor which was heroic and despairing in Beethoven's music, was used by Bach to convey tranquil moods, or moods of deep acceptance. The dirges of the Passion, "So schlafen unsre Sünden ein", "Wer weiss, wie nahe mir mein Ende", and "Ewigkeit", are all written in C minor.[2] Then there were his choruses, with their remarkable dramatic content. More than anything else, they were musical equivalents of a turba,* a crowd shaken by conflicting emotions of fear, love, pride and hatred. If rightly sung, these choruses should have the audience falling on its knees. Or so Mendelssohn felt. Zelter thought otherwise.

The jealous Zelter kept the score of the *St. Matthew Passion* hidden away in a closet. Legend has it that Mendelssohn coaxed Zelter into letting him leaf through it. At any rate, he was fired with the longing to perform this magnificent work. Child of the nineteenth century that he was, he placed great store by anniversaries. The *St. Matthew Passion* had been written in 1729. Now the year 1829 was approaching. Then again, a bit of secret family data was involved (and this was characteristic of many of Mendelssohn's actions). For 1829 was also the centenary of the birth of his great forebear, Moses Mendelssohn.

But Felix was only twenty and could not bring Zelter round. Someone else persuaded Zelter to release the score. This was Eduard Devrient, who was to sing the part of Christ. In his memoirs he gives a fascinating description of the whole affair. Secret rehearsals went on for weeks at the Mendelssohns'. They learned the music and the arias. But where was the double chorus and double orchestra to come from? Zelter would never consent to place his Singakademie at the disposal of any such project.

---

[1] G. A. Huber: *J. S. Bach als Meister der Farben*. 1949.
[2] O. Loerke: *Johann Sebastian Bach*. Frankfurt am Main, 1950.
* The chorus in medieval passion-plays.

Bach was generally considered "unmelodic, mathematical, dry and incomprehensible"—out of the question, to ask the public to listen to such stuff.

"But I could not give up my dream. One evening in January 1829, we sang the entire first part of the work for a small group. I spent a sleepless night afterwards, during which I hatched my plan for putting across a public performance. Felix, the old man's favourite pupil, must win Zelter over. Impatiently, I waited for the late winter dawn, and then set out for the Mendelssohn house. Felix was still asleep. I thought I should leave, but his youngest brother, Paul, volunteered to wake him, and began the operation. Felix lay in his well-known deathlike slumber. Paul took him under the arms, then around the waist, and sat him up. 'Felix, wake up, it's eight o'clock.' He rocked the upper part of his body back and forth, but it was a long time before Felix, who was apparently dreaming of music, murmured: 'Oh, stop it, I always said so, it's sheer squawking.' His brother, however, did not stop shaking and calling him by name, until he had at least roused him a little. Then he allowed him to lie back on the pillow. At this point Felix opened his eyes wide, and seeing me by his bed exclaimed in Berlin dialect: 'Hey, Eduard, what are you doing here?' I told him that I had something I wanted to talk over with him. Paul led me into the low-ceilinged study where Felix's breakfast was waiting on the big white desk, and his coffee on the stove."[3]

While Mendelssohn was breakfasting, Devrient said that he had made up his mind that the *St. Matthew Passion* must be performed at the Singakademie during the next few months. Mendelssohn laughed: "Who is going to conduct it?" "You, of course," Devrient said. Zelter could not refuse to let him have the concert hall. After all, he himself, Devrient, was a star of some note, and surely he could ask a favour in return for his ten years of participation in the Academy's concerts. If Mendelssohn would conduct, and above all if the proceeds of the concert could go to some charity—toward the foundation, say, of a sewing school for poor girls—Zelter would have to say yes. If not, Devrient would complain to the trustees. He wanted Felix to take him to Zelter's at once.

Felix agreed, with some trepidation. "But you know, if he gets nasty I'm going to leave; I musn't squabble with the old fellow." "He'll certainly get nasty," Devrient replied. "But leave the squabbling to me."[4]

They knocked at the door on the ground floor of the Singakademie.

---

[3] E. Devrient: *Meine Erinnerungen an Felix Mendelssohn-Bartholdy.* Leipzig, 1872.
[4] Ibid.

"A hoarse voice called, 'Come in!' We found the old giant sitting at his grand piano with its double keyboards, a long pipe in his mouth, and a dense cloud of tobacco-smoke surrounding him. A sheet of music was before him, and he held the swan's quill, with which he habitually wrote, in his hand. He was wearing his usual short, snuff-coloured, beribboned and betasselled Polish jacket and knee breeches, stockings of coarse wool and embroidered shoes.... He peered at us through his spectacles, and when he saw who it was called out good-naturedly: 'Why, lo and behold! Two such handsome young people so early in the day. To what am I indebted for this honour?' "

Devrient began to talk. About Bach in general and the *St. Matthew Passion* in particular. Zelter's face grew longer and longer. If it could only be done that way. But you couldn't take such a plunge nowadays. If Bach were alive, it would be another matter. Today's violinists didn't understand that music, and for choruses like that you needed the Thomasschule of Leipzig.

Devrient gallantly replied that Zelter himself had built up the Berlin chorus to the point where they could handle it. At which Zelter became properly vexed: "Am I supposed to sit here and listen to such crazy schemes! You snotnoses! What are you thinking of?"

Devrient looked around for Mendelssohn. "He stood at the door, hand on the latch, and with a rather pale and hurt expression gestured that we should go. I gestured back that we must stay, and stuck to my guns with Zelter. 'It was true we were young', I said, 'but we weren't so totally immature. After all, a certain amount of courage and enterprise was proper for the young, and a teacher should be pleased if two of his pupils wanted to attempt something sublime....' "

This argument seemed to take effect. He only grumbled: "And what about the trustees, who have to give their approval? There are so many heads, so many minds—and women's minds to boot; not easy to do anything with them."

"But the lady trustees have been taking part in the rehearsals at the Mendelssohns."

"Humph, women!" Zelter growled. "Today ten of them come to rehearsal and tomorrow twenty of them stay away." The visitors laughed at this joke, and finally Zelter himself laughed. "Oh well, I won't oppose you—and will put in a word for you wherever necessary. Go ahead then, in God's name and we'll see what comes of it."[5]

The pair rushed back to Mendelssohn's house to announce their victory.

[5] Ibid.

And now they plunged into weeks of feverish work. The orchestra had to be rehearsed, the singers—Stürmer, Busolt, Bader, Weppler, Mmes Schätzel and Milkder-Hauptmann—to be personally invited. To call upon the all-important soloists, the friends dressed up in dandyish array: blue jackets, white waistcoats, black scarves, black pantaloons and bright yellow leather gloves. Since Mendelssohn had only a small allowance and had run through his pocket money, Devrient lent him enough to buy the gloves. Thrifty Leah Mendelssohn reproved them for this expenditure. They could have done without the gloves, she said.

Mendelssohn threw all the force of his genius and his fantastic capacity for work into the project. First of all, he compressed the score, omitting a good deal that did not directly relate to the Passion; and by so doing he contributed greatly to the dramatic force of Bach's opus. Moreover, he "modernized" Bach; he filled out the instrumentation and ventured—to this day the purists have not forgiven him—to introduce a good many effects that Bach had never thought of. Thus he instrumented the recitative: "Und der Vorhang im Tempel zerriss". A lightning-flash of sound ran from top to bottom along the two *r*'s and the *i*, so that the listener shuddered with awe.

The performance took place on 11th March 1829. Four hundred persons sang in the chorus. The core of the huge orchestra was the Philharmonischer Verein; it was augmented by many string and wind players borrowed from the Königliche Kapelle. Mendelssohn stood before this army conducting with such ease and naturalness that it seemed as though he had already directed ten Bach festivals.

The audience, as Fanny Mendelssohn related in her diary, sat as reverently as if they were in church. In many places, however, they were absolutely carried away with enthusiasm and would have liked to call for encores. Never had a divine service been so much of a concert, and never a concert so much of a divine service. Soon the whole city was talking about the event. Everybody claimed to have attended or wished he had attended. And so, ten days later, on Bach's birthday, the *St. Matthew Passion* was given again. "The same crowds, only larger; even the lobby was filled with seats, all of which were sold out, likewise the small rehearsal room behind the orchestra."[6] For a select company there was a supper afterwards at the home of Zelter. Zelter, already framing a letter to Goethe in his mind, was in seventh heaven, and took unto himself the lion's share of credit. Therese Schlesinger, Devrient's wife, has given a whimsical description of this dinner party, at which all the celebrities of

[6] S. Hensel: *Die Familie Mendelssohn, 1729–1847*. Berlin, 1879.

Berlin were present. Mendelssohn sat at her right; on her left was an over-eager gentleman who continually tried to ply her with wine, which she refused until a toast to the artist was proposed. Only then would she drink. "He clutched my wide lace sleeve in an unrelenting grip—to protect it, he said! and would every so often turn toward me; in short, he so plagued me with his gallantries that I leaned over to Felix and asked: 'Tell me, who is this idiot beside me?' Felix held his handkerchief over his mouth for a moment—then he whispered: 'The idiot beside you is the celebrated philosopher Hegel!' "[7]

A humorous incident. But the success of a Bach Passion had serious consequences for Mendelssohn. Overnight he became virtually the head of a "school" of historical scholarship in music. And this fact not only helped but also harmed his own work. Although he had written such works as the Octet and the overture to *A Midsummer Night's Dream*, a different kind of music was now expected of him. Music is not only timeless; it belongs very much to a given time—and this was to be true of the *avant-garde* efforts of the Young Europeans, the Wagners, Berliozes and Liszts.

HE IS RATHER TOO FOND OF THE DEAD

But Mendelssohn had been born into a period with little interest in the musical past. The concert audiences were ignorant of such great composers of the seventeenth century as Dietrich Buxtehude and Heinrich Schütz.[1] How could those masters be known when not a note of theirs was available? It was true that Ignaz Sonnleithner, the friend of Schubert, and Forkel, the biographer of Bach, had begun publishing a *History of Music in Documents*, and had issued a volume of *Masses of the Seventeenth Century*; but this enterprise suffered a symbolic fate: the French troops marching into Vienna confiscated the engraved plates of the book in order to melt them down for ammunition. Thus war and Napoleon cancelled out musicology.[2]

This being so, old Zelter's and young Mendelssohn's efforts on behalf of the music of former days opened up a virgin field. Nevertheless, their campaign for the revival of old music did not meet with full acceptance. It was taken for granted that a painter, before he stepped forth on his

---

[7] Th. Schlesinger-Devrient: *Jugenderinnerungen*. Stuttgart, 1905.
[1] H. J. Moser: *Heinrich Schütz*. Kassel, 1936.
[2] J. N. Forkel: *Johann Sebastian Bach*. Leipzig, 1802.

own, would study Albrecht Dürer or Raphael. But antiquarian interests were somehow suspect in a composer. Uhland wrote dramas and ballads on German history—and steeped himself in scholarly investigations of Germany's past. No one questioned his right to do so, or took it as a sign of little talent. But how could a composer voluntarily choose old forms if he desired to speak to his contemporaries?

Had not Mozart done so? But everyone knew quite well that Mozart had not done so of his own free will. The eccentric Baron van Swieten wanted new arrangements of work by Handel and Bach for his private concerts, and Mozart had complied because he was always in need of money. To be sure, Mozart's works had benefited; he had proved once more that he could turn his hand to anything in the realm of music. But that was another matter entirely. Certainly, since the birth of "modern" music—the kind of music written by Chopin, who after all was only one year younger than Felix Mendelssohn—no living composer wanted to be branded as an old fogy. Music was neither painting nor writing. It was supposed to carry the breath of "youth", to be absolutely of the present day. But it had never occurred to Felix that he was endangering his own creativity by concerning himself with the old masters. Richard Wagner, the enemy who already stood at the gates, preparing to destroy both classical and romantic music, could have enlightened him. Just as there was an Art of the Future (1850), so there would also be—ugly though the slogan was—a Music for the Future. Mendelssohn would not have grasped the idea.

What he thought about changing times, and the flimsiness of such changes, came out in a conversation he had during his last visit to England with Sir Julius Benedict, the son of a Stuttgart banker and one-time favourite pupil of Weber. They had been talking about Mendelssohn's religious compositions, and Benedict had asked him what passage in the Old Testament he most prized. Therefore Mendelssohn had gone to the Bible lying on the table and read aloud the famous passage from Ecclesiastes: "Vanity of vanities! All is vanity. What does man gain by all the toil at which he toils under the sun? A generation goes, and a generation comes, but the earth remains for ever.... What has been is what will be, and what has been done is what will be done; and there is nothing new under the sun. Is there a thing of which it is said, See, this is new?" Then Mendelssohn sighed and asked rhetorically who could set that to music. And suddenly, unexpectedly—for he was a man in the prime of life, and physically fit—he had looked absolutely ancient.[3]

[3] H. R. Cox: *Musical Recollections of the Last Half Century*. London, 1872.

None of the Wagnerian Germans knew this anecdote, or they would have pounced upon it, claiming that a man who held such a creed was certainly not a qualified leader of modern music. Yet Mendelssohn's conservative outlook by no means bound him to imitating what had already been done. He turned to old forms for fresh inspiration. Thus, at the time of his last journey to England, he had already done a great deal toward renewing the forms of ecclesiastical music.

Not all, but the greater part of Felix Mendelssohn's works for the Church are extraordinary compositions. He was a Protestant; but his music curiously enough, has a distinctly Catholic cast. As a musician he refused to take a partisan attitude toward the Catholic Church. In the midst of the three pieces of church music which constitute his opus 23 (composed in the autumn of 1830), between the tenor solo "Aus tiefer Not schrei ich zu Dir" (*De profundis clamavi*) and "Mitten wir im Leben sind mit dem Tod unfangen" (*In media vitae*)—we encounter an *Ave Maria*. Mendelssohn was in Rome at the time—and it is pertinent to ask how anyone could be a hundred per cent Protestant there. "The music", Heinrich Dorn wrote in the *Neue Zeitschrift für Musik*, "sings so convincingly of Mary's sanctity that it could lead a non-Catholic to her. The sacredly joyous A major resembles a golden platter upon which the master has laid down this pure hymn. Here we find the tenderest tonal colours of edification, worship, religion; thoughts directed toward heaven and reflected in the eye." Another admirer[4] compared this glorious *Ave Maria* with one of the old German Madonnas turned out by Stephan Lochner's workshop. Yet while still in Rome, Felix rectified the balance by setting texts of Luther's to music. His pieces, "Vom Himmel hoch, da komm ich her", "Ach Gott vom Himmel, sieh darein", "Wir glauben all an einen Gott", and "Verleih uns Frieden" stem from this time. The first three songs are framed as choral cantatas, but the prayer for peace (opus 94) seemed to him too important to be couched in a traditional form which might tend to blur its seriousness. He handled this text with complete freedom, with great vigour but also with great sweetness—as though "peace on earth" were already in sight, or at any rate as though mankind would not have long to wait for this blessing. From the basses the song rises into the alto range and is then taken up by the entire chorus. Flutes, clarinets, bassoon, string quartet and organ glow in soft, changing spectra. Robert Schumann, Felix's friend and admirer, said of this work: "A uniquely beautiful composition; a mere look at the score scarcely conveys its enormous effectiveness. This little piece deserves to be known the

---

[4] R. Werner: *Felix Mendelssohn-Bartholdy als Kirchenmusiker*. Frankfurt am Main, 1930.

world over, and so it will be; Madonnas by Raphael and Murillo cannot long remain hidden from sight. . . ."[5]

The fact is that these small religious pieces did indeed win this fame. They were performed throughout the nineteenth century, and none of Mendelssohn's later enemies was able to expel them from the churches. If there was anything questionable about Mendelssohn's church music, it concerned the strange company in which he found himself. In the past Catholicism had produced magnificent music; but the musical life of nineteenth-century Protestantism was rather parched; and Mendelssohn's songs were sung on Sundays by altogether devout but unmusical congregations. What was more, church music had been sobered up and scrubbed clean of all traces of secular beauty. Thus the Cecilia Club, run by that otherwise excellent citizen of Frankfurt, Johann Nepomuk Schelble, objected to the glorious Masses of Haydn and to Mozart's celestial spiritual music.[6] Mendelssohn found such attitudes appalling. Nevertheless he felt obliged to find out what these people really wanted.

With this purpose he called on the famous zealot Anton Friedrich Justus Thibaut in Heidelberg—had in fact done so a year and a half before the performance of the *St. Matthew Passion*! Thibaut was the jurist who in 1825 had published a strange, much-discussed book, *Reinheit der Tonkunst* ("Purity in the Art of Music"). As we know today, the book did enormous harm; perhaps only a non-musician could have written so wrong-headed a work.[7]

Of Thibaut's ardent love for music, there could be no doubt. He had travelled widely, had spent much time in Rome and especially in Vienna, and everywhere had dug up precious old manuscripts. He spoke of these with wild enthusiasm. Palestrina was his god—though, save for him, the name was scarcely known. He was also enamoured of Orlando di Lasso (1520–94), who had been born in Holland as Roland Lass. King Charles IX of France had commissioned Orlando di Lasso to set the penitential psalms to music, by way of doing penance for St. Bartholomew's Night. "This gigantic work", Thibaut wrote, "still lies in the Munich library, the manuscript ornamented with gold, jewels and the portraits of composers of the time. But what young composer has travelled to Munich to study this work, or any of the other works by this incomparable master? Similarly, the directors of the library of St. Mark's in Venice could write

[5] R. Schumann: *Gesammelte Schriften über Musik und Musiker*. Leipzig, 1891.

[6] H. E. Jacob: *Joseph Haydn: His Art, Times and Glory*. New York, 1950.

[7] A. F. J. Thibaut: *Über die Reinheit der Tonkunst*. Heidelberg, 1825.

on the nails of their little fingers the names of the German virtuosi who during the past thirty years have asked them for the works of Lotti."

Mendelssohn would surely have exclaimed "Hear, hear!" at this protest. For he too loved the old composers and thought that they were unjustly neglected by the moderns. And he would have felt himself in the presence of a fellow-spirit when he found Thibaut, on the very next page, inveighing against the neglect of Handel. Handel, said Thibaut, was as great as the Bible, was the Homer and Shakespeare of Music. His *Samson*, his *Alexander's Feast*, his *Judas Maccabaeus*, *The Messiah*, the *Dettingen Te Deum*, the *Jubilate* of the 100th Psalm—in fact all that Handel had written was pronounced a "true ocean of glories". Thibaut particularly praised the oratorios *Esther* and *Israel in Egypt*. As for Handel's last work, *Jephthah*, Thibaut rated it with his best, insisting that it was composed with "a freshness and liveliness, as if the inspired old man had once again attained to the full strength of youth and manhood."[8]

Curiously enough, the name of Johann Sebastian Bach was scarcely mentioned in the catalogue of the great masters of the past. Thibaut, then, did not see eye to eye with Zelter on the supremacy of Bach. But Felix Mendelssohn, the youth who was soon afterwards to resurrect the *St. Matthew Passion* from its tomb, was drawn to Handel too. Perhaps the texts of Handel oratorios corresponded more closely with his spirit. The Old Testament wrathfulness of the London composer influenced his own major works, the *Paul* and the *Elijah*, far more strongly than the mysticism of the Cantor of Leipzig. Mendelssohn was more impressed by Thibaut's book than he cared to or dared to admit.

But then came the disagreeable side of Thibaut. Proceeding straight from Handel, he pronounced his anathema upon modern music. Mozart had been gifted, it was true. But why had he ruined Handel's *Messiah* by dubious instrumentation, his introduction of courtly flutes, clarinets and bassoons? Thibaut was completely unaware of all the developments that had taken place in the orchestra since the late Baroque period. This archconservative was horrified by the "vainglory of the instruments, their impulse to exceed themselves". "Nowadays every instrument seeks to do everything, and each prefers to be heard where it oversteps the limits of its nature or exhibits its weakest sides. The Jew's harp and the French horn seek rippling runs like violins; the violin imitates the lean exigencies of the piano; the trumpet tries to be delicate as the flute; and the venerable, armoured double-bass has recently tried imitating the graces of all the graceful instruments."[9]

[8] Ibid.   [9] Ibid.

How would Mendelssohn take this—Felix, the romantic instrumentalist who in the overture to *A Midsummer Night's Dream* had gone almost further than Beethoven, Weber and Schubert in exploring the potentialities of the instruments? As for Beethoven, Thibaut grudgingly put up with him. "But what a strained, theatrical and often vulgar text supplies the basis for his oratorio *Christ at the Mount of Olives!*" And he adds: "In the present state of things it seems almost a natural law that all boundaries between the oratorio and opera be erased." This was indeed a difficult aesthetic problem—and Thibaut was not the only one who brooded over it. Nevertheless, the puristic Thibaut overlooked the fact that even his revered Handel had not scrupled to introduce exactly the same type of music into his oratorios, as he used in his operas *Julius Caesar, Rodelinda* and *Alexander*.[10]

But Thibaut's utter lack of comprehension of music as a living organism came to light in his description of how a contemporary composer planned a work: "First a mysterious beginning; then a shot to startle the listener; sudden silence; unexpectedly, a bit of waltzlike music; but just as this is beginning to stir the listener's senses there follows, with equal brilliance, a sudden transition to profundity and mournfulness; then an immediate plunge into a savage tempest; out of the midst of the storm, after a little suspenseful pause, we go over to something playful; and at the end a kind of hurrah, in the course of which everybody embraces heartily all round, screaming universal love in all directions." Thibaut does not specify the composer, but he implies that Carl Maria von Weber's overtures were written in this manner—nervously, disjointedly, and only for sensation. Thibaut is incensed by sudden changes of tempo and accentuation; to him, it is criminal to break off a largo movement before it is musically finished, and to bring an allegro to a sudden halt. Such devices were sheer decadence. But what had brought music to this sorry state? The connoisseur Thibaut thought he knew. Modern composers were pandering to the taste of a mixed public. "If a mixed public has a colourful hodgepodge served up to it, everybody can find something he likes." Contemporary composers were sacrificing their artistic integrity for cheap success.[11]

And nevertheless a leader of the modern school had long and deep talks with such a man, and did not lose his temper. "The man knows little about music", Mendelssohn wrote to his mother at the time. "Even his historical knowledge of it is fairly limited; he acts mostly out of sheer

[10] H. Leichtentritt: *Händel*. Leipzig, 1925.
[11] A. F. J. Thibaut: op. cit.

instinct. I know more about it than he does. *And yet I have learned a tremendous lot from him.*"[12]

It is hard to know which to admire more—Mendelssohn's modesty or his deep charity, which would not let him condemn a person whom he felt to be well-meaning.

Mendelssohn was not a classical composer. As a leader of the Romantic school of music, he could not be. But he was a classicist, and that was quite another thing. His natural inclination was to give his music a retrospective cast. In this he reminds us of one of the foremost architects of the period, Karl Friedrich Schinkel, who was a regular visitor to the Sunday concerts at Felix's home. Schinkel too was retrospective; but he was by no means wedded to any one period.[13] When his classicist building, the Berlin Schauspielhaus, was opened, Goethe composed some verses to celebrate the occasion. He praised the theatre because

> The right proportion strictly measured out
> Puts all disorder in yourselves to rout.

Right proportion, strict measuring—these terms could be applied to certain works of Mendelssohn's. But not to the majority of his works, and certainly not to those highly original ones wherein Goethe's world is transposed into music: *Meeresstille und glückliche Fahrt* or *Erste Walpurgisnacht*. As for the architect Schinkel, he once said that he was fortunate in being able "to look from the wavering present into the past"—but even more so in that he "could choose the century" to look back to. Eduard Grisebach wrote of Schinkel that his greatness "consisted in the fusing of the pagan and the Christian, the Hellenic and the national German, the classical and the romantic".[14]

Historicism can also be eclecticism: that is one of its strengths. Mendelssohn, too, chose his fathers. As Karl H. Wörner has pointed out, "Mendelssohn made a *principle* of style out of the revival and perpetuation of classicism's corpus of historical forms. He was the first to take this approach, which was destined to be carried on by many others."[15] Thus, the work of Brahms is inconceivable without the precedent of Mendelssohn; Brahms too made creative use of the classical and the romantic styles. As for Max Reger, he had little patience with those who deplored Mendelssohn's historicism and eclecticism. Those qualities were the very rock on which he built his own style.

[12] S. Hensel: *Die Familie Mendelssohn 1729–1847*. Berlin, 1879.
[13] H. Grimm: *Rede auf Schinkel*. 1862.
[14] E. Grisebach: *Karl Friedrich Schinkel*. Leipzig, 1924.
[15] K. H. Wörner: *Neue Musik in der Entscheidung*. Mainz, 1954.

Felix was only twenty-one when he perceived this aspect of his mission. "No one can forbid me to enjoy and to develop all that the great masters have left behind them, for there is no sense in everyone's beginning at the beginning again; but it must be a development to the best of my ability, not a lifeless repetition of what has already been."[16] Three years later, and that much more mature, he was the more convinced of this. "Men must come along who will continue on the road—they will lead others further, or else back (though it really should be called forward) to what is old and right." Of course he was conscious of the difficulties he was courting as the leader of a conservative league. For still another three years later he wrote, with more than a trace of self-mockery: "Three organ fugues are to be printed in the next month—me voilà perruque. May God let me hit on a jolly piano passage soon, so that I can wipe out the bad impression."

For of course the New Germans were already starting to sneer. Who would want to go back to Bach in this day and age?

Mendelssohn, on the other hand, was not always capable of understanding his contemporaries. He had tremendous admiration for Liszt as a virtuoso. ("I have never seen a musician in whom musical feeling runs down to the very fingertips, as it does in him, and then pours directly out of them.") Perhaps he was a little partial toward Liszt ever since Liszt had surpassed himself in his performance of Mendelssohn's G minor Concerto (opus 25) in Paris. But Mendelssohn never learned to appreciate Liszt as a composer. Nor could the quiet and unassuming Mendelssohn entirely take to Berlioz, with his bouts of temperament and tendency to act the genius. Superficially, a fairly friendly relationship was established between the two composers. They met in Rome; Mendelssohn played parts of *Walpurgisnacht* on the piano, and Berlioz was much impressed by it. It gave the Frenchman quite a turn when he discovered that this amiable young German could stand up strongly for his opinions. When they discussed old music, Mendelssohn turned into a veritable hedgehog. "You did not know where to touch him without getting your hand pricked. In all other respects, Mendelssohn had an excellent character and the gentlest disposition; he did not mind being contradicted; and I for my part abused his tolerance in the philosophical and religious discussions that frequently sprang up between us."[17]

Apparently Berlioz was not shamming affection for his colleague. There was true feeling in the note he wrote to Mendelssohn from Prague a year and a half before the latter's death. On 14th April 1846 he scribbled:

---

[16] Ibid.   [17] H. Berlioz: *Mémoires*. Paris, 1870.

"Permettez-moi de vous dire que j'ai entendu à Breslau votre 'Songe d'une nuit d'été' et que je n'ai jamais rien entendu d'aussi profondément Shakespearien que votre musique." And in impetuous accents that bear every sign of coming from the heart, the note continued: "When I left the theatre, I would gladly have given three years of my life to embrace you. Adieu! Adieu! Believe me that I love you as much as I admire you— and that is a great deal. I belong to you heart and soul. Berlioz."

Alas—Mendelssohn did not reciprocate this admiration. It is a good thing that Berlioz never knew what harsh judgment Mendelssohn passed on him. "Berlioz's instrumentation is so frightfully filthy, such a confused smear, that you want to wash your fingers after merely holding one of his scores in your hand. Moreover, it is simply disgraceful for anyone to put music together out of nothing but killing and misery and lamentation; for even if it were good, there would be little else in it but suchlike *atrocités*. He really depressed me from the very first, especially the way he passes such clever and sweeping judgments on everybody else, is so utterly reasonable, and often does not seem to be aware of the infinitely unreasonable stuff he himself turns out." And on another occasion he posed the question of whether Berlioz was not, after all, quite boring. Did not his eternal turbulence and excitement end by putting the listener to sleep?[18]

Such remarks were in the spirit of Zelter and Goethe, who detested turbulence in art. It was not fair to judge Berlioz by these criteria. Which piece of music was Mendelssohn referring to? Possibly to the *Symphonie Fantastique*, that attempt at "autobiography" with its wide range of feeling—tenderness, jealousy, rage; with its interpolated scenes: the "idyll in country" and "the ball"; with its imaginary adventures: "walk to the scaffold" and "dream of a witches' night". "A tremendous symphony. I have just written the last note of it", Berlioz reported to his friend Humbert Ferrand in 1830.[19] And so it was, for it alone ushered in Romanticism in France.

How could Mendelssohn have failed to understand such music? "He is rather too fond of the dead", Berlioz once said of him. At any rate Mendelssohn's scathing opinion of Berlioz as a composer was voiced only in a private letter, and never did Berlioz any damage. Mendelssohn was far too courteous to have expressed such an opinion openly. But he was to find that others were not so discreet when, in 1850, the first public attacks were launched against him. The cause of these attacks was not his music, but his origins.

[18] F. Mendelssohn-Bartholdy: *Briefe an Ignaz und Charlotte Moscheles.* Leipzig, 1888.
[19] G. de Pourtalès: *Berlioz et l'Europe Romantique.* Paris, 1938.

THE FRIENDSHIP OF SCHUMANN

Had Mendelssohn been nothing but an "eclectic talent" and a "tasteful antiquarian" (to mention only two of the labels with which his later enemies branded him), he would not have enjoyed the most precious thing in his artistic life: the friendship of Schumann, the admiration of this great master. All his life, Schumann's battle-cry remained "Mendelssohn and Chopin"—while he himself was too modest to place himself alongside or above these contemporaries.

We find Schumann in his letters[1] calling Mendelssohn the "first musician of the present day", one who "is a true god" and one to whom he looks up "as to a high mountain range". Such artistic veneration—bordering as it does on a kind of idolatry—occurs only among artists who are fundamentally very different from one another. For if their talents run along the same lines, they cannot take such a view. Goethe could admire Schiller so strongly only because they were such different natures. And the artistic friendship of Haydn and Mozart was also based largely upon the disparities between the two. The case of Schumann and Mendelssohn was similar. Josef Wilhelm von Wasielewski, an early biographer of Schumann, has left us with a good description of the physical appearance of these two composers which alone makes clear that these were personalities of an entirely different stamp.[2]

"Mendelssohn had a finely built, rather slight frame. His lithe, agile movements were extraordinarily animated, and in keeping with his frequent changes of facial expression. His dark eyes flashed fire. They could quickly take on an amiably benevolent and serene expression, or a sharply penetrating or gravely meditative look.... His high, finely arched forehead was framed by black hair which fell in curls to the back and sides. His face, which narrowed sharply toward the chin, was bordered by a vigorous growth of whiskers. The moderately hooked nose was of the Roman type and betrayed oriental descent. The mouth, extremely well shaped, was strikingly expressive.... Everything in Mendelssohn's nature united to make his whole appearance attractive and prepossessing. It is understandable, therefore, that he was a most popular and respected

[1] R. Schumann: *Briefe, Neue Folge*. Leipzig, 1904.
[2] J. W. von Wasielewski: *Aus siebzig Jahren*. Stuttgart, 1897.

personality, all the more so since his intellectual qualities had an irresistible fascination."

Schumann, however, made an entirely different impression, As Wasielewski described him.

"Most of his time was devoted to his creative work, with the result that he was not often seen in society. By nature he was not inclined toward free, open, communicative intercourse with others. Although he privately took the keenest interest in all the events of the day and all the new developments in the realm of art—as his many articles on music and musicians amply prove—he was for the most part taciturn and apparently self-absorbed while in the company of others. Only when he was with close friends did he emerge from his shell. Then he would to a certain extent disclose his rich spiritual and emotional life, which is so beautifully and significantly unfolded in his music. . . ."

But this description is inadequate and does not take into account another side of Schumann. For people were apt to be struck not by his dreamy blue-grey eyes, so often closed as he listened to talk or music, but by his powerful, jutting cheekbones. These gave his face a vigorous Eastern-European, distinctly Slavonic quality. He reminded people of the Russian revolutionaries, the Dekabrists, who in 1825 took part in the unsuccessful uprising against Tsar Nicholas I. Schumann's character was extremely manly, and his music was too. When he produced, out of the inner core of his being, such works as the already mentioned *Davidsbündlermarsch gegen die Philister* (opus 6), he did more than write great music; he described himself. And the Schumann of such moods no longer held his head at a dreamy tilt. The eyes above the prominent cheekbones flamed defiance. The slow beat of the march advanced like a soldier bearing a halberd, ready to run the hosts of Philistines through.

But who were the *Davidsbündler*, the members of this "League of David"? In his introspection Schumann had early discovered three different egos in himself, three persons whom he named Eusebius, Florestan and Raro. He had become aware that "I am not like myself. Different natures converse within me. But which one shall I regard as my proper self?" We must hasten to point out that this curious division within himself was not initially what we would today call schizophrenia. It was not accompanied by psychic obsessions, but remained on the plane of critical intelligence. Eusebius, Raro and Florestan criticized one another's ideas. They were, to begin with, literary fancies, for Schumann was the son of a bookseller and had read his Jean Paul.[3] Later on, perhaps, the three identities were to take on a more dangerous cast, and by 1854 he daily "heard voices that were not his own". Then madness seemed to hound him, and, despairing, he threw himself into the Rhine. We may wonder whether his love for the "romantic infinitudes" of Jean Paul was not in some sense a preparation for insanity.[4]

But in 1835, when Schumann saw Mendelssohn for the first time, he was twenty-five years old and in full possession of his health and genius. Eusebius, Raro and Florestan were inner voices whose contentions he smilingly adjudicated. In fact, this trio of inner musicians was not enough for Schumann's artistic purposes. He had to incorporate a number of flesh-and-blood friends into his League of David, the only people whose opinion on music counted. The group was an intensely private one and he renamed its members with his own "lodge" names.[5] His Clara was called Chiarina; Ernestine von Fricken, the one-time muse of his *Symphonic Études* (opus 13), was christened Estrella, and he punned on his conviction of Mendelssohn's merits by calling him Felix Meritis. He could not resist letting some private jokes slip into the public domain— and it is amusing to read in his collected writings (*Gesammelte Schriften über Musik und Musiker*, 1854): "Yesterday Meritis conducted a concerto by Mendelssohn."

Effective publicist that he was (the greatest musical publicist of his time, for Richard Wagner furthered no one's career but his own), Schumann let slip no opportunity of fulfilling what he regarded as his duty: to make the world aware of the qualities of Mendelssohn's music. In his voluminous critical writings he discusses, often in great detail, Mendelssohn's concerti for pianoforte, the Serenade for Orchestra, the Preludes and Fugues (opus 35), the Sonata for Piano and 'Cello (opus 45). "This inner well-being, this peace, this spiritual grace everywhere. . . . The sonata", Schumann wrote after Mendelssohn's death, "is one of his last

[3] H. Kötz: *Der Einfluss Jean Pauls auf Robert Schumann*. Wiemar, 1933.

[4] R. Pitrou: *La Vie Intérieure de Robert Schumann*. Paris, 1925.

[5] F. G. Jansen: *Die Davidsbündler. Aus Schumanns Sturm- und Drangperiode*. Leipzig, 1883.

works. . . . It seems to me that it strives to become something more than music; it is all intensely refined, transfigured—if it would not be misinterpreted I would say: intensely Mozartian. . . . This sonata is the purest kind of music, completely valid in and for itself—a sonata as beautiful and lucid as anything that has ever emerged from the hands of a great artist . . . to be enjoyed preferably in the family circle after, say, a few poems by Goethe or Byron."

And Schumann wrote this of a composer who was certainly no master of the sonata, but who could not write a piece of music without bringing his composition to perfection. We can imagine, then, how he would treat Mendelssohn's major works, the *Songs without Words*, the overture to *A Midsummer Night's Dream*, the overture to *Melusina*, the celebrated prayer, *Verleih uns Frieden gnädiglich*, and the 114th Psalm: "Da Israel aus Ägypten zog". In discussing this psalm Schumann records the fact that there was some discussion, in the audience, whether it had not been surpassed by an older psalm of Mendelssohn's, "Wie der Hirsch schreiet nach frischem Wasser".

Schumann's acts of friendship seem all the more extraordinary when compared with the spite of most other artists against a successful colleague. And we must keep in mind how different Schumann's talent and his aims were from those of Mendelssohn. The basic form of all Schumann's music was the sketch, and the predominant mood of his early compositions was a "high-spirited jocularity".[6] Even as a boy he could "characterize the different personalities of the playmates standing around him so precisely and comically in certain figures and passages on the piano that they burst into roars of laughter at the portrait likenesses." This alone underlines the difference in generations which separated Schumann from the classical composers, from Haydn, Mozart and Beethoven. For it would scarcely have been thinkable for these illustrious predecessors to use music for such purposes. To conceive such music you had to be post-Schubertian. And Schumann was. But for Schubert's "Diary Fragments", but for the inspired shorthand of the "Moment Musical" Schubert had invented, Schumann would not have been Schumann. He no longer developed; he sketched. With the bold, swift hand of the draughtsman he dashed out his themes. Mendelssohn, too, was aware of this technique, but only in a theoretical way. Mendelssohn was more impressed by the fact that Schubert in his greatness "shattered the piano sonata only after he himself had created the most beautiful ones ever

[6] W. Gertler: *Robert Schumann in seinen frühen Klavierwerken* Wolfenbüttel, 1931.

written"—a revealing remark for more reasons than one. Not only does it bring to light that Schubert was the last classical composer,[7] but it implies that Mendelssohn would have liked to overcome romanticism in himself and turn toward a new classicism—an attitude that was later to triumph in Brahms.

But in Schumann's *Carneval*, in the *Papillons*, there was no classicism. Life and love rollick along in romantic disguises. Although both composers loved the "ethereal music" of their favourite master, Weber, Schumann never wrote like Mendelssohn and Mendelssohn never wrote like Schumann. The very rhythmic base of their inspirations differed. In spite of *Träumerei* Schumann preferred an iambic-anapæstic rhythm—which corresponds with the nature of the German language, to "Germanism" in general, as Wilhelm Wundt, the psychologist, demonstrated.[8] The verbal accent of the Mediterranean peoples, especially the Spaniards, is different. It is trochaic—and the difficulty with the trochee is that it "ultimately writes itself". (Grillparzer's *Der Traum ein Leben*, Heine's epic *Atta Troll* and Gerhart Hauptmann's *Weisser Heiland* are not, alas, evidence to the contrary.) Goethe and Eichendorff, at any rate, instinctively recognized the dangers of that Spanish-Moorish rhythm, and incorporated caesuras and irregularities into their trochaic poems. Schumann is so distrustful of trochees that when for once he has a genuine, wholly trochaic idea, as in the opening of the *Kreisleriana* (gently rising and then falling in a splendid cadence):

he *expects* the pianist to interrupt the flow, to introduce a hesitancy, a fermata, a slight pause for reflection. (Eugen d'Albert chose the D in the second measure; Rolf Walter Hirschberg syncopated the F following it.) Mendelssohn did not have this timidity about the trochaic accent. He chose freely among the Germanic iambic, the Homeric dactylic or the Spanish-Moorish trochaic rhythms.

Both Schumann and Mendelssohn were great masters of the *lied*, perhaps the greatest except for Schubert. But what differences there were in their choice of texts, and accordingly in their compositions! With Schumann almost every song took on the quality of a ballad:

[7] W. Vetter: *Der Klassiker Schubert*. Leipzig, 1953.
[8] Wilhelm Wundt: *Völkerpsychologie*. Leipzig, 1911–12.

Ein-ge-schla-fen auf der Lau-er o-ben ist der al - te Rit-ter,

(Eichendorff's "Romanze".) The E minor is not a genuine E minor. It is a Phrygian ecclesiastical mode. The rowing slows:

Mu - si - kan - ten spie - len mun - ter, und die

schö - ne Braut, die wei - - - net

Here he uses music to paint the grandeur, the expansiveness of the Rhineland landscape. It is the talent of a born ballad maker. He does the same in his setting of Eichendorff's "Waldesgespräch", with the chilling haste of its beginning: "Es ist schon spät, es ist schon kalt...." In the conversation with the "witch Loreley", who is not a witch at all but a betrayed woman:

Gross ist der Männer Trug und List,
Vor Schmerz mein Herz gebrochen ist—

with what boldness the music expresses the encounter between man and woman, between desire and refusal! Every ballad that Robert Schumann touched became a ten times greater ballad in his hands. In "The Two Grenadiers", for example, how inevitable we find those little drum-rolls throbbing beneath the words, and at the end (something that Heine never thought of) the "Marseillaise" sustaining the words like a gigantic barrel-vault. That was, when it was composed, one of the greatest strokes of inspiration in the whole history of song. . . . Or take the setting of Eichendorff's "Mondnacht"—a poem of simple mood, without plot, without romance. As soon as Schumann took hold of the poem it promptly acquired a chivalric profile. An active will, the very essence of volition, mysteriously enters the poem four times in the first two stanzas. This "will" seems to sustain the firmament.

The innermost core of this will consists of a triviality: the mordent on the G sharp at the word "still". . . . As if there were any such thing as trivialities in a composition. At any rate Richard Wagner borrowed this Schumann phrase for his herald in the second act of *Lohengrin*. Even Wagner could think of nothing more chivalric.

From still another point of view Schumann's setting of "Mondnacht" is one of the greatest miracles of the lied. It is a song for piano, as almost all of Schumann's lieder are. But the piano voice is no mere accompaniment. It enjoys supreme autonomy; so that one might equally well say that the singer does the accompaniment. Before Schumann no composer had ever dared to take such liberties.

Certainly not Mendelssohn. He who was himself so great a pianist (whereas Schumann, as is well known, had tragically ruined his career on that instrument by tying his third finger in order to make his fourth more adroit[9]) would hardly have allowed a singer to engage in a duel, a duet with the piano voice. To Mendelssohn a song was really a song, and the accompaniment at most a guide for one or several singing voices. In this respect he remained a Berliner—though without any admixture of Zelter's philistinism. Another difference between him and Schumann was that in choosing his texts he instinctively steered away from ballads. Even an old German text like Jacob von der Warte's "Maienlied" lost its hard, antiquarian character when he set it to music:

[9] A. Boucourechliev: *Robert Schumann in Selbstzeugnissen und Bilddokumenten.* Hamburg, 1958.

Man soll hö - ren sü - ßes Sin - gen in den Au - en ü - ber - all, lieb - lich hell Ge - sang er - klin - gen, vor - - aus vor der Nach - - ti - gall!

It is true that he did well with romanzas, but he seldom chose to set them. "Es fiel ein Reif in der Frühlingsnacht", that lovely lament, is rather exceptional. Mendelssohn's greatness as a master of the lied—we shall have much more to say about it later on—lay not in the realm of the romanza and the ballad, but in the folk song and the hymnic song.

Schumann would not have admired a composer whose work was too like his own. Mendelssohn, however, reduced him to a state of sheer astonishment. It is now known that Schumann left a diary and that it contains certain jottings, made after Mendelssohn's death, by way of summarizing his relationship with his friend. This diary, kept secret by Clara Schumann, was not published until 1949. It was first put out in a facsimile edition by the Zwickau Schumann Museum and shortly afterwards in a more conventional format edited by Georg Eismann and Gertrud Rudloff-Hille.[10]

In his published writings Schumann was inclined to be verbose—for which reason these diary notes are all the more significant. For once he did not wax eloquent, but set down his memories of Mendelssohn in spare and essential form.

> His judgments in musical matters—especially on composition —the most trenchant imaginable, go straight to the innermost core.—He instantly and everywhere recognized flaws and their cause.—
> He never kept diaries or anything of that sort, he told me.—
> I always considered his praise the highest—he was the highest authority, the court of last appeal.
> If he had unjustly offended anyone—spoken of someone adversely to a third party—he could not rest until he had made amends. His behaviour toward other living composers. . . . When

[10] G. Eismann and G. Rudloff-Hille: *Schumanns Mendelssohn-Tagebuch*. Zwickau, 1949.

he had nothing to praise, he said nothing; but where he un-mistakably found talent, he was the first to say so (thus in the cases of Bennett, Gade and Rietz).

In 1836 when we were talking about ageing composers, he said "how sad is the thought of creativity drying up" and added that he could not be reconciled to this thought.—

He was free of all the weaknesses of vanity.—

The exaltation of associating with him. Highest moral and artistic principles; for that reason intransigent, sometimes seem-ingly rude and unkind.—

He never remained in debt. If you said something good or significant to him, you could be certain of receiving it back twice and thrice over.—

On his relationship to Meyerbeer he said they had never suited each other; if one of them said "Good day" the other would surely have scented some ulterior motive.—

Self-criticism, the strictest and most conscientious I have ever encountered in an artist. He changed some passages five and six times. (Especially the *Elijah*; his fine remark on that: "I think there are a few things I might do better".)—

If all his intimate friends had been writers, each would have had something extraordinary and something different to record; each would have whole volumes to write about him.—

It was as if every day he had been born anew.—

Did he feel that he had fulfilled his mission?

I think so. The trace of melancholia which is so frequently found in all his compositions after the *Lobgesang*.—

His face in death. He looked like a hierophant, like a warrior of God who had conquered.—6th November 1847.

This entry is the last. Schumann was one of the pallbearers at Mendels-sohn's funeral in Leipzig. He survived his friend by nearly nine years. But afterwards a good many persons noted that "he had begun to die at that time".

PARTING WITH GOETHE

Seventeen years before this final farewell there had been another parting. Mendelssohn had bidden Goethe adieu—although neither knew it at the time.

That was the year of Mendelssohn's Italian journey. In the spring of 1830 Felix passed through Weimar. He had not planned to stay long. But Goethe welcomed him with open arms and would not release the young man to whom he had been wont to say: "You are my David. Play for me when I am sad. I will not cast my spear at you." Now he craftily invented all sorts of pretexts to keep Mendelssohn from leaving—in this, no doubt, falling in with Felix's own inclinations. He wanted, for example, to have Felix for his portrait, "in order to add this to a collection of drawings which he had been amassing for some time." He invented amusements for his guest, sending him on an outing to Tiefurt with the ladies of the household, Ulrike and Ottilie. But first Goethe archly warned him: "But you must not go to Berka because there is a beautiful girl living there who might break your heart!" But Felix did not have the makings of a Werther. Besides, the old, old man who daily sat across the table from him was far more interesting than any woman—even capricious daughter-in-law Ottilie who prepared their tea and coaxed Felix into taking part in a magazine entitled *Chaos*. (What could be more inappropriate in the household of Goethe, who in fact made sarcastic remarks about it and proposed that the magazine be renamed.[1])

The old gentleman complained that he had heard little music at home these days. To give him his fill for once, Felix played copiously—mornings for Goethe alone; evenings in a larger company. As always, Goethe was interested in the biological and historical aspects of music. As we know from his correspondence with Zelter and also from Felix's accounts, Goethe regarded music as something "evolvable"; it was to him a part of natural history and fascinated him in the same way as the growth of crystals. Indeed, why should not music be experienced in strata? At that very time Ludwig Spohr was experimenting with a Historical Symphony in which he intended to copy the styles of various eras. The experiment was a failure, of course, but it was an attempt in the spirit of Goethe.[2]

[1] E. Ludwig: *Goethe. Die Geschichte eines Menschen*. Berlin, 1926.
[2] L. Spohr: *Selbstbiographie*. Kassel, 1860–61.

"In the morning", Mendelssohn wrote, "I have to play for him for an hour or so, from a variety of the great composers in chronological order, and must tell him how they have developed the art. While I am playing he sits in a dark corner like a *Jupiter tonans,* his old eyes flashing. He did not want to touch Beethoven at all."[3] Naturally not! For he knew only too well that the historian's attitude which he could bring to baroque music, Bach, Haydn and even Mozart, would be out of the question in the case of Beethoven. With Beethoven a blunt "no" or "yes" was essential. "But I told him", Felix wrote home, "that I could not help him, and played the first movement of the C minor Symphony. It had an odd effect on him. At first he said: 'But it doesn't *move anything at all* ' "—that is to say, he found it chaotic and a man of Goethe's temperament could only respond to ordered material. "But then he continued uncomfortably: '*That only rouses astonishment; it is grandiose.*' He muttered for a while and after some time brought out: '*That is very great, fantastic; one would be inclined to fear that the house would tumble down; suppose everybody played that all together!*' And at table, in the midst of a conversation on something else entirely, he brought the matter up again."

The octogenarian Goethe was highly eccentric. His moods had become redoubtable. A young *littérateur* named Stephan Schütze who had met the great man in Johanna Schopenhauer's salon in Weimar remarked that you could never be sure of how he would behave.[4] One moment you had before you a calm and gentle sage, at another an irate and dismaying autocrat. (Even his feelings of grief were expressed by irateness.) He was now aloof, silent, then again eloquent, loquacious; now displayed an epic tranquility, now a fiery, excitable temperament; or he could be ironically jesting, playfully teasing. . . .[5] Music was essential to this restless spirit whose mood could change four times in the course of an hour. And Felix was still the harper David who knew how to enchant his Saul. But not always. Baroness Jenny von Gustedt, who was often present while Felix played, relates an incident "in which Goethe—all Saul!—lost patience with his favourite because Felix did not understand something". This something had been a matter outside music, of course—some aspect of natural history, perhaps, beyond the ken of a musician. "Quite unnerved, Mendelssohn sat frozen at the instrument, until, almost unconsciously,

[3] F. Mendelssohn-Bartholdy: *Briefe aus den Jahren 1830–47.* Leipzig, 1861.
[4] H. H. Houben: *Damals in Weimar. Erinnerungen und Briefe von und an Johanna Schopenhauer.* Leipzig, 1924.
[5] V. Tornius: *Salons, Bilder gesellschaftlicher Kultur aus fünf Jahrhunderten.* Berlin, 1925.

his fingers touched the keys and he began to play, as if to console himself. Suddenly Goethe came over to his side again and in his gentlest voice said: '*You have enough; hold on to it!*'" These were words that Felix pondered again and again.[6] Yet their meaning was simple: Goethe had ceded the point; he would not ask the young man to think in other than purely musical terms. While Riemer, Eckermann and the other gentlemen of his retinue were required always to follow him on the alpine ascents of his thought, to make all the sudden, dangerous leaps from peak to peak, Felix was exempt.

What Goethe prized in Felix Mendelssohn was certainly not his competence at the piano—for there were others in the circle who could have played for him, had he wished it—but the aristocratic quality of Felix's approach to music: its mixture of modesty and self-assurance. As Goethe remarked to his daughter-in-law Ottilie: "Felix is so clear about his own affair that one can learn a great deal from him." His affair was music, of course—but if Felix had too openly displayed his superiority in this realm, the old Goethe might have been incensed. Felix avoided that danger— and not from superficial prudence, but from that inner balance which all his friends remarked in him.

What attached him to Goethe—not just to Goethe's works, but to Goethe's personality—was the many-sidedness of Goethe's nature, the variety of his interests, any one of which might suddenly come to the fore in conversation. Posterity, Mendelssohn wrote, would some day assert that Goethe had not been a single person, but had consisted of a number of small Goethides: satellites revolving around a central sun, as it were. But what exactly was this central sun? At this question, Felix would fall silent, for there was something staggering about Goethe's craving for knowledge. Logical enough that the talk should turn to Scotland and Spontini—these were topics on which Felix could be informative. But pretty soon Goethe had moved from these to questions of theology. What did people in Berlin think of the dispute that had just broken out between the orthodox party of Geheimrat Hengstenberg's Protestant church newspaper and the anti-Pietists Wegscheider and Gesenius? Was there serious danger of secession?[7] No sooner had Felix replied—his own tastes were not particularly Pietistic—he tended to follow Schleiermacher who pointed out the existence of certain Greek-Pantheistic roots of Christianity—than the old man shifted to Hegel, under whom his guest had studied, after

[6] L. V. Kretschmann: "Erinnerungen der Jenny von Gustedt." *Deutsche Rundschau*, Berlin, 1891.
[7] L. Witte: *Das Leben F. A. Tholucks*. Bielefeld, 1884.

all. What, he wanted to know, did sceptical Berlin think of a man who considered himself the messianic absolute, who believed that there would be no more philosophers after him?[8] This question was difficult to answer, and called for the utmost diplomacy. For who did not know that Goethe, with utter *naïveté*, considered himself the "last poet"? And none the less was astonished by Hegel's hubris. . . .

The versatility of this mind became even more impressive when Goethe started holding forth himself. His thoughts would range from *La Muette de Portici*—Auber's masterpiece, which later in that year of 1830 was to stir up a revolution in Brussels—to Walter Scott, whom Felix had visited at his home in Scotland; from Scott to the pretty girls in Weimar; from the girls to the students, then to *The Robbers*, and so to Schiller. "And now he gaily talked on for a good hour or more without interruption about Schiller's life, his writings, his position in Weimar; by way of that he came to the late Grand Duke and to the year 1775, which he called Germany's intellectual spring. Nobody would ever be able to describe all that as finely as he himself, he said. He had planned to reserve the second volume of his autobiography for that, but what with the botany and meteorology and all the other stuff that no one would thank him for, he never got round to it. Then he told stories about the time he was directing the theatre in Weimar, and when I tried to thank him for these reminiscences, he said: 'It's just chance, you know; all that comes to mind by the way, summoned up by your dear presence.' Those words sounded wonderfully sweet to me; it was one of those talks you don't forget for the rest of your life. Next day he gave me a sheet of his *Faust* manuscript. He had written below: 'To my dear young friend Felix Mendelssohn-Bartholdy, the strong and gentle ruler of the piano, in friendly recollection of glad May days in 1830. J. W. von Goethe.' "[9]

Certainly those days were not to be forgotten. At their parting on the following morning Goethe once again showed him the painting of a *Praying Peasant Family* by Adriaen van Ostade which had made a great impression on the child Felix nine years before. "So, so, now you are leaving," the old man said very gravely. "We must take care to keep ourselves on our feet till you come again. But we do not wish to part without a bit of piety, and so we must look at the *Prayer* together a few more times." Then he tapped his forefinger tenderly against Felix's cheek, kissed him, and pushed him out. That was the last time Felix saw Goethe,

[8] K. Barth: *Die Protestantische Theologie im 19. Jahrhundert.* Basel, 1947.
[9] F. Mendelssohn-Bartholdy: *Reisebriefe aus den Jahren 1830–1832.* Leipzig, 1861.

the "gracious imperial sun of my life", as he later so handsomely described him to Sir Julius Benedict. Grace is unmerited, and he who is vouchsafed it can only be grateful. Mendelssohn showed his gratitude by setting to music—like so many other composers—a part of the Goethean world. But he did so in a manner quite different from that of all others. After having created a new art form in his *A Midsummer Night's Dream* —it is still erroneously called an overture; we might do better to follow Hans von Bülow's suggestion and call such works symphonic poems— after having thus created a new art form, he shaped Goethe's two poems "A Calm Sea" and "A Prosperous Voyage" into a symphonic poem. It would continue to live, Bülow said, when other symphonic poems had ceased to be played. *That* was said by a son-in-law of Franz Liszt!

A CALM SEA AND A PROSPEROUS VOYAGE

The first mention of it crops up in a letter (18 June 1828) of Fanny Mendelssohn to Klingemann in London: "Felix is writing a big instrumental piece, *A Calm Sea and A Prosperous Voyage*, after Goethe. It will be very much worthy of him. He wished to avoid an *overture* with *introduction* and has kept the whole in two scenes standing side by side." Evidently Fanny perfectly well understood the originality of the conception. However, Schubert had already discovered the musical potentiality of one of the poems: on 21st June 1815 he had made the "Calm Sea" into a song, with broken chords and peculiar symphonic breadth.[1]

Schubert's musical instinct was infallible. Although far less cultivated than Schumann or Mendelssohn, he found what, for his purposes, were the perfect texts. If he did not feel at first glance that something belonged to him, he let it go.[2] In this Goethe poem he succeeded, eighty years before Hugo Wolf, in composing what may be called the earliest impressionistic *lied*. He used effects and allusions that Wolf was later to take over and develop in his setting of Mörike's *Du bist Orplid*.[3] The anxiety of the sailors is expressed in the almost quiescent song line and the modulated arpeggios. Goethe never heard Schubert's composition, but he would have preferred J. F. Reichardt's setting of the poem. It was simple, in

[1] W. Dahms: *Schubert*. Stuttgart, 1918.
[2] H. Frh. v. d. Pfordten: *Schubert und das Lied*. Leipzig, 1916.
[3] A. Einstein: *Schubert*. Zürich, 1952.

slow F major and dynamically expanding C major. Reichardt was a pre-Beethoven master who was faithful to Goethe's main principle: the music must follow undeviatingly the stanzaic structure of the poem.

Beethoven, "with whom it was an artistic principle to be heavier than air",[4] could not pass by the "horrendous plasticity" of those two Goethe poems. Unthanked by the author as always, he had made of them a cantata for chorus and orchestra, *A Calm Sea and A Prosperous Voyage*, (opus 112), "respectfully dedicated to the author of the poems, the immortal Goethe". The work was published in 1824, and led even so devout an admirer of Beethoven as Adolf Bernhard Marx into heresy. Writing in his *Berliner Allgemeine Musikalische Zeitung* he called this a case in which "an immortal has extended his hand to the immortal",[5] but admitted that the handclasp somehow had not been achieved.

> *Tiefe Stille herrscht im Wasser,*
> *Ohne Regung ruht das Meer,*
> *Und bekümmert sieht der Schiffer*
> *Glatte Fläche ringsumher.*
> *Keine Luft von keiner Seite!*
> *Todesstille fürchterlich!*
> *In der ungeheuren Weite*
> *Reget keine Welle sich.*

> (Deepest calm upon the water,
>   Sleek and level lies the sea.
> Anxiously the sailor watches
>   For some stirring to the lee.
> Not a breeze from any quarter!
>   Stillness fearsome as the dead.
> In the vast expanse of water
>   Not a wave lifts up its head.)

Marx found the orchestral complement—strings, flutes, oboes, clarinets, bassoons, four horns, trumpets and kettledrums—overwhelming, and no less overwhelming the full chorus which "paints the sleek, malignant calm. The strings lie motionless, drawn far apart from one another, their high and low voices frightened off to opposite ends where they lie in wait":

---

[4] R. Specht: *Bildnis Beethovens*. Hellerau, 1930.
[5] *Berliner Allgemeine Musikalische Zeitung*. November, 1824.

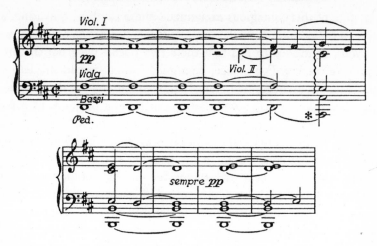

The word *fürchterlich* comes in the dark chord; at *Weite* an alarming fortissimo begins, sending basses and sopranos reaching for the lowest and the highest extremes of their ranges. Then the "Prosperous Journey" begins in a soft, rocking allegro, a six-eight tempo which slowly grows stronger and fuller:

Die Nebel zerreissen,
Der Himmel ist helle,
Und Äolus löset
Das ängstliche Band.
Es säuseln die Winde,
Es rührt sich der Schiffer.
Geschwinde! Geschwinde!
Es teilt sich die Welle,
Es naht sich die Ferne;
Schon seh ich das Land!

(The mists are now sundered,
The sky leaps to brightness,
And Aeolus loosens
    The frightening band.
The winds begin blowing,
The sailor is stirring.
Now rapidly flowing,
The billows are parted.
A shadow draws nearer,
    And now I see land.)

But in spite of this contagious excitement, these rhythms quivering with joy like the Bacchantic final movements of Beethoven's symphonies,[6] A. B. Marx continued to feel that these two poems were not the proper subject for a cantata. For silence, he argued, cannot speak, still less sing. Goethe, Marx contended, had scarcely wished "to use the deathly fear of the forsaken, already half annihilated man for the purposes of a painting." Marx, it will be remembered, was the critic who was always calling for painting in music! Felix Mendelssohn was acquainted with this article of his. It probably contributed to his decision not to set the poems as such, but to consider them as a theme for an epic composition—which indeed turned out to be magnificent. Alongside Mendelssohn's opus Beethoven's seems, as Hans Joachim Moser puts it, "effective but scarcely important".[7]

Music, of course, is movement. But instrumental music can accomplish what vocal music cannot—that is, simulate motionlessness. Long whole notes extending over many measures set up a mood of massive calm. Mendelssohn made use of that strategy. Wagner (who knew his predecessor's concert overtures very well) was to use the same device in *Tristan und Isolde*. On the other hand, the human voice has no way of reproducing "fearsome stillness" except by pauses. But pauses are full of tension, whereas Goethe's picture of the calm at sea was meant to be devoid of tension; it was a *numb* stillness that was being evoked.

Mendelssohn's innate artistry found the right beginning. An Adagio in D, growing out of motionless whole notes:

[6] H. Kretzschmar: *Führer durch den Konzertsaal*, vol. II. Leipzig, 1899.
[7] H. J. Moser: *Goethe und die Musik*. Leipzig, 1949.

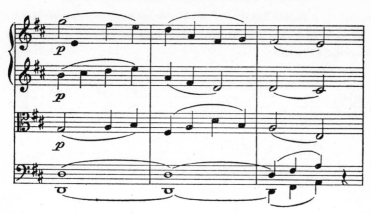

Then that passage in which, as Niels W. Gade has said, "the calm dreams of movement without being able to move." And then the dream loses itself in muteness. Suddenly (scarcely to be believed), the twitter of a flute:

There is a hint of wind in the air. Has it come at last? A long-drawn seventh chord on G sharp and its crescendo affirm that it has. The woodwinds leap up; a *molto allegro vivace* fills the bellying sails; the bass figures begin to roll; rejoicing stirs again and again, with mounting intensity, but not yet forte—on the contrary, piano; the woodwind theme has come in.[8]

Four measures beginning with high F sharp. Soon the theme comes in fortissimo. Then another theme sails to meet it (we are at sea and everything sails. Later, in the "Hebrides" Overture, there would again be this sailing up of themes). It is repeated twice in the course of four measures

[8] W. Dahms: *Mendelssohn*. Berlin, no date.

beginning with high C sharp.[9] For thirty-seven measures now the 'cello's voice speaks. The new theme was to become a code of greeting among Mendelssohn's friends:

Only themes with strong profiles can become such codes. Siegfried's "horn signal" has become a favourite one. But in the days before the revolution of 1848 people preferred more subdued themes, in order not to startle. Otherwise Mendelssohn's friends could have picked the concluding Allegro Maestoso—the trumpet signals of arrival at port. The chords thud and the anchor is dropped with a rattling of chains in triplets. Drums roll a salute. And in the midst of this triumphant Finale we suddenly realize with amazement that for some time a Beethoven theme has been dominating the scene. It is the march from *Fidelio*:

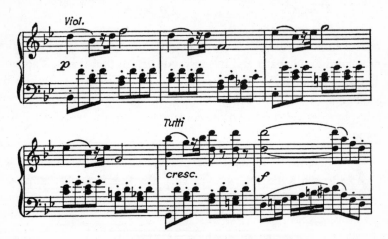

How does one master come to quote another? And what is quoting and what is plagiarism? The composer Wilhelm Kienzl has had some sharp and pointed things to say about hunters of "reminiscences". But there is no help for it: in music we constantly encounter a phenomenon that looks frightfully like outright borrowing. The well-known theory of wandering melodies which Wilhelm Tappert propounded in 1868 only partly explains

[9] B. Bartels: *Mendelssohn-Bartholdy, Mensch und Werk*. Bremen, 1947.

the phenomenon. Tappert suggested that Darwin's principle that "all animal and plant forms are descended from a few organisms which have evolved in the course of time by natural processes" might also be applied to music. In the realm of music, he argued, there are so many plagiarisms which are not plagiarisms at all, but rather "transmutations in the evolutionary sense".[10] According to Tappert, every "melody, no matter how developed and elaborated, has a simple foundation". It is this basis that speaks to the hearts of the people, that passes from the concert hall into the factories and out to the highways, making mock of political and geographical boundaries. The artist's ear hears the stray melody, takes it in and changes it. Or rather, it changes itself, although its bone-structure does not undergo change.[11]

No doubt that is frequently so. But the case of the final theme of *A Calm Sea and A Prosperous Voyage* was different. This was a deliberate quotation, like the quotation from Weber at the end of the overture to *A Midsummer Night's Dream*. In both places the quotation was legitimate. A legitimate quotation of one master by another must simultaneously be a variation of one's own idea. Mendelssohn would have hit upon the theme even without Beethoven because it developed from an idea of his own. If the jubilant Finale nevertheless sounded so much like Beethoven, it was because Mendelssohn was treating the same psychological situation. The theme is liberation: Pizarro's prisoners were liberated, and the rising wind at sea had liberated the becalmed ship. In both Finales, the *angina pectoris*, constriction of the heart, was shattered. That accounts for the powerful pulsation of those measures.

Such, probably, is the genesis of the final quotation from Beethoven in Mendelssohn's symphonic poem. For the rest, there were of course elements of programme music in the work—although Mendelssohn would scarcely have admitted it. Setting a programme to music, distracting the listener from the music by extra-musical ideas, was to his mind a barbarous practice. Not on grounds of excessive naturalism, but for entirely different reasons which Wagner later deals with in his important essay, *On the Overture*.[12] The working-out of themes, Wagner wrote, should always correspond solely to their purely musical qualities. A working-out must never lose itself in details, never tie itself to the course of events, "because any such procedure ... would promptly abolish the uniquely effective character of a musical work." Music should be addressed to

[10] W. Tappert: *Wandernde Melodien*. Berlin, 1868.
[11] H. E. Jacob: *Joseph Haydn: His Art, Times and Glory*. New York, 1950.
[12] G. Ernest: *Richard Wagner, sein Leben und Schaffen*. Berlin, 1915.

musical persons alone, and not to those who are merely curious, who afterwards want to know what the composer thought about when he wrote this or that phrase. So Wagner argued, and Mendelssohn would have agreed whole-heartedly with him.

In his *A Calm Sea*, Mendelssohn had succeeded to a remarkable degree in creating music not out of the detailed events, but out of the whole psychological situation. Begun in the summer of 1828, the relatively short work was many a month in the writing. Mendelssohn seems to have considered it unfinished for a number of years. It was not publicly performed until 1832, "after it had received those innumerable corrections and alterations and afterthoughts which Mendelssohn always gave his works," as Sir George Grove admiringly comments.[13] For Mendelssohn was no Mozart; his airy attitude toward his work was only seeming. He brooded long over his compositions and was eternally dissatisfied with what he had done.

WALPURGIS NIGHT

"This is Italy!" Felix wrote rapturously on 10th October 1830 when he first set foot on the soil of that southern land. "And now there has begun what I have always thought, ever since I could think, to be the supreme joy in life. And I am loving it. Today was so rich that now, in the evening, I must collect myself a little, and so I am writing to you to thank you, dear parents, for having given me all this happiness, and I want to think intensely of you, dear sisters, and to wish you here with me, Paul, so that I can rejoice again in your rejoicing...."[1] The young man of twenty-one was in Venice. A flood of impressions almost swept him off his feet: the Piazza San Marco, Titian's *Peter*, the *Assunta*, paintings, churches, the crowds.... Had Goethe not prophesied this when, during Felix's stay in Weimar, they had discussed the Italian journey?

Goethe had predicted a good many things to him, but not the most remarkable feature of this journey. For it was not the "Italianate" Goethe who loomed large in Felix's thoughts: not the Goethe of the *Roman Elegies*, the *Venetian Epigrams*, the Goethe who had grown ecstatic over Florence, nor the Goethe of Mignon's songs. That delicate chemical

---

[13] Sir George Grove: *Dictionary of Music and Musicians*. London, no date.

[1] F. Mendelssohn-Bartholdy: *Reisebriefe*. Leipzig, 1861.

balance in Felix's mind, which so often governed his creative life, prompted him to think of a wholly nordic Goethe while he stayed in Italy, a Goethe of the misty Harz mountains, wrapped in a flowing pagan cloak. Felix set to work composing his *Walpurgis Night*.

This strange poem is called the *First Walpurgis Night*—to distinguish it from the two other *Walpurgis Nights*, the ones in *Faust*. Goethe counted it among his ballads, though strictly speaking it is not one. Written probably on 30th July 1799, it was very close in time to the far more famous *Bride of Corinth* which closed with the verses:

> When the sparks go flying
> And the embers are dying
> We hurry toward the old, the ancient gods.

Toward *the ancient gods*. Both poems, then, as the Goethe scholar Erich Trunz remarks,[2] were written at the time of Goethe's most forthright rejection of Christianity. For the Christian priests in the *First Walpurgis Night* cut a very poor figure indeed. Their behaviour is so weird and eccentric that it becomes comical. Goethe alternately loved and hated such folklore pieces, and so his attitude toward his own poem changed with the passing decades. He sent the poem to Zelter on 26th August 1799, with the comment: "I am enclosing a production which may seem rather odd. It arose out of the idea: would it not be possible to write dramatic ballads in such a way as to provide a composer with material for a longish vocal piece? Unfortunately the present example does not have enough dignity to justify so much effort." Not enough dignity? Zelter's reply was written four weeks later: "The verses are musical and singable. But I *cannot find the atmosphere* in which the whole is enveloped, and it will be best if I let it lie for the present." An honest man's answer. For that atmosphere was ironic—and how would a simple soul like Zelter compose anything ironical?

The text was set aside for thirteen years. On 21st November 1812 Zelter reported that he was at last beginning to set the poem to music but was unclear about its meaning, and would like to know which particular historical event had been the nucleus of the poem! Historical event? Goethe began to smile. Must all fables contain "a kernel of fact"? Oh well, he conceded (for this was 1812, and the new science inaugurated by the Grimm Brothers was flourishing), perhaps there really was an element of reality underlying his poem. "One student of the German past has posited a historical basis for the legend of the gatherings of witches and

[2] E. Trunz in a letter to H. E. Jacob dated 29th March 1958.

devils on the Brocken, a legend which has been current in Germany from time immemorial." According to this theory, Goethe went on to say, the German heathen priests retreated to this mountain with their followers when Christianity was being imposed by force upon their people. There on the Brocken, every spring, they had worshipped their formless god with prayers and flames. "In order to be safe from the armed missionaries who were tracking them down, they had found it advisable to disguise some of their number, thus frightening off their superstitious enemies. Protected by diabolic masks, they carried out their wholly pure services to their god. . . ."[3]

When Zelter read this and realized that the poem dealt with "mockery against mockery", he again felt the musical ground slipping away from under his feet: this time for ever. No more was heard of the *First Walpurgis Night* until 5th March 1831, when Felix Mendelssohn reported that he had begun setting it to music. On 28th August he wrote to Goethe that the work was finished and that he hoped to have it performed soon.

He, at any rate, had not been frightened off by the strange will-o-the-wispishness and the wild humour of the story. More decisively than even Goethe had (at least, so the music reveals), he regarded the poem as a candid profession of Germanic paganism.

What is the story of Goethe's "ballad"? Druids are celebrating the first of May by igniting a bonfire on a high mountain peak. But the fire is forbidden under penalty of death. The Druids remind one another of the laws set by their harsh conquerors, of the traps waiting everywhere for pagans and for sinners, of their wives and children slaughtered on the palisades and the certain fate awaiting all of them:

> *Kennet Ihr nicht die Gesetze*
> *unsrer harten Überwinder?*
> *Rings gestellt sind ihre Netze*
> *auf die Heiden, auf die Sünder.*
> *Ach, sie schlachten auf dem Walle*
> *unsre Weiber, unsre Kinder.*
> *Und wir alle*
> *nahen uns gewissem Falle.*

The poem deals with the manner in which the people overcome their fear and once again "serve the old gods"—and in doing so find a way to terrify the Christian guards, so that they run away.

It is grotesque that this particular tribute to Germanic paganism should

---

[3] L. Geiger: *Briefwechsel zwischen Goethe und Zelter.* Leipzig, 1902.

have been composed in Italy. In the same way Richard Wagner began
writing his "dearest dream of Germany", his *Meistersinger*, in Paris—
perhaps the reality of Nuremberg, the petty-bourgeois German atmosphere, would have been only too disillusioning from closer up. The
Walpurgis Night cantata certainly did not play the same part in Mendelssohn's life as the *Meistersinger* in Wagner's—but the phenomenon is a
similar one. Under the bright blue sky of the south, the unchanging blue
sky, Felix began a symphonic poem with "description of bad weather",
followed by "transition to spring". He could not have put it more
modestly. In reality this overture contains music every bit as vivid as
Wagner's spring storms in *Die Walküre* were to be. It was a very early
"breakthrough into the elemental". For the first time Mendelssohn
revealed himself as "Richard Wagner's elder brother".[4]

The best analysis of the work is still that written by Ernst Wolff in
1909, on the occasion of Mendelssohn's hundredth anniversary. The first
Allegro begins *con fuoco* with three incisive chords in the winds. Immediately thereafter comes an inrush of strings in rushing semiquaver
figures in A minor that paint the howls of the storm wind. Then violins
and horns separate out of the tonal mass with the characteristic principal
theme.

Motif development in E minor; second principal idea of the Allegro in
oboes and bassoons:

Very remote keys are touched. A lightning-flash of a figure in F sharp
major unleashes wild, elemental thunder which mounts to a *fortissimo
assai*, something seldom found in Mendelssohn. A mighty F major chord
tutti apparently concludes this passage of thunder, and harbingers of
spring can be heard in the horns and bassoons: the May motif of the first
chorus.[5] But the storm has not yet subsided; it raises its hoary head
once more. Only then can an A major passage, both sweet and majestic,

[4] H. S. Oakeley: *Reminiscences*. London, no date.
[5] E. Wolff: *Felix Mendelssohn-Bartholdy*. Berlin, 1909.

describe in intricate quaver figures the sudden warming of the world under the spring sun. And now the voices can begin:

This overture, incidentally, was the part Felix wrote last, after the body of the work was already complete. He had a great deal of trouble with its form—although he had made up his mind about the character of the piece from the very beginning. Should this overture be a grand symphony or only a short introduction?[6] He decided upon a middle course, after having explained the plan to Goethe himself:

> What has been occupying me almost exclusively for several weeks has been the music to your Excellency's poem "First Walpurgis Night". I want to compose it with orchestral accompaniment as a kind of grand cantata, and the serene springlike opening, then the witchcraft and diabolism and the solemn ritual choruses in between could provide opportunities for the most beautiful music. I don't know whether I shall succeed, but I feel how big the task is and with what collectedness and reverence I must attack it. . . .

Goethe's response from Weimar on 9th September 1831 was surely one of the most curious messages Felix ever received from him. It was moreover a document that showed to what extent Goethe was involved in his geological studies. These were the years in which his interest in natural science, in neptunism and vulcanism, overflowed even into *Faust*. In 1830, in a tremendously excited session of the Paris Academy, two great scientists, Cuvier and Saint-Hilaire, had clashed on the question of whether the world must be explained as an accumulation of isolated mechanistic phenomena, or whether it had been built up on a unified plan of organization.[7] (Goethe took the latter view.) Consequently, his letter to Felix was strangely couched in the terminology of natural science. He

[6] F. Mendelssohn-Bartholdy: *Briefe aus den Jahren 1830–47.* Leipzig, 1861.

[7] H. Loiseau: *Goethe et la France.* Paris, 1930.

talks of "old, well-founded, tested" elements, of "upthrusting innovations" which "press, shift, displace"—as though he were dealing with an earthquake. And yet the poem itself dealt with human, not geological matters, with political and historical phenomena which not everyone could understand. Zelter certainly did not. The language and the imagery struck him as too bizarre. But Mendelssohn truly understood the poem, realized that it dealt not with a private fantasy, but with a universal theme which had more than once emerged in the course of history.

Goethe's letter read: "In its real meaning this poem is intended to be highly symbolic. For in the history of this world it has necessarily happened repeatedly that the old, well-founded, tested, settled elements are pressed, shifted, displaced and, if not annihilated, then driven into the narrowest space by upthrusting innovations. The medial period, in which hatred can and may still produce its counter forces, is depicted in the poem with sufficient pregnancy, and a joyful, indestructible *enthusiasme* once more blazes up in radiance and clarity."

Radiance and clarity were in the music, too, and indestructible enthusiasm. Not that the letter influenced the music, for it arrived too late; the composition was already finished, except for the overture which Felix composed in Paris in 1832. We can only wonder whether Goethe would have been satisfied if he had heard the whole. He was no friend of modern music and probably would scarcely have understood how well his highly symbolic intentions had been realized. Ten years after Goethe's death in 1843, Felix revised the score and published it as opus 60, using the provocative words of Goethe's letter for a motto.

It was extraordinary music, and shows a different Mendelssohn from the romantic creator of the *Octet*, *A Midsummer Night's Dream*, *A Calm Sea*, *Fingal's Cave*, and the A minor "Scottish" Symphony—although these last were already "expression music". And certainly it was a different Mendelssohn from the historically-minded Protestant and reviver of Bach. This third Mendelssohn was indeed Richard Wagner's elder brother. If the name were erased from the title pages, it would be hard to guess that *Walpurgis Night* was by Mendelssohn. "Goethe", Hermann Kretzschmar wrote,[8] "compressed the description of a whole long epoch into a single event... and in so doing made himself the advocate of a doomed world. All the light in the poem falls upon the Druids and the pagan people, upon their fresh, elemental religion of nature, upon their inspiration, their cunning, their courage and their suffering. They

[8] H. Kretzschmar: *Führer durch den Konzertsaal*, vol. II. Leipzig, 1899.

celebrate a triumph over the Christians that mingles grandeur and humour. The Christians themselves appear only in the distance, cruel and cowardly."

But Mendelssohn introduced even stronger accents. The one thing that checked and subdued his emphases was his wisely apportioned humour. For he was as good a humorist as Wagner—though a more subtle one. Led spiritedly by the tenor soloist, the flock of pagan women welcomes the new spring "in one of the most glorious spring songs we possess."[9] Formally speaking, the passage is a model of the division of labour between human and instrumental voices. The second and longer part of the movement takes up the religious element. The soloist calls on the people to climb to the peak of the mountain and there kindle the sacrificial flames in gratitude to All-Father. For it is Odin (unnamed) who has after all given his faithful people the spring:

This is set in a chivalric A major, key of victory and courage. The accents are brief and concentrated. The womenfolk fear the Christian God. An old woman tremulously warns them:

> Dare we risk it? We are weak.
> Is it death you boldly seek?

A chorus of women takes up the warning: D minor in three-four time; strings and oboes in strangely rocking chromatics convey the people's fear of the conquerors. But the Druid priest—Mendelssohn had, as he wrote, composed this part "right for the larynx" of his singer friend, Eduard Devrient—reproves the women for their timidity, and bids them not to hold the men back. For the moment it seems as if we are in the midst of a secular oratorio, an art form that had disappeared since Haydn's *The Seasons*. But we are able to think of Haydn only very

[9] Ibid.

briefly. For what follows goes far beyond the eighteenth century. Trombones urge the laggards on. The command in recitative, "Go to your posts, stout-hearted men!" is answered by the Druid guards in a four-voiced mixed chorus whose rich palette of orchestral colours—with pungent staccato of the violins, signal motifs in the horns, and swift-moving parlando song—evokes the scurrying figures in the twilight of the woods. After the song has slowly ebbed away, a guard calls out to the people in a brief recitative (which the Metternich censorship in Vienna wanted to have changed!):

> Let the Christian fools come near us!
> We will teach the dogs to fear us,
>> Make them see the very devils
>> They've invented in their fables.

In response there blasts forth that infernal din which Felix had already envisioned in Naples when he wrote home about his possible instrumentation. The *gran cassa*, the bass drum, piccolos, cymbals and kettledrums thunder the grotesque noise to the words of a male chorus in G minor:

> Come with forks and come with prongs,
> Come with torches and with gongs!
>> Like a thousand roaring forges
>> Clamour in the rocky gorges.

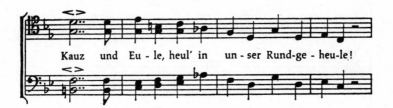

Goethe had the Witch's Kitchen from the first part of *Faust* boil and bubble over once again in these passages. And Mendelssohn followed his lead. What chromatic runs as the Christians turn tail and flee from the diabolic spectacle (see following page).

Neither Wagner, Berlioz, nor Liszt could have written any more grotesque triplets of rage and terror. And then the witches' sabbath is over. The music lifts us out of the sinister mists into the light-filled atmosphere of worship and transfiguration. The worship is pagan. The Druid has just finished lamenting the lot of his people in A minor; Christianity has driven them so far that they are compelled to sing their

hymns to All-Father secretly, at night. But then the A minor changes to
a C major hymn:

> But day has dawned when we may bring
> A pure heart unto Thee.

And in a glorious eight-voiced chorus, the hymn concludes:

> As the flame its smoke dispels,
> So may our faith be purified.
> The foe our ancient custom quells,
> But ever shall Thy light abide.

"It is tragic", Hans Joachim Moser wrote,[10] "that Goethe himself did
not live to enjoy this magnificent fulfilment of his poem in music. It is a
choral structure such as Germans today might use to great effect at
Goethe festivals—a tonal work of art in which romantic colour and
classical control of form merge in the happiest possible manner."

Well, why not perform it at festivals? Take this national work out of
the concert halls where it leads a miserable sham existence, if it is not
entirely forgotten. Stage it, put these Druid singers in pagan, Wagnerian
costumes. . . . It would not do? Does it seem embarrassing that Mendelssohn should have so well expressed the ancient Germanic attitudes for,
after all, his forefathers were not born and buried in the Teutoburg
Forest? But descent in the flesh is not so simple a matter, or has not been
since the Gospel of St. John: "That which is born of the flesh is flesh,
and that which is born of the Spirit is spirit. . . . The wind blows where
it wills, and you hear the sound of it, but you do not know whence it
comes or whither it goes; so it is with every one who is born of the
Spirit." The spirit blows where it wills; it is not bound to flesh and bone.
It makes its free choices out of love. Beethoven and Wagner were not
great German artists because their ancestors came into the world among
Flemings or Saxons. They might have freely chosen another people for
themselves. Mendelssohn chose Germany for his homeland. After he had
travelled through the countries of Europe for several years, he reported to
his father: "Thinking of what you proposed to me before my departure,
and commanded me to keep in mind—that I ought to look carefully at
different countries *in order to choose the one in which I would like to
live and work* . . . it gives me a joyful feeling to be able to say to you now
that I have done so. *The country is Germany*; I am quite sure about that

[10] H. J. Moser: *Goethe und die Musik*. Leipzig, 1949.

now within myself. . . . "[11] This was a free choice, made out of love. And the spirit which "bloweth where it lists" inspired him to present the German people with a May Day cantata such as it had never possessed.

[11] F. Mendelssohn-Bartholdy: *Briefe aus den Jahren 1830–47*. Leipzig, 1861.

BOOK THREE

THE LIMITS AND THE HEART OF AN AGE

How hard it is for us to rise above
our times, our families, our own
selves.

—FANNY MENDELSSOHN-HENSEL

BIEDERMEIER: MAN AND WOMAN

We must ask ourselves whether Mendelssohn's contemporaries wanted this kind of "expression music", these *avant-garde* compositions? The answer is certainly no—for the age was one that wanted no kind of advances at all. The age was quite content with itself, and wanted no revolutions, not in politics and certainly not in art.

The Biedermeier era has been called the Second Rococo Age. The parallel is apt. First of all, both ages had the same desire for rest. In both cases the society and its culture needed to recover from a fearful blood-letting. The age of the religious wars and the wars of conquest were finally wiped from memory by the rococo. And in similar fashion the Biedermeier era drew a veil over the grim Napoleonic Wars. People did not paint, sing or talk loudly in the rococo age, between approximately 1720 and 1789; a similar tempering of emotions and behaviour marked the span between 1815 and 1848, or what is generally termed the age of Biedermeier. Intimacy was its characteristic note.[1]

Life and art both sought quiet accents. The roar of cannon, the thunder of battle, were no longer desired. Only Beethoven presumed to charge the salons in a Napoleonic manner. On that score alone he was a genius too big for his times. Goethe's naïve fear of him was shared by contemporaries. Instead the Biedermeier era chose Mozart for its darling, the good bourgeoisie having first taken all the sting out of him. In fact they made themselves a counterfeit Mozart, all charm and grace.[2] They did not want the real Mozart of *Don Giovanni*, with his demonic insight into the strains between man and woman. In the Biedermeier age no one was permitted to speak of the "volcano of sexual love".

In this matter the age was far removed from the rococo.[3] Under Louis XV the French spirit recovered from the strains of war by strenuous attendance in the boudoir. The weapons of womankind reached their highest development: rouge, powder, hoop skirt, tournure and low-cut bodices. These bits of costumery are evoked again and again in poems and even more in suggestive chansons. The nudes of Boucher[4] and his

[1] G. Hermann: *Das Biedermeier im Spiegel seiner Zeit*. Berlin, 1913.
[2] O. Jahn: *Mozart*. Leipzig, 1856–60.
[3] M. Osborn: *Die Kunst des Rokoko*. Berlin, 1929.
[4] E. Michel: *François Boucher*. Paris, 1886.

pupil Fragonard looked down from the walls and were multiplied in mirrors: the misdemeanours of Diana, Aurora, Thetis; pink and white nakedness; *The Stolen Shift, The Birth of Venus, Bathing Women, The Eavesdropper*, an aroma of youthful but practised women's bodies. If you looked at them more closely, you recognized an actress you had often seen on the stage, or the king's mistress.[5]

The mores of the Biedermeier era could not be in greater contrast. First of all, the cultural climate was pervaded by the old German sanctification of woman. Month after month more treasures of the Middle Ages were brought to light. Minnesang and chivalry were enjoying a tremendous vogue: The historians, of course, had their own bias, and were quite upset when their excavations into the past brought up some story which had un-Christian or possibly obscene overtones. It is interesting to read what was thought of the story of *Tristan und Isolde*:

> The content of the poem is completely coarse: the story of the seduction of a married woman who sacrifices her honour and her soul to adulterous pleasure. A polite dandy who curries favour with ladies, such as we might no doubt find at any time among idlers of Paris, is the hero. Finally there is a weak husband who is not merely hoodwinked but disgracefully deceived and who in the end is supposed to bear all the blame because he had the impertinence to try to guard his loose wife. . . . Treacherous cunning is praised as a cardinal virtue, persistence in sin as faithfulness, and the conduct of courtiers who mean well and wish to help the deceived husband is branded as disloyalty. . . .

And what about the love-potion which makes the protagonists innocently guilty or guiltily innocent? Its significance is utterly lost upon this critic of *Tristan und Isolde*:

> A glistening chain of abominations. . . . A creed of absolutistic sexual love, to which all else must yield. . . . Stupefying fragrance of poisonous flowers. . . . It makes mock of the sanctity of the oath, of prayer, of the ordeal. . . .

In short, *Tristan und Isolde* is a piece of pornography! And the author of these words was none other than the poet Eichendorff.[6] He was condemning not Wagner's *Tristan*, which had not yet been written, but the

---

[5] Josz: *J. A. Fragonard, Moeurs de XVIIIᵐᵉ Siècle*. Paris, 1866.
[6] J. Frh. v. Eichendorff: *Geschichte der Poetischen Literatur Deutschlands*. Paderborn, 1857.

"shameless" work written by the great medieval German poet, Gottfried von Strassburg. The rigid idea of propriety that dominated the decades after Waterloo, the ideal of the Christian household, was a force to which art had to bow. Painting submitted readily—the paintings of the late Nazarenes, among whom was Felix Mendelssohn's cousin Philipp Veit, were studiously pure and edifying.[7]

In his excellent book on the period, Ernst Heilborn has some interesting things to say about the era's concept of the perfect woman.[8] The ideal was based on the character of Queen Louise of Prussia, only recently dead. Here was a heroine entirely without traits of intellectualism or eroticism. Endowed with extraordinary, even saintly beauty, Louise thought of herself first and foremost as a *Hausfrau* and mother of a family. But those were difficult times, with Napoleon threatening the kingdom, and the royal family often forced to take flight from the French armies. The Queen remained beside her husband even on the field of war. Once, after the battle of Jena, when the fortunes of Prussia were at their lowest ebb, Queen Louise herself paid a secret visit to the French headquarters to make a personal petition to Napoleon. If he would only be so kind as to return Magdeburg, she implored. Napoleon was gallant but unmoved. One did not discuss fortresses with gracious ladies, he answered. "Then she fell silent, but turned her eyes heavenward," Rückert wrote, in his poetic reconstruction of the scene.

It was during these dark days that the Queen, quartered in a Tilsit inn, used her diamond ring to engrave the famous Goethe quatrain on one of the window panes:

> Whose tears have never mingled with his bread,
> And who has never sat through grievous hours
> Of night, weeping upon his bed,
> Knows naught of you, ye heavenly powers.

Yet the young Queen's staunchness was an inspiration to her whole people. When she died in 1810, she was mourned throughout the land. The country had not yet been liberated, and her death was felt to be in some way a sacrifice to that end. The army of volunteers which marched off in 1813 to meet and vanquish the forces of Napoleon murmured her name as though invoking a patron saint.

She was entombed in the castle garden of Charlottenburg. Christian

[7] M. Spahn: *Philipp Veit*. Bielefeld, 1901.
[8] E. Heilborn: *Zwischen zwei Revolutionen. Der Geist der Schinkelzeit 1789–1848*. Berlin, 1927.

Daniel Rauch was commissioned to design her monument, and he rendered the Queen so beautifully in marble that people fell in love all over again with the limpid beauty of that effigy.

> You sleep so still, your gentle features brushed
> By only the sweeter dreams you had in life.[9]

But as early as 1789, Novalis had called for some kind of canonization for this woman whose life struck him as so inspiring. He felt that the picture of the Queen belonged in every home—every careful mother should try to raise her daughter in consonance with the Queen's example. For the state was only a larger household, in which the Queen occupied the place of housewife. Therefore her virtues might be emulated by every private citizen. Novalis also recommended that young women serve several years of apprenticeship, after the manner of Natalia's apprenticeship in *Wilhelm Meister*. In fact he decided that the character of Natalia in *Wilhelm Meister* was "the chance portrait" of Queen Louise.[10] And more than fifty years later Liszt, though south-east German and Hungarian, nevertheless modelled his "Legend of Saint Elizabeth" along the lines of the Prussian queen. The spirit of Queen Louise reigns over the Andante theme at the beginning:

dolcissimo

Around the year 1800 a woman like Karoline Schlegel had still been the idol of Early Romanticism. She, née Michaelis, widow of Boehme, and unmarried Forster, had divorced August Wilhelm Schlegel. When at the age of thirty she took her fourth husband, the philosopher Schelling, she wrote, sighing, to a woman friend: "Alas, I was born for fidelity."[11] But not too long afterwards all that had changed. In the Biedermeier era, divorce became improper and shame attached even to an unhappy family life. As for public display of free love, that became utterly unthinkable. Passion was equated with looseness.

It was an age of profound respectability. King Frederick William III, widowed and lonely, adored the opera. He raved about Henriette Sontag, the greatly gifted singer, and commanded that she be paid an enormous

---

[9] E. Belling: *Die Königin Luise in der Dichtung*. Berlin, 1890.
[10] Novalis: *Gesammelte Werke*, ed. by Carl Zeelig. Zürich, 1945–46.
[11] M. v. Boehn: *Die Mode, Menschen und Mode im 19. Jahrhundert*. Munich, 1908.

salary, to the astonishment of Director Count Brühl. But there is no record that the King ever exchanged a word alone with Henriette Sontag. The bright light of graciousness that, as Börne expressed it, the King "shed upon the seventh day of the week" (*Sonntag* = Sunday), turned the Berliners for the first time into opera fans, and attendance at the opera became as important as it had been in Vienna and Naples.[12] But the private lives of their favourites had to be pure. Scandalous love affairs among singers and actresses were frowned upon. An actress named Clara Stich was boycotted because her lover had killed her husband in a duel.[13]

The King also loved ballet. He made his dancers princely gifts of precious shawls and inlaid combs; but again there were never any whispers that he had spent an evening alone with a dancer. Sitting paternally in the prompter's box with General von Witzleben, he discussed the personal problems of the ballerinas and asked after the health of their parents. His Chamberlain Timm would give small intimate suppers, with delicacies and good wines; Frederick William would casually drop in and joke with the girls—but at midnight he would leave. After all, he was a family man, even though his "dearest Louise" had left him a widower. No gossip must touch him.

And then came the day on which his family—grown sons of thirty and daughters not much younger—burst into tears of incomprehension. Their father had demeaned himself, had become "an ordinary man", for he informed them that if they had no objection he, an old man now, would take Fräulein So-and-so for his morganatic wife and confer upon her the title of Duchess of Liegnitz. The lady was waiting in the adjoining room, he said, and he would be obliged if they would give her a friendly reception.

The future Emperor William I later told this story, describing how the children were so shocked at the news. That same day they went out to their mother's grave and knelt by Rauch's Sleeping Louise, to consult the spirit of that saintly spouse who had been dead for fourteen years.[14] They returned from that expedition no more reconciled to the new marriage than before. The Prussian people, and in fact all of Germany, simply ignored the Duchess of Liegnitz, so monogamous was the age.

Once again we can only be amazed at the disparities between the

[12] F. Tietze: *Bunte Erinnerungen aus Berlins Theaterleben*. Berlin, 1859.

[13] E. Dronke: *Berlin*. Frankfurt am Main, 1846.

[14] *Jugendbekenntnisse des Alten Kaisers*, ed. by K. v. Jagow. Leipzig, 1939.

Germans and the French. For in France at that very same time the tone was being set by George Sand, the lover of Chopin and Alfred de Musset, awakener of great passions and frenzied despairs. "How distasteful this George Sand is!" Chopin had said when he first met the celebrated lady. "Is she really a woman? I am inclined to doubt it." But then she took him by storm,[15] shook him with her intensity and threw his spiritual and physical life into total disorder for eight years.[16] Her effect upon Musset was equally drastic. She lured him away to Venice and there, while he lay sick, deceived him with his doctor. In his *Confession d'un enfant du siècle* (1836) Musset fashioned a monument to that period of turbulent emotions.

At the same time this nymphomaniac, this cigar-smoking woman who swept through Europe in masculine clothes, was Europe's first suffragette.[17] But in Germany the outlook for female emancipation was scarcely bright, as is evident from Karl Gutzkow's dreary novel of 1835, *Wally, die Zweiflerin*, in which a lady strips to the skin in order to show a man she is basically free of prejudice.[18] True, the topical novels of Countess Hahn-Hahn are somewhat more advanced. But the author became a Catholic convert in 1850, and renounced her sinful notions. Instead she preached the beauty of a life devoted to domestic service and a nunlike waiting for death and the hereafter.[19] There remained only Fanny Lewald-Stahr, the first German suffragette worthy of the name, who towered head and shoulders above her Biedermeier contemporaries.[20]

Women's rights were a matter for the future. The greatest fulfilment a woman could have was to be adored by men as their queen and idol. If a woman were not a queen, these "chivalrous" men with their nostalgia for the Middle Ages, saw her only as a servant in the household. For alongside the Biedermeier ideal of Louise there stood the image of the "Katie"—taken from Heinrich von Kleist's drama, *Käthchen von Heilbronn*. Kleist's reasons for having the Emperor's daughter serve Count Strahl as a maid might be mysterious and ambivalent—for Kleist's mind operated by a strange dialectic. The implications are made more subtle by the author's couching the whole play in dreamlike terms.[21] At the end

---

[15] A. Cortot: *Chopin, Wesen und Gestalt*. Zürich, 1954.
[16] W. and P. Rehberg: *Chopin*. Zürich, 1949.
[17] A. Maurois: *La Vie de George Sand*. Paris, 1952.
[18] H. H. Houben: *Gutzkow-Funde*. Berlin, 1901.
[19] P. Haffner: *Gräfin Ida Hahn-Hahn*. Frankfurt am Main, 1880.
[20] K. Frenzel: *Erinnerungen und Strömungen*. Leipzig, 1890.
[21] B. v. Wiese: *Die Deutsche Tragödie von Lessing bis Hebbel*. Hamburg, 1948.

Katie of Heilbronn abandons her humble role, and rises triumphant like a
Cinderella from the ashes. But in general the men of the time were quite
in favour of the subservience of women. Wilhelm von Humboldt was an
exception; he sometimes remarked on how ridiculous it was that a woman
should be made a glorified sort of serving-maid and always considered
subsidiary to man.[22]

When women themselves rose up in their own defence, they were apt
to choose the wrong occasion. Thus, when Wagner's *Lohengrin* appeared,
they protested that the hero had acted abominably toward poor Elsa. To
desert a woman because she asked him about his origins and family on
the wedding night! As his wife, did she not have a right to know, and
was it gentlemanly not to answer? Wagner, of course, was not in the least
put out. Lohengrin, he wrote,[23] was not a man, but a classical demigod
who had condescended to have commerce with a mortal woman, like
Zeus with Semele. And Wagner was right: his Christianized hero (taken
from the medieval poem *Loherangarein*[24]) was essentially a mythic character. Like all knights of the Grail he obeyed a different set of laws from
ordinary mortals.

But the pre-1848 poets accepted the assumption of the man's innate
superiority; to them, it was a fact of nature. Adalbert von Chamisso
travelled over half the globe, knew many countries, seas and kinds of
people.[25] But as a poet—and doubly a German poet because he had immi-
grated from France—he knew so little about women (or did he know
them so well?) that he wrote poetic cycles like *Women's Life and Love*,
in which "He, the lordliest of all" men is thus addressed by his wife:

> As against the firmament
>   Glows that bright and splendid star,
> So he shines in my own heaven
>   Bright and splendid, high and far.
>
> Sweep along thy destined orbit;
>   Let me only watch thee shine,
> Watching in humility,
>   Bliss and sorrow shall be mine!

[22] W. and K. v. Humboldt: *Briefwechsel*. Leipzig, 1906–13.
[23] R. Wagner: *Gesammelte Schriften und Dichtungen*. Leipzig, 1907.
[24] F. Panzer: *Lohengrin-Studien*. Halle, 1894.
[25] K. Fulda: *Chamisso und seine Zeit*. Leipzig, 1881.

Do not hear my silent prayer:
That all may be well with thee.
Star above, in thy high splendour,
Mayst not stoop to maid like me.

She alone is worthy of thee
Who is worthiest of all;
Blessings on her I will shower,
Her on whom thy choice may fall.

Then I shall rejoice, and weeping,
Of her bliss I shall partake.
And if my heart should be breaking,
It is nothing—let it break.

To us in the twentieth century, such sentiments are incomprehensible. But Robert Schumann set the verses to music,[26] and did it beautifully, expending all his gifts of melody on the song. A prisoner of the attitudes of his time, he saw nothing false in the text. Yet we might imagine that he of all people would have objected, for his wife was an emancipated woman. He had married Clara Wieck, the most celebrated woman pianist of Europe. She might not have been that at the time of their marriage, but she was soon to become it. At one of her concerts in Vienna a gentleman innocently asked Herr Schumann: "Are you musical *too?*" It was Clara's superb performances of her husband's works which made Schumann famous as a composer for the piano. She was the breadwinner in the household. Here was a marriage in which the wife could scarcely echo the words of Chamisso's maiden. Or could she? In our times it is arresting to hear the voice of a happy wife, herself a great artist, who nevertheless subordinated herself to her husband: "Often I am overcome by a feverish anxiety when I think that I am a woman happier than millions of others, and then I often ask Heaven whether I may not have been given too much happiness. What are all the cares of livelihood compared to the joys and the hours of bliss that I am vouchsafed by the love and the works of my Robert. . . ." And she had a full share in those works.

Robert Schumann was a genius. Perhaps it is a rare kind of experience to serve a genius. There was a contemporary poet named Heinrich Stieglitz who was nothing of the sort. Whatever he put his hand to was unsuccessful. He searched in vain for an experience that would lift him

[26] A. Boucourechliev: *Robert Schumann in Selbstzeugnissen und Bilddokumenten*. Hamburg, 1958.

above his triviality, would supply him with the theme for a major work of art. One evening his wife Charlotte sent him out of the house and stabbed herself through the heart, leaving behind a farewell letter: "Here, Heinrich, you have your experience!"[27] There were such marriages in those days, marriages of silent, humble love. Any reference to passion, however, was banned.

CÉCILE—THE WOMAN WITHOUT PREDECESSORS

Felix Mendelssohn's marriage was the very model of passionlessness. The sober manner in which this exemplary alliance came about is almost incredible. And it is hard to realize that the transports of Werther, the abandon of the Rousseauian decades, lay only fifty years behind. It is as if a thousand years had elapsed between young Goethe and the youthful Mendelssohn who declared: "And now I am going to get married."

The lucky girl had not yet been discovered. And so Felix started looking for a bride in a manner quite unwonted for an artist. There is something particularly touching about this, too. For behind the precipitate decision lay a wish of his father's—and his father had just died. Abraham Mendelssohn had often expressed the fear "that Felix may miss the right time for marriage, and along with marriage the gaining of a centre of gravity for his life". The boy, he felt, stood in particular need of such a centre of gravity. "I remember", Devrient has related, "that in connection with Felix's finicky requirements for an operatic poem his father said to me: 'I am afraid that Felix with his fault-finding will no more obtain an opera libretto than he will a wife. . . .'" But his father died suddenly on 19th November 1835, and Felix at once felt the full force of the fact that the older generation had been extinguished, and that he himself had an obligation to carry on the line. It was, Devrient observes, "the thought that every well-bred person takes away with him from the grave of some departed one." In Felix's case it took the form of a resolve to find a wife.[1]

"Nothing suitable" was found either in Berlin or in Leipzig. But in Frankfurt, Felix was introduced into the home of Madame Jeanrenaud, the beautiful young widow of a deceased minister of the French

[27] Th. Mundt: *Charlotte Stieglitz, Ein Denkmal*. Berlin, 1835.
[1] E. Devrient: *Meine Erinnerungen an Felix Mendelssohn-Bartholdy*. Leipzig, 1872.

Reformed Church. This was a family of Huguenots—a type of family to which the Mendelssohns felt naturally attracted, for they too stemmed from a small, ardent minority group. (Later, Rebecca Mendelssohn also married a Huguenot.) Madame Jeanrenaud's daughter, Cécile, was a gentle, blue-eyed girl, whose face was so pure and lovely that when she entered the room "you thought she had been painted by a painter of the Düsseldorf school."[2] Did Felix find her appealing? He gave no signs of that, at first. And even after he declared himself and the engagement was a settled thing, Felix behaved "as if he would never take off his gloves. ... His visits", Hiller[3] relates, "to the still youthful mother became ever more frequent, but he treated the girl with such restraint that for several weeks it did not occur to her to refer Mendelssohn's visits to herself; she thought he came only to see her mother, who was indeed vivacious, intelligent, cultivated and extremely attractive."

If he said little to Cécile when he was with her in these early days, he spoke all the more of her when she was not present. Lying on the sofa as was his habit, hands clasped under his head, he sang her praises—but never, Hiller observed, in an ardently passionate way. "Frankfurt society followed with curiosity Mendelssohn's half-disguised courting, and a good many of the remarks I heard made it plain that in some circles it was not enough to possess genius, cultivation, fame, charm and fortune and to belong to an important, not to say a distinguished family. All such attributes did not entitle a young man to aspire to a young woman of patrician background. But I don't think that any such talk ever reached Mendelssohn's ears."[4]

"I am more frightfully in love than I have ever been in my life, and I do not know what I should do", Felix wrote on 24th July 1836 to Rebecca in Berlin. "I am supposed to leave Frankfurt the day after tomorrow, but I feel as if it will cost my neck to do so. In any case, before I go to Leipzig I intend to come back here in order to see this much too sweet girl once more; but what I don't know is whether she sees anything in me, and as I say, I also don't know what I should do...."

What he did was rather childish. To test his feelings (we can imagine what Byron, Stendhal or Wagner would have done in his place), he set out for Holland in order to think of her at a distance, on the beach at Scheveningen. Schadow, the director of the Düsseldorf Academy, was with him.[5] Felix had always loved the beach: the straight green lines of

[2] J. Hübner. *Schadow und seine Schule*. Bonn, 1869.
[3] F. Hiller: *Felix Mendelssohn-Bartholdy*. Cologne, 1874.
[4] Ibid.   [5] J. Hübner: op. cit.

the waves, the shells and seaweed washed up on the sand—but now the scene seemed to him dreary and prosaic. It did not improve his mood to be recognized and stopped by a Dutchman who addressed him in a ridiculous mixture of Dutch and German. "And here is where you collect majestic ideas", the officious stranger said. And so Felix rushed back from The Hague to Frankfurt and in a burst of enterprise asked Cécile Jeanrenaud whether she would marry him.

When she "whispered" her consent, Felix's good, childlike, unharmed heart was filled with happiness. Unharmed—that is the word. He was twenty-eight years old. Unlike so many other composers, however, he had never suffered harm from women. Exceedingly handsome, rich, not at all shy, he had always been spoiled by the fair sex—but it had not mattered to him. All his relationships had remained on a superficial social basis; he had rather feared that a serious liaison might disturb his work. And yet he was not cold, far from it. In keeping with the spirit of his age, he was all "feeling". No one can write music which so strongly appeals to women, so softly vibrant and full of such smiling accents, without knowing a good deal about women. But he did not need women; he was not dependent on their favours. In a letter to his mother he criticized the way a greatly gifted musician like Chopin was "succumbing to the Parisian craze for despair and mania for passion".

We may well ask to what extent he had been interested in women before he met Cécile Jeanrenaud. He had been allured by their spirit, their atmosphere, especially if they were ladies of culture. There was, for example, Delphine von Schauroth of Munich "whom everyone here adores". At a grand soirée "ministers and counts trot around her like domestic animals in the hen yard; artists, too, and other cultivated persons". So he wrote to Fanny on 11th June 1830. What a simpering tone he manages to project in these few phrases, though in fact he rather respected Delphine, for she was a good pianist. "Her mother is a baroness; she is an artist, and very cultured. In short, I made sheep's eyes. We played Hummel's four-handed sonata beautifully, to the delight of the company; I melted and smiled and pounded and held the A flat at the beginning of the last movement for her because 'my small hand cannot reach it'...." It was during his morning calls upon Delphine that the outlines of his G minor piano concerto (opus 25) came to him—the concerto that Liszt was later to present as a stunning concert piece. The concerto is in fact dedicated to Delphine von Schauroth. It shows Mendelssohn at his best; engaging, grave, and for all its lyricism, epic. In it, he experiments with a device he was later to use in his "Scottish" Symphony: the three movements of this concerto are not separated by

pauses. All in all, this piano concerto is a masterly work: the first movement with its proud octave staccatos, Weberesque in its bravura; the
second movement a songlike Andante; the third a roaring presto Finale
in G major. How youthful and blithe the whole work is. And yet he was
not in love with Delphine. He assured Fanny of that in his letters, to
quiet her sisterly jealousy. What reasons had he to fall in love? There was
also a girl named Josephine Lang in Munich, who had a great talent for
composition. He devoted an hour a day to teaching her counterpoint, and
remained her lifelong friend. She married Professor Köstlin, a Swabian
jurist, and Felix Mendelssohn became the godfather of her firstborn son.[6]

There are no traces of a *femme fatale*. All his relationships were *scher-
zando*, emotional "capriccios". Felix was neither a Cherubino nor a Don
Giovanni. He was not dull, but he was distinctly not passionate and
not enslaved by the curse of the flesh. Above all he was concerned about
social status. It is hard to escape the feeling that the only women who
attracted him were those whom he could present to his sisters, Fanny the
musician and the worldly-wise Rebecca with her extraordinary gift for
languages. When he lost his heart, he always lost it to the background as
well as to the girl: the music room, the distinguished gathering, the trees
in the garden, night, the interesting talks with men. He was not particularly keen on being alone with women. Another letter from Munich is
typical of him:

> Yesterday was the day of the university ball that I've men-
> tioned to you. I wish you could have seen me waltzing with the
> President's wife. It was lovely. A section of the garden was
> floored and the area canopied and garlanded with flowers; there
> we danced. The trees were hung with colourful Chinese lanterns;
> after full darkness fell there were fireworks, then a transparency
> representing the University, along with grand illuminations. The
> Papal Nuncio was there too, in addition the tutor of the Duke of
> Bordeaux, a Mr. Martin, who asked many questions about Aunt
> Henriette Mendelssohn and gave me a thousand messages for
> her.... From a dark lane Johann Nepomuk von Ringseis turned
> up [he was a great diagnostic physician of the time; Bettina von
> Arnim describes him as a man with the physiognomy of a
> medieval knight; his face seemed moulded of bronze and his
> eyes blazed up at the sight of disease[7]]. I had myself introduced
> to Ringseis.... To my right people were talking Russian; the

[6] H. A. Köstlin: *Josephine Lang*. Leipzig, 1881.
[7] B. v. Arnim: *Sämtliche Schriften*. Weimar, 1853.

loveliest burgher girls, their hair all done up in ringlets, were walking under the big trees; farther up in the circle sat the Austrian Ambassador and the wife of Soandso and Baroness Soandso and Moritz Saphir without a cravat, also a number of professors and insipid officers; trumpets and drums accompanied the student songs—in short, a brilliant celebration. I went home alone, did not know my way and cut boldly across cornfields in the direction I fancied was that of the city, still hearing the dance music in the distance. It was utterly delicious walking on the footpath under the brightest of starry skies, the corn on either side of me, the strange land underfoot. The path did not lead me astray; I came to a high embankment on the shore of the Isar.... The river roared energetically, and before me the lights of Munich lay outspread; behind me the lamps and lanterns of the ball still gleamed. I thought about all of you a great deal.

Night breezes, bright and light thoughts—those of a twenty-one-year-old. Along with all this there was a brief mention of a Scotswoman with whom Felix talked English at the ball. One more woman—he brought her in to show how unimportant they all were. Above all he did not want to be involved. These charming letters of Felix speak the language of a happy man. And Adolf Bernhard Marx, who was also present at the fête —after a penniless youth now soundly established as a professor of music history and for the first time enjoying the delights of prosperity—wrote in tones of intoxicated happiness to Fanny in Berlin: "Who can write all the details, count the innumerable leaves on the tree of joy and of love?"

It is quite certain that Cécile Jeanrenaud, daughter of a Frankfurt patrician house, had had no predecessors. The woman Felix married was his first and last love. And yet Felix was a virtuoso in offering consolation to women suffering from loneliness. There was Ottilie von Goethe, so much older than he, who looked back with pride upon a sad, sweet past. On 27th June 1834 Felix wrote to her from Düsseldorf, where he had an opera engagement, in answer to a letter of hers:

The days which I spent with you are among the dearest, best days I have ever known; and although all that, too, is long since past, it remains with me and cannot be taken from me.... If only we could arrange things so that I might see you again this summer! You say that you also wish it, so let us see whether you will write me a line in answer to the following question: Where can I meet you at the end of August, or the end of September? [He suggests various possibilities: Berlin, Kassel, Düsseldorf.]

But I rather think I shall go by way of Frankfurt, and if we were again to miss each other, perhaps even in the same hotel, that would be altogether too awful. . . . If you were to be coming to Bonn some time before then, I would naturally set out at once, leaving music-paper and work in the lurch; only I cannot very well travel farther now and cannot be long away from Düsseldorf—therefore I beg you once more, really do write, so that I can arrange my itinerary accordingly. In all probability you will not do it and we will miss each other by a few miles, but I don't want to be to blame for that. . . . You say not a word about Ulrike—how is she and what is her life like now? Many greetings to the children, and my best to you. And now I must pester you for a reply: where shall I meet you in the summer?[8]

This was how Felix addressed a relict of Goethe's "court"—but it was also the way he paid his respects, in his own droll way, to an ageing, aristocratic lady. Was he in love with Ottilie? Heaven forbid. But he played the game according to its rules; women love to be adored. Bringing passion into their lives was another matter, and most of the women of the age would have found it disquieting.

Among the many fortunate aspects of Mendelssohn's life, perhaps this was the most fortunate: that he did not spend a single day of his life suffering the pangs of "unrequited love". He never underwent the fearful humiliations because of women which were the lot of others. There was Schubert serving only as minstrel for his friends, when they went a-courting. When he sang, "Softly do my songs implore", he sang not for himself—others received the reward and the kisses. What crimes women committed against this shy, inhibited man. And when he did once venture to love a girl of the aristocracy, as happened in Hungary, she—Countess Esterhazy—did not condescend to notice. And so he went to bed with her maid, caught a mysterious disease that is not so mysterious to us nowadays, and died only a few years afterwards.

Mendelssohn found flattery and pretty caresses easy—for no pangs of love were involved. It is proof of his artistic and psychological prudence that no woman could imperil him. And yet, as conductor, pianist and connoisseur of singing, he was naturally subject to the temptation of beautiful singers. It was something of a thrill to appear in London as escort of the divine Malibran, the woman who could simultaneously

[8] Unpublished manuscript in the possession of the International Felix Mendelssohn Society, Basel.

"weep and sing" on the stage.[9] This Spanish singer brought a South European springtime to the English; her interpretations of Rossini's heroines, and especially of Bellini's *Norma* and *La Sonnambula,* sent audiences into a frenzy. Salons and hurdy-gurdies rang with her melodies. Felix Mendelssohn performed with her at a soirée, and his father, who was with him at the time, wrote an account of the occasion in a letter dated 7th July 1833: "Malibran sang a Spanish song, then, at Felix's request, two others, then an English rowing song and a French troubadour song. . . . What a torrent, fountain, eruption of vigour and spirit, of mood and dash . . . what boldness and sureness of touch this woman displayed in those little songs!" She stirred Felix too—but only his feeling for his art, not his heart.[10]

There were other singers who filled him with joy and admiration. But there is no evidence that he ever poured out passionate epistolary sighs, or lost a day of work over such emotions. On the other hand he was by nature inclined to daydream. In his boyhood his mother used to call out to him, "Felix, haven't you any work to do?" because he seemed so suspiciously silent in his room. He dreamed of a great many things—but visions of great love never played a part in those reveries. It was his good fortune that his life was not to be half shattered like the lives of Musset or Chopin. Goethe had said, "Passion is suffering". Mendelssohn escaped both.

Feeling was another matter. Feeling, not passion, was the watchword of the Biedermeier decades, of the people who rejected the extravagant sensuality of Wagner. Franz Grillparzer was musician enough to understand Beethoven and Schubert—he spoke at their funerals and wrote magnificently about them. But *Tannhäuser* horrified him, for he was quite alive to the erotic atmosphere of the work. He dissimulated his feelings by a curious kind of carping:

> One person said that the music expressed the Russo-Turkish war, in which the trumpets and drums of the Christian chorale symbolized the intrepidity of the Russians, and the quivering of the violins the fear of the Turks, although in truth the Turks did not seem to have been so terribly afraid. A second listener thought it probably represented the ice-jam on the Danube. Two others heard it as the creation of the world, a third as the world's doom. Finally a good man gave us the author's programme

[9] H. Kühner: *Genien des Gesanges aus dem Zeitalter der Klassik und Romantik.* Basel, 1951.

[10] S. Hensel: *Die Familie Mendelssohn 1729–1847.* Berlin, 1879.

notes, though unfortunately not until the overture was over. Only then did we understand what it was all about and resolved not to miss this "glorious overture" at any future performance.[11]

This humorous tone was an evasion, or as we would say in present-day terminology, a repression. The phallic element in the bacchanal, the depiction of an erection:

was an abomination to this man of feeling. Schumann, too, could not endure it. And Mendelssohn, though he loved *The Flying Dutchman*, drew the line at *Tannhäuser*. For him, the happy exponent of the age, the "bourgeois artist", the central problem of the opera had no meaning. Venus and Elizabeth? The conflict between depravity and sanctity seemed arbitrary. The whole story was an unpleasant business. There were no Venuses in the world of the Biedermeier—hence there were no Elizabeths, nor any of the unnaturalness inherent in the ideal of chastity.

No ecstasy, then—but also no flagellation. For Felix, Cécile Jeanrenaud was not the fulfilment of passionate dreams, but of tranquility, of home and children. She was surrounded by a melodious stillness. You scarcely noticed that she was in the room. Eduard Devrient praised the lovely light of her eyes and the fact that she always spoke softly and slowly. To have children by such a woman would be bliss indeed. And after the birth of his first child—his wife having been in grave danger for four days—Felix wrote:

> Now that all the fear is past, and wife and child are well, I feel so gay and yet not one bit philistine. . . . I cannot help myself, it is a dear and warm feeling to look at such a tiny little fellow who has brought into the world with him his mother's blue eyes and button of a nose and knows her so well that he smiles at her when she enters the room, and then when he lies at her breast and drinks like mad, and both enjoy it so—I cannot help myself, I am beside myself with happiness. Carl Wolfgang Paul is the little fellow's name. . . .[12]

[11] F. Grillparzer: *Sämtliche Werke*. Stuttgart, 1872.
[12] F. Hiller: op cit.

GENRE PAINTERS OF CHILDREN AND FLOWERS

The parents' joy in children was an essential component of marriage in 1830. A swarm of children crying their happiness to high heaven.... This may seem like a self-evident matter, but it is not, not at all. The marriages of the older Romantics, even when these happened to have been legalized, seemed more like love affairs in which children resulted by accident. Dorothea Mendelssohn had children by Veit, the banker, but none by Friedrich Schlegel, the great love of her life. Karoline Schlegel had none by Schelling. In spite of all his philandering Clemens Brentano never became a father—yet he put together a wonderful anthology of verse for children, his *Des Knaben Wunderhorn.*

But Biedermeier people actively wanted children. The tenuousness and temporariness of romantic alliances struck them as indecent. Around 1800 the ego and freedom were the goal of all desire; in 1830 and 1840 permanent ties and offspring were the thing.

If women around 1750 also bore many children, they did so because infant mortality was so high and families wanted at least two survivors to continue the stock. A hundred years later, however, in an age of improved hygiene, Biedermeier families had four, six, often eight children who grew to man's estate. All Mendelssohn's friends were married and had numerous progeny. The feeling was that artists should also be good citizens, which was synonymous with being family men. Bachelors and childless couples were somehow suspect. Grillparzer and Nikolaus Lenau who remained unmarried, were always looked at a bit askance by their contemporaries.

Robert Schumann was immensely taken up with his composing, was solitary by disposition, was the prey of inner torments, and thus hardly what we might call an ideal father. And Clara, the great pianist, had to help earn their living. Nevertheless the pair had six children who brought great happiness into the household. Mendelssohn loved the role of father. Cécile bore him five children: Carl, Maria, Paul, Felix and Lili. Each time he waited for their birth with trepidation, and was immoderately happy afterwards. But he loved children in general. Max Reger's wife has related how her grandmother, a singer, once surprised Felix Mendelssohn sitting with her two-year-old daughter on his knees, at the piano, pounding away. "What can I do when your Gustel wants to hear a bear dance?" he apologized.[1]

The painters and draughtsmen of the Biedermeier era discovered the child as subject matter. This statement may sound a little wild—after all, for more than a thousand years Christian art had painted the child in the form of the Holy Infant. But the Italian school had concentrated on the sanctity of childhood, and presented an idealized type of childish beauty, white and dimpled. The North knew better, but northern artists were slow about showing the child as they saw him, touchingly droll, realistically ugly. The genre masters of the Biedermeier era were complete realists: they saw children as high-spirited, mischievous, imaginative, defiant. tractable—but never as beautiful. Speckter and Ludwig Richter saw them thus. And so did Schumann, who presented his children with a lovely sketchbook, the *Album for the Young*. Though these, of course, were sketches set to music.

These piano pieces have always been great favourites, but as works of art they have often been underestimated. This is particularly true for the later *Scenes from Childhood*. It has been suggested that the titles were quite accidental—as if the master had first composed the piece and then "as an afterthought added a poeticizing allusion which was in itself superfluous and which could easily have been something else entirely". How wrong this was has been evident ever since William Stern and Karl Groos disclosed some of the secrets of the psychology of childhood.[2] Robert Schumann's pieces for children are perfect reproductions of actual psychological states.

Schumann, then, did not write children's songs. As Franz M. Böhme has shown, a children's song is the constant repetition of two beats; the piece moves ahead monotonously, now in the fifth, now in the tonic, also touches the upper harmonic, and often concludes on the third.[3] What Schumann produced, however, were highly complex psychological portraits. The child, still unacquainted with the mixed feelings and disturbances of adulthood, seems to be experiencing everything for the first time. Sören Kierkegaard's *Story of Youth* speaks of the awakening of man in the state of childhood—he is hurled into existence not knowing whence or why. This experience is accompanied by anxiety feelings, though joyousness on the whole predominates. Bernard Groethuysen's remarks on the

---

[1] E. Reger: *Mein Leben mit und für Max Reger, Erinnerungen*. Leipzig, 1930.
[2] K. Groos: *Die Spiele der Menschen*. Jena, 1899.
[3] F. M. Böhme: *Deutsches Kinderlied und Kinderspiel*. 1894.

nature of childhood[4] cast considerable light on Schumann's *Scenes from Childhood*. This is "expression music", but not tone-painting (which Robert Lach later drew upon in order to explore the nature of children's musical reactions).[5] Schumann was after something different. His underlying point was that the child, untroubled by memories (that is the key factor) has an absolute relationship to every one of his experiences.

In "Morning Walk", for example, the child moves with a tremendous rush out of the garden gate and down the road. He wants to discover the world. Never in his adult life will he be so unburdened. Or that immensely spirited "After the Theatre": no adult will ever feel the excitement of a roused imagination as anything so *absolute*.

On the other hand: if "Curious Tale" and "Important Event" are comical, their comedy is not the sort that a grown-up ascribes to a child. Instead, Schumann has found the primal levels of comedy, those that are experienced by the child himself. How the throat bubbles with laughter in "Curious Tale":

Or "Important Event", with its travesty of the incomprehensible activities of the grown-ups:

"Wild Rider" and "Happy Farmer", too, are not actual portraits of a rider or a farmer, but the way the child reacts to them; the first sends shivers up the child's back, the second fills him with enormous gusto.

Mendelssohn painted a water-colour of himself, Cécile and two children standing in a large room. The painter Bendemann objected that the children looked too stiff. "That may be", Felix said, "*but perhaps they are afraid!*"[6]—Compare that insight with Schumann's "Fright", which is keenly realistic:

[4] B. Groethuysen: "Über den Kindersinn." *Die Wandlung* II, Part 7. Heidelberg, 1947.

[5] R. Lach: *Studien zur Entwicklungsgeschichte der ornamentalen Melopöie*. Leipzig, 1913.

[6] J. Schrattenholz: *Eduard Bendemann*. Düsseldorf, 1891.

Eugénie Schumann, the long-lived daughter of Robert and Clara, has described this matter of fear in the nursery: "One evening, we younger children were playing together in the dining-room. Then it occurred to us that we wanted to go to Mama and ask her for chocolate. But to do so we had to pass through a room that to our children's minds seemed enormous, where a large yellow fur coat hung on a stand in the corner; our father had once worn this coat on a trip to Russia. We were as frightened of this coat as if it were a wild animal, and it took all our courage to venture past it. We held hands, ran together across the dark room and stormed into Mama's room. She was sitting at her desk in the bright lamplight— I can still see her slender figure in black velvet bodice and silk skirt. How safe we felt after passing through such perils! She kept us with her a while, produced the sweets we craved from one of the desk drawers, and dismissed us again."[7]

It was, then, the reality of childhood that Robert Schumann depicted. We have further testimony to that from Ludwig Richter, who in 1848 designed the title page for the first edition of *Forty Piano Pieces for the Young*. Clara Schumann played the pieces for him. "During the playing the composer sat with bowed head and half-closed eyes at his wife's side. Before each piece he whispered its title and a few explanatory remarks. Schumann's explanation of 'Wintertime' ran somewhat as follows: Woods and fields are covered with snow; snow lies thickly on the road. Twilight. Scattered snowflakes begin drifting down. In the cosy room the old people sit, watching the children play with their dolls. . . ."[8]

Such parental participation in the children's pleasure probably started in the Biedermeier epoch. Classicists and romanticists had paid little attention to children. And in the baroque age the father was a dignified gentleman who never even entered the nursery. The nursery was the mother's domain. A letter such as Martin Luther's "To his son Hans" on the

[7] E. Schumann: *Erinnerungen*. Stuttgart, 1925.

[8] L. Richter: *Lebenserinnerungen eines deutschen Malers*. Frankfurt am Main, 1886.

pleasures of toys in paradise was a great rarity. It is impossible to conceive of the bewigged dignitaries of the age of Bach joining in childish play. Such antics began to happen in the Biedermeier period—Felix Mendelssohn would get down on his knees, forgetful of his good clothes, to crawl whinnying around the room as a pony, or to pull a toy ship by a rope.[9] He, too, composed pieces for children. Perhaps they had more finish than Schumann's, but they were no less sincerely felt. As late as the year of his death, 1847, he took his inspiration from children at play; their quick ecstatic breathing can be heard in his opus 72, *Six Songs for Children*:

When little Beckie was quite small, Felix (in imitation of Haydn?) had written a children's symphony which was performed in the orangery to gales of laughter. His second children's symphony has since been lost.[10]

But just as Mozart did not write the most beautiful children's song of his time: "Schlafe, mein Prinzchen, es ruhn" (for this song was written by Bernhard Fliess[11]—though people are still reluctant to admit it!), so Mendelssohn did not write the most beautiful lullaby of his era. For "Schlaf in guter Ruh, tu die Äuglein zu" was composed by Wilhelm Taubert, one of his Berlin friends:[12]

> Sleep, my love, and rest,
> Close your eyes, my best.
>> Listen to the rain, and mark
>> How the neighbour's dog does bark.
>
> Neighbour's dog has nipped the man,
> Oh my, how the beggar ran.
>> The dog has torn the beggar's vest;
>> Sleep, my love, and rest.

[9] C. E. Horsley: "Reminiscences of Mendelssohn." *Dwight's Journal of Music*. Boston.
[10] S. Hensel: *Die Familie Mendelssohn 1729–1847*. Berlin, 1879.
[11] M. Friedländer: *Das deutsche Lied im 18. Jahrhundert*. Stuttgart, 1902.
[12] W. Taubert: *Lieder*. Berlin, 1840.

The secret of this song is that really it lulls not the children but the grown-ups to sleep. Before the March Revolution of 1848 all sorts of things were happening: neighbours' dogs bit beggars, who were soon to be called "proletarians", while outside the rain fell. But inside the good bourgeois slept, taking their well-deserved rest.

Such were the limits and the sensibility of an age! Second in the hearts of the good bourgeois (after the innocence of childhood) came the innocence of flowers. Roses, tulips, carnations, each flower with its symbolic import, turned up in hundreds of thousands of album verses and amateur drawings.[13] No doubt about it, flowers did mean something: as long as men give women flowers they symbolize fragility, short-lived, imperilled beauty.

There was genuine feeling in Heinrich Heine's eight lines:

> *Du bist wie eine Blume*
> *so hold und schön und rein;*
> *ich schau dich an, und Wehmut*
> *schleicht mir ins Herz hinein.*

> *Mir ist, als ob ich die Hände*
> *aufs Haupt dir legen sollt,*
> *Betend, dass Gott dich erhalte*
> *so rein und schön und hold.*

The text for the song "sent out to greet a rose", which Felix Mendelssohn composed (opus 19, 3), was not so beautiful:

Lei - se zieht durch mein Ge - müt

Granted the beauty of the swinging, swaying, bell-ringing thirds of the beginning[14]—but what about the continuation! The poet addresses his own song—now, is that proper? And asks it to fly off into the distance and bring his regards to the dweller in a country house. The sentiment is silly, and the music does not make it any better. But perhaps today we are unjust to a song that has been sung too much, and so sung to shreds. Moreover, Heine's artful simplicity has had a thousand imitators.[15]

But the people of 1839 idolized flowers for other, deeper reasons. For it

[13] G. Hermann: *Das Biedermeier im Spiegel seiner Zeit*. Berlin, 1913.
[14] E. Hoffman: *Das Wesen der Melodie*. Berlin, 1924.
[15] K. Kraus: *Heine und die Folgen*. Munich, 1910.

was an age when the dominance of cities was beginning. The smoke of factories and locomotives clouded and shrouded the age—most monstrously in England. London and Manchester were swathed in the soot of industry. The fog settled down and stagnated over the crowded counting houses and banks of the City of London. The bourgeoisie sought salvation in the "English" garden.[16] There flowers were no longer symbols, but an aspect of reality—of better reality—intensely experienced.

To Germans in the period before the March Revolution of 1848, flowers had a significance which has been more or less lost in our day. As early as 1828 Adolf Bernhard Marx spoke of the "orchestral music of flowers" in his *May Day Greeting to the Philosophers of Art*. The whole essay is based on the conceit of a composer's dream:

> Since the beginning of the world [the rose tells the composer], we flowers have been making music. Only your deaf ears do not hear it. We have the most delicate instruments on which to play ...although the wind sometimes disturbs us slightly. The sunflowers are the trumpets, the tuberoses the drums; the hydrangeas play the horns, hyacinths the clarinets, tulips the oboe and lilies the flutes; violets are the bassoons. All the grasses and the leaves of trees play the fiddle; chestnut leaves take the viola, the long-needled pines are the bass violins.[17]

All this is utterly in the spirit of Jean Paul. And why should we doubt that Mendelssohn felt the same way when he wrote home from London in explanation of the genesis of his *Three Fantasias* or *Caprices* (opus 16): "I shall always remember my stay with the three Taylor girls. . . . I shall never forget the meadows, the wild flowers and the murmur of the gravelly brook." For the eldest girl he composed an *Andante con moto* meant to depict pink carnations and red roses:

For the youngest, he set to music the yellow trumpet blossoms in her hair.

[16] C. Holme: *The Gardens of England*. London, 1907.
[17] A. B. Marx: *Maigruss an die Kunstphilosophen*. Berlin, 1828.

But to the middle one "I gave the brook which so pleased us once when we were out riding that we dismounted and sat down beside it. This last piece is, I think, the best; it flows so slowly and gently and is a bit tediously simple, so that I played it for myself every day and waxed quite sentimental over it."[18]

As soon as a person realizes that he is being sentimental, he is aware of the faint ridiculousness of the situation. And as a musician Mendelssohn seldom if ever deceived himself; he knew what he was saying when he called his piece tediously simple. For there is something curious about flowers. If their beauty is to move us, they need a counter-accent. And that counter-accent is *death*! Great poets have always known that. How does Ophelia die in *Hamlet*?

> There is a willow grows aslant a brook,
> That shows his hoar leaves in the glassy stream;
> There with fantastic garlands did she come
> Of crow-flowers, nettles, daisies and long purples...
>
> There, on the pendent boughs, her coronet weeds
> Clambering to hang, an envious sliver broke,
> When down her weedy trophies and herself
> Fell in the weeping brook.

In the *Nibelungenlied* there is a single verse that shows the dramatic value of flowers. When Siegfried is suddenly transfixed through the back by Hagen's spear, there comes the line:

> *Do viel in die bluomen der Chriemhiltes man*
> (Then Kriemhild's husband fell among the flowers)

—and it is as if until this moment flowers had never existed. For the flowers into which Siegfried falls are the counter-accent to his death. Only one of two things can be real: the innocent flowers or the act of treachery. But the fact that both are nevertheless real: dearest life and most vicious death—this is what creates the counterpoint.

The genre masters of the Biedermeier era, the poets, painters and musicians, were not always aware of this law. They loved—and with some justification—the weakness, the lack of accent in the gentle motion of flowers stirred by a soft breeze. They loved, that is, the things that had been ignored by the sensibilities of more heroic eras. Yet these masters might have learned from the folksong collections of their day, from *Des Knaben Wunderhorn*, for example, about the antithesis of flowers and

[18] S. Hensel: op. cit.

death, and what it means. They might have discovered it in that tremendous song in minor key that Mendelssohn set:

Es ist ein Schnit-ter, der heißt Tod, hat Ge-walt vom höchsten Gott.

Heut' wetzt er das Mes-ser, es schneid't schon viel bes-ser, bald wird er drein schnei-den, wir müs-sen's nur lei-den.

Hü-te dich, schön's Blü-me-lein!

> There is a reaper, Death his name
> Whom God has given power and fame.
> > His scythe he is whetting,
> > Soon he will be cutting,
> We cannot defer it,
> Must bravely endure it.
> > Care, take care, thou blossom fair.

There is the lovely catalogue of all the flowers which must be woven into the harvest wreath:

> The elegant lilies,
> The low-growing gillies,
> > The drooping bluebell,
> > The angel-eyed speedwell,
> The fragrant melissas
> And noble narcissus.

And the resounding bravery of the challenge: "I defy thee, Death, and fear thee not."

> My hope shall be granted
> And I be transplanted
> > To that garden in heaven
> > Where all is forgiven.
> Rejoice, have no care, thou blossom fair.

What composer before Wagner could have carried off such a composition—for that matter, could Wagner have handled it before the *Meistersinger*? But Mendelssohn wrote it at the age of eighteen, in 1827. He was sensitive to the verbal values of older German poems, to their angular unsentimentality and charming thrift. He was, as we know today, well acquainted with the philological researches of Uhland, Lachmann and Grimm. His familiarity with these matters was no less than that of Brahms, and considerably more than Schumann's—although the latter seemed predestined to write the music which would match the incisiveness of the old lyrics. And indeed Schumann could achieve the necessary hardness in songs; but in larger forms he often became unbearably soft. Mendelssohn was aware of this and would undoubtedly have warned his friend against that secular oratorio, *The Rose's Pilgrimage*, if he had lived. But in 1853 Mendelssohn was already six years dead.

The author of this unfortunate affair was a poetaster named Moritz Horn. Though the story was incredibly silly, Schumann was seduced by the smoothness of the verses. A rose aspires to become a human being. The queen of the elves grants her wish. A miller and his wife thereupon adopt the human rose as their daughter; she falls in love and marries the forester's son; but after the birth of her child she voluntarily departs from earth. She has experienced the supreme joy and can expect nothing greater. That, in essence, was the story. It had, to be sure, genre scenes such as the Biedermeier era doted on, cosy German-village things. Instead of retreating in alarm—from, for example, "a mill standing between green trees"—Schumann artfully composed an "Ei Mühle, liebe Mühle!" in whimsical imitation of Schubert's songs in "Die schöne Müllerin". He also had a male chorus singing to the accompaniment of horns: "Bist du im Wald gewandelt?" But Mendelssohn had already written "Wer hat dich, du schöner Wald" and the trick of tender parody does not bear repetition.

Wagner, the foe of Biedermeier and especially the foe of Schumann—wrote some excessively harsh words to his pupil Theodor Uhlig about *The Rose's Pilgrimage*.[19] And Nietzsche once described the ageing Schumann as spinsterly. Wagner and Nietzsche were sick and tired of the everlasting flowers and the precious little children. They hated the nursery atmosphere of the age. "Why are our poets always whispering as though they did not want to wake us up?" wrote Theodor Mundt, a member of the Young Germany movement.[20] Another enemy of Biedermeier, the

[19] R. Wagner: *Briefe an Theodor Uhlig*. Leipzig, 1888.
[20] Th. Mundt: *Geschichte der Literatur der Gegenwart*. Berlin, 1842.

dramatist Friedrich Hebbel, joined in the attack upon the school of flower poets. Contemptuous of miniaturism and delicacy, he hammered out some distichs which, in German verse, are the time-honoured mode for epigrams:

> Why do you manage so well with beetles and buttercups?
> Because you know little of men and never look up at the stars!
> If you looked deep into hearts, you would not be raving of beetles.
> If you regarded the heavens, would bunches of posies so stir you?
> Yet it must doubtless be thus: That you might so well provide the small,
> Nature in her wisdom, has removed the great from your grasp.

This was directed not only against the now-forgotten writer Leopold Kompert, the "gentle depicter of character",[21] but also against a far greater man, Adalbert Stifter. And it was Stifter who came forth to defend the *art of the miniature* against Hebbel and Wagner; praising the "art of absolute stillness, because tranquillity is true monumentality". In movement, he argued, life flows away; all movement is in itself falsification.[22]

But if that were intended as a theory—and Stifter did so intend it—it was something monstrous, and certainly had no application whatsoever to music. "Music is movement," Eduard Hanslick wrote in 1854,[23] and only recently Ernst Kurth has added: "Melody is movement."[24]

As composers, both Schumann and Mendelssohn would have given short shrift to this call for a "motionless world". Yet Stifter was as much an exponent and a product of the Biedermeier spirit as these two composers. His timid, grave, side-whiskered face peers out of the same stiff high collars as those worn by the masters of the Leipzig music school and the Düsseldorf school of painters.

Everywhere, this shunning of human conflicts; everywhere, this painting of dawns and sunsets, of mountain woods, strangely shaped rock formations, the steppes—all sorts of idyllic nature scenes in which man was only an intruder. It was a Goethean world without Goethe, that is to say, without the demonic element. Because the demonic would have been "falsification". A masterly style had led Adalbert Stifter into a world of magnificent resignation, a world of contemplation without action. To him the only real subjects lacked tension, were motionless.

[21] L. Kompert: *Gesammelte Schriften*. Berlin, 1882.
[22] A. Stifter: *Briefe*. Pest, 1869.
[23] E. Hanslick: *Vom Musikalisch-Schönen*. Leipzig, 1854.
[24] E. Kurth: *Grundlagen des Linearen Kontrapunkts*. Berlin, 1922.

Nevertheless he acted. Racked by infernal pain, he did not wait submissively for disease to complete its work, but seized a razor and cut his own throat—leaving the orderly cosmic idyll through which he had moved so deliberately, contemplating colours and stones. Like Nikolaus Lenau and Robert Schumann, he too was ambushed by the demons whose existence he had long refused to recognize.

DOMESTIC PROBLEMS—FANNY AND WILHELM

At the time Felix married Cécile, Fanny, his elder sister, had already been married for six years. Her choice had been, for her family, an unusual one.

Richard Wagner, Mendelssohn's opposite, once professed his delight that he came from no "family", that he had virtually engendered himself and had no need to be thankful to anyone. "In total anarchy . . . life has made me my sole mentor."[1] It is the statement of a self-made man, a man of genius. The sentiment could never have been voiced by an aristocrat, or, for that matter, by a Jew—for Jews were above all the "people of the heritage".

The Mendelssohn children were heirs in every sense of the word. Young Felix did not have a thought of which his parents would not have approved. Everything he composed had to have the sanction of his family; and if he had ambition, it could be traced to the mettlesome spirit of his grandfather which lived on in him.

Brahms once joked that one of his Jewish friends, who was an excellent composer, had wished to make a change in a score of his; but then, Brahms reported, "the whole family was against it", so the passage stayed the way it was.[2] The fact that a family council could be called on such a point as that seems comical enough on the surface. There is, however, a hidden meaning to such family solidarity which Brahms the individualist could not have understood. The Jews had lost their country two thousand years before. Because of that they, more than other people, were forced to fall back upon life in the *family*.

It was true that Jewish family life with its excessive emotionality sometimes bred strange phenomena. In 1829, when Mendelssohn was in England for the first time, the thought struck him that he must get back

[1] H. v. Wolzogen: *Wagnerbrevier*. Berlin, no date.
[2] M. Kalbeck: *Johannes Brahms*. Berlin, 1908–13.

to Germany for his parents' silver wedding anniversary. Perhaps any young man of twenty might have felt the same. But Felix had had an accident; his carriage had been overturned and his knee had been badly injured.[3] Nevertheless, he set out on the journey, limping heavily on a cane and fearful that he might arrive too late with the anniversary gift he was bringing. This gift was a *singspiel*, the text written by his friend Klingemann. It was pretty much hit or miss as far as the words went: a mediocre story, with much ado about disguises. The libretto bore a certain resemblance to Dittersdorf's *Doktor und Apotheker* of 1786 and to Schenk's *Dorfbarbier*—in other words, was pretty antiquated. But the village magistrate and his wife sitting under the linden tree and waiting for the "homecoming son from abroad", was a happy touch. In short, it would do splendidly for the purpose. Felix's jestingly sentimental music was far better than is normally to be found in such occasional pieces.

Felix reached home during the first week of December. The silver wedding celebration was to take place in two weeks. His *singspiel*, *Die Heimkehr aus der Fremde*, was secretly put into rehearsal. The female parts were taken by Felix's sisters, who had quite good voices[4]; the principal role was reserved for Devrient, that devoted friend of the family. Then a request came from the King that Devrient appear at a command performance the very evening of the Mendelssohn celebration—which upset the arrangements for the *singspiel*. When the bad news reached Felix, who had been limping about the house in a highly nervous state, he seemed to go altogether out of his mind. He fell to the floor, started to stutter, suddenly could no longer understand German and stammered instructions in English. His father came to the rescue; he had the young man carried to bed, where a profound twelve-hour sleep restored Felix to normal. Devrient, knowing how much it meant to Felix, managed to get away early from his engagement at the court; he turned up at the Mendelssohn house and the show could go on. The *singspiel* was a great success and soon Felix was being importuned to let it be performed publicly. The idea did not at all appeal to him. He felt the work was purely a piece of family history. He would not release it, and so it was not until 1851, four years after his death, that it was performed: in Leipzig and concurrently, in an English version, at the Haymarket Theatre in London, where it long occupied a place in the repertory under the title of *Son and Stranger*. In 1884 Richard Strauss, writing to his own parents, praised the

[3] L. Geiger: *Briefwechsel zwischen Goethe und Zelter*. Leipzig, 1902.
[4] S. Hensel: *Die Familie Mendelssohn 1729–1847*. Berlin, 1879.

overture as a masterpiece.[5] In Germany the work has been forgotten, but it continues to appear on programmes of the Italian radio.

A family anniversary gift, then, would be devalued as soon as it was exposed to the public gaze. That was typical of the aristocratic Mendelssohnian temper, and demonstrated—not for the first time—the peculiarly "inbred" quality of the family. Fanny had violated family solidarity when, a few months before her parents' silver anniversary, she married the painter Wilhelm Hensel. The marriage had come after a long secret engagement: Leah Mendelssohn had disapproved of Hensel as a suitor. But the marriage came none too soon, for family friends like the Partheys and Ebertys had already been making jokes about Fanny's forthcoming marriage to Felix. In artistic matters the brother and sister always acted as a couple. And that went on; until quite late in life Felix scarcely wrote a note that he did not submit to Fanny for approval.

The secret engagement to Wilhelm Hensel had gone on for more than six years.[6] Their love story was among the most touching of the period. Leah Mendelssohn was certainly no fierce beldame, no blighter of her daughter's happiness. But the romantic waiting period she insisted on (hoping, of course, that time would bring the lovers to their senses) was asking a good deal of two young people.

Wilhelm Hensel, the son of a poor Protestant country clergyman, had come to Berlin almost penniless, aspiring to be a painter. He had taken part in the war against Napoleon from 1813 to 1815 and had twice marched into Paris. In keeping with the taste of the time, he had done a painting showing Tsar Alexander I of Russia as the Archangel Michael and Napoleon as Lucifer. The painting was an excellent propaganda piece for the Holy Alliance—and conservative forces were to prove helpful to Hensel in his further career.[7] In January 1821 there was a great festival in Berlin, one that was to be remembered for decades afterwards. The Russian heir-apparent, Nicholas, and his wife were visiting the Prussian court. Relations of the imperial family came from Vienna, and the Duke of Cumberland was likewise present. Thus the entire Holy Alliance was assembled in Berlin, and the King of Prussia planned a round of entertainment. It was an age when pantomimes were all the rage and so theatricals were planned in which the high-born guests would take part. Before the wonder-struck populace, the Russian prince and princess, Crown Prince Frederick William IV of Prussia and his brother who as William I was later to be first monarch of a united Germany, the Duke of

---

[5] R. Strauss: *Briefe an die Eltern*, ed. by Willi Schuh. Zürich, 1954.
[6] S. Hensel: op. cit.   [7] S. Hensel: op. cit.

Cumberland, and many other members of the highest aristocracy appeared on the stage. The climax of the week-long festivities was a series of *tableaux vivants* representing the famous English epic *Lalla Rookh*.[8]

The poem was by Thomas Moore, who was one of the "horde of Byron's friends", not quite so dear to him as Shelley, and not so great a poet. Nevertheless, Byron was friendly with Moore, the grocer's son from Dublin, lover of wine, women and Irish songs, whose personal charm sometimes contrived to win important people to the cause of Ireland. From Venice, Byron had written to him:

> Tell me what you are doing, O Thomas Moore!
> What are you doing now, O Thomas Moore?
> Sighing or suing now, O Thomas Moore?
> Rhyming or wooing now, O Thomas Moore?
> Billing or cooing now, O Thomas Moore?
>   Which, Thomas Moore?
> The Carnival's coming, O Thomas Moore!
> The Carnival's coming, O Thomas Moore,
>   Masking and humming,
>   Fifing and drumming,
> Guitaring and strumming, O Thomas Moore!

But Thomas Moore did not only write melodious verses in the Irish style; he also tried his hand at epics. *Lalla Rookh* was one of the most famous of these the story of how the ruler of Delhi, Aurengzeb, betrothes his daughter to the prince of the Buchars and sends her to Kashmir for the wedding. During the journey a singer named Feramors appears and by telling fairy-tales so endears himself to the princess that the engagement is imperilled. At the moment of arrival she realizes with joyous surprise that Feramor has disguised himself; he is her fiancé. How the period thrilled to this happy ending! For otherwise it would have been a Tristan and Isolde story, an "extremely immoral" tale and highly unsuitable for an entertainment in which princely personages were taking part.

Caroline de la Motte-Fouqué, the wife of the well-known poet, described the fabulous costumes that were worn, the silks, pearls, diamonds, scarves, daggers and turbans.[9] The little spectacle, however, was not altogether innocent. The Duke of Cumberland, of course, would be reporting in detail to London. And though this implication had been furthest from

[8] G. Vallet: *Thomas Moore, sa Vie et ses Œuvres*. Paris. 1886.
[9] Anonymous: *Briefe über Berlin*. Berlin, 1821.

the poet's mind when he wrote his sultry Oriental epic, its presentation now served principally to emphasize English interests in the Orient as against Russia's—this a good many decades before Disraeli conceived the plan of making Queen Victoria actual Empress of India.[10]

The costumes for the tableaux had to be historically authentic. A painter was called in to make the sketches. This painter was Wilhelm Hensel, and he designed the whole performance. When the play was over, the Russian grand duchess who had played Lalla Rookh herself, exclaimed: "Is posterity to have no memorial of our happiness?" Frederick William III heard her, and nodded gallantly. The laconic King, who spoke mostly in verbs, said merely: "Is to have."[11] In the ordinary course of things, *tableaux vivants* are patterned after paintings; the King decided to pattern paintings after the tableaux. Could Hensel handle it? He could. The royal personages sat for him for individual portraits in their Lalla Rookh costumes. Before the paintings were sent off to St. Petersburg, they were on exhibit in the artist's studio for a few days. And Fanny and Felix Mendelssohn came to the studio with their parents to see the paintings.

Two things happened at once. With Fanny and Wilhelm it was a case of love at first sight. And secondly, the self-taught artist was awarded a government stipend for a stay of several years in Rome, that he might study classical antiquity. The happy artist wanted to become officially engaged at once. But he encountered distinct coolness on the part of Fanny's parents. An artist, Leah Mendelssohn commented, could not base excessive hopes on a single success. Fortune was fickle. How did he intend to support his wife? Let him spend a few years in Rome, and with that background "really conquer Germany". In the meantime, however, she forbade him even to write letters to Fanny. That was making it hard indeed. What did she really have in mind?

Felix, too, had had to prove himself before his parents permitted him to think of composing as a vocation. It was only natural that they expected something similar of Hensel. The fact that he was a Christian was in no way against him. The Mendelssohn family did not exclude non-Jewish in-laws. But there was always the suspicion that he might be on the look-out for a wealthy match. Again and again Leah pointed out how insecure the times were. Even banking houses could collapse, as had happened in Leipzig to the Reichenbach's bank, and in London to the firm of Goldsmid.[12] But it soon became evident that Hensel was no

[10] A. Maurois: *Disraeli*. Paris, 1927.
[11] R. F. Eylert: *Charakterzüge aus dem Leben König Friedrich Wilhelms III*. Magdeburg, 1843–46.
[12] S. Hensel: op. cit.

fortune hunter. There was something else that made Leah wary of him. Something rather odd which formed a part of the Mendelssohnian idea of loyalty. The Mendelssohns were baptized Protestants; they did not want anyone in the family to whom there clung any suspicion of crypto-Catholicism.

How had any such rumour come to be fastened upon Wilhelm Hensel? It seems that he had a talented sister, the poetess Louise Hensel, who had actually become a convert. In 1818 this daughter of a Protestant minister's family had gone over to Catholicism. Clemens Brentano was blamed for having lured Louise to Catholicism. But the truth of the matter was just the reverse; Louise had become a Catholic in order "to make Clemens devout and human".[13] Soon the two went their separate ways. He offended against her ideal of chastity—and she was, like her poems, a profoundly virginal soul. Though a convert, she did not become a zealot.[14]

Wilhelm was as close to this gifted sister of his as Felix was to Fanny. And certain astute people claimed they could detect in Wilhelm's works —not so much in their content as in their technique, which was reminiscent of religious painting—that he was on the point of renouncing his Lutheran faith. And to make matters worse he was now about to set off for Rome! What kind of people would he meet there?

Abraham Mendelssohn was not worried about such matters. His own sisters were Catholic—Henriette in Paris, Dorothea Schlegel in Vienna— and the family were proud of his nephew Philipp Veit, the Catholic church painter in Rome.[15] But Leah took a different view of it. She was determined that Fanny must not marry a Catholic. The Berlin branch of the family must remain Protestant. Probably this obsession was connected with her brother, Jakob Bartholdy, the diplomat.

Bartholdy, whose original name, like Leah's, was Salomon, had become a Protestant in 1805. In 1813 he served his apprenticeship in diplomacy under the Prince of Hardenberg, the Chancellor of Prussia, and rose rapidly; only two years later he was consul-general in Rome, and after the Congress of Aachen in 1818 he became Prussian chargé d'affaires in Florence. He took an anti-papal stand and was an arch-opponent of Barthold Georg Niebuhr[16] who seemed too yielding toward the claims of the Curia. Bartholdy's secret reports were highly esteemed at the Berlin

[13] J. B. Diel and W. Kreiten: *Clemens Brentano*. Freiburg, 1877–78.
[14] F. Bartscher: *Der innere Lebensgang der Dichterin Luise Hensel*. Paderborn, 1882.
[15] M. Spahn: *Philipp Veit*. Bielefeld, 1902.
[16] F. Eyssenhardt: *Barthold Georg Niebuhr*. Gotha, 1886.

Chancellory. He also helped German artists of any faith by having the Casa Bartholdy in Rome decorated with fine frescoes—he was rich and could afford to patronize the arts.[17] Soon Hensel received such a commission from him. Alongside more successful men like Cornelius, Overbeck and Veit the young Hensel did not cut too bad a figure at all.

We do not know whether Bartholdy also sent secret reports on the young man's activities to his sister Leah in Berlin. Since Wilhelm was not permitted to write to Fanny (he had had to promise on his word of honour), he did something else, by way of maintaining their bond: he drew the whole Mendelssohn family from memory, portrait after portrait —parents, even Rebecca and little Paul, and sent these portraits to Fanny's mother. They were pure, Raphaelesque little pictures. The love for Fanny concealed and made so plain by the portraits evidently softened Leah's heart. She wrote to him expressing her cordial thanks.[18] Thus the ban on letters was circumvented, for Leah read the letters from Rome aloud to Fanny, and in the end she came to understand the love between the two.

For five long years Hensel remained in Rome without a word of the engagement leaking to the outside world. Meanwhile Jakob Bartholdy died, and his fortune was bequeathed to Leah. (The Mendelssohns had earlier adopted the name of this uncle from whom they expected to inherit, calling themselves Mendelssohn-Bartholdy.) The family had now become even richer. Wilhelm, who had been appointed executor of those portions of Bartholdy's will dealing with the disposition of his art collection, was kept busy for a while. At last he came home. He scarcely recognized his Fanny. She was now twenty-three—no longer quite young, by the standards of the time. Intelligent, gifted, she had shed some, though not all, of her redoubtable sharpness in repartee. She was a fine composer by now, though she gave her works to Felix. He published her settings of Goethe songs in opus 8 and 10: "Heimweh", "Italien", "Suleika und Hatem", "Sehnsucht", "Verlust" and "Nonne". She was also one of the best and most original letter writers of the day.

The engagement was announced on 22nd January 1829, and on 7th October Wilhelm and Fanny were married. For many years to come Fanny had to steer a narrow course between the jealousy of her brother and of her husband—and Wilhelm often felt himself a stranger. As his son Sebastian later revealed, this intruder from the outside world found the "coterie language" of the family incomprehensible. But he and

[17] L. V. Donop: *Die Wandgemälde der Casa Bartholdy.* Berlin, 1889.
[18] S. Hensel: op. cit.

Fanny could always laugh over the English poem, *Lalla Rookh*, which had brought them together.

On the other hand, England was no laughing matter. For the island kingdom was for them beginning to assume a new importance—in connection with Felix's fame.

ENGLAND OR FRANCE?

After the battle of Waterloo every intellectual European was faced with a sort of decision. Was he going to choose France or England? The one seemed to exclude the other. Everyone has his native land, but besides this everyone also has a fatherland of the mind and heart. If he does not, he remains a provincial. People became European-minded only if they responded to the defeat of France in 1815 by a conscious action. Either they chose England for the land of their hearts, because they regarded the victory at Waterloo as a judgment of God, or they sympathized with France, feeling that the better cause had been crushed and that men of good will must come to the aid of a humiliated ideology.

Conscious action? Are we right in saying that this choice has to be made consciously? Perhaps many of those who opted for England or for France were quite unconsciously following a political fashion. Very well —but what is a fashion really? It is observable that after every war or great political upheaval people wear a different cut of clothes. After the famous storming of the Bastille the liberated bourgeois started wearing the long trousers which had previously been the garb of galley slaves; and the Napoleonic wars inspired ladies to dress in what was felt to be the style of classical antiquity. The Polish Revolution of 1830 affected modes in France, so that fur collars became all the rage and tiny mazurka hats ("Chopin has recently composed a hat here", wrote a scoffer at the time). And that most popular of uprisings, the Hungarian struggle for freedom in 1848, though suppressed, brought to the whole of the Western world the corded Magyar jacket—which became even more popular after Berlioz's wild Rákóczy March. . . . What does conscious or unconscious mean in such contexts? With the same naturalness with which he wore "political" clothes, the intellectual of pre-1848 days asked himself: "What is going on in Paris? What is going on in London? And what attitude should I take?" He could be a partisan only of one side or the other. If he believed in one nation, he seemed, strangely enough, to have only hostile feelings for the other.

There was, for example, the case of Heine, and his impressions of London. Walter Scott had recently written a book about Napoleon,[1] a distinctly pro-English, anti-imperial book; Heine was so vexed by it, and its apotheosis of Wellington, that the street-scenes themselves became hateful to him. Always an acute observer, he saw everything with great distinctness: the lords on the riding tracks, the cabriolets with pink-and-white ladies inside, the Stock Exchange, Parliament and the lively doings in the House of Commons—and he hated it all as he hated the poverty and the shame of poverty, the "blackish, olive-green chimneys that thrust like pulled teeth into the joyless sky". He forgot that though the French cry was *liberté*, the English also valued liberty and that this was by no means hypocrisy and had, in the course of history, conferred infinite benefits upon humanity. But if he did not forget, Heine consciously excised all mention of such matters: the same Heine who spoke to the Germans about the French more wisely and sincerely than any other German has ever done. And who also ventured to teach the French truths about the intellectual history of the Germans which they could learn from no one else. The much-berated Heine did more for rapprochement between the Germans and the French than a hundred other writers before or after him. But his mind was closed against the English. There is no indication that he was impressed by such contemporaries as Dickens, Thackeray, Emily Brontë, Thomas Carlyle or Macaulay.[2]

Vice versa: the German of the period who opted for England was not interested in Paris. On the contrary, he did not understand the French and felt a sharp distaste for them. They were to him a dissolute people. From the time of Lessing on—he was the first to represent the French upon the stage in an unflattering light—German literature was not just Anglophile, but Anglomaniac. Nothing but English books stood on young Goethe's desk, and that was long before the French Revolution. The fact that Schiller's works would have been impossible without the influence of Racine and Corneille[3] was concealed from the nation. And German composers moved into the English orbit even more readily than the writers. Haydn, Mozart, Beethoven and Weber wrote music celebrating English victories or partial victories. Thus, we have works with such titles as *Neptune Cantata*,[4] *The Battle of Vittoria*, *Struggle and Victory*, expressive of the most uncritical worship. The underlying feeling seems to have

---

[1] W. Scott: *The Life of Napoleon Buonaparte*. London, 1827.
[2] H. Heine: *Gesammelte Werke*. Berlin, 1956.
[3] F. Strich: *Goethe und die Weltliteratur*. Bern, 1957.
[4] H. E. Jacob: *Joseph Haydn: His Art, Times and Glory*. New York, 1950.

been that the English had a monopoly of political and personal dignity, liberty and true humanity.

How have the English themselves borne up under the burden of this admiration? Eric Blom, keen critic of English musical life that he is, observed that the Victorian Age scarcely merited so much admiration.[5] No really creative musician lived in England at the time. There were no Purcells around, and certainly no Handel—who though German by birth did indeed become a true Englishman. Victorian England distinguished itself musically in another way. For decades London had had the finest concert halls, the richest associations of amateurs, the most luxurious opera houses. Musical life in London—directed almost entirely by foreigners—flourished ever more vigorously. The city rang with Italian, Scottish and German music. When Victoria was crowned on 28th June 1837, the wonderful dance music of Strauss père was as essential to the festivities as the cannon salutes punctuating the Coronation Oath.[6]

Mendelssohn has been jestingly called the first Early Victorian, because he appeared on the scene *before* Victoria. The appellation is absolutely right. When he arrived in London, that "symphony of smoke and stone", for the first time on 21st April 1829, his confusion was as great as Heine's. But what a difference—he loved it all! He called it horrible, insane and nevertheless wonderful. "I am confused and topsy-turvy! London is the most grandiose monster on the face of the earth.... In the whole of the past half-year in Berlin I did not see so many contrasts and such variety." During the past half-year he had revived the *St. Matthew Passion*—but what did antiquarianism amount to, what were the glories of the past to this present London? It tossed him about like a whirlpool; like a swimmer he plunged into arcaded Regent Street. He saw shops with signs in lettering tall as a man, brushed past the omnibuses from which people hung like clusters of grapes. The press of carts made walking dangerous. Heine, wedged in the crowds on this same spot, had had the most unpleasant sensations; admirer of Napoleon that he was, he thought of the French crossing the Beresina river. Mendelssohn, however, was fascinated to see "a horse rearing up because the rider has acquaintances in that house—and people going about carrying placards promising us (O animal-loving London!) the most gracious artistic performances by trained cats.... And the beggars and the Moors and the well-fed John Bulls with their slender beautiful daughters in pairs on their arms...."[7] If the world were to be

[5] E. Blom: *Music in England*. London, 1949.
[6] H. E. Jacob: *Johann Strauss, Vater und Sohn*. Hamburg, 1956.
[7] S. Hensel: *Die Familie Mendelssohn 1729–1847*. Berlin, 1879.

governed from any place in the world, let it be from this fundamentally sound, complacent, mighty city of London.

He was overcome by "John Bullism", as he wrote to his friend Johann Gustav Droysen in Berlin. Merely to sit before an English fireplace, legs outstretched comfortably, an enormous English newspaper in his hands, seemed to him the height of pleasure. Nor did he ever change his mind; in ten journeys to England, his enthusiasm for that country never wavered. Yet at the beginning he did not properly understand the rhythm of English life; the laws of the Season, the ebb and flow of social life, were alien to him—as is indicated by his letter to Zelter, here reproduced in facsimile for the first time. The text runs:

23 June 1829

Herr Novello has just informed me that he is first going to France. I am therefore sending these lines by way of the Embassy, and promise to write you a better and longer letter shortly. Dear Herr Professor, if you accept my proposal I am convinced that your songs will soon be favourites among the English, and that would be very nice indeed. Here, music is beginning to vanish from the scene right now. No one goes to concerts, and the theatres are closed. The season will be over in two weeks. I have made many acquaintances among the musicians, and believe I have assured myself a pleasant reception, in case I should return. Now everyone is leaving the city. I have bought a ticket for a long trip and am setting out for Scotland, which I long to visit because I expect to compose a good deal there. The bagpipes and the echoes are said to be altogether strange. But there is no music to be heard in London, and the art itself is alien to the people. More and better in my next. Yours, Felix M.

Although Felix could count his first concert a grand success, he decided without more ado that there was "no music" in London. Soon he would be changing his mind. For the time being he went to Scotland in order "to understand the English" from that point of vantage. After all, he knew that Haydn had arranged one hundred and thirty-eight national songs for the Edinburgh publisher, George Thompson,[8] and he also knew that Beethoven had followed in his footsteps.[9] The windy north, he reasoned, must be more receptive to music than any other part of the

[8] K. Geiringer: "Haydn and the Folksong of the British Isles." *Musical Quarterly*. New York, 1949.
[9] A. W. Thayer: *Ludwig van Beethovens Leben*. Leipzig, 1911

British Isles. We shall have more to say about Mendelssohn's experiences when he reached the latitude of the "Hebrides" and the "Scottish" Symphony.

Felix's predilection for England had already come to light in his attitudes toward French music. One might say that he had first become an Englishman in Paris. His lack of comprehension of French musical life was more than amazing; it was incredible. When we hear Mozart alternately complaining and fuming (and Wagner later, in almost the same words) about the soulless shallowness and brash sensationalism of Parisian musical circles, we know that extremely personal and grave disappointments lay behind that verdict.[10] Despite his hazardous admission that in 1830 everybody in Europe who had any future had been attracted to Paris by the July revolution, Wagner's love of Paris remained unrequited. The fact that Wagner's music did not register with the French was actually nothing but bad luck. His *Rienzi* had certainly been fiery enough, sweeping, oratorical and flamboyant—for he had learned a great deal from Méhul and Spontini. And the French knew the meaning of *élan*; nowhere had Beethoven's "Ninth" been given such performances as Habeneck's at the Paris Conservatoire.[11]

But why should Mendelssohn have taken so stern a line toward the Parisians? He had been treated just as well as he could wish. His Octet had even been performed in a church in his honour. But he had not been pleased—he had not meant it for ecclesiastical music. What would Mendelssohn have said if he had been alive in 1950 and had heard one of his favourite pieces, the horn Adagio from the overture to *Freischütz*, played in California as a *hymn*, with interpolated text in English! To the French musicians, good music was good music wherever it was played. But to Mendelssohn with his strict principles of what was tasteful and correct, his Octet in a church seemed sacrilege—and no doubt roused in him some ancient German feelings about France. Lasciviousness in music surely corresponded to licence in morals. Quite apart from politics (and in 1831 all Parisian life revolved wildly around politics, a topic which young Mendelssohn detested), what upset him greatly was the over-emphasis upon eroticism in the theatre. The shadow of Meyerbeer seemed to him to darken the whole of Paris. Yet what did he have against Meyerbeer, who was in no sense a rival of his?

Meyerbeer was no Frenchman; he was a Berliner like Felix himself. But he had the remarkable knack of representing at peak intensity the

[10] R. Sternfeld: *Aus Richard Wagners Pariser Zeit*. Berlin, no date.
[11] R. Wagner: *Gesammelte Schriften und Dichtungen*. Leipzig, 1907.

nation in which he happened to be living for the time being. When not yet thirty he had begun writing Italian operas like *Emma di Resburgo* and *Il Crociato in Egitto* so perfectly that Rossini was astonished. Five years later he wrote his most successful French opera, *Robert le Diable*. In 1836 he added *Les Huguenots*, whose expressive and glittering arias aroused universal enthusiasm. With the same facility he became a Prussian and Berliner again in 1842, when King Frederick William IV called him home to succeed Spontini as head of the Berlin opera. Once on German soil, Meyerbeer promptly proceeded to compose his *Ein Feldlager in Silesien*, basing it on songs of Frederick's army. Perhaps there is a "Meyerbeer case" as there is a "Tschaikovsky case"—here, perhaps, were composers whose talent lay in assimilating and transmuting materials from outside themselves. However, we have no right to talk loosely of Meyerbeer's career with its multiple adaptations to environment as a "tragedy of rootlessness". Compared with the operatic sun that Mozart was, Meyerbeer was of course a minor planet. But why should we praise Mozart for his unifying of the German, Italian and French strains, in his work, and call that *Europeanism*, while we denigrate another composer for his mining of the three national strata of European opera? It will not do at all. Meyerbeer's weakness was solely that he did not dig deeply enough, that he aimed only for success, and that even his best music was never really great.

But when Mendelssohn despised Meyerbeer as a super-Frenchman, and condemned his type of opera, he was concerned with other than purely musical questions. As he wrote to his father in Berlin:

> The main point is one of those ... which we must take our stand against: it is the point of immorality. When in *Robert le Diable* the nuns come one after the other and try to seduce the hero, until the abbess at last succeeds; when the hero enters his mistress's bedroom by magic and throws her to the floor in a tableau, the Parisian audience applauds. . . . And when she then begs for mercy in an aria; when in another opera the girl undresses, meanwhile singing an aria about how she will be married by this same time next day—it made a sensation, but I would not have that sort of thing in any opera of mine. For it is vulgar, and if that is the sort of thing that spells success these days, I prefer to write church music. . . .

This letter was written in 1831, when Mendelssohn was barely twenty-three. A few weeks later Felix wrote to the theatre director Karl Immermann in Düsseldorf in even sharper terms about Meyerbeer and his librettist Scribe.[12] Meyerbeer's rival and heir, Wagner, had a more mature attitude on this question, and felt called upon to write personally to Meyerbeer professing his "ardent veneration" for his work. Some of this was, of course, flattery, but Wagner also wrote a long essay (which, read nowadays, may strike us as excessive) analysing the fourth act of *Les Huguenots* and praising it as an unsurpassable masterpiece. He declared that this "German fellow-countryman" of his, whom he compared with Gluck and even with Mozart, had brought contemporary French opera to the peak of achievement—and called himself Meyerbeer's "subject, eternally devoted to you with heart and blood".[13]

Mendelssohn was not so susceptible. Glittering orchestration could not blind him. The "heroic sexuality" that played so large a part in Meyerbeer's works disgusted him, violating as it did a deep streak in his nature. This innate chasteness of Mendelssohn's was one of his ties with Robert Schumann. After attending a performance of Meyerbeer's *Le Prophète*, Schumann laconically noted the title in his diary and inscribed a graveyard cross after it. This was the same Schumann who felt that *Tannhäuser* was not only "indecent" but also *Meyerbeerian*.[14] Yet if the libretto of *Le Prophète* had not contained so dubious a mixture of religion, eroticism and communism, Schumann would unquestionably have admired the music.

Mendelssohn's accounts of Parisian musical life aroused considerable apprehension at 3 Leipziger Strasse, for his father was still hoping that Felix would some day become a Paris "opera man". Evidently Felix had learned nothing since his earlier stay in Paris at the age of sixteen, when he had written to his sister Fanny (9 May 1825):

> The land of milk and honey? Reconsider, I beg you. Are you in Paris or am I? I really ought to know the place better than you! Is it like me to judge music out of prejudice? And even if it were: is Rode prejudiced when he says to me: "C'est ici une dégringolade musicale!" Is Neukomm prejudiced when he says to me: "Here the public understands and enjoys nothing but variations." And are ten thousand others who denounce Paris prejudiced? You, you are the prejudiced one, because you won't believe my altogether unpartisan reports but insist on clinging to

[12] F. Mendelssohn-Bartholdy: *Briefe aus den Jahren 1830–47*. Leipzig, 1861.

[13] J. Kapp: *Meyerbeer*. Stuttgart–Berlin, 1924.

[14] R. Schumann: *Gesammelte Schriften über Musik und Musiker*. Leipzig, 1891.

a pretty dream of Paris as an Eldorado fashioned according to your own fantasies.

It was true, of course, that a good many foreigners could not abide Parisian musical life for all too obvious reasons. But how did Felix Mendelssohn feel about those aspects of French music in 1831 which were not Meyerbeer or of the Meyerbeer school? How did he feel about the most engaging contribution the French had made to Europe, French light opera? What about Daniel François Esprit Auber,[15] the great master of comic operas, whose works had long been given in Berlin? Even the intransigent Wagner who in those days called "bombast and pedantry the arch-evils of German opera" (this from Wagner!),[16] was so enchanted by the realism of French light opera that he wrote in 1836: "From Grétry to Auber *dramatic truth* has remained one of the main principles of the French." No such tributes are to be found in Mendelssohn's letters. Nor any comments on Adolphe Adam's overture to *Si j'étais Roi* or his rendering of the tramp of horses through the village in *Postillon de Longjumeau*.[17]

Felix understood this type of opera so ill that in a conversation with young Gounod, who was later to compose his great *Faust*, he contended that the French nation had no future in opera at all. The French ought to apply their energies to composing oratorios, he said! Were they to do penance, then? It would have been hard for any critic to make a worse mistake. Plainly, a man of Mendelssohn's tastes belonged in England, which would always take him in with open arms, as composer or conductor. And, in fact, at the mere mention of England Felix would shiver rapturously.[18] True, for the past two generations the country had brought forth no great musicians. But it had produced two immortal songs: *The Last Rose of Summer* (on which Mendelssohn wrote some very fine variations and which Friedrich von Flotow later incorporated into his light opera *Martha*) and Bishop's *Home, sweet Home*, which many decades later was to become a beacon light for Sousa and American music.[19]

To Mendelssohn, England was life itself, was greatness, activity. There was a land of men, no morass of womenfolk. The English heroes and English scenes of Walter Scott's novels were the darlings of the Continent.

[15] H. Weber: *Daniel François Esprit Auber*. Zurich, 1881.
[16] R. Wagner: op. cit.
[17] B. Pougin: *Adolphe Adam*. Paris, 1867.
[18] C. Graves: "Some Recollections". *The Times*. London, 1894.
[19] J. P. Sousa: *Marching Along*. Boston, 1928.

In Italy Donizetti wrote *Lucia di Lammermoor,* and in *La Donna del Lago* Rossini tried his hand at Scott's "The Lady of the Lake". In Germany Heinrich Marschner leaned heavily on *Ivanhoe* for his opera *Templer und Jüdin.* And in the days of Victoria's coronation Schumann wrote his stormiest youthful work, the *Symphonic Études*—with the magnificent variation, "Proud England, rejoice!" He dedicated it to an Englishman, young William Sterndale Bennett.

VICTOR HUGO AND HORACE VERNET

Mendelssohn has been rebuked for not knowing that the Paris he was visiting was also the Paris of Victor Hugo.[1] But Mendelssohn could not have had the historical perspective that informs Hugo von Hofmannsthal's famous essay written in 1901.[2] Hugo's heroic role still lay in the future: his seventeen-year-long exile, during the reign of Napoleon III, and his triumphal return to exercise the moral leadership of the late nineteenth century.

The Victor Hugo whom Mendelssohn knew was a wild and grotesque author, a kind of Meyerbeer in poetry and prose. His two early novels, *Han d'Islande* and *Bug-Jargal,* abounded with that class of deformed beings, hunchbacks, sadists and power-mad dreamers who play so large a part in French literature. His volume of poetry, *Les Orientales,* purported to celebrate the struggle of Greece against Turkey; its real impact lay in its voluptuous description of a dream-Orient and its portrait of the beauties of the harem. His *Marion Delorme* (1829) deals with a courtesan transfigured by a pure love: the first appearance of this theme upon the stage. Then, on 25th February 1830, came the première of Victor Hugo's *Hernani*—which turned out to be a tremendous and deliberate theatrical scandal. The theatre was the scene of impassioned outcries—the whole demonstration being engineered by Hugo's disciple Théophile Gautier.[3] After the battle over *Hernani,* the reign of classicism was overthrown. Henceforth *romantisme* held the field; Delacroix rightly commented: "Qui dit romantisme, dit art moderne."[4]

[1] P. Levin: *Victor Hugo.* Copenhagen, 1902.
[2] H. v. Hofmannsthal: *Versuch über Victor Hugo.* Berlin, 1901.
[3] P. de Saint-Victor: *Victor Hugo.* Paris, 1885.
[4] *Delacroix devant ses Contemporains.* Paris, 1886.

No doubt Mendelssohn observed—for he was almost a greater reader of books than Wagner or Schumann—how anti-romantic (for a German!) French romanticism was. The difference did not lie in the French partiality for harshly horrible, pathological elements—for German romanticism went in for that also; the Germans after all had E. T. A. Hoffmann, whom the French adopted as their favourite German author a few decades after his death.[5] French romanticism was linked to highly practical aims. It was nostalgically pro-Napoleon, and not at all disinclined to reversing the *status quo* achieved by the Anglo-German victory. This was why French poets and musicians treated the occupation of Algeria and the victory over Abd-el-Kader as a great triumph;[6] in the next few years France was almost literally flooded with Oriental paintings, poems and hymns. When Johann Strauss the Elder brought his orchestra to France in 1835, he could not present his programme until he had led off with the "Marseillaise". "Vive la France! Vive l'armée! Vive le général Damrémont, le vainqueur de Constantine!" the Strassburg audience cried.[7] The triumphal return of Napoleon's remains and their interment in the Invalides was only a few years in the future (1840).

Art had to have political overtures if it were to stand a chance in the France of that period—and Victor Hugo perfectly exemplified this axiom. Poor Mendelssohn could never have understood an art of this sort. For him, art was something pure, outside controversy. Since he lacked any knowledge of the conflict from which Hugo's poems were born, the poems awoke no echo in his heart. He found them affected and hollow. Later, Hofmannsthal showed almost inspired insight, when with one stroke he uncovered the historical truth that underlay so much of Hugo's work.[8] Hugo had not been lying; it was all authentic; it could all be traced to his childhood experience. His father, a high army officer, had moved into conquered Spain under King Joseph Bonaparte. But the country was never wholly conquered; the menacing and mysterious Spanish treated the French occupying forces as upstarts.[9] The years in Spain account for much that is strongest in Hugo's imaginative creations: thus Hernani, Ruy Gomez, Ruy Blas, all show a Spanish-Gothic Moorish sultriness. All these characters, Hofmannsthal points out, "were antitheses of themselves, simultaneously possessed an alien and a native being, lived

[5] W. Harich: *E. Th. A. Hoffmann*. Berlin, 1921.
[6] A. Nettement: *Histoire de la conquête d'Alger*. Paris, 1856.
[7] H. E. Jacob: *Johann Strauss, Vater und Sohn*. Hamburg, 1956.
[8] H. v. Hofmannsthal: op. cit.
[9] E. Depuy: *La Jeunesse de Victor Hugo*. Paris, 1902.

in a jungle of disguises, of changed and concealed names, of mistaken killings and poignant insights—all this enveloped in mysterious etiquette and glorious taboos. . . ."[10] Even the Hunchback of Notre Dame belonged to Hugo's childhood experience. On his first morning in his Madrid boarding school a hunchback had come to help him dress; a hunchback attired in a red linen jacket, breeches of blue velvet, and yellow stockings —what a livery! When the pupils were annoyed with this servant they called out to him, "*Corcova!* Hunchback!" When they were pleased, they used the diminutive: *Corcoveta.* And meanwhile the cripple's eyes were clouded by profound grief and abysmal scorn.

Adultery and poisoning, mistaken identities, nobility of spirit and bombast of language—the whole crazy structure came tumbling down upon Mendelssohn when, in Leipzig in 1839, he suddenly found himself forced to read Victor Hugo's *Ruy Blas* and compose an overture for it. The assignment had to be completed in a few days; it was needed for the theatre's pension fund. "I read the play", he wrote to his mother; "it is so utterly horrible and beneath anyone's dignity that it is simply incredible." And then he wrote an overture that is one of his most enchanting and imperishable creations.

After four lento bars, with all the strings silent, the *allegro molto* of the flutes and strings begins in tripping semicircles

which impart to the whole work a curious gaiety in the minor mode. The motif is entirely without pathos—a quality Hugo would have wanted— but it incorporates the macabre drollery of the play, which is what gives it its Shakespearian overtones. Again and again the woodwinds try to assert their independence; the bassoon struts a grotesque dance. Mendelssohn's dotted capriccio notes come in, and others scurry along to cover them up; a staccato begins just where it is not expected; suddenly there is a kettle-drum fortissimo; and before the listener has fully realized what is happening, everything is woven up again in the semicircle of the initial motif.

[10] H. v. Hofmannsthal: op. cit.

... Most wonderful of all are the figures of high-spirited laughter, in the second part, with the oboe:

Was there, then, a streak in Felix's personality that gave the lie to what he had written to his mother? Was there something in him that actually loved this play? But what do we know of an artist's sympathies and antipathies? All such feelings fall by the wayside when "the spirit calls". And here the spirit had called. Mendelssohn's overture has become so integral to the play that *Ruy Blas* is never performed without it.

Mendelssohn had, altogether, an innate sense of balance of a sort possessed by few other geniuses. The more he rejected Gallicism as "shallow and orgiastic", the readier he was to be delighted, even carried away, by the charm and manliness of individual Frenchmen. Henriette Sontag, who came to France for a guest performance in 1851—long after she had left the stage—wrote a few sentences which perfectly expressed Mendelssohn's feeling: "The English nation is magnificent, the individual chilly, egotistical, calculating. In France it is just the other way round. The whole nation is wretched, the individual *charmant, spirituel, facile à vivre, aimable*."[11] Mendelssohn had discovered the same thing. Hard though he tried to resist it, he was utterly won over by a certain kind of French virility and bravado. Had he lived until 1900 he would have found these characteristics epitomized in Rostand's *Cyrano*. As it was, he encountered them in a painter, the remarkable Horace Vernet, whom he met in 1830 at a ball in Rome given by Prince Torlonia. He describes him as a "little skinny Frenchman with a mane of gray hair and the ribbon of the Legion of Honour". A month later Felix, at a

[11] H. Kühner: *Genien des Gesanges aus dem Zeitalter der Klassik und Romantik*. Basel, 1951.

smaller gathering, played from *Don Giovanni* for him. As might have
been predicted, the duel scene with its whistling rapiers

was Horace Vernet's favourite music. Afterwards Felix fell to improvising. Vernet rose and whispered something very odd to him: "We must
make an exchange now, Maître—for you see, I can improvise *also*!" Felix
raised his eyebrows but obediently followed the painter into the adjoining
room. "I have a canvas ready stretched," Vernet said. "Have you a little
time for me?" Smiling mysteriously, and then turning suddenly modest,
he said that he would have to pull himself together a bit for this improvisation, for he was not really an improviser. But it was bound to turn out
well, wasn't it? And before Felix could object, the painter began sketching at a breakneck pace, and turned out one of his most apt and charming
masterpieces.[12]

The portrait is extraordinarily true to character. If we look at a whole
flock of Mendelessohn portraits (Max F. Schneider has assembled seventeen of them in one small volume[13]) we are struck by the realism of the
brilliant painter of battle scenes. A good many of the paintings of Mendelssohn, even including one by his brother-in-law Wilhelm Hensel done
in 1829, show him wearing an inquiring look which was hardly characteristic. But Vernet, the romantic, painted him accurately. The brow is
Moses Mendelssohn's handsome brow, which descended to all the Mendelssohns. The lower eyelids are somewhat swollen—a trait no other

[12] F. Mendelssohn-Bartholdy: *Briefe aus den Jahren 1830–1847*. Leipzig, 1861.
[13] M. F. Schneider: *Felix Mendelssohn im Bildnis*. Basel, 1953.

painter had noticed. The mouth is small and pleasant, but by no means feminine; it is the mouth of a man accustomed to talking a good deal. The most handsome features are the dark, arched eyebrows: the eyebrows of a listener, and yet having also a close relationship with the mouth. The hair is curly, but not excessively so. The most curious aspect of the portrait is that the face seems to be bathed in sweat. As a matter of fact, Felix was perspiring when it was done—he was wearing too warm clothes. The account of this incident that Felix sent home was dated 17th January 1831. He reported that the winter was already over and the young girls of Rome were wearing violets and bunches of anemone in the streets. But he himself had not counted on such an early spring and was dressed in vest, cravat and *redingote* as though he had gone to Russia rather than Italy. His costume is faithfully reproduced in the painting.

An enviable fellow, this sharp-eyed Vernet. Felix watched his behaviour with astonishment: "Everyone can learn something from him. He is the very personification of ease and nonchalance in creative work. The moment he sees a figure that says something to him, he poses it, and while we others are still considering whether the picture deserves to be called beautiful, whether it should be admired or criticized, he has already done something new and given our aesthetic standard another jolt." The way of it could not be learned, Mendelssohn went on to say. But "the principle is a splendid one; and the serenity that arises out of it, and the eternal freshness of the work, are quite matchless."[14] The location of Vernet's studio was easy to discover. He lived amid a continual din; wherever the most shouting was going on, or dogs were barking and trumpets blaring, there he would be found painting. "The most magnificent disorder prevails everywhere—guns, a hunting horn, a long-tailed monkey, palettes, several recently shot hares, dead rabbits; all over the walls finished and half-finished pictures." Portraits of the Pope or of a group of Moors, of Cain and Abel, of Felix Mendelssohn and the sculptor Thorwaldsen, and finally pictures of the studio itself, hung about this studio. The nonchalance of it all appealed tremendously to Felix. Did he not have that same quality of nonchalance himself, and had he not fought too hard against it with his affection for the dead, for fugues, for church music and Bach? Mightn't it have been a good thing after all to be French and rely on nothing but colours and temperament? But of course it was impossible for him to shed his own skin.

Some nine years later (5th April 1840), when Fanny Mendelssohn Hensel met Horace Vernet at a party in Rome given by Ingres, she was

---

[14] Mendelssohn-Bartholdy: op. cit.

fascinated by him much as her brother had been. The affair was not a masked ball, but Vernet had just come over from Algiers, and made a point of dressing like an Arab. With his sun-browned skin, he might almost be taken for one. He would talk of nothing but Algiers and Tunis, for he insisted: "I am an Oriental and only pretending to be here in Rome."[15] Fanny felt that he radiated the grand casualness of the French character, as well as the torrid sun of the East. The Hensels had an animated conversation with Vernet, who had taken it into his head that Hensel must come back with him to Algiers at once. The future of art lay in Africa, he told them. And a flustered Fanny wrote in her diary: "Wilhelm really might have done it. . . . Why do we Germans always put things off! Always miss the right moment! Always come too late. *How hard it is for us to rise above our times, our families, our own selves.* This affair moves me and stirs me to the quick. . . ."[16]

SALON MUSIC?

Felix would not have subscribed to Fanny's complaint that it was so hard to rise above the times. He was a piano virtuoso, and his piano compositions were among the most successful of the age. His *Songs without Words* were precisely what the times, the middle class, the salons, demanded of him. But did this mean that he wrote salon music? Far from it. He merely adjusted, as Schubert had before him and Schumann and Chopin along with him, to a cult of the small form which was based upon the existence of the salon.

We should not think of a Biedermeier salon as something soft and enervating. It was not an overfurnished room, as the rococo boudoir had been, with its profusion of cushions and silk hangings. Since the time of Napoleon the European bourgeoisie, especially in Germany, had become impoverished. Hence they welcomed the new and plainer style of furniture which had come over from England. The idea was that rooms could be attractive without an undue show of luxury if the reflection of a garden were allowed to fill a small apartment, and if the walls were papered with sunlight. As a pupil was to write of Moritz von Schwind, the painter, decorator and friend of Schubert: "To accomplish much with

[15] A. Dayot: *Les Vernet.* Paris, 1898.
[16] S. Hensel: *Die Familie Mendelssohn 1729–1847.* Berlin, 1879.

little was his watchword in art and life."[1] It was the watchword of an entire school. The fundamental principle of the Biedermeier style, "beauty is simple, simplicity inexpensive", created a new look in interiors. Curtains were of cotton, the same material as women's clothes. Wood showed its natural colours. Green, pink, yellow—flower colours made their way indoors, into salons in which the grand pianos stood awaiting the touch of fingers. ... Lightness, grace, comfort, these were the dominant qualities. There were no longer the *Appassionatas* and *Pathéthiques*, the stormy griefs and blows of destiny that characterized the embattled decades when Napoleon made all Europe tumble.

Space creates its own special kind of music. Cathedrals, market-places and theatres do so; so do military terrains over which armies march to a set beat. The salon had its own music. Schumann, Mendelssohn and Chopin, not to speak of their friends and imitators, provided music tailored for the salon. Within the four walls of the family domain, this music was cherished. The atmosphere, however, though intimate, was never suffocating. The windows stood open to the garden. Mendelssohn used to add little notations to his compositions, such as "to be played in the open air", "to be sung in the open air". In this, Anglo-German taste was in no wise like that of the French, who revelled in psychology and never had this cult of nature. When we read a description of Schumann's music in a Maupassant novel written as much as fifty years later—*Fort comme la Mort* (1889), we cannot escape the impression that Maupassant has missed the point, and substituted paper flowers for real ones.

Music had never been so natural as it was in 1830, never more sincere in its love of the newly discovered small form. Such music was a far cry from the classical sonata developed by Haydn, Mozart and Beethoven. The sonata was a large form of four movements (Allegro, Andante, Minuet or Scherzo, Presto) in which the classicists had fully expressed themselves. Despite enormous differences of temperament, choice of thematic material, ideas and accent, they had all treated the sonata as a *strict* form. From the very first movement it became evident that no arbitrariness was allowed: the first theme was always set in the fundamental key, the second in the dominant or parallel key. After the exposition came the development, the recapitulation and the coda. In these works there was no more freedom than there had been in the fugues of a hundred years before.[2]

Romanticism did not abandon the classical sonata out of a mood of

[1] M. von Schwind: *Briefe und Bilder*. Stuttgart, 1923.
[2] H. Leichentritt: *Musikalische Formenlehre*. Leipzig, 1952.

irresponsibility.[3] Schubert was still eager and able to master the sonata form. But the inner tension of the "moment musical" which Schubert had invented was intolerant of these long elaborations and elaborate lengths. It was as though something within Schubert had spoken: "No! Life is too short. Every motif has the same right to existence. We cannot develop all of them in an orderly fashion." The age of unrestricted "inspiration" had come.

Nevertheless, the new masters were aware that every form has its own exigencies. Even as allowance was made for momentality, the piano music of 1830 developed an apparent counterpoise: the *étude* raised to the level of art. It would be better to call it "study". For such masterly *études* as those written by Czerny or Moscheles are anything but mere finger exercises. That they developed the flexibility of the fingers was a side-effect. In reality they were more in the nature of "characteristic pieces", a genre which had really been initiated by the sonata master Muzio Clementi, the son of a Roman silversmith, who "made the piano sound silvery". He was famous throughout Europe for the gaiety and force of his pianistic studies, the so-called sonatinas which he collected and published in 1818 under the title of *Gradus ad Parnassum*. But force was not quite what was wanted in the Biedermeier salon. The new piano music was more in the nature of a "dreamy diary-piece". Here was music which luxuriated in its depth of feeling. Chopin's *Preludes*, Schubert's *Impromptus*, Mendelssohn's *Songs without Words*, Schumann's *Carnival*, *Kreisleriana* and *Fantasies*, all belong to this psychologically so significant genre.

Perhaps it should be traced to one John Field,[4] a remarkable though not enormous talent; an Anglo-Irishman born in Dublin in 1782, who later became Clementi's pupil in London and died in Moscow in 1837. Field spoke of "standing music". He put forth the theory that the only real melodies were "melodies in a state of rest". It was possible, he contended, to hold a single tone on the piano (he was a first-rate pianist) for so long that the impression of sculptural calm would be achieved. This device was crucial to the effectiveness of the desired short form. Also significant was Field's contention that "composing is possible only at night". The bustle of day, he held, made tonal truth unattainable. This same thought is expressed in Novalis's *Hymns to Night*:

> I turn away, turn to the holy, inexpressible, mysterious night. The world lies far off—buried in a deep vault—where it had been is waste and solitude. . . . Must the morning always return again?

[3] P. Egerth: *Die Romantische Klaviersonata*. 1934.
[4] G. Smith: *John Field*. London, 1901.

Will earthly things never lose their power? Accursed bustle blights the celestial approach of winged night. Will it never be that love's secret sacrifice will burn forever? Time was measured out for the light; but the dominion of night is eternal and infinite.

In that spirit, Field wrote nocturnes. Perhaps they are forgotten today, but Chopin knew them and the world knows what Chopin made of them.[5]

There was another ancestor of salon music besides John Field. It is hard to believe the name—but it was *Beethoven*. Beethoven found himself encumbered with a host of motifs which did not lend themselves to regular use. However, he worked them up as best he could. The end result were the three collections of "trivia" which were issued under the names of *Seven Bagatelles, Eleven New Bagatelles* and *Six Bagatelles* (opus 33, 119, 126). At the time of their publication they brought the composer nothing but grief.[6] For his admirers among his contemporaries did not understand how a man of Beethoven's force and passion could squander his powers on such nonsense. His own publisher, Peters in Leipzig, sent opus 119 back to him, with the comment that it was "altogether unworthy" of Beethoven. (Significantly enough, it had to be published by a Parisian house. The French were more hospitable towards anything experimental.) Hans von Bülow later wrote that these minor works of Beethoven were as great as his major works, that there was such a wealth of imagination and charming subtlety in them that no one should presume to speak of a Homer nodding. But this was in the heyday of the Biedermeier era, when salon music had come into its own and was challenging the cult of passion —which is to say, the other Beethoven. Before that the *Bagatelles* could not have been appreciated.

Friedrich Hebbel, a foe of Biedermeier, had only recently written: "A Beethoven symphony and a thunderstorm rest upon the same premises."[7] The *Bagatelles* rested upon altogether different premises; nevertheless, Beethoven was extremely fond of them. We do not know whether or how he performed them publicly. Perhaps, if he did, he did not do well with them. People who heard Beethoven for the first time did not think him a good pianist. It took a second or a third hearing to realize what sort of man was playing. He did not go in for little tricks of the trade, ignored the refinements of technique.[8] But the same "thrusting and pressing"

[5] F. Niecks: *Frederick Chopin as a Man and a Musician*. London, 1888,
[6] P. Bekker: *Beethovens Bagatellen*. Munich, 1920.
[7] F. Hebbel: *Tagebücher*. Berlin, 1885–87.
[8] O. Bie: *Das Klavier und seine Meister*. Munich, 1898.

which E. T. A. Hoffmann singled out as forming the real content of his symphonies, dominated his technique as a pianist. He was a "naturalist in piano-playing". He conceived all technique in terms of the rhythm. This rhythm, however, was determined in his mind by spiritual, psychological elements—and that (along with a hundred other things) set him apart from the school of temperament, in the sense Liszt gave to the word. If Beethoven had carried out his intention of writing a "School of Piano", his pedagogue would have had little to do "with the fingers and the wrist".[9]

Perhaps Beethoven wisely preferred to have his *Bagatelles*, with their tranquil rhythms, played by others. Certainly we cannot picture him rendering a *Moment Musical* or an *Impromptu* of Schubert, with their strangely intimate and delicate alternations of harmonic darks and lights. It took the Biedermeier age, it took the Viennese friends of Schubert, to do justice to this master of pianistic miniatures. Germany was quite slow to take up the Schubert cult, although once the cult reached there it became firmly implanted in the circle around Schumann.

Schumann, the poet of the piano, was by no means in direct line of descent from Schubert. Not only his melody, but his harmony is of a different order. The alpine broken sixth and the typical Schubertian third[10]—that is to say, the truly Austrian elements—were alien to Schumann, the Saxon. But Schumann's *Papillons*, breaking out of their silk cocoons in the Biedermeier salon, had a Schubert waltz as their antecedent. Few of Schumann's listeners knew what the circling and fluttering of these butterflies meant to Schumann. Only friends with whom he had been corresponding could have known that he had been steeping himself in his beloved Jean Paul's *Flegeljahre* when he wrote the music. The mood of the piece—a blend of highest seriousness and infinite laughter—was quite his own. Certainly Schumann misunderstood Schubert when, writing to Friedrich Wieck from Heidelberg in 1829, he explained: "When I play Schubert, I feel as if I were reading a novel of Jean Paul's set to music." For Schubert was definitely no Jean Paul; the contrast between tobacco pouches, laundry lists, roasts of mutton and heaven-shaking ideas—a contrast Jean Paul revelled in—did not at all attract Schubert. He was too grave, too melancholic, plunged too deep in the sorrows of love. And there was nothing in the least philistine about his wonderful grace and the terpsichorean power of his forms.

Mendelssohn, the elegant cosmopolitan who brought the piano music

[9] Ibid.
[10] E. v. Hornbostel: *A Theory of Intervals*. London, no date.

of his age to its highest peak,[11] was also no philistine. Between 1840 and 1890 probably no piece of music was played so often as his *Songs without Words*. But what a curious title he had given them, with an airy manner à la Heine! Yet no title could be apter. For those forty-eight piano pieces were really based upon the song form; and it was equally true that anyone could write his own text to them. Now that the form has been sedulously imitated by composers of all nations, we can scarcely imagine how original the *Songs without Words* were to Mendelssohn's contemporaries.

"Songs without words? What can they be?" Moritz Hauptmann wrote in some alarm to the singer Franz Hauser.[12] "Is it possible? *Does Mendelssohn mean it seriously?*" And yet Hauptmann was the greatest theorist and contrapuntalist of his time, and in 1853 was to publish an important book on *The Nature of Harmony and Metrics*. Thus Mendelssohn's idea that piano pieces could be written in strict song form but without texts to accompany them—taken for granted today—was regarded by his age as a new discovery. It was, if nothing else, a romantic fusion of forms. The writing of these songs went on throughout the entire second creative period of his life. The first volume (opus 19) was published in 1834. Seven more series followed up to his death (opus 30, 38, 53, 62, 67, 85, 102). How was it that Mendelssohn so frequently returned to this diary form which might well seem the most private of all forms of music?

Unlike Wagner, who carried the practice of confession to almost monstrous lengths, Mendelssohn hardly ever attempted to explain his art to others. But he did make some important statements about the *Songs without Words*. In a remarkable letter to Marc André Souchay, a relative of his wife who was then in Lübeck, he wrote from Berlin on 15th October 1812:[13]

> People usually complain that music is so ambiguous; that they
> are doubtful as to what they should think when they hear it,
> whereas everyone understands words. For me, it is just the
> reverse. And that is so not only for whole speeches, but for single
> words also: they too seem to me so ambiguous, so indefinite, so
> open to misunderstanding in comparison with real music which
> fills one's soul with a thousand better things than words. To me,

[11] C. W. Wilkinson: *How to Interpret Mendelssohn's "Songs without Words"*. London, 1930.

[12] M. Hauptmann: *Briefe an Franz Hauser*. Leipzig, no date.

[13] M. F. Schneider and Willi Reich: *Felix Mendelssohn-Bartholdy*. Basel, 1947.

the music I love does not express thoughts too indefinite to be put into words, but too definite. . . .

If you ask me what I thought [in connection with one or another of the *Songs without Words*], I must say: the song itself as it stands. If, with one or the other of them, I had a specific word or specific words in mind, I should not like to give them these titles, because words do not mean the same to one person as they mean to another; only the song says the same thing, arouses the same feeling, in one person as in another—a feeling that, however, cannot be expressed in the same words.

Resignation, melancholy, praise of God, a foxhunt—these are words which everyone interprets differently. What is resignation to one person is melancholy to another; a third thinks of both as lifeless. For a man who loves hunting, the foxhunt and praise of God might well be equivalents; he would feel that the winding of horns was really and truly the right way to praise God. To us a foxhunt is merely a foxhunt, and no matter how much we discussed the matter, we would get nowhere. The word remains ambiguous; but in music we would understand one another rightly.

The incorruptible Hans von Bülow said bluntly of this music: "To me a *Song without Words* by Mendelssohn is just as classical as a poem of Goethe's." That the pieces are imbued with feeling for feeling's sake, in other words that they are highly sentimental, was not considered a defect by Mendelssohn's contemporaries. They admired the pithiness of the themes, the formal completeness and the perfection of pianistic style. A whole world of feeling had been captured with remarkable conciseness, without romantic vagueness; the image was clear and sharp. Mendelssohn's considerable gift for drawing—his artist brother-in-law Hensel called him a walking sketchbook—emerged in these songs.

Schumann's piano pieces surpassed Mendelssohn's in humour and surprise; Mendelssohn's surpassed those of his friend in flawless formal purity. And, it must be said again, in brevity. Since salon music was bland music, and could not seek effect by strong fortissimos and energetic overemphases, Mendelssohn's salon pieces might have been boring. But that was precisely what they were not—because their author possessed the secret of grace as had scarcely any other composer since Mozart.[14]

Mendelssohn habitually relaxed from composing by drawing. His travel sketches too—Max F. Schneider has collected the sketches of a trip in

[14] Wilkinson: op. cit.

Switzerland undertaken in 1842—show a distinct impulse toward realism. And his rendering of mountains, lakes and trees reveals a fondness for the miniature. This miniaturistic realism sometimes emerges in the piano pieces. As Felix said, he did not want to be confined by titles or "contents". Yet sometimes a song will not conceal its inspiration. Number 29 in A minor of his *Songs without Words* was really a Venetian Gondola Song in which the gondolier

returns, above the gently rising, plucking six-eight beats of the rocking water, as a tremendously forceful motif:

And similarly Number 34, in C major, is undeniably a Spinning Song. The nervously vibrating thread is clearly in evidence, the G trembling between A flat and F sharp:

What *does* that remind us of? In 1843 *The Flying Dutchman* was produced. It is interesting to compare the spinning songs of the two composers, Mendelssohn's little song for piano and the gigantic choral work
from the second act of Wagner's opera. Mendelssohn avoids large intervals
—why startle the listener! But Wagner very soon ventures an unexpected
leap of a ninth. He was not in the least interested in drawing and
miniaturist realism. What he wanted was expression at any cost.

But Mendelssohn clung to his dependable skill, and indeed his musical
skill remained unsurpassed. "He actually varied the simplest formal
pattern, ABA (without the trio), forty-two times in a succession of
inspired new variations, a brilliant demonstration of his command of
form," wrote Hugo Leichtentritt.[15] A student could learn much about
effective recapitulation by examining the manner in which Mendelssohn
arrived at a reprise. The return to the beginning at the end, and the
subtle thematic elaboration of the coda, still strike us as masterly,
Leichtentritt points out.

Granted. Yet it is strange that up to the beginnings of naturalism and
the victory of symphonic tone-poems (which, after all, Mendelssohn had
fathered), the *Songs without Words* were taken as representing the
essence of Mendelssohn. His contemporaries were victims of an amiable
deception, induced perhaps by the impressive manner in which Mendelssohn himself played these little pieces on the piano. Clara Schumann, who
should have known, regarded Felix Mendelssohn as the greatest pianist of
the age. His expressive power, she thought, far outranked Thalberg's
virtuosity. In a letter to her husband describing Felix at the piano, she
reported: "He played so consummately and with such fire that for a few
minutes I really could not restrain my tears. When all is said and done, he
remains for me the dearest pianist of all. . . ."[16]

It may be that the famous dreaminess and inner tranquillity of a
Mendelssohn passage strikes us as lacking in accentuation only because we
do not know the counterpressure the composer supplied in his own

[15] H. Leichtentritt: op. cit.
[16] B. Litzmann: *Clara Schumann.* Leipzig, 1925.

interpretations of these pieces. There was no sighing, no vagueness about
Mendelssohn's playing. His attack was vigorous, decisive and clear. He
even did without arpeggios, as Hans von Bülow observed with surprise.
Joseph Joachim marvelled at the way the composer could electrify these
pieces, almost from the first note he played. He praised Mendelssohn's
pungent staccatos and the remarkable effects he could extract from his
Spring Song, the most beautiful of the *Songs without Words* (opus 62,
No. 2) by the detached figures of the accompaniment:

   The reticence with which Brahms hid feelings simply did not exist in
Mendelssohn's time. The Biedermeier man loved sentiment and it was
no disgrace to give vent to feeling in the salon. Oscar Bie is surely unjust
when—though paying tribute to the technical brilliance, the broken
accompaniments, and the polyrhythmics of the *Songs without Words*—
he calls the whole "a goldsmith's kind of lyricism, lacking the disconcert-
ing honesty of a Bach or a Schubert". In point of fact, the hidden
presence of the baroque spirit of which Mendelssohn was so much the
partisan, kept many of the *Songs without Words* from melting away into
emotional vapidity. Schumann saw far deeper into the situation when he
spoke of Bach as his grammar which provided him with a moral framework. "The poetic, the humoristic, the profoundly combinatory quality
of modern music", Schumann wrote in 1840, "derives mostly from Bach.
The music of Mendelssohn, Bennett, Chopin, Hiller, in fact of all the
so-called Romantics, is far closer to Bach than to Mozart. Indeed, they all
know Bach very thoroughly. I myself daily make my confession to this

supreme master, with the aim of purging and strengthening myself through him."[17]

It is significant that Schumann names Mendelssohn first. For his supremacy was hardly contested. In general, the salon wanted no fugues, no well-tempered claviers. The salon wanted salon music: the good bourgeois did not ask where the composer went digging to find the elements he then worked up so artfully. If he satisfied the requirements of the salon, he was a power. More than anyone else Mendelssohn satisfied the requirements of the salon and so he was a great power, pianistically speaking, in the Germany of 1840. He would have been one on the basis of the *Songs without Words* alone. His *Rondo Brillant* for piano and orchestra (opus 29) would have made him one; and more than anything else, his seventeen *Variations Sérieuses* on the melancholy andante theme

which leads with chromatic insistence to transformations that dialectically combine simplicity and virtuoso *élan* and are resolved at last in a scintillating Finale. Of these *Variations Sérieuses* Moritz Mayer-Mahr wrote in 1924: "They occupy the same position in the whole of his piano *oeuvre* as the *Symphonic Études* do for Schumann, the *Goldberg Variations* for Bach, and Beethoven's paraphrases of a theme by Diabelli. These *Variations Sérieuses* form the romantic bridge from the classicists to Liszt, to Brahms's variations on Handel and Reger's paraphrases of Bach and Telemann."[18]

[17] R. Schumann: *Gesammelte Schriften über Musik und Musiker*. Leipzig, 1891.
[18] M. Mayer-Mahr: *Mendelssohn's "Variations Sérieuses"*. Berlin, 1924.

Salon music began to degenerate even during the Biedermeier era. Part
of the reason for this was the onslaught of the "New Germans". Partly,
too, Liszt was hammering at the gates. Liszt, after all, was a "Paganini
without a fiddle" whose wildly temperamental pounding at the keys
shattered the miniature forms favoured by Mendelssohn and Schumann.
But mainly salon music decayed inwardly when Kalkbrenner (the
developer of modern octave-playing and pedalling) and those like him
began writing unspeakable piano potpourris "since we are no longer
bound by the sonata". Today no military band would dare to play such
pieces. Kalkbrenner was once asked what he had been thinking of when
he wrote *Charmes de Berlin*. He replied, in a broad Berlin accent: "Well,
you see, the whole thing is a dream, a kind of reverie; it starts off with
love, if you like, passion, desperation, despair, and it ends up with a
military march."[19]

The audiences did not protest against this vulgar claptrap because
Kalkbrenner was one of the most celebrated pianists of the era. He was
protected by the power of the salons and the sympathy of women. The
salon was indeed omnipotent, as Schubert demonstrated in a strange way
only ten months before his death. He wrote a four-movement sonata, but
then dissected it into four impromptus in deference to the taste of the
time. Robert Schumann uncovered this incredible tale.[20] Present-day
biographers of Schubert, such as Alfred Einstein[21] and August Vetter,[22]
also vouch for its truthfulness.

What about Chopin, then? Chopin who personified the year 1830, who
was the echo in France of the Polish uprisings? Surely the passion and
political nature of his music would have branded him as the antithesis of
a Biedermeier personality. Nevertheless, there was no help for it. If he
wanted to be heard in the salons, he had to address his age in Biedermeier
language, with muted accents and expiring airs. Perhaps he never could
have achieved that tone had he not been able to fall back, especially in his
Préludes, on "Slavic monotony" and the melancholy fatalism that came
so naturally to him.[23] In spite of all the surprises of rhythm, in spite of
the boldest chromaticism and harmony, how deliberately monotone is
such a piece as No. 15 of the *Préludes*, the so-called "Raindrop Étude" in
D flat major. It has a sweetness, even a banality, of which we would
scarcely have believed Chopin capable: proof that even this intense in-

[19] O. Bie: op. cit.
[20] R. Schumann: op. cit.
[21] A Einstein: *Schubert*. Zürich, 1952.
[22] A. Vetter: *Der Klassiker Schubert*. Leipzig, 1953.
[23] W. and P. Rehberg: *Chopin*. Zürich, 1949.

ventor of the mazurka and the cracovienne was forced to bow to the superior might of the salon. And Chopin was very well aware of this cultural force. In a letter to a friend (14th November 1829) in which he speaks of one of the polonaises he had composed at the estate of Prince Radziwill he writes: "I have written an Alla Polacca with violoncello. It is nothing but a bit of glittering tinsel *for the salon, for the ladies.* . . ."[24]

[24] B. Scharlitt: *Friedrich Chopins gesammelte Briefe.* Leipzig, 1911.

BOOK FOUR

THE ASCENT TO THE SUMMIT

Mendelssohn was one of those halcyon composers who because of his lighter, purer, more radiant soul was quickly forgotten—the beautiful interlude in German music.

—FRIEDRICH NIETZSCHE

Richard Wagner used to call Mendelssohn (in conversation, at least) the greatest specifically musical genius the world has had since Mozart.

—HANS VON BÜLOW

I would gladly give all my works if I had succeeded in writing a piece like the "Hebrides" overture!

—JOHANNES BRAHMS

The real day of revolution, the nativity of the New Music, came at the première of *The Flying Dutchman* in Dresden. When the winds sounded their first chords, the music of the past was extinguished, and along with it the generations of major and minor. For the third was missing from those rumbling, hollow fifths:

This was virtually forbidden. If such effects had occurred in music heretofore, they had been unintentional, or else meant for special colour, a disharmony to be resolved by harmony again. But they had never been presented as a tonal ideology, as the doctrine of the void-in-itself. This motif of the phantom ship is an evocation of water and air; human beings are not yet present. They remain to be created. The human world is absent until the redemption motif rises above that of the sea in a congenial F major, and struggles with the motif of the curse:

This has a familiar ring—and is indeed familiar from Weber's *Freischütz*. But as Wagner uses it here, it is in utter accord with the dramatic situation. Senta hopes to save the Dutchman and trusts to the same consolations that Agathe offers Max.

The Dutchman and Senta are human. But they are also elements. And consequently Wagner needed to create an elemental music to do them justice.

O laß   Hoff - nung   dich be-le - ben,

und ver - trau - e, ver - trau-e dem Ge-schick!

We may assume that technique is a necessary component of all expression. But it was something new for a composer to deform technique in
order to make it capable of expressing the raw materials of the cosmos.
When Richard Wagner died in 1883, Algernon Charles Swinburne wrote
an epitaph in which the composer is identified with the wild elements
themselves:

> ... Winds that make moan and triumph, skies that bend,
> Thunders, and sound of tides in gulf and firth,
> Spake through his spirits of speech....

For in his music he had churned up the depths of the sea, the night, the
storm and the thunder: had created chaos out of which form arose again.[1]
    The dramaturgical artistry with which Wagner developed his music in
The Flying Dutchman, making it pour from its single source into every
scene, excluding any alien colouring, refusing the help of any graceful
operatic flourishes which might bridge a difficult transition—this drama-
turgic artistry was almost greater than the music itself. The core of the
whole work of art was Senta's "Ballad of the Dutchman", which she
sings to the other maidens while they are at their spinning. All the motifs
of the opera are contained in this one song.[2] Even a seemingly spontaneous lyric such as Steuermann later sings, with its yearning exclama-
tion: "Ach lieber Südwind, blase doch!" is actually fabricated out of the
beginning of Senta's ballad. And the sailors' dance is a variation on the
same theme—though this is cleverly concealed behind a reminiscence of
the Tsar's hymn, "God be the Emperor's Shield"—which Wagner knew
from his experience as a conductor in Russian Riga.[3] Similarly, the
rousing, masculine:

[1] M. Moser: *Richard Wagner in der englischen Literatur des 19. Jahrhunderts.* Bern, 1938.
    [2] A. Einstein: *Geschichte der Musik.* Zürich, 1953.
    [3] J. A. Glebow: *Boye Zarya Krani.* Petersburg, 1895.

Fürch-ten we-der Wind noch bö - sen Strand,

wol - len heu - te 'mal recht lu - stig sein!

is one more variation of the Dutchman motif.

The astonishing congruence between the drama and the music was what was hardest for the Biedermeier era to comprehend. *Rienzi* with its clash of arms, that opera of the Roman tribune, pleased them more—it was more in the vein of the heroics to which they had been accustomed from Gluck to Spontini. But *The Flying Dutchman* was a literary production of such high quality that it could have been performed on the stage without music. It was Wagner's first excursion into the theme of doomed passion. For just as Senta is the Dutchman's fate, so he is unconditionally hers. From the moment she confronts him, nothing else matters—neither father nor bridegroom, neither the ties of blood nor the biddings of affinity—in the face of such compulsion.

That compulsion is elemental—and if it were to be set to music, the music had to be elemental too. The aspect of Wagner that was later to become so disturbing—his over-estimation of folklore—had not yet entered in. In *The Flying Dutchman* nothing is sheer prop, or worse still, sheer ritual, as so much is in *Lohengrin*—where a great to-do is made over the fact that some of the Saxon knights drive the point of their swords into the ground in front of them, while the men of Brabant lay their swords flat. (As though that had anything whatsoever to do with the truth of the music and of the theme!)

The Flying Dutchman needed none of the trappings garnered from historical studies to be convincing; its music was as sublimely ruthless as only the elements can be, and now and then the human soul. Wind and sea appear in the *Dutchman* with primordial violence, just as later fire and thunder were to appear in the *Ring*. In *Tristan* the elemental power is Eros, the "undefeated in the battle", as Sophocles called it. For Brangäne's love-potion is a force far more ancient than any archaeological trappings, than any national modes and customs.[4]

The unnatural length, the sham infinitude of narratives and dialogues,

[4] L. Spitzer: *Wagner's Tristan, a Method of Interpreting Literature.* Northampton, Mass., 1949.

made their appearances in *Tannhäuser*; in the *Ring of the Nibelungs* they reached such a pitch that they became a real menace. Had Wagner only been a dilettante as a poet—as many persons think—everything would have been much simpler.[5] For then the musical giant would have sent the poet packing. But Wagner was in fact a talented poet,[6] and never stopped being one even where he made serious mistakes—such as reviving the long-outmoded Germanic alliterative verse, in order to simulate the simplicity of the Eddas. The result was that his highly complex orchestra fought the alliteration with every breath. He was a poet in *Meistersinger* too, and produced a credible imitation of the wooden explicitness of sixteenth-century verse, while at the same time the brilliant and warm music makes raucous fun of the inept poetry. But precisely because he remained a poet in spite of all his mistakes, Wagner made monstrous demands upon his music, which was after all his greatest gift. The two did not get on very well together. The poet insisted upon demonstrating the psychological verity of his epic subjects; his heroes had to explain how they felt about one another, why they did this or that, and forebore to do something else. But the dramatic musician, who really knew what he was about, who had at his disposal an orchestra greater even than Beethoven's —Wagner the dramatic musician had no patience with his approach, took the bit in his teeth and tried to shake off Wagner the poet.[7]

However, none of these cross purposes came to the surface in *The Flying Dutchman*, Wagner's most perfect work. There word was music and music word. The two were not yet at war with one another. Those who attended the première of the opera on 2nd January 1843 both understood it and did not understand it. Wagner had been extremely anxious at the rehearsals, and with good reason. The great dramatic singer Wilhelmine Schröder-Devrient had shrugged and declared that she did not hope for much in the role of Senta: "I don't know what to do with the stuff." At the beginning of the ballad she actually stumbled. The chorus of spinners also did not come right.[8] But the ensemble dominated everything. The flustered, incredulous master (he was not yet "great Richard") was called before the curtain again and again, got tangled in the furnishings of the spinning room and took a tumble. The curtain fell. But the reverberations of the applause reached Berlin, and a few months later the work was performed there. In the director's box sat a man who hurried backstage while the audience was still roaring applause and

[5] E. Ludwig: *Wagner oder die Entzauberten*. Berlin, 1913.
[6] P. Stefan: *Die Feindschaft gegen Wagner*. Berlin, 1912.
[7] H. Bulthaupt: *Dramaturgie der Oper*. Leipzig, 1902.
[8] G. Ernest: *Richard Wagner, sein Leben und Schaffen*. Berlin, 1915.

showered congratulations on the successful composer. He was a man with a pale complexion, light sidewhiskers, dark eyes: the composer Felix Mendelssohn.

THE HEBRIDES

Fourteen years before this scene, which Wagner himself described,[1] Felix Mendelssohn had had a decisive encounter—not with music-drama, but with the sea. (His experience closely parallels that of Wagner, who had come to appreciate the elements in the course of a voyage from Riga to London.) And at the same time the encounter was one with himself also. In order to understand the importance of this episode for Mendelssohn's future, we must first look into a lively travel letter written by his friend Klingemann at the time—a letter that speaks only of bad weather, not the elemental powers. Klingemann wrote from Glasgow on 10th August 1829:

> When you are sitting, as we are now, in the best hotel in a commercial city of 160,000 inhabitants, which boasts a university and cotton factories, and coffee and sugar delivered straight off the boat, you tend to look back with pleasure on discomforts so recently endured: the Highlands and the sea together brew nothing but whiskey, fog and foul weather. . . . Three days ago we were on our steamer and things were very different. The lower the barometer fell, the higher the sea rose. It stretched its myriad tentacles ever more brutally and churned more and more. . . . The ladies went down like ninepins, and one or two of the gentlemen followed their example. I wished my fellow-traveller in misery, Felix, had not been among them; but as an artist he gets along better with the sea than does his stomach. . . . An eighty-two-year-old woman sat calmly by the smoke stack, warming herself in the cold wind. She was determined to see Staffa before she died. Staffa, with its silly basalt columns and caves, is in all the picture books. We were put out into boats and clambered past the hissing sea on stumps of columns up to the odiously celebrated Fingal's Cave. I must say, never did such green and roaring waves pound in a stranger cave. The many pillars make the inside resemble a monstrous organ. Black, resounding, and utterly without any purpose at all, it lies there,

[1] R. Wagner: *Gesammelte Schriften und Dichtungen*. Leipzig, 1907.

the broad gray sea inside it and in front of it. The old woman clambered along the rocks with difficulty; she still had her mind fixed on being able to say she had seen the cave of Staffa before her death. . . .[2]

Felix was profoundly impressed by the natural phenomenon. On 7th August 1929 he wrote home: "To give you an idea of how strange I felt in the Hebrides, the following occurred to me":

These notes were the beginnings of a magnificent composition that seemed to spring suddenly into being. Nothing in Mendelssohn's previous works had hinted at it, not even *A Calm Sea and a Prosperous Voyage*, that programmatic tone-poem whose conception was literary. Of course Felix was a great reader, and literary associations with Ossian, Macpherson and Fingal may have played their part in this. But this part was fairly negligible. Wind, water and rocky beach directly shaped Felix Mendelssohn's "Hebrides" overture (opus 26).

"He would have won enough fame with the *Midsummer Night's Dream* overture", Schumann raved. "The other pieces should bear the

[2] S. Hensel: *Die Familie Mendelssohn 1729–1847*. Berlin, 1879.

names of other composers."[3] Be that as it may, the "Hebrides" overture significantly bore the name of Mendelssohn. The boundless loneliness of man in the vastness of nature was its theme (not its programme). The overture brings the perils of nature straight into the concert hall, and the audience is forced to respond on the sheer physical level. For although the minor figure in the bassoons in the first and second measures is a descending and melancholic motif, in the third and fourth measures we are suddenly compelled to take a deep breath; the initial tone leaps upwards in thirds toward A, and in the fifth and sixth measures actually reaches C sharp. The effect is indescribable: the motif, beginning so sombrely and pessimistically, grows, leaps beyond mere mood. It leaves all human limitations behind it, becomes as elemental as Nature herself. Here, before Wagner, was a Wagnerian motif!

At this point the accompaniment becomes more and more violent. But at the same time—and this is altogether strange—the movement of the water does not remain the same. It alternates between a cajoling and a threatening mood. Sometimes it seems to recede; at another place it gathers strength and hurls itself with tremendous power against the cliffs. (Later there is a staccato march of wind and water advancing upon the land.) Then again, the water subsides entirely in an incredible anticipation of the hollow pauses of the prelude to *The Flying Dutchman*, and only the wail of the wind can be heard.... Pianissimo kettledrums.... Glissandi of instruments had not yet been invented.... The powerful second motif follows:

This motif was destined to have an enormous influence upon European music in the nineteenth century. We find it in Denmark in the music of Niels Wilhelm Gade; in Holland it turns up in the work of Johannes Verhulst, and in England in William Sterndale Bennett's *Naiads*. But its effect was greatest among the Slavs. We come upon it in the work of Mikhail Glinka[4], in orchestral poems such as the *Kamarinskaya,* and it

[3] R. Schumann: *Gesammelte Schriften über Musik und Musiker.* Leipzig, 1891.

[4] F. M. Bojarksi: *Mikhail Glinka.* Petersburg, 1904.

is particularly distinct in Smetana's *Moldau*.[5] When the Czech master set out to describe his native river, he had recourse to memories of Mendelssohn.

Mendelssohn was not a naturalist composer. In his typically balanced manner, he was a classicist one week and a romanticist the next—"and just this was the perfect blending", as his pupil Chorley declared.[6] He was no more committed to realism than any of his predecessors had been. But the realism of the "Hebrides" tone-poem went far beyond anything that either classicists or romanticists had ventured heretofore. Mendelssohn not only went beyond realism but went beyond himself, pushing on into a future which he could barely sense. A present-day Scottish critic, W. Gillies Whittaker, has pointed out how magnificently modern Mendelssohn was in his tonal depiction of the contest between water, wind and grotto. But—Whittaker points out—life is there, in the form of bird cries. There is the hoarse screech of the gulls tossed about by the wind, hovering above the waves with heavily beating wings. And there is the forlorn twittering of a much smaller bird, performed by clarinets and flute:

Then there is the gliding of great albatrosses. Who will be the victor? Probably the storm; some day, we sense, the furious sea will overwhelm the islands. But that day has not yet come. Mendelssohn leaves the world as he finds it. A ray of sunlight breaks through the cloud. A clarinet imitates a gull, which is then joined by another; happy companions; they soar above the subsiding ocean. For many measures the storm has raged; now the trumpets begin a mild pianissimo octave. A few last chords crash. Then the clarinets once more take up the principal theme. A flute, so thin and delicate that it sounds as if it may be blown away, rises lightly and gracefully, and with a gentle roll of the kettledrums and the strings playing pizzicato in unison, the whole scene dissolves.[7]

[5] O. Hostinsky: *Bedrich Smetana.* Prague, 1901.
[6] H. F. Chorley: *Modern German Music.* London, 1854.
[7] H. G. Whittaker: *Introduction to the Hebrides by Felix Mendelssohn.* London, no date.

To reap the full meaning of this work, we must turn from music and consider two English painters who were contemporaries of Mendelssohn. John Constable (who died in 1837) had recognized that air was "not colourless and never completely transparent", and so he painted the sky shimmering in all the colours of the spectrum, like a smeared palette.[8] He was a forerunner of the Impressionists as was Mendelssohn in his "Hebrides" tone-poem. . . . William Turner, the painter of illuminated mists, went even further. He set himself subjects that no one had thought of before him: *Sun rising through Vapour* was the title of one of his paintings; before his day people had thought that sun and fog were mutually exclusive. Similarly, Mendelssohn made tonal combinations in the "Hebrides" overture that no one had hitherto thought possible. Scarcely appreciated by anyone save Ruskin, the great painter died in 1851, only four years after Mendelssohn.[9] Felix, too, would probably not have understood the revolutionary implications of Turner's paintings. But the "Hebrides" was as much a breakthrough in music as Constable's and Turner's experiments with light in painting.

It is in these terms that we can understand Mendelssohn's feelings in 1843, when he was present at the Berlin première of *The Flying Dutchman*. It was like an encounter with himself—enlarged. He was hearing what he had never dared to hope for: elemental music, the respiration of the cosmos, being performed upon an operatic stage! Certainly envy was an emotion wholly alien to him. But he did turn pale. There may have been a certain amount of truth in Wagner's somewhat malicious story that Mendelssohn, in congratulating him, had "lisped his praises". For whenever Felix was excited, he was overcome by the stammer from which his grandfather had suffered.

COLOURIST OR SCULPTOR?

"If you reverse the first measures of *The Flying Dutchman*", James Gibbons Huneker said in one of his 1912 lectures, "if you play them backwards as it were, you arrive almost note for note at the initial theme of the 'Hebrides' overture."

The New York music critic saw it as a case of simple imitation. Richard

[8] C. R. Leslie: *Memoirs of the Life of John Constable*. London, 1912.
[9] C. Mauclair: *Turner*. London, 1949.

Wagner, impressed by Mendelssohn's melancholic, Ossianesque motif, had stowed it away in his memory and fetched it out fourteen years later. Turned around, it served excellently for the beginning of his Senta ballad. For whether it is played in normal order or in reverse, it vividly invokes an endless waste of waters.

But what would the two composers have said if confronted with Huneker's discovery? The facts were compromising but scarcely deniable. In 1843 Mendelssohn was a famous man; Wagner was nothing of the kind. Mendelssohn was being generous when he showered compliments on Wagner. Wagner could only look up to his eminent visitor. Along with Schumann, Bülow, Reger and Richard Strauss, Wagner must have been aware of the historic importance of the "Hebrides" overture, although he never would have been guilty of such an extravagant utterance as Brahms's: "I would gladly give all my works if I had succeeded in writing a piece like the 'Hebrides' overture."[1] Still, he held it in esteem. "It is one of the finest pieces of music we possess," Wagner said to Wolzogen. "Mendelssohn is a first-class landscape painter, and the 'Hebrides' is his masterpiece. There is a magnificent intellectual vision throughout, a fine sensibility, and the observations of both reproduced with the greatest art. The passage where the oboes alone rise wailing through the other instruments like the wind above the waves of the sea, is of an extraordinary beauty. . . ."[2]

Wagner particularly loved the oboe and always assigned special tasks to it in his scores. The instrument does not lend itself to solo work, Theodor W. Adorno, the authority on aesthetics, has written in his *Essay on Wagner*; it does not have the beautiful loneliness of the flute's tone, nor the friendly quality of the clarinet.[3] The oboe has, we might add, an inbreathing quality, as though it drew its tone in rather than breathed it out. Certainly that is the effect of the oboe passages in the "Hebrides". Yet we are surprised to find that Wagner, in singling out the oboes for praise, did not also comment on the novel treatment of the trumpets. It would be difficult to find such a trumpet effect in any composer before Mendelssohn. "The trumpet", said Karl Sargans, the Berlin trumpeter, in 1830, "is not an orchestral instrument. When it sounds, all else must fall silent."[4] Naturally he was thinking of Beethoven's trumpet signal in the next-to-last act of *Fidelio,* which derived from the trumpet motif

[1] J. Brahms: Letter to Theodor Engelmann, quoted by H. J. Moser: *Geschichte der deutschen Musik*, vol. III. Stuttgart, 1928.

[2] H. v. Wolzogen: *Wagner-Brevier*. Berlin, no date.

[3] T. W. Adorno: *Versuch über Wagner*. Berlin, 1952.

[4] A. Carse: *The Orchestra from Beethoven to Berlioz*. Cambridge, 1948.

in Haydn's "Military" Symphony (opus 100). The trumpet, in fact, had been used to "announce heroes and rulers" ever since Aeschylus wrote his famous verse describing the battle of Salamis in *The Persians*: "The trumpet sounded and kindled all with its rays." Mendelssohn knew the Aeschylus passage well, since his friend Johann Gustav Droysen had only recently translated the work.[5]

But Mendelssohn's trumpets are different. He had filtered out their incisive, brassy clangour; they sounded, as Adolf Fredrik Lindblad commented, like "underwater trumpets", trumpets of the deep.[6] The English critic Onslow remarked that the trumpets in Mendelssohn's tone-poem sounded as if they were playing "through a curtain of water". "There is something indirect, veiled about them, which has nothing to do with their dynamics, with their forte or piano."[7] But if the tonal colour was not created by the dynamics, by what was it created? What strange trick was involved and where had Mendelssohn learned it? We have discovered only recently that Mendelssohn had borrowed it from himself,[8] from the work which the family called the "Trumpet Overture" in C. Felix had written this at the age of sixteen, before *A Midsummer Night's Dream*. And it had contained the same tonal phenomenon: the curious blurring of the trumpets. The trumpets are sounded together with horn and kettle-drums, even together with the trombone. Only after a while do the strings come to life, at first very low and faint. The whole structure rises in a bold, strange manner, with the subdued trumpets of the opening playing round the other instruments. Felix himself thought little of the work (unlike his father, who rightly judged the overture remarkable), and so it was not published until after Mendelssohn's death (as opus 101).

Wagner, therefore, could not have known that experimental work at all. What he praised about the "Hebrides", Mendelssohn's colouristic skill, was something that Felix had in common with Weber, Spohr and Wagner himself. But that was not the essential quality of the work. "Wagner's music is action and sculpture," Paul Bekker has commented. "The colouristic element in it is altogether a subsidiary matter."[9] And Wagner himself emphasized that his aim was to have "every colour become action"—which was not the case with the Romanticists.

In general Romanticism was unsculptural and hostile to action. The romantic composers loved transitions, rising and fading colours; to this

---

[5] Äschylos: *Werke*, trans. by J. G. Droysen. Berlin, 1832.

[6] *The Times*. London, September 1880.

[7] *Monthly Chronicle*. London, 1840.

[8] Giehan: *Wind Instruments in the Romantic Era*. New York, 1926.

[9] P. Bekker: *Wagner, das Leben im Werk*. Berlin–Leipzig, 1924.

predilection the Biedermeier era added absence of accentuation: pouring, gliding movement, or dreamy stasis. But the "Hebrides" overture made use of leitmotifs, was accentually strong; it was a piece of music with distinctively sculptural qualities. It represented the historic link between Beethoven the epic composer and Wagner the dramatic composer.

We may well ask how Mendelssohn, ordinarily a lover of rapid and capricious movement, conceived the desire for the reposeful quality of sculpture. Little has ever been said of his meeting with the greatest sculptor of his age. In Rome at the age of twenty—the same visit during which he made the acquaintance of Horace Vernet—he had met Bertel Thorwaldsen. The Danish sculptor, by then sixty, had come to Italy as a man of twenty-six, to study classical antiquity. In his early days he had been much addicted to pastoral subjects:[10] Amor stung by a bee; Amor as lion-tamer. By and by the sculptor observed that he did better with lions than with shepherds, and so he did a figure of the hero Jason, winner of the Golden Fleece. The statue evidently did not arouse enthusiasm. The sculptor flew into a rage and smashed his model to smithereens. On second thoughts, however, he decided that size was needed to make such a statue impressive and he redid his Jason, this time on a colossal scale. Again no one in Rome liked it, and Thorwaldsen, seething with indignation, was on the point of taking ship for Copenhagen when an Englishman named Sir Thomas Hope fell in love with the huge sculpture, bought it, and commissioned additional works from the sculptor. As a result, Thorwaldsen remained in Rome producing the statues that made him famous throughout Europe—his *Mercury as the Killer of Argus* and (when Napoleon came to Italy, in tribute to the Emperor) his *Triumphal Procession of Alexander the Great in Babylon*, his *Ganymede*, the *Bust of Lord Byron*, and the monument for Napoleon's step-son Eugène de Beauharnais.[11]

When Mendelssohn met Thorwaldsen, the sculptor had just completed a monument to Copernicus, for the city of Warsaw. Felix saw only the sketches. But he was enormously struck by Thorwaldsen's style, whose power was in striking contrast with the narrow, timid prettiness which was in vogue. As always, Felix communicated his impressions to his family:

> Thorwaldsen has just completed the clay model of a statue of
> Lord Byron. The poet is seated amidst ancient ruins, his feet

[10] J. M. Thiele: *Thorwaldsens Leben nach eigenhändigen Aufzeichnungen*. Leipzig, 1852–56.

[11] S. Müller: *Thorwaldsen, Hans Liv og Hans Verker*. Copenhagen, 1890–95.

resting on the capital of a column, and is gazing into the distance. He holds a tablet in his hand and is on the point of writing something. He is not wearing Roman costume, but is represented in the simplest contemporary dress, and this seems to me excellent and not at all disturbing. The whole work has that natural air which is so wonderfully achieved in all his statues, and yet Byron looks sufficiently gloomy and elegiac (and thus not at all affected). One of these days I must write you a whole letter about the *Alexander's Procession*; for never has any sculpture made such an impression upon me as this one. I go to see it every week, look at it and nothing else, and march with it into Babylon. . . .

In another letter he wrote:

Thorwaldsen is a man like a lion. It refreshes me just to see his face. It is immediately evident that he must be a glorious artist; there is a lucidity shining from his eyes, as though everything were transformed by them into form and image. In addition he is extremely gentle and friendly, because he stands on such a pinnacle; and yet I imagine that he takes joy in every little thing. It is a profound pleasure for me to see such a great man and to think that he is the creator of things which are destined to last. . . .[12]

To "last forever", in fact. The hope of indestructibility is contained within all sculpture. The youthful composer went frequently to Thorwaldsen's studio, encouraged him with his work, and played, softly or loudly, pieces from the *Walpurgis Night* and even more frequently, perhaps, the slowly gestating "Hebrides".[13] Did the deliberate blows of the sculptor's chisel punctuate the music, reminding him that art is a struggle to wrest form out of rock?

There was something highly educational about this friendship. It foreshadows an important meeting which was to take place in Paris eighty years later between the German poet Rilke and the French sculptor Rodin.[14] Rilke, with his inclination toward soft-fibred fantasy, attached himself to the rugged Rodin, not only to admire him, but to learn from his example. As a young man Rilke had a dangerous relationship to rhyme. Or rather, rhyme represented a peril to him. The tendency is

[12] F. Mendelssohn-Bartholdy: *Briefe aus den Jahren 1830–47*. Leipzig, 1861.

[13] A. M. Reissmann: *Felix Mendelssohn-Bartholdy*. Berlin, 1872.

[14] R. M. Rilke: *Briefe*. Wiesbaden, 1950.

apparent in his early poetry, even in such masterpieces as the *Book of the Hours*. Rilke loved language only too well. The stanza might be finished, the thought pursued to its conclusion, but euphony and rhyme continue to lead the poet on.

Such faults disappeared after Rilke met Master Rodin. The single mighty blows of the chisel were a reprimand to the facile, pleasing, over-ornamented verse. The encounter left its mark upon the hard *Neue Gedichte*: rhymeless poems that were sheer verbal sculpture, stripped of everything that was mere charm or floweriness. Rilke began carving a tremendous frieze of associations that no longer arose out of the rhyme.

The blows of Thorwaldsen's chisel produced precisely the same effect upon Felix Mendelssohn. He never afterwards forgot the lesson he had learned in the sculptor's studio. In all his subsequent great work, the sculptural quality was present. It is to be found in the *Walpurgis Night*, in the "Hebrides", in his tremendous choral songs, in symphonies and concerti, in the *St. Paul*, in the *Hymn of Praise*, in the *Elijah*.

BERLIN AND DÜSSELDORF

The stage, as we have seen, had failed him, or he had failed the stage. But the passion and hardness which were by no means alien to his character sought another outlet, and found it in the oratorio—the form which is half cantata and half drama.

We can scarcely comprehend the popularity of this intermediary form in the first half of the nineteenth century. It died a quick death in the eighties when Wagner's music-drama came to the fore. But in the earlier years of the century every composer of any rank wrote oratorios. Loewe produced them, and so did Spohr, Bernard Klein and Friedrich Schneider. But Mendelssohn alone wrote oratorios that were a success on all five continents. Like Haydn's *Creation* and *The Seasons*, his *Paul* and *Elijah* were performed in the farthest corners of the world.[1]

But strangely enough, the *Paul* would never have been written if Mendelssohn had remained in the bosom of his family and in the city of Berlin. He had to leave the place where everyone spoiled him, had to drive himself into self-imposed exile in the harsh outer world. That was what was meant by entering professional life. And so he went to Düsseldorf, where he had to prove himself and even engage in wrangles. Yet he

[1] A. Schering: *Geschichte des Oratoriums*. Leipzig, 1911.

would never have left Berlin but for an intolerable insult to his self-esteem. At the age of twenty-four something happened to him that was worse than his previous failure with *The Wedding of Camacho*. Or at least so he imagined.

Hamburger though he was by birth, Felix was really a born Berliner and never ceased to be one. From his early boyhood he had been conscious of Berlin surrounding the spacious Mendelssohn gardens on Leipziger Strasse: Berlin with its inland ports, its Spree river, its barges piled high with fruit and vegetables; Berlin with the Havel, the Pichelsberg, the pale beer, the *Konditoreien*; with its sardonic inhabitants who parodied everything and were no respecters of persons. That joy in mockery helped shape Felix's psyche. He delighted in the humour of the Berlin artisan who "shot off his mouth" when the rest of the nation primly held its tongue. He and his brother-in-law Hensel knew Louis Angely's vaudeville hit, *The Festival of the Artisans*, almost by heart—they would sing it to one another at home. When in 1842 King Frederick William IV asked Mendelssohn for some stage music to *A Midsummer Night's Dream* (the overture having been one of his enthusiams since his days as Crown Prince), Mendelssohn wrote the Scherzo in the form of a genuine jest between "rude mechanicals":

The Berlin "pavement loafers" were entertaining people, and great fanciers of the hurdy-gurdy, which they called a "whimper box". Let the organ-grinder pause a moment to rest his arm and they would instantly be bawling. The city had not only these loafers, but a fantastic variety of occupations. There were, for example, the "funeral notifiers"—a peculiar institution of Berlin. Death notices were not published in the newspapers in those days; instead one of these funeral notifiers went the rounds, usually drunk, informing relatives and friends of the impending solemn occasion. Gulping and pretending tears, the drunkard would announce: "It has pleased the Lord to call So-and-So the Saddler to his Heavenly home." Once, when Felix heard the announcement couched in verse— "Too good he was for this vale of tears, the choirs of angels now he hears"—he almost choked with laughter.[2]

Mendelssohn loved this lively irreverent city. And this devoted Berliner who never wanted to live anywhere else (unless he were globe-trotting or visiting friends) left his native city in resentment. After Zelter's death he had let himself be persuaded to apply for the vacant post of Director at the Singakademie. But on 22nd January 1833 the members of the Sing-akademie decided to give the post to a nonentity named Rungenhagen. This Karl Friedrich Rungenhagen, an unimportant musician but a skilled administrator, received 148 votes to Mendelssohn's 88. Eduard Devrient, who has described the proceedings in considerable detail, assumes that anti-Semitic intrigues were involved.[3] This is, however, highly unlikely; in the first place, the singers appointed Mendelssohn Rungenhagen's deputy, in other words vice-director; and in the second place racial preju-dice did not yet play the role it was to play a generation later, especially in the field of the arts. The real reason was Mendelssohn's youth. Felix had acquitted himself gloriously in the performance of the *St. Matthew Passion*; but a director of the Singakademie was more than just a con-ductor. He would have had to carry out a great variety of duties. The somewhat elderly members of the Academy had just lost their elder statesman Zelter. They could not quite see replacing him by such a young fellow, who was extremely rich and who, perhaps without being aware of it, was somewhat dandified in dress. Eight days before the vote was cast, Felix's mother had written to Ferdinand David, the violinist: "Humdrum, pity and mediocrity will certainly decide this appointment as they do most official posts here. Moreover there is the fact that no female minor and nobody who has been a member for less than two years

[2] L. Lenz and L. Eichler: *Berlin und die Berliner*. Berlin, 1840.
[3] E. Devrient: *Meine Erinnerungen an Felix Mendelssohn-Bartholdy*. Leipzig, 1872.

is allowed to vote; the elders cling to their traditions and cannot adjust to the idea of seeing a lively young man at their head."[4] Leah had undoubtedly hit on the truth. And the fact that Felix pleased the young ladies only too well—they went into ecstasies over him, which is a thing that parents notoriously cannot endure—may also have contributed to his defeat. Felix, however, with his soaring ambition, regarded this vote as a shameful disgrace. He actually fled from Berlin and did not return for years.

A Lower Rhine Music Festival in Düsseldorf three months later somewhat took the sting from the defeat. For he was asked to direct it. He obtained from England the original score of Handel's *Israel in Egypt*, and secured for Handel a triumph almost as sensational as that scored by the *St. Matthew Passion* in Berlin. Altogether the festival was an unprecedented success. People came from Holland, from Hesse, from as far up the Rhine as Basle and the rest of Switzerland. Abraham Mendelssohn, who attended, wrote proudly home that "four hundred singers and musicians of all sexes, classes and ages, drifted together like snow, permitted themselves to be guided and directed by one of the youngest among them, one without titles or dignities, and obeyed him like so many docile children."[5] In addition to the Handel oratorio, the programme consisted of Beethoven's "Leonore" Overture and "Pastoral" Symphony as well as Felix's own "Trumpet Overture" in C major, which he himself treated so cavalierly. His father boldly wrote that in the future that trumpet overture would always usher in the Handel work. The proud and happy populace of Düsseldorf wanted to bind their youthful visitor to the city for years to come; they offered to engage him as Municipal Music Director at a salary of six hundred talers. The three-year contract was to take effect on 1st October 1833; it provided for an annual three-month vacation any time between May and November, which Felix fancied he would spend in England. Without much hesitation, he signed.

Thus Felix became the colleague of another man of stature, the theatre director and writer Karl Immermann.[6] This rather heavy, brooding Saxon often felt himself completely out of place in the Rhineland. He could not, for instance, throw himself into the spirit of things at Carnival time, as the true Rhinelander can. Immermann found it repugnant, and said so for all to hear, to have to put on a fool's cap for weeks at a time.

[4] J. Eckardt: *Ferdinand David und die Familie Mendelssohn-Bartholdy*. Leipzig, 1888.
[5] F. Mendelssohn-Bartholdy: *Briefe aus den Jahren 1830–47*. Leipzig, 1861.
[6] H. Mayer: *Immermann: Der Mann und sein Werk*. Munich, 1921.

But Immermann looked forward to a happy collaboration with Mendelssohn. He was particularly fond of Jewish people: their wit and mental agility complemented his own slower-moving spirit. His closest friends were Jewish. Among them were Karl Rosenkranz, a well-known pupil of Hegel and historian of literature;[7] Michael Beer, a poet Heine thought well of, and whom Immermann admired as the author of the *Paria* and *Struensee*.[8] Then there was Heine himself, who was indebted to Immermann for his encouraging reviews.

Mendelssohn, however, made no effort to reciprocate Immermann's admiration. Immermann showed him a libretto for an opera—based on Shakespeare's *Tempest*, as it happened—only to have Felix return it. Of course Felix turned down every operatic libretto, for reasons we have already discussed. But in addition he displayed a rather pointed indifference toward Immermann's other works. He was obliging in small ways, it is true; he wrote a song for use in Immermann's *Trauerspiel in Tirol*, and another, the "Death-song of the Boyar", for the tragedy *Alexis*. That he could write these songs is proof of Mendelssohn's signal capacity to adjust to subjects quite alien to him. But when Immermann's prose works were discussed, such as his *Münchhausen*—a highly respected work which "rolled along like a heavily-laden ship between the shores of Goethe and Jean Paul"—Felix remained obstinately and significantly silent.[9] The only book of Immermann's that Mendelssohn truly liked was the comic epic *Tulifäntchen,* in which he recognized echoes of his beloved Englishmen, Swift and Sterne.[10] This was a mock epic of a Tom Thumb who associates with giants. Since Felix himself loved fairy-tales and parody, he was taken with the subject. Little Tulifäntchen had the intelligence and the ambition of full-grown people. He rode forth in the ear of a horse, with a penknife blade for a sword, a silver coin for shield, and a nutshell for helmet. In the first canto he killed flies; in the second he felled a huge giant; and in the third canto fairies released him from his unfortunate marriage to Princess Balsamine, who was twenty times his size. Felix was greatly entertained by all this, as well as by the topicality of the satire: Tulifäntchen represented the age of the Restoration after Waterloo, which tried to seem bigger than it was and marched on in the giant's boots of the *Freiheitskriege*.[11] Perhaps Mendelssohn would have

---

[7] R. Jonas: *Karl Rosenkranz*. Leipzig, 1907.

[8] M. Beer: *Briefwechsel*, ed. by E. von Schenk. Leipzig, 1837.

[9] F. Mendelssohn-Bartholdy: *Briefe*, op. cit.

[10] M. Windfuhr: *Immermanns erzählendes Werk. Zur Situation des Romans in der Restaurationszeit*. Giessen, 1957.

[11] T. Kreutz: *Immermanns Politische Satire*. Münster, 1928.

liked to turn Immermann's epic into a comic opera or else, since he was always shy of opera, into a symphonic tone-poem. But nothing came of the impulse.

Instead, relations soured between the theatre director and the musical director. Immermann, who was really a quiet and modest man, behaved with every appearance of arrogance; and Mendelssohn showed that he too was not entirely amiable when crossed. For years Immermann's private life had been unhappy. In an age that looked askance at such affairs he lived in irregular union with a divorced woman, Elisa von Ahlefeldt, the former wife of Baron Lützow, the famous leader of the Free Corps. This woman, who exercised an almost diabolic domination over him, was considerably older than Immermann. He repeatedly offered to marry her; but out of a romantic scorn for the conventions she always refused to take the step. All Düsseldorf knew of the affair, which complicated Immermann's relations with the people who counted in Düsseldorf, and made the writer himself suspicious and irritable.[12] Finally the tensions produced a break between him and a number of his friends in the theatre, and above all the squabble with Mendelssohn. The imbroglio came so suddenly that Mendelssohn threw up his contract. A biographer of Immermann, Werner Deetjen, has given an interpretation of the events which reflects badly upon Mendelssohn:

"The news that Mendelssohn wanted to resign from his post as director of the opera came as a shattering blow to Immermann. Mendelssohn, spoiled by good fortune, unfortunately lacked the seriousness, the capacity for renunciation and self-mastery, which Immermann so notably possessed." From the start, Deetjen relates, the younger man had taken a cool attitude toward Immermann's plans for injecting new life into the Düsseldorf theatre and combining theatre and opera into a joint enterprise. Negligent, frivolous, inconsiderate, concerned only with his personal glory, he had undermined the good cause and the position of his older friend. Immermann had repeatedly tried to arrive at a good understanding with his confrère. Only when Felix Mendelssohn, long after he had resigned his post, continued to intrigue against Immermann from afar, and had slandered the purity of his character—only then, Deetjen concludes, "did Immermann, his sense of honour and justice profoundly offended, turn away from Mendelssohn."[13]

This version cannot possibly be true. Mendelssohn was the last person on earth to engage in backstage intrigues. Backbiting was alien to his

---

[12] A. Wien: *Liebeszauber der Romantik*. Berlin, 1920.
[13] W. Deetjen: *Immermanns Werke, ein Lebensbild*. Leipzig, no date.

nature. And as for his seriousness about work, his diligence and sense of responsibility toward duties he had assumed—ten years later in Leipzig he literally worked himself to death—although there, it is true, he did not have to co-ordinate his plans with anyone else's.

The people of Düsseldorf, at any rate, formed a different estimate of Mendelssohn. Otherwise they would scarcely have put up a handsome statue of him in front of the opera house. For Düsseldorf had the honour of being the first to hear his *St. Paul*, whose première fell on 22nd May 1836. And the city on the Rhine has basked in the reflections of that fame ever since.

Mendelssohn afterwards came to the Rhine frequently to direct music festivals. He seems to have had the warmest memories of his sojourn in Düsseldorf. Was he concerned exclusively with his own reputation? He spoke of the "twilight whispering of the river, the beautiful trees, the riding, the walks with Düsseldorf painters"—with Schadow, Hübner and Bendemann. He himself took lessons from one of these painters, a man named Schirmer, and "water-coloured to my heart's delight".[14] "And do you know what the finest thing about Düsseldorf is?" he would say with his engaging smile, "that it is so close to London."

THE STORY OF PAUL OF TARSUS

Julius Schubring, the author of the text of *St. Paul*, was born in 1806—that is, he was three years older than Mendelssohn. Their friendship dated from the time the young philologist of Dessau had lived in Berlin as the tutor of Schleiermacher's children, and had been in and out of the Mendelssohn household. In 1830 Julius Schubring returned to Dessau, and about the same time Mendelssohn, then in Rome, began considering an oratorio on St. Paul. He had looked at a great deal of Titian and Raphael in the galleries of Rome, and perhaps this was the source of his inspiration. In December 1832 he sent a highly detailed outline of *St. Paul* to Dessau, and in January 1833 Schubring's first counter-proposal arrived —still more detailed. For years thereafter the plan was weighed, gone over scene by scene, speech by speech, word by word. One fortunate aspect of the matter was that Julius Schubring, a dry and cautious man, was well acquainted with Friedrich Schneider, composer of the oratorios

[14] *Düsseldorfer Künstlerbriefe*. Düsseldorf, 1858.

Last Judgment and *Jerusalem Liberated*, who also lived in Dessau. Thus Schubring did not lose the thread; he was forever mindful that where an oratorio was concerned, the music was primary and the religious aspect must come second. Where another preacher might have been reluctant to surrender "one jot or tittle" of the Biblical text, Schubring on the contrary cried out: "Let's keep it short." He himself mercilessly cut anything that might hinder the composer. Nevertheless almost four years passed before the *St. Paul* was ready for rehearsal.[1]

The subject, then, was the great Paul, the propagandist for a new conception of the world. Mendelssohn could easily have explained why he chose Paul for the hero of his first oratorio. But when this great work was launched in 1836, explanations were not in order: the explanatory age of Richard Wagner had not yet dawned. Mendelssohn talked as little about his intentions as Bach, Handel or Beethoven had done before him. To his mind, either a work of art justified itself or it could not be justified.

Though he preserved this admirable silence, we ourselves are sorely tempted to examine the psychological attractions that the subject of St. Paul had for him. The figure of Paul was of tremendous importance to Felix both personally and in terms of his own times. *"Mea res agitur"*, he might well have said. For Paul, the founder of a supranational religion, was the first man of classical antiquity who denounced the mysticism of blood and race which characterized the peoples of antiquity. To Paul, the Jews were not God's chosen people. Neither were the Greeks, Romans or other pagan peoples rejected by God. Paul attempted to equate all human beings by the symbolic act of baptism. His was an act of tremendous boldness, for in rejecting pro-Semitism he simultaneously rejected anti-Semitism. If all men were equal in Christ, the Jews too need no longer be zealous sons of their fathers, clinging to a law that separated them from their fellow-men. They ceased to be either chosen or persecuted by their birth. And the same applied to all others: Scythians, Germans, Greeks, Black, White and Yellow men, need no longer feel themselves to be separate nations. What Paul proclaimed was nothing less than pan-humanism. What a powerful appeal would such a doctrine as "the nullity of the fleshly heritage" have to someone like Mendelssohn! With what enthusiasm would he seize upon the gospel of that tentmaker of Tarsus who after his conversion—which came upon him like a bolt of lightning —had changed his name from Saul to Paul. The intoxicating joy of re-birth: "He who is in Christ is new—the old in us has passed away!"

[1] *Briefwechsel zwischen F. Mendelssohn-Bartholdy und J. Schubring.* Leipzig, 1892.

resounds from the lyrical parts of the score. The narrative portions of the text did not turn out so well.

Mendelssohn's old friend Adolf Bernhard Marx, who later turned against the *St. Paul*, penetrated the reasons that had impelled Mendelssohn to set this subject to music. He made some acute comments on the theme that "the subject chooses us, not we the subject". Even though the mind seemingly leaves us infinite freedom to choose a subject, the ultimate decision is not free. "What draws the artist ... to this particular subject, and no other, is a product of his whole way of thinking; in such decisions a mutual relationship, a magnetic rapport, is operating."[2]

"I must not make any mistakes," Felix resolved at the time. Along with his correspondence with Schubring, he pursued Biblical and historical studies. In Düsseldorf Felix happened upon a history of early Christianity, Gfrörer's *Geschichte des Urchristentums*. The book so fascinated him that he took it with him when he went riding in the woods—where he and it suffered severely from rain. He was reading everything he could find on Greek history and daily life in the period of Paul. As a result of all this study he knew a good deal more than might have been thought necessary for his task. He was aware, for example, that at the time of Paul an effective Greek religion no longer existed. Everything had turned to syncretism; the Oriental religions had been thoroughly shaken up in the melting pot. Ever since the third century B.C. when Euhemerus in his travel novel entitled *Sacred History*, had contended that the gods had in truth been mortal men (they had been called "immortal gods" in honour of the good they had done humanity), ancient religion had really been nothing more than a cult of heroes.[3] So it was not too difficult for Paul to smash it. The reformer had much harder work dealing with the Jewish faith, which still had a religious character. It is possible that Felix also studied purely Jewish sources on Paul. The Jews of the oratorio who oppose Paul are vehement but devout men, not the mob of Bach's *St. Matthew Passion*. Mendelssohn was far more just to them; perhaps it was due to his origins that he understood Paul's adversaries.[4] Paul himself, after all, had been one of those stern and pious Jews.

At Whitsuntide in 1836 *St. Paul* was presented to the world. It proved to have an amazing wealth of forms—arias, choruses and recitatives—and a mingling of the lyrical and the heroic moods. The separate elements were old, but the combination was new, and so the whole was novel and

[2] A. B. Marx: *Erinnerungen aus meinem Leben*. Berlin, 1865.
[3] G. Murray: *Five Stages of Greek Religion*. Oxford, 1930.
[4] M. S. Enslin: *The Ethics of Paul*. New York, 1930.

surprising. No contemporary doubted that here was a specimen of "very great music". The work provoked a flood of essays which did not abate for years. Johann Theodor Mosewius, a Bachian, praised it to the skies,[5] and the comments of Otto Jahn, archaeologist and biographer of Mozart, were almost equally laudatory.[6] Certain features aroused some alarm or astonishment, it is true, but these were never taken as defects, but only served to keep the discussion alive. Thus, a number of persons soon asked: What in the world had Mendelssohn in mind when he represented the voice of the Son of God by a quartet of women's voices? He himself made a principle of unyielding silence; he never even attempted to answer the question. But it is probable that he was motivated by the Old Testament Commandment: "Thou shalt make thee no graven images", the prohibition against carving or painting any image of God. Given the close relationship that Mendelssohn felt between music and pictorial art, he probably felt it would be impious to entrust a male singer with the task of imitating the voice of God. Even a chorus of men would be impossible. For, since we conceive of God as masculine, the temptation to imitation would be present. Only the greatest possible distance from God's real voice would not offend—and with a women's chorus Mendelssohn could achieve this distance.

August Reissmann, one of his earliest biographers, was clever enough to fathom this.[7] He wrote: "Mendelssohn assigned the voice that speaks to Paul from Heaven to a quartet of women. If the master had chosen a single voice, and particularly a male one, the listener could only have assumed that this voice represented the physical voice of Christ, which in this situation would have been a gross misunderstanding. . . . It was necessary to bring out not a particular *human* voice, but the element of the *supernatural*, and for this women's voices are best suited—especially as Mendelssohn uses them. The miraculous phenomenon of Christ speaking from Heaven is rendered by the wind instruments which sound sustained or quavering chords. The women's chorus is so closely linked with them that it really seems as if the words were floating bodilessly out of the Appearance itself."

Mendelssohn had found the ideal strategy for circumventing the religious taboo that a divine figure must not sing realistically. Actually, the composer had even had compunctions over the propriety of his women's chorus. On a musical journey to Cologne—where he had gone

[5] J. T. Mosewius: *Zur Aufführung des Oratoriums Paulus*. Berlin, 1857.
[6] O. Jahn: *Über Felix Mendelssohn-Bartholdys Oratorium Paulus*. Kiel, 1842.
[7] A. Reissmann: *Felix Mendelssohn-Bartholdy*. Berlin, 1866.

Saul!

Saul!   was verfolgst   du   mich!

to dig up old ecclesiastical music for his Düsseldorf concerts—he had made the acquaintance of a young canon of Cologne cathedral whom he queried about the role of women in the Early Christian congregations. Had not women been relegated to an exceedingly minor place? Had not the Fathers of the Church fulminated against women, Tertullian calling woman the "gate to hell" and Clement of Alexandria exclaiming: "Every woman should be filled with shame at the thought that she is a woman"?[8] The canon had shaken his head over such naïve questions. It was not very probable, he said, that Paul had heard the "Saul, Saul, why do you persecute me?" as women's voices. But the Early Church had certainly not rejected women. St. Paul himself had travelled about with a woman missionary, the virgin Thekla of Ikonia, who followed him to Antioch, barely escaped martyrdom, and performed prodigies in the conversion of the pagans.[9] This information reassured Mendelssohn, for although he held firmly to the principle of the primacy of music, he did not want to be unhistorical if he could help it.

[8] S. Drinker: *Die Frau in der Musik*. Zürich, 1955.
[9] C. Schlau: *Die Akten des Paulus und der Thekla und die ältere Thekla-Legende*. Leipzig, 1877.

As a matter of fact, however, historians were disturbed by the boldness of *St. Paul*. Adolf Bernhard Marx, by now a distinguished theoretician and professor of musical history, considered the use of chorales in the structure of the work as unhistorical. Chorales belonged in a "Passion" and were a private preserve of Bach. They had no place in the grand oratorio as developed by Handel. Others concurred, refusing to recognize that Mendelssohn had created a magnificent synthesis of the intensity and gravity of Bach with Handel's rounded characterization and operatically powerful instrumentation. But this remained a minor cavil, even if voiced by such noted musicians as Karl Loewe[10] or Ludwig Spohr.[11] In general, the response of the musical world was very favourable. Soon after the English première in Liverpool, *The Times* wrote: "It is incomprehensible that the great landscape-painter of 'Fingal's Cave' and of *Calm Sea and Prosperous Voyage*, and the vigorous humorist of the overture to *A Midsummer Night's Dream* has been able to create so powerfully religious a work as the *St. Paul*."[12] But it was not really incomprehensible. Although the eternal comparison with Mozart is by now a nuisance, the two composers did have one thing in common: an astonishing versatility and inability to be boring. Why do most people dislike religious music? Chiefly because it bores them by repetitions. It takes too literally the injunction that God must be praised "without ceasing". And the Mendelssohn who wrote the *St. Paul* was a master of brief forms.

Apart from the magnificence of the music, we must ask ourselves whether a composer of the present day would take on a text marred by such obvious faults. In spite of endless discussion between Felix, Schubring and other friends, the libretto did not turn out well. An effective text should really have begun with the dramatic situation of the zealot Saul persecuting the Christians and then suddenly being overtaken by the lightning-bolt of conversion on the road to Damascus. A real dramatist such as Handel, for example, would have seized upon this situation. Moreover, an oratorio on Paul should not have had a second hero in Stephen the Martyr, who is stoned in the first part of the work and monopolizes the listener's sympathies to such an extent that Paul has a hard time competing for attention. But the greatest mistake of all, from the dramatic point of view, lay in the failure to conclude the oratorio with Paul's martyrdom. This was ruled out because the stoning of Stephen had been depicted in the first act and a similar scene of horror could not be

---

[10] K. Loewe: *Selbstbiographie*. Berlin, 1870.
[11] L. Spohr: *Selbstbiographie*. Kassel, 1860–61.
[12] *The Times*, London, August 1840.

repeated. But there was another reason, characteristic of Mendelssohn: his fidelity to the letter of the Bible. Paul's death is not reported in the Acts of the Apostles. To be sure, we know that he will die a martyr, and he himself knows it—but Mendelssohn could never have brought himself to invent Biblical texts. And so he deprived himself of an effect that a less scrupulous artist (such as Wagner), one who was a *real* dramatic composer, would certainly not have foregone. To be sure, there is a wealth of poignant implication in the great farewell song in which the 'cello becomes a human voice: "Sei getreu bis in den Tod, so will ich dir die Krone des Lebens geben" ("Be faithful unto death, and I will give thee the crown of life").

In simple words the apostle has told his friends of his decision to go to Jerusalem, where tribulation and bonds await him. The Ephesian fellowship attempts to dissuade him, urging him: "Spare yourself. Let this not be your lot!" But they can do nothing; Paul abides by his resolve to die for the name of the Lord Jesus. They accompany him to the ship and say farewell. The heartfelt, gentle A flat major chorus speaking of the love "which the Father showeth us" invokes God's paternal care, which is greater than brief suffering. The final chorus is framed as a double fugue, whose splendour rivals the great fugues of Bach.

Bach or Handel? Mendelssohn's contemporaries found it difficult to decide which of these two influences they should admire more in the *St. Paul*. In the Bach Passion, as is well known, three elements predominate and carry the action forward: the narrating evangelist, the individual dramatic hero, and the chorus, which supplies the moral commentary, not unlike the choruses in classical tragedy. To be sure, the chorus likewise sings the chorale, which brings in the fourth element, a divine force

which seems "no longer to have anything human about it". Handel's
oratorios, on the other hand, are musical dramas, if not music-dramas.
They are, as Davison once remarked, an opera rehearsal for which the
principal singers and the choruses have not yet put on their costumes.[13]
Handel eliminates the epic narration; all the persons of the oratorios, both
those who mourn and those who act violently—victims, fighters and
victors—always speak for themselves. Even the choruses and the arias
always refer to the action, and further that action. There is none of the
"otherworldly contemplation of Bach", and certainly no trace of the
miracle of the chorale. How could such contrasting approaches be combined? Felix Mendelssohn, who adored both these great predecessors,
continued to do so.

His prelude starts off completely in the style of Bach, with the mighty
choral melody, "Wachet auf, ruft uns die Stimme der Wächter sehr hoch
auf der Zinnen, wach auf, du Stadt Jerusalem." ("Awake! The voice of
the watchman calls from the high pinnacle. Awake, thou city of Jerusalem.") In canon style as in the *St. Matthew Passion*, the "false witnesses"
appear, repeating each others' lies which will bring about the death of
Stephen. At this point Handel's influence is predominant; accompanied
by the strings, Stephen begins to defend himself with vigorous oratory.
But the inflamed populace shouts him down: "Weg, weg mit dem!"
The crash of stones begins; the music surges murderously. . . . But then,
mysteriously, in a *pianissimo espressivo*, with a prayer for his foes, he
dies. Devout men carry him away and tend to the body: "Wir preisen
selig . . ."

[13] H. Davison: *From Mendelssohn to Wagner*. London, 1912.

Only then does Saul appear, raging and inveighing against the accursed Christian sect. He is punished, he falls, is blinded. "Saul, Saul," comes the supernal, gentle voice, "Warum verfolgst du mich!" ("Saul, Saul, why do you persecute me?") And then the repentance. Saul becomes Paul. He regains his sight, is healed. Accompanied by tremendous music, all fire, fervour and celestial jubilation ('cellos, violins and trumpets of unearthly beauty), Paul sets off to win the whole world to Jesus Christ.

There is fierce contention with the Hebrews. But what about the Gentiles? In treating this part of the story, Mendelssohn shows great inventiveness. Perhaps the handling of the high-spirited scene where Paul and Barnabus are taken for gods by the people of Lystra, may be traced to the influence of a close friend of Mendelssohn, the famous historian J. G. Droysen, a professor at Berlin University, who had just published a *History of Alexander the Great*.[14] Felix was deeply interested in the book. Thorwaldsen's sculpture, too, had given him important insights into the world of Alexander. Now he made his Greeks jubilantly sing: "Seid uns gnädig, hohe Götter!" ("Have mercy upon us, ye high gods!")

But Paul, doubly indignant, cries out against their error.

And so scene follows scene, chorus follows chorus, to the gentle conclusion of the work: "How sweet are the messengers of the Lord who proclaim peace! Their sound has gone out into all lands and into all the world their words."

"O what a profundity of riches!" Astounded contemporaries quoted from one of the chorales to comment on the whole oratorio. "The music of *St. Paul*", Walter Dahms said, "possesses a tremendous range, expressing everything from fanaticism to piety, from hatred to the highest dedication, from ugly menace to entrancing grace and sweetness, from sober rationalism to dreamy romanticism." It was a *tour-de-force* which had no precedent.

The work was unthinkable without Bach, but at the same time it was

[14] J. G. Droysen: *Geschichte Alexanders des Grossen*. Berlin, 1933.

more modern, more appealing to romantic feeling than Bach. Mendelssohn's *St. Paul* had no sooner left the printer than sixty-one German cities put on performances of the work. In the next two years it was also performed in Sweden and Russia, Holland, Poland, Switzerland, England and America. Amid the chorus of praise, only one man stood with arms folded, and sourly refused to add his tribute. Not yet well known, still extremely dependent upon the favour of the mighty, in 1836 he did not have the right to say the things he could say in 1850. He was the adversary, the enemy of old music and above all hostile to the cult of Bach, which Mendelssohn had introduced as a young man. "Bach's musical language", Wagner wrote, "was formed in that period of our musical history in which the general language of music was still struggling to find its way to surer, more individual expression. Music was still imprisoned in the bonds of pedantry, the purely formal elements, so that in Bach, human expressiveness . . . was just beginning to emerge. The language of Bach stands in the same relationship to the language of Mozart and finally of Beethoven as the Egyptian Sphinx to Greek human statuary: as the Sphinx with its human face is just striving for release from the animal body, so Bach's noble human head strives for release from the wig. It represents a fantastic benightedness in the luxuriant musical taste of our time that we should simultaneously allow the language of Bach to speak to us alongside that of Beethoven, and should be persuaded that in the languages of the two there exists only an individual and formal difference, but by no means a real disparity."[15]

Wagner wrote these lines about the dead composer Bach after Mendelssohn, too, had died. Do they concern us here? They do. For in any book on Mendelssohn, Wagner must be the second hero. And he may grow to such vast proportions that he will soon overshadow the first.

BUT WHY IS EVERYBODY DYING?

When a creative artist devotes a full quarter of his life and art to composing under the aegis of another—we are speaking of Mendelssohn and Bach—it might be assumed that he had also shared the other's central experience. With Bach, that experience was death and its place in life. Bach's theme was the conquest of the fear of death by religious belief.

[15] R. Wagner: *Gesammelte Schriften und Dichtungen*. Leipzig, 1907.

Every note of Bach's asserts an unshakable faith in God and a life after death.

Was that also true for his disciples? Strangely enough, it was not. Mendelssohn wrote a good deal of comforting music in the Bachian spirit, but he was only too prone to modern ideas, modern nervous tensions. He tended to concur with Goethe's well-known remark to Eckermann about the unreasonableness of death: "Death, you know, is something so strange that despite all experience we do not think it possible in connection with any being dear to us, and when it happens it is always something un-believable and unexpected. It is a kind of impossibility that suddenly becomes a reality...."[1] There is no acceptance here, certainly no hailing of death as a stage in the soul's route to the hereafter. Goethe's distaste for death and its "unjustified claim" resembled that of Tolstoy in old age, who seemed to think that death would make an exception of him and preserve for the world a physical and moral force such as he was.[2]

Felix might accept it as part of the order of things that old people should die. Goethe died at eighty-three, and had lived a full life to the end. Hearing of Goethe's death, Felix had exclaimed that it left *him* feeling so impoverished. He had felt considerable sadness, too, at the death of Zelter. But why were so many *young* people dying? It was as though the Reaper were lying in wait especially for the young in city and country, everywhere. The death of the young violinist Eduard Rietz, who was carried off by consumption, plunged Felix into days of depression. He subsequently struck up a close friendship with Rietz's brother Julius and engaged him to work in the Düsseldorf opera. This was a typical example of Felix's consistent loyalties, and at the same time his answer to death—he would act as if Eduard were living on in Julius. For one had to deny death, evade it, even trick it. But this became difficult, for at the time thousands were being killed by an invisible foe: cholera. "But why is everybody dying?" This perplexed cry was Mendelssohn's response to an unprecedented situation.[3]

The strange disease had first come from Asia in 1829, had subsided, reawakened, and moved about by fits and starts, staying until 1837. Vomiting, diarrhoea were its symptoms. But no one knew more than that; no one knew how to deal with it. The disease wrought frightful changes on its victims within a few hours of infection: faces were drawn,

[1] J. P. Eckermann: *Gespräche mit Goethe in den letzten Jahren seines Lebens*. Leipzig, 1939.

[2] T. Mann: *Leiden und Grösse der Meister*. Frankfurt am Main, 1957.

[3] F. L. Bunn: *Stories of Music and Musicians*. London, 1852.

Mendelssohn at the age of twenty-two, painted in Rome by
Horace Vernet, 1831. (*Photo Handke, Bad Berneck*)

Cécile Jeanrenaud Mendelssohn, Felix Mendelssohn's wife. Painting
by Eduard Magnus, circa 1837. Property of the Mendelssohn family.
(*Photo Handke, Bad Berneck*)

eyes started horribly, and voices turned hoarse. The pulse moved jerkily; the body was racked by incessant vomiting and dysentery. The end came shortly after. Medicine was helpless (fifty years were to pass before Robert Koch discovered the bacillus responsible for the disease). The police undertook to protect the populace by setting up cordons against all persons coming from the East—not knowing that the disease was not transmitted from person to person, but through the intestinal discharges of the sick. Everyone fled the big cities. But wherever people went for safety, the ground-water became infected, and it was months before people realized that they had to boil water before drinking it or even washing with it. To reassure its citizens, the government in Berlin issued false statistics on the epidemic. Today we can guess how grave it was by examining the toll it took among various professions. Along with General Gneisenau, four other generals died.[4] In addition to the most famous philosopher at the University of Berlin, hundreds of students perished. Well-meant dilettante hygienic measures only added to the panic. At the suggestion of Privy Councillor Rust, the Commissioner of Health, some people took to wearing wax masks when they went about the streets. Neighbours did not recognize one another, mistook the masquers for ghosts or burglars, and there was a rash of violent incidents. "Fumigate! Lock the doors! Disinfect money and goods!" All these measures were virtually useless.[5]

The Mendelssohn family turned for advice to a doctor who was a specialist, in so far as anyone could be called a specialist on the subject at the time. Dr. Gottfried Christian Reich was writing a book on cholera. He had lived for a long time in Poland and knew how Eastern Europe instinctively fought the disease. Washing with vinegar, camphor, garlic, all these offered some protection. The great prescription was bodily cleanliness, internal and external. Reich had his office at 13 Mauerstrasse.[6] He came to the Mendelssohn house, examined the family, found them all in good health, and instituted a strict quarantine. Even letters that came from the outside world were to be washed with a tincture before being read. A few of the letters were from Felix, who was bedridden in Paris.[7] Before the family could start to fear for him he had proceeded on his way to London.

[4] G. H. Pertz: *Das Leben des Feldmarschalls Neithardt von Gneisenau.* Berlin, 1864–80.

[5] K. Gutzkow: *Aus der Knabenzeit.* Frankfurt am Main, 1852.

[6] G. C. Reich: *Die Cholera in Berlin.* Berlin, 1831.

[7] F. Mendelssohn-Bartholdy: *Briefe aus den Jahren 1830–47.* Leipzig, 1861.

As for Paris, "The cholera came upon us like a grim clown," Prosper Mérimée wrote later;[8] an incisive description. For despite the horror of the plague, there was something preposterous in the way human beings were being carried off *en masse*. Early in the history of Paris, probably as early as the fourteenth century, the *danse macabre*, the dance of death, had been painted on the walls of cemeteries: pictures of shrivelled corpses in shrouds dancing among the living, and skeletal Death himself leading the procession, blowing his fife. The figures of the *Death of Paris* dated from those ancient days of plague, as well as the still more famous *Death of Lübeck*, and the most famous of all, the *Death of Basel*, which had been painted by Holbein the Younger.[9]

This present "Death of Berlin" was not dissimilar. Could there be anything more preposterous than Hegel's dying of cholera? This untimely death could not be classified in the *Phenomenology* or in the *System of Dialectics*. Here was no synthesis following upon thesis and antithesis; this was only an indecent practical joke at the expense of Spirit.

Felix Mendelssohn was a Hegelian, and had taken extensive lecture notes on the master's teachings. But he was also a great artist with an innate suspicion of the finality of philosophy. The bolts of lightning that struck close to home affected him more than the death of the great Hegel. Felix had not been intimate with Ludwig Robert, Rahel Varnhagen's brother, for they were of different generations. (Robert was almost fifty-four when he died in 1832.) But Felix thought highly of Ludwig Robert for ideological reasons. While still a very young man, Robert, who was a writer of some note, had chosen to become a Protestant. He had done so on the score of politics and nationalism rather than religion. It was the spirit of the Wars of Liberation that had led Robert, as he himself put it, to "take Fichte's hand" and join the German nation. He subsequently felt intensely bitter about the ill-will that was soon displayed towards himself and his fellow converts, and in many of his poems he attacked this attitude.[10] Influential groups had protested against the granting of the rights of citizenship to the Jews, and two hard-bitten noblemen, Baron Friedrich von der Marwitz and Count Karl von Finckenstein had appealed to the King, asking whether "old, honest Brandenburgian Prussia is to be turned into a new-fashioned Jews' state". Whereupon the Prussian government headed by Prince Hardenberg had answered the

[8] P. Mérimée: *Lettres à une Inconnue*. Paris, 1873.
[9] J. Langlois: *Essai sur les Danses des Morts*. Rouen, 1851.
[10] F. v. Oppeln-Bronikowski: *Koreff*. Leipzig, no date.

question in a manner that both gentlemen instantly understood: the pair were arrested and transported to the fortress of Spandau.[11]

In 1819 (Felix was then ten years old) Ludwig Robert published a play which was much discussed—in the Mendelssohn household, too. It was called *Die Macht der Verhältnisse* ("The Power of Conditions") and was in fact a problem play which called upon the nobility to take into account the social changes of the nineteenth century. The drama centred about the institution of the duel: if the new bourgeoisie, to which the converts also belonged, were to enjoy equal rights, its members must be entitled to give and receive satisfaction from the nobles on the duelling ground. The play stirred up a great deal of dust at the time, for it was based upon an actual incident: a poet who was a nobleman had insulted a member of a Jewish family; he had compounded the insult by refusing the proposal of a duel, and had been given a good beating before witnesses in a Berlin bath-house.

But that was all long ago. The cholera levelled all classes. In July 1832 Robert, who already felt ill, had fled from Berlin to escape the epidemic. In Baden-Baden death caught up with him. Was it cholera, or a nerve fever? Seven years earlier Rahel had had a premonition of her brother's death. She had had a frightful dream in which she had seen her room filled with a red glow like sunset, had cried out, "Robert, where are you?" and thought that she too was about to die with him, before she awoke, gasping for breath.[12]

Felix Mendelssohn was deeply shaken when he heard of Robert's death. He was even more shocked when Ludwig Robert's wife, Friederike, followed her husband only a few weeks later: beautiful Friederike Braun, the "Swabian maid", as Felix called her. At the time of the overture to *A Midsummer Night's Dream*, Ludwig and Friederike Robert had been staying in the Mendelssohns' garden house. A. B. Marx has described how Friederike would often sit silent and apparently indifferent to everything. But if another pretty woman entered the garden, she would suddenly kindle. "Then woe to the newly-arrived beauty! She would be outshone by Friederike who, craving victory and sure of her power, could never tolerate a rival."[13] But "Riekchen", as the Mendelssohns called her, Berlin-fashion, was not only decorative; she was also a poet whose theme was nostalgia for her native Swabia. She never achieved the

[11] S. Jaznelson: *Beethovens Ferne und Unsterbliche Geliebte.* Zürich, 1954.

[12] R. Varnhagen: *Ein Buch des Andenkens für ihre Freunde.* Berlin, 1834.

[13] A. B. Marx: *Erinnerungen aus meinem Leben.* Berlin, 1865.

loveliness with which Mörike was later to invest Swabian poetry, but she did write some charming pieces. She had a way, for example, of attaching a "le" to most nouns—and that quaint bit of Swabian dialect tinkled in the poem that Felix set to music:

And now the lovely poetess was dead. Unsightly, shrivelled, laid in the ground. "The elegant lilies . . . the low-growing gillies . . . Care, take care, thou blossom fair." What was happening? Felix could not come to terms with it.[14]

And many whom the cholera spared were carried away, during that same decade from 1830 to 1840, by the epidemic of suicides. Was it possible that hundreds, thousands even, were taking their lives out of sheer boredom? For the fad began where life was most peaceful, where people had undergone no sufferings at all: in Denmark. From there it quickly spread through all of Europe. Philosophers, theologians, physicians and economists hunted for the cause and could find none, apart from the theory that the age of the restoration and the "overlong peace" seemed to be addling men's brains.

The noted singer Adolphe Nourrit had not been a friend of Mendelssohn, but Felix had known him well as a friend of Ferdinand Hiller. Nourrit had sung Pylades in Gluck's *Iphigenia*, had taken the leading rôles in Rossini's *Tell* and in Fromental Halévy's *La Juive*. He then became convinced that he had lost his voice. On a visit to Naples he threw himself from the top of a building and plunged to his death—only thirty-seven years old.[15] The news was a dreadful shock to Felix. In 1835 the French painter Leopold Robert drowned himself in the lagoon of Venice, out of unrequited love for a Princess Bonaparte. From his *Correspondance Inédite* it has been deduced, though never proved conclusively, that Mendelssohn's "Italian" Symphony was influenced by Robert's demi-realistic paintings such as the *Sleeping Brigands* and the *Fishermen*

[14] W. Haape: *Ludwig und Friederike Robert*. Karlsruhe, 1895.
[15] Quicherat: *Adolphe Nourrit*. Paris, 1867.

of the Adriatic Sea.[16] To throw away his life for a woman! These insane Parisians! But the peak of senselessness was reached by little Daniel Lessmann. This professional Diogenes had probably never known an hour of real hardship in his life. Everyone who knew him loved to hear of his experiments: he had, for instance, set out for Italy on foot, dressed in a tail-coat and successfully begged rides from drovers or from the rich people in their carriages. He would come to the Mendelssohns on Sunday and stuff himself with so much food that he could well wait until the following Wednesday before going to the Meyerbeers for his next meal. . . . And in the autumn of 1831 this little jester was found hanged in a forest near Wittenberg. Could it have been a crime?—but who would want to kill a man who had no money in his purse, no rings on his fingers, no watch in his pocket? Heine's brother Maximilian had another explanation: "The little humorist is bored, sings a farewell ditty under his breath; a pretty tree is an invitation to hanging. Lessmann does not think twice about it, pulls off his silk scarf, knots it; he regards the act as a bad joke, the crowning jest of his gallows' humour."[17]

This wave of voluntary deaths probably drew Mendelssohn even closer to Bach. Between 1830 and 1840 he wrote a great number of spiritual compositions, such as the "Five Psalms for Solo Voices, Chorus and Orchestra" (opus 31, 42, 46, 51, 91) masterpieces of polyphony, works that were at once lyrical and passionate. Had he then made Bach's fundamental experience, the confrontation with death, his own? He had—and he had not. For neither he nor his contemporary Chopin was genuinely a musician of death. . . . When Chopin wrote his funeral march, the famous sluggish and somnolent one from the B minor Sonata, he was by no means exhibiting his best vein. And when Mendelssohn composed a funeral march (in A minor, opus 103) for a fellow-composer and friend of Immermann, Norbert Burgmüller, he did not make very much of the assignment; it in no way bears comparison with Mozart's *Requiem* or *Maurerische Trauermusik*. Nor with Schubert's *Death and the Maiden*. The reason for this is that Mendelssohn's most profound religious experience was not with death at all, but with the Word. He was forever deeply moved by the letter of Scripture, whether the Word was that of the New Covenant or the Old.

[16] Clément: *Leopold Robert d'après sa Correspondance inédite.* Paris, 1874.
[17] M. Heine: *Erinnerungen an Heinrich Heine.* Berlin, 1868.

IN THE BEGINNING WAS THE WORD

Mendelssohn's father Abraham had often made it clear to all about him that he did not believe in "revelation" in either the Old or the New Testament. Like other members of the Enlightened generation, he regarded the books of the Bible as mythology and moral precept. The younger generation, and Felix Mendelssohn in particular, took quite a different view. Felix once had a talk with the noted preacher Bauer and expressed his surprise that Goethe should make Faust say: "I cannot think so highly of the Word. . . . In the beginning was the Deed."[1] Perhaps, Mendelssohn thought, that statement might be quite in character with Faust, but it could not have been Goethe's view. So great a poet would surely have had to subscribe to the first line of the Gospel of John.

In 1830 the tricentennial of the Augsburg Confession was to be celebrated. Felix reflected on the life of Luther and was overwhelmed. That a persecuted man hiding in the Wartburg under the pseudonym of Junker Jörg, in peril of death, should have set himself the task of translating the Bible for the German people, seemed to him a miracle. And to pay tribute to the greatness of Luther as the translator of the Bible, he wrote his "Reformation" Symphony (opus 107). It was one of the mightiest of his orchestral works, though he was only twenty when he undertook it.

Felix did not concern himself with Luther's later political behaviour. Perhaps the Reformer had had sound reasons for being for the peasants one day and against them the next; for having wanted to join with Hutten and then turning against him; for insisting on the principle of monogamy and then sanctioning bigamy in the case of Landgrave Philip of Hesse. Such vacillations, like all politics, were an attempt to find the lesser evil. . . . Facts of this sort could not spoil Felix's image of Luther. He had always cherished Luther as translator of the Bible, musician, genial host and paterfamilias. Luther was the man at whose table one broke bread as though one were in Heaven, where righteousness became the music of the lute and all laughter was praise of the heavenly Father.[2] A strong, exhilarating wind sweeps through the four movements

---

[1] K. Weiss: *Der Prolog des Johannes-Evangeliums, eine Apologie in Antithesen.* Frieburg, 1899.
[2] J. Mackinnon: *Luther and the Reformation.* London, 1925–30.

of the symphony. There is something autumnal about it, an October clarity and crispness. We will look in vain here for the typical Mendelssohnian effects of delicate pianissimi. Alertness and disputatiousness are the moods of the first movement. It is not a march, yet we may hear the footsteps of a sentinel as he walks the parapets of a city wall. We can also hear the Luther Amen (the so-called "Dresden" Amen) that Wagner incorporated in his *Parsifal* so much later. In Mendelssohn the measures go:

The second, extremely concentrated movement, is likewise bright as day and filled with vigour and zest. The Andante, as Kretzschmar[3] comments, is brief and resembles an agitated recitative, and the Trio has a Christmas carol quality. The most powerful section is Mendelssohn's magnificent paraphrase of Luther's hymn, "A Mighty Fortress is our God". Mendelssohn of course was not the only one to use such a device. But in order to appreciate what he made of it, we must consider what others did with the same idea. Think, for example, of the initial bars of *The Huguenots*, in which Meyerbeer inexcusably hurried the song through the orchestra in order to suggest something of the atmosphere of the Wars of Religion. He failed completely: the atmosphere he conjured up was not that of St. Bartholomew's Night, but of Paris grand opera in 1836.

Paris behaved in character and gave short shrift to Mendelssohn's far too serious "Reformation" Symphony. The "archaic" work was given only one reading at the Conservatoire; the musicians then shrugged and set it aside. But it is strange to find that people did not care for the symphony even in Germany and England.[4] Ultimately, Mendelssohn himself lost faith in it. He did not have the tenacity of Wagner, who stuck by every one of his major works through thick and thin, preferring to hate his adversaries rather than admit that their criticism might be just. He felt that if people did not like his symphony, they might be right: "I sometimes wonder that I did not make a better job of it," Mendelssohn later wrote, and filed the work away. (It was not published until after his death.)

[3] H. Kretzschmar: *Führer durch den Konzertsaal*, vol. II. Leipzig, 1899.
[4] *The Times*. London, April 1850.

But was this only a decent submitting to criticism, or was there some-thing else behind it? It would not have been the first time that Felix hid his deeper thoughts behind a screen. Once the celebration of the Reforma-tion was over, Mendelssohn must have asked himself why he had taken a theological stand in this occasional piece. He had intervened in the smouldering war between Protestants and Catholics. But why? He was a Christian, a Pauline Christian, baptized as a Protestant but in reality above all, spiritually centred upon Christianity as a whole. Did he not love Palestrina's Masses and Mozart's great ecclesiastical music? Why then had he written a symphony which might be taken as a defiance to Catholicism? What had led him to such sectarianism? It was no excuse to point to the example of Bach: no, none at all. Bach's situation had been entirely different. We have no statements of his on this question, but perhaps Mendelssohn realized that no religious composer of the nineteenth century should contribute to an intensification of the divisions within Christendom.

Perhaps this was his feeling. For certainly he felt no guilt at having produced an occasional piece. He did magnificently with occasional pieces. As Chorley has remarked, Mendelssohn was wont to write a work either in ten years or in ten days.[5] Once, meeting the nineteen-year-old Felix in the Mendelssohn garden, Alexander von Humboldt, who was on his way to the observatory he had set up on the premises, asked whether Felix would care to set to music a poem Ludwig Rellstab had written for a festive gathering of scientists. A few days later the opus was ready and "Alexander the Great", as the scientist was called, took pride in having it produced for the Berliners. Six months before, in April 1829, the Society of Graphic Artists had asked Felix for a cantata for the Dürer Festival, and Felix had obliged them with a splendid one.

The classical composers, too, would not have refused such assignments. But Felix Mendelssohn had more than that in mind. For he regarded himself as not only a composer, but also as a man of culture who in spite of antiquarian enthusiasms believed in Progress and modern inventions. Had anyone thought to ask him, he would have gladly provided steamship companies and railways shareholders with occasional music—although his contribution would not have included the hiss of steam and the clatter of rails, as a present-day Russian composer's does. Yet in 1840 he threw himself whole-heartedly into the task of writing a *Festgesang* to com-memorate the five hundredth anniversary of the art of printing. There was a true subject for him: Meister Gutenberg in Mainz! In preparation

[5] H. F. Chorley: *Modern German Music*. London, 1854.

he read through Wetter's history of the art of printing[6] and conjured up
the image of the wizard who invented cast type and the printing press:
Johann Gensfleisch zum Gutenberg, printer of the forty-two-line Paris
Bible. What a modern figure! And with his faith in all things progressive,
Felix set to work composing a piece worthy of its subject.

Again and again the composer stretched out his hand for the living
Word, the word pulsating with Spirit. In that year of 1840—the most
fecund year of his productive life—he also set the 114th Psalm to music,
showing the extent of his religious sensibility. On 6th January 1840 he
had set Eichendorff's "Des Jägers Abschied", with its solemn words:

> Wohl den Meister will ich loben
> so lang noch meine Stimm' erschallt!

That, too, was no purely secular song. And now the 114th Psalm, which
he set for a chorus of eight voices:

> The sea looked and fled,
> Jordan turned back.
> The mountains skipped like rams,
> The hills like lambs.

It had struck Moritz Hauptmann that Mendelssohn seemed to hear more
than other people in certain texts.[7] What did he hear in this one, that he
never spoke of it without emotion? Sir George Grove could boldly assert
(though a German might not do so, once the anti-Semites had decreed
that Mendelssohn could have no place in German art): "The Jewish
blood of Mendelssohn must surely for once have beat fiercely over this
picture of the great triumph of his forefathers...."[8] For an Englishman
would not find it hard to credit that a man with Jewish blood could also
be a good Englishman. Moreover, Mendelssohn the psalmist was also a
Christian. It must have been the irradiation of that Judaeo-Christianity
that caused a man like Thackeray to make the staggering remark to
Richard Doyle, the artist: "Mendelssohn's face is the most beautiful face
I ever saw. I imagine our Saviour's to have been like it."[9]

But Mendelssohn shows his religious side most convincingly in his
Second Symphony (opus 52). This work, also written in 1840 and performed at the Leipzig Festival Week on 25th June of that year, merged

---

[6] J. Wetter: *Kritische Geschichte der Erfindung der Buchdruckerkunst.*
Mainz, 1836.

[7] M. Hauptmann: *Briefe an Franz Hauser.* Leipzig, no date.

[8] Sir G. Grove: *Dictionary of Music and Musicians.* London, no date.

[9] R. Doyle: *A Sketch Book of Reminiscences.* London, 1880.

the symphonic form with that of the spiritual cantata. We do wrong to compare Mendelssohn's *Hymn of Praise* with Beethoven's Ninth Symphony, for the composer had something entirely different in mind. When Beethoven has the tenor introduce the final movement with the words: "O friends, no more of these sounds!" Wagner and his followers decided that that meant: "From now on, instrumental music has come to an end." No interpretation could be more far-fetched. Far from renouncing the symphonic form, Beethoven had begun to sketch a tenth symphony, which was to be purely instrumental once more.[10]

But to return to Mendelssohn's symphony-cantata (the term is Klinge-mann's, and seems an apt one) the issue was scarcely instrumental versus vocal music. Mendelssohn was experimenting with a romantic fusion of forms, and he succeeded admirably. The purely symphonic part is brief, though it contains three movements; the sung part is larger, built around phrases from the Bible selected by Mendelssohn himself. A beautifully sculptured motif, "And let all flesh magnify his might and his glory", emerges brilliantly from the trumpets:

[10] K. Nef: *Die Neun Sinfonien Beethovens.* Leipzig, 1928.

This motif was closely related to the piece Mendelssohn had recently completed for the Gutenberg festival.[11] Mendelssohn made the second movement a Scherzo because "the pious man's heart so joyously beats". Then comes the Chorale in G major, and then an *Adagio religioso* in D which leads in a soaring crescendo to the beginning of the vocal section. Here we find a wealth of forms and brilliant inspirations: some lovely women's choruses such as "Lobe den Herrn", deeply felt soprano duets, a tenor aria in C minor, wherein the anxious question is thrice repeated with rising intensity: "Hüter, ist die Nacht bald hin?"—and finally the joyous tidings from above:

Die   Nacht   ist   ver - gan - gen,   ver - gan - gen.

Mighty fugues play with the words, "Und ergreifen die Waffen des Lichts" and "Preiset seine Herrlichkeit." In the ten final measures the work recapitulates the motif of the beginning.

No religious work of Mendelssohn's, not even the *St. Paul* or the *Elijah*, found more favour with his contemporaries. The symphony-cantata had a triumph throughout Germany. Its arias immediately travelled from concert hall to the church and to the household. King Friedrich August II of Saxony, who had been present at the première, insisted on hearing it again and again. The entire royal family of Prussia was equally en-raptured and there was talk of coaxing Mendelssohn away from Leipzig and back to Berlin. In England the work was tremendously popular; Felix conducted it in Birmingham shortly after the Leipzig première. The "civilizing and optimistic quality of this music"—Anglican bishops spoke in such terms in those days—won all hearts for the *Hymn of Praise*.[12]

[11] E. Wolff: *Felix Mendelssohn-Bartholdy*. Berlin, 1909.
[12] *Fraser's Magazine*. London, 1848.

SCOTTISH SYMPHONY

Mendelssohn had made ten trips to England—so packed with events, emotions and impressions that they seemed like twenty. John Edward Taylor, the musician, was struck by how well Mendelssohn spoke English. His speech was more colourful than that of Englishmen themselves because, like every continental, he had an unusual choice of words. Whereas other Germans could not manage the *th*, Mendelssohn put to good use the speech defect he had inherited from his grandfather. He was enormously popular in society, among musicians, with the nobility. Once when Sir George Smart, the famous conductor, one-time friend of Haydn and later of Weber, was asked in company to play something on the piano, he laughingly refused: "No, no, do not call upon the old post-horse, when you have a high-mettled young racer at hand."[1]

The "Hebrides" overture had established Mendelssohn as virtually an English composer. How charming of him to have written such a glorious piece of music on Fingal's Cave! Any other artist would have followed up this success with a second piece in a similar vein. Mendelssohn, however, took ten years. It was 1842 before he completed the A minor Symphony (opus 56) known as the "Scottish", his major achievement in the symphonic form. Strangely enough, what characterized it was its complete remoteness from Beethoven. This "Scottish" Symphony was no instrumented sonata with theme, counter-theme and working-out, which, fundamentally speaking, all classical symphonies had been. It was a truly new form: a symphonic arrangement of song themes, of intricate variations upon *lieder* which somewhere and sometime had been sung by the people. True, a great instrumentalist, a master of the piano and a connoisseur of the most involved effects, was constantly manipulating these borrowed themes. Nevertheless, it remains astonishing that the raw material of the symphony consisted of songs.

Mendelssohn himself was well aware of this, for at the beginning of the Andante he introduced a melancholy song from his own *St. Paul*, which still later he was to use in the *Elijah*:[2]

[1] H. R. Cox: *Leaves from the Journal of Sir George Smart*. London, 1907.
[2] H. Kretzschmar: *Führer durch den Konzertsaal*, vol. II. Leipzig, 1899.

The first principal theme quickly follows. It is a genuinely Mendelssohnian inspiration, rapid and nervous, while at the same time both the rapidity and the nervousness are *muted*. This theme is unmistakably the beginning of a ballad:

That is to say, once again a song. How intensely songlike it is may be shown when we compare it with the passage in *Fidelio* where Marzelline, Rocco's daughter, begins a similar ballad of longing as follows:

In the third line, however, with the moralistic comment, "A girl can say what she thinks, after all," she drops back into the eighteenth century at its most bourgeois. Mendelssohn carries out the ballad idea with much greater verve. His sense of tone does not desert him. Never abandoning the yearning quality of the minor, the cautious, crouching, muted feeling, he produces a melody that seems to have its eyes half shut.... Listening to these *strings*, we involuntarily recall Lindblad's remark about Mendelssohn's "underwater trumpets". Suddenly, completely unexpectedly, there enters in a hint of rage, that brief but dangerous anger which Mendelssohn's friends knew him to be susceptible to. But even this touch has a ballad quality—and the movement ends in melancholy.

Is this not a song? It is almost Schubert's: "Gute Ruh, gute Ruh, mach die Augen zu"—the brook's fatal lullaby in the "Schöne Müllerin". It is as heartbreaking here as there. Perhaps both inspirations go back to the same migrant folksong.

We do not know the songs that Mendelssohn transformed and ennobled in his "Scottish" Symphony. There is, however, no doubt that they were really Scottish melodies. He was drawing on impressions he had gathered on his trip through the Highlands in 1829. The feat of memory is amazing. But it is even more amazing that not a measure of the "Scottish" Symphony had previously been used in the "Hebrides". Mendelssohn's travels in Scotland had yielded so rich a harvest that he had more than enough stored up to meet his needs. (As a matter of fact, he had enough for three Scottish pieces, for he had also written a *Sonate Écossaise*. But it was neither a sonata nor conspicuously Scottish, and rightly recognizing this, he had crossed out the title and called it instead: Fantasy in F sharp minor.[3])

We know something, as we have seen, about the circumstances that gave rise to the "Hebrides" overture. We possess similar information concerning the A minor Symphony. On 30th July 1829 Mendelssohn wrote from Edinburgh:

> Today we went in dense dusk to the palace where Queen Mary lived and loved. There is a small room to be seen, with a winding staircase leading up to it; they went up there, found Riccio in the little room, dragged him out, and three rooms away is a dark corner where they killed him. The roof is gone from the

[3] W. Edwards: *The Times*. London, 1863.

adjoining chapel; a great deal of grass and ivy are growing in it; and at the shattered altar Mary was crowned Queen of Scotland. Everything is decayed and smashed, and the clear sky shines straight into it. I think I have found the beginning of my Scottish Symphony today.[4]

He had indeed found it. In ruins, time stands still. Or rather, old times look helplessly at the present time swirling about them. Ruins belong to eternity; they do not know the passage of the days and nights. For that reason the most derelict of ruins gives us a greater sense of bygone ages than any monument in perfect preservation.

Here, then, in the roofless palace, Felix Mendelssohn felt the emptiness and sadness peopled with shadowy beings. But he did not try to deal directly with their story, or write what would have been an equivalent of Liszt's *Mazeppa* or Strauss's *Don Juan*. Instead, he summoned up the echoes of the ballads that the people sang or might have sung about Mary Stuart and Riccio and Darnley.

The Romantics were particularly drawn to the story of Mary Stuart. She was their perfect heroine, wilful and passionate, widowed young, heroic in her struggle against adversity, and finally dying loyal to the Catholic faith. In Béranger's:

> Adieu, charmant pays de France,
> adieu, te quitter c'est mourir[5]

Mary Stuart was recalled to life, as she was in Mendelssohn's symphony, and was to be again in 1852, a few years after Mendelssohn's death, when Schumann set to music the *Poems of Mary Stuart*, her "Prayer after the Birth of a Son", her "Address to Queen Elizabeth", and her "Farewell to the World".

Mary herself, then, was a song—and the Scottish people were a music-loving people. Especially they loved the music of the bagpipes.

Felix's ear had registered this characteristic sound. In his Scherzo he used the clarinet to simulate a bagpipe:

It was a true Scottish motif, devoid of fourths and sevenths. Then again came a complete change of mood: a hymnic, lyrical Adagio in A major,

---

[4] S. Hensel: *Die Familie Mendelssohn 1729–1847*. Berlin, 1879.
[5] Janin: *Béranger et son temps*. Paris, 1866.

with pizzicato accompaniment of the violins. This was followed by an onrushing *Allegro guerriero*, like a veritable war-dance. (For there was nothing languid about Mendelssohn as a musician. His piano-playing, for example, abounded in spells of "fury" as violent as Liszt's.)

The symphony unfolds and we become aware that we are not hearing themes struggling against one another, but the initial lines of songs. In the *Allegro guerriero* there are actually five. At the end, in tremendous crescendo, comes an *Allegro maestoso* which strangely enough employs six-eight time. Felix was worried that this end might sound too much like a male chorus and asked Ferdinand David whether he should not omit the kettledrums, strengthen the horns and sharply limit the violins. Fortunately his friend, who liked the "roaring and buzzing", argued for keeping things just as they were.[6]

If the "Scottish" Symphony is full of changes of mood, it is because Felix's trip through Scotland had also been full of contrasts. For he was travelling with his dear friend Klingemann, the liveliest and best of travel companions. Though not much of a poet, Klingemann could record their experiences in fairly vivid vignettes, such as the following:[7]

> Lofty mountains rise toward the heavens,
> And the moors stretch black as pitch between them.
> Castles, gorges, precipices, ruins
> Tell their tales of ancient, bygone days.
> Mind and senses reel, for we, the moderns
> Dream of the past, but understand it scarcely.
> Yet by the gates of their fair land dwells one,
> A wise man, who unlocks the ancient riddles
> And brings to light anew all that is gold.
>> Now we go gladly
>> Peering and hearing,
>> Walking and talking,
> Beholding and the meaning unfolding
> Of castles and gorges, precipices and ruins.
>> But the wise man still mines
>> More and more treasures
> And mints them into golden, tinkling coins!

The "wise man" whom Klingemann gently pokes fun at was none other than the famous Sir Walter Scott, who received them hospitably at

[6] J. Eckardt: *Ferdinand David und die Familie Mendelssohn-Bartholdy*. Leipzig, 1888.

[7] S. Hensel: op. cit.

Abbotsford. They walked in the park under the mighty elms; but unfortunately their visit lasted only an hour, for Sir Walter was on the point of departure. That was a considerable disappointment to the two friends, for they had no chance to discuss music, or even learn a bit about Sir Walter's musical preferences. They might have been surprised by their discoveries, for the great novelist who was supplying half of Europe with musical subjects was himself entirely unmusical.[8]

BLUE SKY IN A MAJOR

To this day Felix Mendelssohn's "Italian" Symphony (opus 90) is always mentioned in conjunction with the "Scottish". The explanation is that it was actually commissioned by the English. Mendelssohn had won the Londoners' hearts with his "Hebrides". In August 1832 the firm of Erard in London made him a present of a concert grand piano. In November the Philarmonic Society asked him to compose a symphony for them. He was offered one hundred guineas. Mendelssohn accepted the commission, and wrote the symphony out of his "Italian Sketches", which he had probably had for a long time. The only phrase to describe what he produced is "a blue sky in A major". He was painting Italy as a travelling Englishman might see her. Italy did have its idyllic side, after all, though it was not exactly the real Italy.

Mendelssohn begins his *Allegro vivace* with a burst which Richard Strauss might have emulated:

[8] A. Hadley: "Was Sir Walter Scott Musical?" *Music and Letters,* XVII. 1936.

This then ascends on a note of manly cheerfulness. A melodic second
theme enters, but does not add any profundity to the whole:

As always, Mendelssohn was writing good music—but it was too transparent, too crystalline, too beautiful. If this was Italy, it was an Italy seen
by an Englishman who never left the terrace of his grand hotel, unless it
was to take a little outing in a carriage.

Yet young Mendelssohn had had his spell in Italy. True, he had associated chiefly with Germans there. He had given a wide berth to the
professional Bohemians of the *Cafe Greco*, who somehow struck him as
unsavoury. "There they sit around on the benches, wearing wide hats, big
butcher's dogs beside them, their necks, cheeks, their whole faces sprout-
ing hair, sending up dreadful clouds of smoke, saying rude things to one
another. The dogs contribute to the spread of vermin; a cravat, a tailcoat,
would constitute an innovation; whatever part of the face is left free of
beard is covered by eyeglasses. And so they drink coffee and talk of Titian
and Pordenone as if those artists were sitting beside them likewise
wearing beards and sou'westers. What is more they paint such sickly
Madonnas, such feeble saints, such weakling heroes, that at times one
feels like slashing away."[1]

Felix was far more in his element at the home of Baron von Bunsen,[2]
the Prussian Ambassador. His wife was Fanny Waddington, an extremely
rich Englishwoman who was ready to give a nephew of the noted diplomat

[1] F. Mendelssohn-Bartholdy: *Briefe aus den Jahren 1830–47*. Leipzig,
no date.

[2] F. v. Bunsen: *Bunsen aus seinen Briefen und nach Erinnerungen
geschildert*. Leipzig, 1868–71.

Bartholdy, the benefit of her many important connections. Josias von Bunsen, son of an impoverished noble family, had originally hoped to emigrate to New York as tutor to John Jacob Astor, the millionaire's son.[3] Subsequently he had become a diplomat in Rome, having been launched on that career by the great Barthold Georg Niebuhr. Through these distinguished connections Felix Mendelssohn made the acquaintance of Abbate Giuseppe Baini, the head of the Papal Choir, and of the great collector, Abbate Fortunato Santini. Thus Felix was enabled to fulfil his passion for old music.[4]

But apart from these learned abbots, and a few nobles to whom he had been recommended by letters of introduction from Berlin, Felix knew no Italians. He was totally unaware of the political currents of Italian life—for which we cannot blame either him or Ambassador Bunsen. Bunsen did not think it appropriate to discuss politics with an artist, and all his life Felix, with wise instinct, had kept clear of things political.

But in this case was it so wise not to know where he and others stood? Perhaps the "Italian" Symphony that Felix wrote a decade later would have been more Italian if he had tried to sound out the cultural aspirations of the Italian people. But he knew nothing of these. He was equally ignorant of the secular struggles of the Papacy, the ambitions of Austria, which was at that time firmly established in Lombardy, and of France's preparations for expelling the Austrians from Italy. Balzac's great novel *Massimila Doni*, which penetrates this complex situation to the heart, had not yet been written. Stendhal alone might have given Mendelssohn a little pertinent information[5]—but Felix, though a passionate reader, probably was not familiar with Stendhal. Felix might, it is true, have learned something from Rossini's *Moses*, for that tempestuously political opera[6] was already written (and no doubt served as an encouragement to Verdi to write his idealistic *Nabucco*). Rossini, who was regarded as a pleasant and ingenious melodist—especially in Germany—at any rate knew what was stirring beneath the surface of his native land.

We may therefore ask whether the "Italian" Symphony really had anything to do with Italy at all. But it had. In the second movement the composer brings in a group of pilgrims. A minor mood dims the blue sky. It is not the great minor of the "Hebrides", nor the nordic sombreness of the "Scottish" Symphony; but it is minor enough to make us feel the

[3] J. Parton: *Life of J. J. Astor*. New York, 1865.
[4] G. Baini: *Palestrina-Studien*. Leipzig, 1834.
[5] L. Farges: *Stendhal diplomate; Rome et l'Italie de 1829 à 1842*. Paris, 1892.
[6] Stendhal: *Rossini*. Paris, 1892.

justice of Vaughan Williams's comment: "Mendelssohn is great in melancholy, and his majors affect us chiefly when they are suddenly opposed to the minor." In the first movement there is no opposition to the major mood at all; it is a sunniness too easily attained. But the second movement, the pilgrims' movement with its deliberate pace, with the mournful, subdued melody in the violas, oboes and bassoons, the monotony of the quavers, is really extraordinary art. The mood is penitential; we sense the weary steps of the pilgrims along the stony road. It is hard to feel that a symphony is being performed—so strong is the sense of a choral work, as is always the case with Mendelssohn:

With pianissimo murmuring, the pilgrims' chorus fades away in the distance. Somewhat abruptly, the A major blue sky returns, but in a Germanic three-four time whose justification is hard to see. Certainly there is little about this that is Italianate. Perhaps Mendelssohn is suggesting that he is bored, is reminding himself and us, with a few horn fanfares, that it is possible to take the post-chaise and be back home in the German forests. . . . In Italy, after all, there were no real forests.

The fourth movement, however, is incontrovertibly Italian. With the *Saltarello* he transports us to the heart of Naples.[7] A more and more violent presto—the dance waxes furious and every head is spinning:

Now and then the tempo slackens, and little spaces open out in the music, moments of tenderness and intimacy—and then the current of the dance sweeps high again and all delicacy is drowned in its rough

[7] G. Roccoli: *Saltarello e Tarantella*. Milan, 1901.

exuberance. Here is the clearest instance of Mendelssohn's insight into foreign folk modes. The authenticity of the *Saltarello* redeems whatever is weak in the "Italian" Symphony.

ANYTHING BUT NATIONAL MUSIC

Whenever he travelled, Felix's ear was open to the characteristic qualities in the music of different peoples. He was keenly aware of Italian, English, Swiss folk modes. And yet his finely balanced mind sensed something false in music with a strongly local flavour. For music transcended nations. It was, to use Romain Rolland's phrase, *audessus de la mêlée*; or as Benedetto Croce has even more trenchantly put it: "Like the air, music mocks at national boundaries. For a while it may be caught in a national forest or isolated valley, but ultimately it rises again into the ether whence it came.... Music has no fatherland."

Still, we cannot but think that Mendelssohn was in a strange mood on 25th August 1829 when he wrote the following from the town of Llangollen in Wales: "Anything but national music! Ten thousand devils take all such nationalism. Here I am in Wales, and, O how picturesque, a harpist sits in the hallway of every reputable tavern playing so-called folk melodies, that is to say, infamous, vulgar, rotten trash, while at the same time a hurdy-gurdy is also grinding out its melodies; enough to drive one mad; it has given me a toothache. The Scottish bagpipes, the Swiss cow-horns, the Welsh harps, all of them peddling their hunters' choruses and gruesome variations—the songs in the hall—all this eminently respectable music! It's unspeakable. Here I am unable to bear Beethoven's nationalistic songs, and I come here and have to listen to the cawing of these screechy nasal instruments accompanied by ludicrous, asinine singers, and don't even swear!"[1]

He is joking, of course—for do we not know that Felix consciously followed the examples of Haydn and Beethoven when he set out to explore Great Britain and gathered material for the "Scottish" Symphony? He owed as much of his inspiration to the national music of various countries as Weber had, and certainly more than Beethoven. And yet there was something else besides an antic disposition at play: Felix was touching on certain deep convictions of his. It was not so much a matter

[1] S. Hensel: *Die Familie Mendelssohn 1729–1847*. Berlin, 1879.

of aesthetics as of ethics. What lay behind this cult of folk music, and this movement for the revival of venerable national instruments? What was the content of these folk songs? *My* mountains, *my* valley, *my* Alps, *my* Rhine. How possessive and exclusive it all was!

Yet there were great things among these native strains. There was the alpine cowherd's song, the *ranz-des-vaches*, with its magnificent melancholy, its clanging of bells and long lament. In 1831, while staying in the Simmental, Mendelssohn transcribed a Swiss folk melody and sent it to his sister, and on the Rigi he heard the alpenhorn, which in all probability he had hitherto known only as a poetical reference.[2] Only now could he appreciate the effect of the alpenhorn upon a Swiss peasant impressed into army service, who in a wave of homesickness tries to desert ("Zu Strassburg auf der Schanz, da ging mein Trauern an"). And what about his own male choruses which had captured the dark-green tone of the German forests? Was that not folk music?

Nevertheless, this grandson of the Enlightenment could not but feel the peril inherent in all such national manifestations, whose effect was to separate peoples rather than unite them. Behind the swelling of the heart at the thought of home, lurked politics, and other dangerous passions. Music could be turned into a weapon. The ethical repugnance that the artist Mendelssohn felt for any partnership between art and war, that deadly enemy of spiritual life, sometimes took the form of an aesthetic distaste for all manifestations of nationalism and racialism.[3] When fine words were bandied about concerning the musical genius of the folk, he was sometimes forced to ask himself, "What do these people whose chief business is distilling whiskey, planting potatoes, or herding cows really have to do with music, the goddess of my own life?" This or that country was beautiful, but would it not be more beautiful if it consisted only of high mountains that conversed with the clouds and had no inhabitants at all? Then these strange national forms of music which touched his heart so deeply would not exist; he would never hear the Highlanders' harmonies without sixths or the untrammelled octave yodelling of the alpine dwellers, which for all its pride sounded like a cry of grief. There was an insoluble contradiction here, and Felix could not master it. Once, when he was again discussing an opera subject with Devrient (probably *William Tell*), Felix wrote: "Show Switzerland in its full might and enormous

[2] A. E. Cherbuliez: *Die Schweiz in der deutschen Musikgeschichte.* Frauenfeld, 1932.

[3] Sir G. A. Macfarren: *Mendelssohn's Antigone, Recollections.* London, 1865.

freshness."[4] With his tremendous gift for abstraction, Schiller had made the people in his drama of Tell talk in images and metaphors such as ordinary folk would never have used—and nevertheless he had miraculously rendered the emotions and the emotional language of the Swiss. *Tell* is a tremendous drama of democracy, a theme which Rossini was never equal to and which possibly should have been treated by a Wagner. It was not a theme for Mendelssohn. His aristocratic honesty even led him to doubt whether anything that pleased the masses could be good art at all.

He was reinforced in this idea when a storm broke out over a song whose composition was wrongly ascribed to him, possibly with the idea of luring him into setting it. It was a loathsomely political song by Nikolaus Becker, written in 1840 and aimed at stirring up war-fever against France; for a "defensive" war, of course. The text went:

> Sie sollen ihn nicht haben,
> den freien deutschen Rhein,
> ob sie wie gier'ge Raben
> sich heiser danach schrei'n.[5]
> (They shall not have it, the free German Rhine,
> though they hoarsely scream
> for it like greedy ravens.)

Of course the French were chiefly to blame for the dispute over the Rhine. Their pseudo-romantic school had for years been calling for revenge for Waterloo.[6] Now France was having political and military difficulties in the Orient and—since she did not dare to turn upon powerful England—her exacerbated feelings turned with fresh fury against the then ally of the English, the Prussians. The cry arose that France must have the Palatinate, her border on the Rhine. German poets and German newspapers were quick to retort. Old Ernst Moritz Arndt wrote "Alldeutschland in Frankreich hinein", Max Schneckenburger "Die Wacht am Rhein", and Nikolaus Becker, the trashiest of the lot, "Sie sollen ihn nicht haben". Whereupon he was answered by Alfred de Musset in an aesthetically far superior poem: "Nous l'avons eu, votre Rhin allemand".[7] With all this excitement, it was a wonder that war did not break out, that 1870 was not anticipated in 1840.

[4] E. Devrient: *Meine Erinnerungen an Felix Mendelssohn-Bartholdy.* Leipzig, 1872.

[5] L. Waeles: *Nikolaus Becker.* Bonn, 1896.

[6] E. Friedell: *Kulturgeschichte der Neuzeit,* vol. III. Munich, 1931.

[7] Barine: *Alfred de Musset.* Paris, 1893.

We must remember Felix Mendelssohn's longstanding dislike for France in order to appreciate the cultural consciousness and the pan-European spirit of his attitude towards all this. Was he to contribute his own talent to something that would sharpen tensions between two hot-tempered nations? Romain Rolland, that apostle of peace, never wrote anything finer than the words Mendelssohn sent from Leipzig to Klingemann in London:

> The whole city is ringing with a political song aimed against the French, which the newspapers are doing everything in their power to make popular. Since very little else is going on, they are succeeding admirably. Everybody is talking about the "Rhine Song", or the "Colognaise", as it is significantly called. The thing is typical, for the verses begin: "They shall not have it, the free German Rhine", and "They shall not have it" is repeated at the beginning of every stanza. As if that were at all apposite! It might at least have been put: "We want to keep it!" But "they shall not have it" seems to me altogether fruitless, useless, juvenile. If something is ours beyond a doubt, we don't have to go about singing that we won't let it belong to anyone else. The verses have had a great success at court in Berlin, and in the casinos and clubs here. Naturally the musicians have leaped into the breach and are scribbling away, composing themselves into immortality. The Leipzig composers have written no less than three tunes for it, and every day the newspapers carry some item or other about the song. Yesterday it was said, among other things, that I had done a setting of the piece, whereas I would never dream of putting such defensive chauvinism to music. There you have it, people lie like troopers, here, where you are, and everywhere.[8]

He expressed his opinion even more plainly in a letter to his brother Paul:

> I could write you a long lament about the aforesaid Rhine song. You have no idea what a fuss they are making about it here, and how repulsive this newspaper *enthusiasme* is to me. In addition, the whole idea of raising such a din to assert that the others shall not get what we have! It would be worth a real din and real music to describe it. . . . Little boys and timid souls scream about

[8] F. Mendelssohn-Bartholdy: *Briefwechsel mit Klingemann*. Wiesbaden, 1909.

such things, but real men do not make a to-do about what's theirs; they have it and that's an end of it. I am vexed that, among other things, they have said in the newspapers that apart from the four settings of these glorious words which Leipzig has already supplied, there is another one by me. . . . There stood my name, printed out in full. . . . And I cannot call anyone a liar; it wouldn't do. My publisher Härtel has also sent me word that if I did compose it he's sure he can sell 6,000 copies in two months. No, Paul—I'm not doing anything of the sort![9]

Can we imagine Wagner ignoring such an opportunity? On the contrary, he would have leaped at such a chance to ingratiate himself with the *demos.* In fact, thirty years later he did exactly that, and taunted the defeated French with a so-called comic pamphlet entitled, *A Capitulation* —in the judgment of Thomas Mann "an incredibly tasteless, in every sense self-betraying satire".[10] Is this, then, the lesson: that the lonelier an artist is, and the more elevated his creative work, the more eagerly he must seize the chance to merge his outlook with the multitude, even if the path they are taking is as ethically questionable as that of the Bismarckian German Reich? (Such was the argument raised at the time by Geoffrey Schultz, who was certainly no enemy of Wagner.) Would the vast public be more receptive to the remarkable chordal structure of *Tristan*, the poignant shepherd's song, the ecstasy of the love-death—if it was known that the author also wrote marches for the Kaiser?

Mendelssohn, at any rate, would never have stooped to that. The thought of war with France made him shudder. Not the least horrible part of it was to have the air poisoned with narrowness and hate. Perhaps another Jahn would come along, and harangue the German nation: "Anyone who has his children taught the French language is a madman; anyone who persists in doing so, sins against the Holy Ghost; but if he has his daughters taught French, it is just the same as if he had them taught whoredom."[11] Mendelssohn was German and realized what had been at stake in 1814 and 1815. The war had had to be won. But had there been any need for some of the things that happened when the Allies marched into Paris? The Mendelssohn family was well acquainted with that episode in recent history. They had kept a packet of letters from their Parisian aunt, Henriette: "As a German I have had the pleasure of having

[9] F. Mendelssohn-Bartholdy: *Briefe aus den Jahren 1830–47.* Leipzig, 1861.

[10] Th. Mann: *Leiden und Grösse der Meister.* Frankfurt am Main, 1957.

[11] A. Streckfuss: *Fünfhundert Jahre Berliner Geschichte.* Berlin, 1880.

to listen to all the complaints about *vos Prussiens*, who are out to prove that they are real avengers. They rob, scorch, burn and kill as though they had learned it all out of some legend of the Middle Ages. But what most disturbs people here seems to be the lack of courtesy. I have frequently heard people say: 'Les soldats des autres nations prennent, mais poliment, ce n'est pas comme ces Prussiens!' "[12]

So Felix could have little sympathy with the warmongers of 1841, and with the sponsors of that abominable Rhine song. He even had some words on the subject with his clerical friend Julius Schubring, who in all innocence was also trying to set the thing to music. Felix couched his reservations in aesthetic language, and had to ask his friend to treat the matter as a confidential one: "For Heaven's sake let us keep this between us; the journalists as it is print every scrap of news on the subject, and I might find myself being booted across the border as a French sympathizer."[13] For the atmosphere was such that to say anything against either the words or the music of the Rhine song was to proclaim oneself a Francophile. Schubring, however, was the author of the text for Mendelssohn's *St. Paul*, and would soon be helping and advising him on the *Elijah*. And so Felix took his friend gently by the ear and led him away from politics into a realm in which both of them were more at home: the realm of religious art.

THE WRATH AND THE GRIEF OF THE PROPHET ELIJAH

If Mendelssohn had lived around 1900, rather than in the days before the Revolution of 1848, he would probably have been made to feel it as something of a fault that he had written an *Elijah* ten years after his *St. Paul*: a work based upon the Old Testament after his New Testament oratorio. Later times would have regarded that as eclectic, and around 1900 the charge of eclecticism was a harsh one. Unjustifiably so. A great artist naturally selects. He is not enslaved to any one philosophy or ideology. He affirms the richness and variety of the world, and takes from it what he can. The authenticity of *Electra* was in no way compromised because Hofmannsthal employed Catholic and Calderònian elements

[12] S. Hensel: op. cit.
[13] *Briefwechsel zwischen Mendelssohn und Schubring*. Leipzig, 1892.

along with his archaic material. Nor was the authenticity of Mendelssohn's work compromised when he, a Protestant and Bachian, composed a work for intensely Catholic Liège, basing it upon a text by St. Thomas Aquinas, *Lauda Sion Salvatorem*. The occasion was the six-hundredth anniversary of the institution of the Corpus Christi festival. And if Mendelssohn chose in that work (opus 73) to be as Italian, as sensuously joyous as Rossini or even Verdi, we can only conclude that a really great artist refuses to confine himself within narrow philosophical limits. Everything that is great and strong makes its claim upon him.

Such was the case with the Biblical oratorios *St. Paul* and *Elijah*, beneath which throbbed an intense faith in the Divine Word. A man named Mendelssohn could not create a New Testament oratorio without matching it with a companion piece glorifying the Old Covenant. The fact that his *St. Paul* antedated his *Elijah* by ten years was mere chance. The succession might equally well have been the other way around; there was no question of preference, certainly not of "conversion". Old Testament and New: to Mendelssohn God's Word was God's Word.

In purely musical terms, however, he had taken a step forward that we must regard as amazing. *Elijah* far more than *St. Paul* anticipates the future, the victory of the art of expression. *Elijah* is elemental music. It is not especially enlightening here, any more than in the cases of the *Walpurgis Night*, the "Hebrides" or the "Scottish" Symphony, to describe Mendelssohn's achievement in terms of some such convenient slogan as Romantic Classicism, to say that Mendelssohn found a creative intermediary position between classicism and romanticism. For the true core of this oratorio is the landscape of Palestine, charged with elemental forces. Just as the depths of the Rhine and the rocks in Wagner's *Ring* are not merely the scene of the human and divine drama, but help to shape the drama, in fact form the basis for it—similarly, the soil of Palestine in *Elijah* shares the stage with Elijah himself. It is a land of drought, thirst and hunger, and also of lightning, thunder, blue-black torrents of rain; of earthquakes, fires, raging storms, green oases and golden deserts, of leathery palm leaves and aromatic shrubs, and whistling winds "in which is the Lord". Such is the ground on which Elijah walks, and he himself, the zealot, quick to wrath and subsiding into sorrow, has the character of the soil itself. *St. Paul* lacked this true local colour: the scenery evoked might be the rural landscape outside Cologne or Düsseldorf, not the Orient in which the story of Paul of Tarsus actually took place.

Felix Mendelssohn had never seen the actual Palestine—for that matter neither had Handel. But both men had an inner vision of the land, and perhaps an affinity for the extremes which are characteristic of its climate and geography.[1] Like Handel in *Israel in Egypt* Mendelssohn began with elemental music, a bare recitative. This is no narrator, however, but Elijah himself speaking—and we seem to see the prophet standing there with girded loins.

Winds and kettledrums remain piano for the time being; a more economical and more powerful introduction could not have been found. And now the overture begins, describing the effect of Elijah's curse. ("As the Lord the God of Israel lives, before whom I stand, there shall be neither dew nor rain these years, except by my word.") A fugue. A fear-stricken crowd creeps along, on winding paths; this is not a march but a slow, dragging movement of dying creatures who fall out by the wayside —we can almost see it! This is drought. And it is something else, some-thing other than mere failure of rain in Europe; it is impotence, dread, despair and repentance. "Wilt Thou destroy us, O Lord?" Choruses cry out to heaven. Nature—the same divine nature which in Noah's day drowned the sinful generations of men in the Flood—stops all rain for three years. The Israelites languish and die.

Even the bringer of the curse is endangered. But the word of God comes to him, bidding him to retire to a brook where the ravens feed him with heavenly nourishment. But he cannot remain there. He goes to the home of a widow. Being the man of God, he is able to resuscitate this widow's child which (though the Bible glosses over this point) has died of thirst. Mendelssohn and the author of his text have been criticized for having included this episode in the oratorio. They could not have chosen

[1] H. Leichtentritt: *Händel.* Berlin, Leipzig, 1925.

a more effective one! For this scene is the only one that does not take place under the open sky. It has the dramatic value of an interior scene. Moreover, the death of the child and the grief of its mother affect us far more than the deaths of thousands who have perished in the drought. And when, trice-repeated, with rising intensity:

the prophet's prayer recalls the child's departed soul to the body, it is as if he has done the same for thousands.

After this proof of God's grace to Elijah comes the contest between him and the priests of Baal, who are dominant in Israel. Two altars are erected; two bulls are butchered and wood made ready: one altar for Baal and one for Jehovah. And Elijah proclaims: "The God who answers by fire, he is God." The priests of Baal and their followers now begin a moderato round-dance around their altar. The musical depiction of their increasing uneasiness, as Baal does not answer their plea, is a psychological masterpiece: "O Baal, hear us. Turn to our offering! . . . Send us thy fire, destroy the foe." Then follows Elijah's biting mockery: "Cry aloud, for he is a god; either he is musing, or he has gone aside, or he is on a journey, or perhaps he is asleep and must be awakened." They cry louder; their staccato invocations are full of fear and rage. They cut themselves with knives, so that their blood may placate Baal. "Limp around the altar which you have made, cry and prophesy!" Elijah mocks. "O Baal, answer us, answer us!" the priests shriek for the last time. Then their mouths freeze open—and here is one of the most dramatic grand pauses in musical literature, when it becomes evident that they will receive no response. Elijah breaks this silence with his prayer, "Lord God of Abraham!" in E flat major. He calls upon the Lord to send his fire to consume the offering. There is a tremendous clap of thunder—and a sea of flames is raging around the altar. Jehovah has won. The priests of Baal are led away to their deaths. A fanatical song of triumph in A minor, rigid and inexorable, proclaims that "the Word of the Lord is as a fire."[2] This is a highly problematical scene. For the Mendelssohn of the *St. Paul* would have signalized the defeat of the priests by making them fall down and worship the true God; he would not have had them massacred. But the Old Testament text was explicit on this point.[3]

After the wicked priests have been removed, God gives another telling demonstration of His power. Elijah sends a boy to the top of a hill. Is there no cloud in sight? "I see nothing", the boy calls down. "The sky is brazen above my head." And again: "I see nothing. The sky is brazen above my head," the dreamy words are repeated. "Is there no rushing as of rain? Do you still see nothing over the sea?" Elijah asks in dark and gentle tones. A pause. The boy repeats: "I see nothing." Then Elijah raises his arms to heaven: "Answer the prayer of thy servant! Remember thy mercy, O Lord!"

Then the gates of Heaven open. At first there is only a little cloud, no bigger than a man's hand. Then the heavens grow black with clouds; a fragrant wind arises. There is a rushing and rustling. The heavens rumble their affirmation; the people shed tears of joy. Above the E flat major of the whole orchestra soars the final chorus of the people. Semi-quavers paint the rain descending in torrents. The rolling cadences of the thanksgiving are worthy of Handel at his greatest: "Thank thee, O Lord, that thou drenchest the thirsty land! The streams of water rise, the waves of water roar mightily; but the Lord is still mightier in His greatness."[4]

Here the first act ends, but not the story of Elijah. Mendelssohn and Schubring would have done well to begin the second act with a narrative: of how King Ahab and his people forgot the miracle of the rain and lapsed again into idolatry. And of how Queen Jezebel in particular could not forgive the deaths of the priests of Baal. . . . But who was there in the oratorio to tell the story? The epic narrator is no longer on the scene. Direct action in Handelian manner might have been employed to show events as they took place.[5] But Mendelssohn distrusted such a method; his reverence for the Biblical text was too great to allow him to invent action not based upon the authentic words of Scripture. Hence the listener is obliged to deduce what actually took place from arias and phrases from the psalms, and this is a matter of some difficulty. Victorious, Elijah is again threatened with death, it would seem. Very well. But it is not

[2] E. Wolff: *Felix Mendelssohn-Bartholdy*. Berlin, 1909.
[3] Ibid.
[4] F. G. Edwards: *History of Elijah*. London, no date.
[5] F. Chrysander: *Georg Friedrich Händel*. Leipzig, 1858–67.

logical that the people should cry out to him once more: "He must die. *Why is he permitted to lock the portals of heaven?* Why is he permitted to prophesy in the name of the Lord?" These protests come long after the heavens have opened. Handel, with the feeling of dramatic climax, would not have permitted such an inconsistency. Nevertheless, this situation— God once more snatches Elijah from danger—affords the composer an opening for a passage of such grandeur that it makes us forget the dramatic weaknesses of the second act. For now Elijah no longer wishes to serve. He is overcome by that weariness, that deep sadness, that Mendelssohn himself knew so well. He feels that he has lived in vain. He has been unable to extirpate the worship of Baal. All his anger has accomplished nothing. Profound melancholy overpowers him. He wishes to die. He pleads with God to grant him death. It is no Bachian death he desires, no consoling entrance into Eternal Life, but a quiet passage into nothingness. His "It is enough! I desire to live no longer; my days have been in vain," moves us deeply by its contemporary tone. And at the same time these words are exceedingly ancient. Mendelssohn had already found the musical equivalents of them in the *St. Paul* and in the "Scottish Symphony". They are not only Jewish and not only Christian. The Greeks, too, had their *mataion*, the melancholy of vain effort. It is seen in the sorrowing expression of their Farnese Heracles as he leans upon his club. What is the sense of ever lifting the club again? The world is too full of monsters, and there is never an end to the deeds that must be done.[6]

But God will not permit Elijah to die. For the present he is still needed on earth. "Behold, he who keeps Israel will not slumber," a chorus encourages the emissary of God. "Thou walkest in fear, but he refreshes thee." Elijah continues to hold back, but an angel leads him to Mount Horeb. He is warned to cover his face, for the Lord will approach him. and now there begins the greatest, the most inspired chorus that Felix Mendelssohn ever wrote: "The Lord has passed." But the Lord was not in the great and strong wind that rent the mountains, nor in the earthquake, nor in the fire (see following page).

That is elemental music, begotten of the Palestinian landscape; and at the same time it is spiritual music. Greater intensity is scarcely possible than the intensity achieved in the "Ascension of Elijah". God send his chariot of fire and carries the prophet off to Heaven. There are flashes of jagged lightning in the orchestra; the winds are like molten metal; the chorus accompanies the miracle with stormy rhythms and long-drawn-out cries. Then, as suddenly as it has come, the vision passes. Mendelssohn

[6] O. Gruppe: *Die griechischen Kulte und Mythen.* Leipzig, 1887.

Medallion struck at the command of Frederick William IV to commemorate the *première* of the *Antigone* in 1841. Property of the International Felix Mendelssohn Society.

Felix Mendelssohn on his deathbed. Property of Geheimrat Hensel, Marburg. (*Photo-Marburg, Marburg an der Lahn*)

allots only twenty measures for the whole episode, and the act ends in shuddering chords.

Elijah is one of the major peaks of religious music between Beethoven's *Christus am Ölberg* and Wagner's *Parsifal*. *Parsifal*, that wonderful mystery-drama, is mentioned advisedly. As early as 1834 Wagner had written in his essay, *German Opera*: "Is it not a patent misunderstanding of the present day for a composer to be still writing oratorios *in whose content and forms no one any longer believes*?"[7] This was directed not against Mendelssohn, but against Friedrich Schneider, Schubring's friend, who had represented the life of Christ in four oratorios: *Christ the Child, Christ the Master, Christ the Redeemer, Christ the Glorified*.[8] Denouncing the ludicrousness of religious subjects, Wagner continued: "For let it be said once more, we do not believe him, since the work *certainly does not represent his own convictions*." This outburst in the spirit of Young Germany was phrased with deplorable lack of caution. For in 1841 Wagner himself came forth with an oratorio, the *Liebesmahl der Apostel*, an excellent piece of music which must unquestionably be regarded as a predecessor of his religious music-drama *Parsifal*. A great artist may very well worship tomorrow what he yesterday rejected as bosh. Such inconsistencies can spring from his personal development. Rather, the strange thing is that every word of Wagner's as a *writer about music* should still be considered canonical—and that such *pro domo* opinions, which to Wagner himself were but products of a given time and to which he was in no way permanently committed, are in some circles taken as absolutes, along with his music and his poetry!

The *Elijah* was intended for the music festival to be held in Birmingham in 1845. Its première therefore was in England, and perhaps the music was more closely correlated to the English translation by Bartholomew than to the original text by Schubring. For example, the stress in the first recitative, "Vor dem ich ste*he*," is impossible in German, but perfectly natural in the English "before whom I stand", where it rightly ends on a fermata. The part of Elijah was taken by the Austrian singer Staudigl, whose majestic bass was the very embodiment of the hero. As might have been expected, the work was a tremendous success. At the première, four choruses and four arias had to be repeated. The psychological impact of Elijah was even greater than that of *St. Paul*, though it is hard to say just why. Were the English flattered by the element of national religious consciousness in the story? Yet that could not have been

[7] R. Wagner: *Gesammelte Schriften und Dichtungen*. Leipzig, 1887.
[8] A. Schering: *Geschichte des Oratoriums*. Leipzig, 1911.

K

uppermost in their minds, for neither the contemporary notices nor later criticism ever mention this point, neither Edwards' *History of Elijah*[9] nor W. S. Rockstros, Ellis, Wells, Haskers, nor Davison's *From Mendelssohn to Wagner*.[10] One thing is certain: its purely musical qualities were highly valued. As late as 1880 Thomas Baxter wondered: "Where have the New Germans and Young Europeans, where have Wagner, Liszt, Berlioz, been bolder than in the transverse chromatic design of the

miracle God performs for Elijah when 'the mountains were rent, the rocks were broken in pieces, the earth quaked, the sea roared'?"[11] This question seems to us a valid one.

And how would a composer of the present day have written an *Elijah*? This, too, is no idle question. Times have changed since 1870, when Wagnerian music-drama drove the oratorio from the field—so thoroughly that even Wagner's own oratorio could no longer be played. The oratorio has come back again. In 1921 the Swiss composer Arthur Honegger wrote a *King David*, and followed it with Paul Claudel's *Joan at the Stake* and a *Dance of Death*.[12] Many other composers have followed his lead; Stravinsky's *Oedipus Rex*, for example, is a reversion from "static opera" to the oratorio.[13]

[9] F. G. Edwards: op. cit.
[10] H. Davison: *From Mendelssohn to Wagner*. London, 1912.
[11] T. Baxter: "Mendelssohn's Elijah". *The Times*. London, 1880.
[12] W. Tappolet: *Arthur Honegger*. Zürich, 1954.
[13] A. Liess: *Die Musik im Weltbild der Gegenwart*. Vienna, 1949.

We can conceive of new *Elijahs* being composed in Israel, where Biblical subjects are popular and where Mendelssohn's *Elijah* is a favourite item in the musical repertory. A present-day text for an oratorio on Elijah would, however, be radically different from that which Schubring prepared for Felix Mendelssohn. Perhaps it would not deal with the Biblical Elijah at all, but rather with the strange afterlife that the prophet enjoyed in Jewish popular thought during the late classical period and the Middle Ages. By then the figure of Elijah had undergone an extraordinary change; he was no longer the fanatical prophet.[14]

The Elijah of the Middle Ages was a kind of Wandering Jew who appeared to individuals of his race, the devout as well as the renegade, and brought them to union with God.[15] He was a mediator between God and man. This portrait of Elijah might prove more interesting to the present-day composer than the old prophet and wonder-worker of the Bible. Chiefly, however, the twentieth-century composer would feel that his oratorio should contain many reminiscences of Hebrew music. Mendelssohn followed another policy. He set out to be a German composer writing a work with the available musical vocabulary of his *time*; the setting was to be foreign, but he did not want any exotic accents. After all, he had not borrowed from Greek music for his *Antigone*, *Oedipus* and *Athalia* (composed at the request of King Frederick William IV). Why, then, base the *Elijah* on the characteristic E-F-G-A tetrachord and the typical modulations of ancient Jewish music?[16] He could have done so, of course. But—here is an amazing fact—he left the writing of synagogal music to those of his colleagues who were Christian born!

This may sound improbable, but it is so. In June 1828 Franz Schubert, a lifelong Catholic, wrote a 92nd Psalm with Hebrew text, with mixed chorus and baritone solo, for the Vienna synagogue on Seitenstettengasse. It was written as a favour to the chief cantor of the synagogue, Salomann Sulzer, who was a close friend of Schubert's.[17] Sulzer was deeply concerned with reforming the whole tradition of Jewish temple singing. He was striving for "a form of worship regenerated in terms of religion and of the *spirit of the times*". He felt that Schubert was just the man to help him with his task. He also enlisted other composers of smaller gifts but greater reputations: Beethoven's friend, Ignaz Ritter von Seyfried, and

[14] M. W. Levinsohn: *Der Prophet Elias. Nach den Talmudim- und Midraschquellen*. Zürich, 1929.

[15] I. Bergmann: *Die Legenden der Juden*. Berlin, 1919.

[16] A. Z. Idelsohn: *Jewish Music in its Historical Development*. New York, 1948.

[17] A. Einstein: *Schubert*. Zürich, 1952.

Tobias Haslinger, a publisher who commanded a great deal of influence. No one, apparently, felt any embarrassment at contributing their services to the improvement of Jewish worship. Just ten years after Schubert's death all their music was collected and published in a volume entitled *Schir Zion*.[18]

In Berlin, Cantor Louis Lewandowski, and in Paris, Cantor Samuel Naumburg, were engaged in similar activities. They "Europeanized" Jewish divine services. As a result, many thousands of Christians poured into the synagogues to hear beautiful old music. This whole development was abruptly cut short when, in 1850, an anonymous lampoon appeared in Germany, *Judaism in Music*. Thereafter only an occasional Christian composer ventured to set some portion of Hebrew liturgy—as Max Bruch did with the *Kol Nidre* for 'cello and orchestra. In a letter written in 1889 apropos the genesis of this deeply felt work, the composer remarked that he regarded folk songs, and thus traditional Jewish liturgical songs also, as the source of all melody. For many years this forthright statement of an obvious truth—that the writing of Hebrew music by a non-Jewish composer was in no way different from other composing in a folk medium —was deliberately overlooked.[19] As though Beethoven had not used a march of the janissaries in his *Ruins of Athens*,[20] and as though Mozart had not done the same in his A major Sonata (K. 331). As a pupil of Abbot Vogler, Weber, who was a great folklorist, knew that comic operas like *Abu Hassan* needed to be coloured with Oriental music.[21] In Russia, Anton Rubinstein discovered the magic of Persian and Tartar songs.[22] And Mendelssohn made use of Scottish melodies when he wrote his symphony in memory of Mary Stuart. Ever since Herder had created a sensation with the *Voices of the Peoples in Songs* and Lord Byron had put out a collection of poems called *Hebrew Melodies*,[23] it had been altogether natural for composers, wherever they could, to follow these pioneers into the realm of folklore. Just as Byron imitated the note of lamentation and heroism in his synthetic Hebrew lyrics, so also non-Jewish composers felt that a Jewish subject called for musical Hebraisms. But the grotesque conclusion that non-Jews should not compose in Hebrew modes, nor Jews in the German manner, was already implicit in

[18] A. M. Rothmüller: *Die Musik der Juden*. Zürich, 1951.
[19] A. Z. Idelsohn: op. cit.
[20] A. W. Thayer: *Ludwig von Beethoven*. Leigzig, 1907-17.
[21] M. M. v. Weber: *Carl Maria von Weber. Ein Lebensbild*. Leipzig, 1864-66.
[22] N. D. Bernstein: *Anton Rubinstein*. Legzig, no date.
[23] Lord Byron: *Poetical Works*. London, 1898–1905.

the above-mentioned pamphlet. And long before Goebbels proclaimed, "When a Jew speaks German, he is lying," the composer Gustav Mahler, singer of German glories, of the "Auferstehn, ja auferstehn", the "Urlicht", and the "Kindertotenlieder", was bluntly told to go back to the desert.

BUCKINGHAM PALACE

Eighteen hundred and forty-one. Queen Victoria and Prince Albert, her German consort, were seeing the northern part of their island for the first time. Scotland burned with autumn colour. The Queen found it easy to feel that this was her country, for she was proud of the Stuart blood in her veins; and the Prince sat beside her in the carriage, and gazed at the landscape.[1] "It reminds me of Thuringia", he sighed again and again. The hills of Scotland were higher, however, and wilder and more mysterious.

Before the visit was over, the Prince Consort was thoroughly converted to Scotland. What pleasure to be a guest at Lord Breadalbane's,[2] to eat porridge and finnan haddie, to hear all about tartans, bagpipes and sword-dances. Victoria and Albert were thoroughly enjoying their stay—and needed the holiday. For they were gravely concerned about imminent developments in their land.[3] Sir Robert Peel, the new Prime Minister, had promised to bring about a reconciliation between capital and labour, and to improve the lot of the common people. But who could say whether he would succeed?[4] By contrast, how pleasant it was to visit the nursery, and see the children. They were already old enough to be taught some little songs. They must learn some of Mendelssohn's songs, of course, which the Queen and the Prince Consort were so fond of.

Really, they ought to know the composer personally. After all, Mendelssohn came frequently to London. Nothing would be easier than to make his acquaintance—only a matter of appealing to Herr von Bunsen, the Prussian Ambassador, who had adjusted so well to English ways. Previously he had been the Prussian envoy in Rome—his present post was far more congenial to him and he was already well entrenched in the best English society. Theological interests were highly esteemed in England—

[1] E. F. Benson: *Queen Victoria*. London, 1930.
[2] M. Wilson: *Early Victorian England*. London, 1932.
[3] *The Letters of Queen Victoria*, vol. I. London, 1908.
[4] W. Walker: *Sir Robert Peel*. London, 1899.

and Bunsen, that demon of industry, was engaged in writing a profound book, *Christianity and Mankind*. In addition he held an honorary doctorate from Oxford.[5] His wife, Fanny Waddington, was English too. She was one of London's most brilliant hostesses. Mendelssohn was a frequent visitor at their house. A gentleman, this Mendelssohn; no word had ever been said against him. Naturally one had to be careful about musical people. So many of them drank and were involved with women. Certain French habits, running around with singers—that sort of thing would not do at all in England. But Mendelssohn was a good family man. Even English bishops had social relations with him and invited him to their homes. Only recently the Bishop of Chichester[6] had had him to dinner and the composer had most amiably consented to play something for the company after dinner. The Bishop had mentioned it to Her Majesty, and had had nothing but praise for his talented guest.

And so on 19th July 1842 a well-bred young man with a southern cast of countenance stood before his Royal hosts in one of the great rooms of Buckingham Palace. Both the Prince and the Queen were slightly ill-at-ease, for they generally had little to do with artists. But they loved music. The Prince was quite proficient at the organ, and Victoria had a small but pleasing voice.[7] Decorative French blinds kept out the heat of the summer's sun. The room was cool, and the young man stood beside the parlour organ and praised Their Majesties' music-making with eloquent gestures. His expression was forever in flux; he seemed unable to keep his face still for a minute at a time. He succeeded in so charming his hosts that they were unwilling to let him go. He was a man of the world, excellently dressed,[8] and seemed to know precisely what he owed to his own position and to his hosts. Soon they sat down to tea.

Felix gave his own circumstantial account of the visit to Buckingham Palace in two letters to his mother. As always, when he was in England, he was in a state of "dry intoxication". He moved from concert to concert, from party to party. When he improvised on the organ in Christ Church, he thought he would suffocate, so great was the throng and so closely did his listeners crowd around the organ bench. A few days later he played to three thousand persons in Exeter Hall—and was greeted with deafening hurrahs, waving handkerchiefs and stamping feet. He could hardly believe the applause was meant for himself until Sir Robert Peel

[5] *Bunsens Leben, aus seinen Briefen und nach eigener Erinnerung geschrieben von seiner Witwe.* Leipzig, 1868–71.

[6] *Recollections of Dr. Charles Graves.* London, no date.

[7] E. Sitwell: *Victoria of England.* London, 1936.

[8] Ibid.

and Lord Wharncliffe clapped vehemently right under his nose. His wife Cécile, whom he had taken with him, was almost overcome by the surge of applause. Sir Edward Bulwer paid court to lovely Cécile with her violet-blue eyes, and Samuel Rogers said that he hoped she would teach her children to speak English as well as she herself spoke it....[9]

To crown it all came this invitation to Buckingham Palace! At first Felix had been received by the Prince alone. Later, when the Queen entered, looking girlish in a simple morning dress, the draught from the door had sent dozens of sheets of music from an untied bundle flying to all corners of the room. The Queen exclaimed, and knelt to gather up the scattered sheets. The Prince hastened to forestall her. Felix promptly made a third crawling about the room. Then he dusted off his knees and looked amusedly around. What a reception! The atmosphere became even more informal when the Queen apologized for being dressed as she was. She had not dressed up because she would have to change to a travelling dress afterwards; they were leaving this very day for their summer residence at Claremont. It was much too hot to stay in London.

Then Mendelssohn was asked to play the organ, and began his chorus from the *St. Paul*: "How lovely are the messengers." Even before he had finished played the first verse, the royal couple had joined their voices to the well-known chorus. Prince Albert pulled the stops so skilfully, always swelling for the forte and dropping into the diminuendo at the right moment, that Felix was altogether delighted. "Then the Prince of Coburg-Gotha came; we began conversing again, and among other things the Queen asked whether I had composed any new songs; she so loved to sing the printed ones. 'You ought to sing one for him,' Prince Albert said, whereupon she offered to try the Spring Song in B flat major. 'All very well, if it were only here!' the Prince said. 'All the music is already packed up for Claremont.' "[10].

Prince Albert went out to look for the music, but returned saying that it was no longer around. "Would it be possible to unpack it again?" Felix Mendelssohn asked. The Queen gave him a look that plainly said this would not be easy. "We must send for Lady So-and-So," she replied (Felix did not catch the name). The bell was rung, the servants ran busily here and there, but the sought-for lady-in-waiting could not be located. Shaking her head, the Queen went out, and returned to say: "She has left and taken all my things with her—I find this very shocking indeed." But if they wanted to hear a song she would sing something else that she knew

---

[9] S. Hensel: *Die Familie Mendelssohn 1729–1847*. Berlin, 1879.
[10] Ibid.

by heart. Perhaps something by Gluck? "The Princess of Coburg-Gotha had meanwhile joined us, and so the five of us went down the corridors to the Queen's living room, where alongside the piano stood an enormously fat hobby-horse and two large bird cages, and such beautiful pictures on the walls"—among other things Mendelssohn noticed several originals by the great Dutch animal painter Paul Potter. Splendidly bound books lay around on tables and bookshelves, and there was a great pile of music on the piano. The Duchess of Kent joined them, and while they were all talking Mendelssohn looked among the music and found his first published songs (opus 8). With pretended petulance he remarked that this was probably a sign that the Queen would not really like to sing Gluck. Everyone laughed. The Queen amiably posted herself beside the piano, and the composer took his seat on the stool.

"Wait, the parrot must go out!" Victoria exclaimed. "Otherwise he screams louder than I do."

Thereupon the bird was carried out—by none other than the Prince of Coburg-Gotha. Mendelssohn, however, caught up with him, exclaiming: "Your Highness, permit me to do it." A dozen astonished servants outside the door witnessed this scene. Then Mendelssohn sat down at the piano again. And the Queen began singing. "She sang", Mendelssohn wrote to his mother, "the song that begins 'Schöner und schöner', sang it with utterly charming purity, strictly in time; only where the song descended to 'der Prosa Last und Mühe' and then harmonically ascended, she hit D sharp both times, and because I corrected it twice she took it as D the last time, though this time it really should have been D sharp. But except for this oversight it was really utterly lovely, and I have never heard an amateur produce the last long G better, more purely and naturally."[11]

Now, however, he had to confess that the honour of authorship did not really belong to him. Actually his sister Fanny had composed the song, he said—a revelation that brought forth many Ahs and Ohs. Quite right, she was Mrs. Fanny Hensel, the wife of the painter—and Mendelssohn added that he believed Her Majesty owned Hensel's painting *Miriam*.

"But now I want to sing something of *yours*, Mr. Mendelssohn," Victoria said, and she sang his "Lass dich nur nichts dauern". Then Prince Albert sang in his pleasant voice the old German song that Felix had set, "Es ist ein Schnitter, der heisst Tod". Felix felt strangely stirred. The ladies of Kent and Coburg-Gotha looked very sad at the thought of

[11] F. Mendelssohn-Bartholdy: *Briefe aus den Jahren 1830–47*. Leipzig, 1861.

so much death and perishability. The Prince Consort appeared to notice, for he asked Mendelssohn to improvise. That was said to be one of his great talents, was it not?

Mendelssohn complied; he played masterfully, winding the theme of the organ chorus in with that of "Schnitter". Soon, however, he gave both themes a gayer turn. The Queen asked him for a potpourri, and Mendelssohn obliged with a medley of the following: First, a free improvisation on "Rule Britannia", then "Lützows wilde, verwegene Jagd" by Weber, and finally the academic song, "Gaudeamus igitur", which Brahms later incorporated into his *Academic Festival Overture* written to thank his Breslau *alma mater* for the degree of honorary doctor.[12] Felix Mendelssohn was honorary doctor of the University of Leipzig—and so now he thudded away in honour of the universities. Everyone applauded. The Princesses bade good-bye and the Queen shook hands with him. The time for her departure was approaching. "I hope that you will soon visit us again in England," she said, becoming somewhat stiff.

He thought this was his dismissal. But the Prince Consort detained him. "Let us sit for a while longer," he said with rather embarrassed gravity.

"And where will you be going next?" he asked. Whereupon Mendelssohn began an enthusiastic account of Leipzig, his "artistic kingdom", where he had been ruling unchallenged these past six years. And he spoke of tasks that the new King of Prussia, Frederick William IV, had in mind for him.

At last the Royal Consort rose. "She asks you"—he did not speak of Her Majesty, but in an intimate tone of his wife—"to accept this gift from her. As a memento." And he handed Mendelssohn a small jewel-box. When Mendelssohn opened it, he saw in it a gold ring engraved with *Victoria Regina 1842*. When he looked up, the Prince had already left the room. In his place was a secretary or steward—the same one who had shown Felix in. He bowed, and let the guest out of the palace. Down galleries, past rows of waiting footmen, he was guided to the door. Outside, a train of carriages waited in the courtyard: a dozen chaises which were to take the Royal couple and its entourage to Claremont. Red-liveried postillions, ostrich plumes, resplendent crests of lion and unicorn and *Dieu et Mon Droit* made a glittering scene in the summer sunlight.

In a curious dreamlike mood, Mendelssohn walked along the line of carriages and turned to where his own hansom cab was waiting to drive him back to his friend Klingemann and his wife Cécile. Suddenly he

[12] M. Kalbeck: *Johannes Brahms*. Berlin, 1908–15.

heard a fanfare; the flag on the palace roof was lowered; and next day the court calendar noted: "Her Majesty left the palace at 30 minutes past 3."[13]

Now, however, he felt such exaltation that he could scarcely bring himself to enter the carriage. He dismissed the cab and set out for home on foot. Since this was English weather, a light rain had begun to fall. He walked through summery London in a dream.

Next day he conducted his D minor Piano Concerto and the "Hebrides" overture, and had to repeat both. What higher triumphs could he hope for?

[13] Sir S. Lee: *Queen Victoria*. London, no date.

BOOK FIVE

ZENITH AND FALL

A distinguished Dane said to me: What do the Germans really want with their hatred for the Jews? In my country almost everyone loves the Jews. We know that they are the most dependable patriots; we know that they lead an upright private life; we respect them as a kind of aristocracy. What do the Germans want? I should have answered him: They want hatred.

—JAKOB WASSERMANN: *My Way as a German and a Jew*

LEIPZIG AND THE TALENT FOR FRIENDSHIP

Once when Liszt, the aristocrat, started complaining about missing the "toilettes of countesses and princesses" in Leipzig, Schumann retorted: "We have our aristocracy here too: one hundred and fifty bookshops, fifty printing plants and thirty periodicals—let him take care!"[1] The city in which Robert Schumann published his *League of David* magazine was vibrant with life, art, the future. And there were salons there too, although perhaps not so many as in the more snobbish cities. Musical affairs in Leipzig were conducted by the bourgeoisie—who, however, received guidance from above; unlike the situation in Berlin, groups of the petty bourgeoisie also participated. Such women as Livia Gerhardt, the wife of the barrister Professor Frege, and Henriette Voigt, wife of the merchant, provided the cosmopolitan note.

The suggestion that Mendelssohn assume the enviable post of director of the Leipzig Gewandhaus came from the Voigt brothers, who won the backing of the Leipzig municipal council—Mendelssohn having been already sounded out by Konrad Schleinitz, a prominent jurist. The annual salary was fixed at a thousand talers, and he was promised an annual leave of six months—this stipulation being of particular importance to Felix.[2]

Mendelssohn held his Leipzig post a full twelve years, from 1835 to 1847. He loved Leipzig, the city of booksellers, with its comical dialect which he himself never mastered. He liked the mood of the city—the compound of a slightly philistine spirit with unflagging industry and good intentions. It was a city of enterprising citizens, where almost everyone prided himself on being a "vigilant" fellow—a word that signified wide-awake and on the go. The city had half forgotten Bach, but responded well to Mendelssohn's campaign to put up a monument to the master. Money was collected, committees formed and benefit concerts given until it was impressed on every Leipziger that Bach and Leipzig were inseparable.

As early as 30th August 1835, from the moment his travelling carriage first clattered into the city, Felix Mendelssohn had a premonition that he would make the hall of the Gewandhaus the very heart of Leipzig, and

[1] K. H. Wörner: *Robert Schumann*. Zürich, 1949.
[2] E. Wolff: *Felix Mendelssohn-Bartholdy*. Berlin. 1909.

Leipzig, perhaps, the heart of Germany. Or of German music, at any rate; for Berlin and Vienna were no longer what they had been. In a letter to Schubring, in fact, Felix had called Vienna "a dissolute and jaded den of eating and drinking",[3] and recalled Berlin as consisting of "barracks and sand".[4] When friends asked him what he intended to do in Leipzig, he replied significantly: "Everything." And in fact he quickly took control. From the day he reached the city the musicians of the orchestra, the choruses, soloists and pianists no longer led a life of their own. He united everything in his own hand, and with infinite diligence tended the whole of Leipzig's musical life. Perhaps the only parallel to his activity is that of Richard Wagner, many years later, who so closely supervised everything in Bayreuth that not a nail was hammered or a set erected without his knowledge and approval.

There was, however, a great difference in character between Mendelssohn and Wagner. Felix Mendelssohn had declared that he would "accept the post only if he were not displacing anyone else".[5] This was an astonishing condition, in which an ethical standard was paired with worldly wisdom. He wanted no enemies. And he himself wanted to be nobody's enemy. To the New Germans of a somewhat later period, such an attitude was slightly suspect. "A real man must have enemies" and "many enemies, much honour", the German proverbs have it. Mendelssohn, on the other hand, was of such a conciliating disposition that he sent orders to English festival officials not to dismiss musicians, with whom he may have been annoyed the previous year.[6]

But this gentleness of his had a hard core. Mendelssohn's presence in Leipzig produced the most vital musical seasons the city had known for many years. We can reconstruct the incredible programme Felix managed to provide for the city from Alfred Dörffel's *History of the Gewandhaus Concerts.*[7] For his first concert, Felix presented the C major Symphony of Schubert, newly discovered by Robert Schumann. The poetic-minded Schumann saw all manner of rich imagery in this precious work. "Vienna with the tower of St. Stephen's, its beautiful women, its girdling Danube, a city set in a fruitful plain which gradually mounts to higher and higher mountains, perfumed by the faint odour of incense—where Beethoven's eye no doubt often swerved restlessly toward the distant

[3] *Briefwechsel zwischen Felix Mendelssohn-Bartholdy und Julius Schubring.* Leipzig, 1892.
[4] S. Hensel: *Die Familie Mendelssohn 1729–1847.* Berlin, 1879.
[5] E. Wolff: op. cit.
[6] Sir G. Grove: *Dictionary of Music and Musicians.* London, no date.
[7] A. Dörffel: *Geschichte der Gewandhauskonzerte.* Leipzig, no date.

range of Alps. . . ."[8] He extolled the Schubert symphony for "its heavenly length". All very well. But we know also that the length was not wholly self-dictated; young Schubert had felt it necessary from Haydn's example to develop themes to exhaustion, and to make endless repetitions.[9] It was no simple task to perform this symphony without causing yawns. Mendelssohn, with his ardour and his magnificently developed feeling for proportions, succeeded in counterfeiting a sense of brevity where it did not exist. The Schubert work was wildly hailed. Hans von Bülow later wrote: "How ever did he manage to slide over the various steps of the endless allegretto so that at the end the audience had no idea of how long these acoustic phenomena had actually lasted?"

The fact was that if a composer were really great, Felix was always ready to help him along with a pious fraud. To how many did he lend his conductor's magic through those years: Bach in altogether unknown secular works; Mozart in many a half-forgotten symphony; even the mighty Beethoven. He persuaded the public to listen to Schumann, who at the time was far more popular as a writer on music than as a composer, and to a group of lesser figures. As for himself—the compositions of Felix Mendelssohn took barely tenth place in his programmes. But audiences listened happily when Clara Schumann—at that time still Clara Wieck— played Mendelssohn's B major Capriccio (opus 22). This *Capriccio Brillant* was colourful and brilliantly instrumented, though as always in the case of Mendelssohn's concerto music it lacked the conflict of two sonata themes. There is a soft Introduction in B major, an *Allegro con fuoco* in B minor. The piece is full of pathos, coquetry, gaiety; it plays with arabesques and march rhythms. For years it remained Clara's bravura piece.

It was always a brilliant evening when Mendelssohn himself sat at the piano. He had no ambitions as a virtuoso, and for all his admiration of the breed he had serious doubts about Liszt, Thalberg and other lions of the concert stage. But his own incredible facility—the product of hard work—astonished everyone who heard him play. Ferdinand Hiller described it poetically: "He played the piano as a lark soars, because it was his nature. He possessed great adroitness, sureness, strength, fluency, a soft full tone . . . but when he played one forgot these qualities; one overlooked even the more spiritual gifts which are called ardour, inspiration, soulfulness, intelligence. When he sat at the piano music poured out of

[8] R. Schumann: *Gesammelte Schriften über Musik und Musiker*. Leipzig, 1891.
[9] H. E. Jacob: *Joseph Haydn: His Art, Times and Glory*. New York, 1950.

him with the richness of inborn genius—he was a centaur and the piano his steed...."[10]

In his position of responsibility Mendelssohn was quite well aware that he must sponsor composers whose talents were perhaps not to his liking. He did not regard his own taste as absolutely binding. There were some composers with whom he was not in sympathy, although perhaps he should have been; he was quite ready to admit that. His attitude toward Chopin's art was none too cordial. But when the question arose of putting on a Chopin festival in Leipzig, he became an enthusiast. And Chopin was surprised at how warmly he was received. Felix likewise gave a wonderful reception to Berlioz, whose musical language was distinctly foreign to him although, as we have seen, Berlioz in many respects revered Mendelssohn. Felix mistook Berlioz's great talent for pose and hysteria, but he placed the orchestra and chorus at the French composer's disposal, and Berlioz scored a triumph. Overflowing with joy, the Frenchman thereupon exchanged batons with Mendelssohn. "Le mien est grossier, while yours is more delicate," Berlioz joked as he examined Mendelssohn's ivory baton. Exchanging batons was a pleasant custom which Berlioz also practised on another occasion, remarking: "May these batons strike root and some day become trees lavishing shade." To Mendelssohn he added: "Be my brother!... When the Great Spirit calls us some day to the eternal hunting grounds, may the warriors of our tribes hang our two tomahawks together above the entrance to their council wigwam!"[11]

Mendelssohn's welcome to Liszt was in some respects even handsomer than his reception of Chopin and Berlioz. Liszt had been hissed by the Gewandhaus audience at his first appearance in Leipzig—for reasons altogether extraneous to his musicianship. His pupil and manager Puzzi Hermann (George Sand had given the little fellow his silly nickname) had ventured to raise the price of tickets from sixteen groschen to a taler. He felt he could ask this high admission fee for the deified virtuoso.[12] Liszt himself was certainly not to blame. For no matter what might be said about his peculiarities and extravagances—he was passionately interested in women, in Hungarian nationalism, in the Countess d'Agoult, Lamartine, Lamennais, Saint-Simonism, Catholicism, and so on—the one thing he certainly did not care about was money. Like Paganini who gave away a small fortune to Berlioz, Liszt was the type of the *grand seigneur*, accustomed to giving, not receiving. But indignation ran high in Leipzig

[10] F. Hiller: *Felix Mendelssohn-Bartholdy*. Cologne, 1878.
[11] G. de Pourtalès: *Berlioz et l'Europe romantique*. Paris, 1937.
[12] P. Raabe: *Liszts Leben*. Stuttgart, 1931.

and the newspapers came out strongly against Liszt. Then Felix Mendelssohn conceived the diplomatic plan of organizing a grand social evening in the Gewandhaus, at which Liszt could show himself the consummate man of the world *and* artist which he was. It was a real soirée for three hundred and fifty persons; no admission fee was asked, and the guests were plied with punch, cake, and above all music. Liszt, Hiller and Mendelssohn gave a virtuoso performance of Bach's triple concerto. Liszt himself played a fantasia on Donizetti's *Lucia de Lammermoor*, his transcription of Schubert's "Erlkönig"; in addition Mendelssohn's *A Calm Sea and a Prosperous Voyage* were performed, and some choruses from the *St. Paul*. The Leipzig public was appeased—and Liszt's subsequent concerts were greeted with storms of applause, as in the rest of Europe.[13]

The crowning glory of Felix Mendelssohn's work in Leipzig was the foundation of the Conservatoire in 1843. There was nothing to compare with it in Germany; and it soon surpassed even the Paris Conservatoire. The creation of the Conservatoire was due to Felix's efforts; his spirit maintained the institution and continued to inspire it after his death. The honorary doctorate which the University of Leipzig had earlier awarded him—in 1836, at the outset of his work at the Gewandhaus—was well earned. For he had taken upon himself a truly enormous burden. "His correspondence", his friend Hiller wrote, "costs him the most time. He must have written a fabulous number of letters."[14] Felix admitted to his mother that there were sometimes as many as eighteen letters a day. Did he assume this responsibility gladly? We must realize that it gave him considerable satisfaction. Felix was by nature a dreamer—and when dreamers become hard workers, they sometimes do so to excess. He had long ago adopted the motto that Goethe gave to his homunculus: "So long as I exist I must be active."[15]

It was only natural that he should enlist his favourite musicians for the Leipzig Conservatoire. These included Julius Rietz, whom he had previously lured to Düsseldorf; Ferdinand David, the violinist; Niels Gade; and later Ignaz Moscheles. All these men, and many others, taught at the Conservatoire, which in those days was with justice called the "Mendelssohnianum".[16] He himself gave his time and strength to teaching with the greatest generosity. At the same time he blamed himself for being too impatient. He chafed at having to repeat a passage two or three times

---

[13] F. Mendelssohn-Bartholdy: *Briefe aus den Jahren 1830–47*. Leipzig, 1861.
[14] F. Hiller: op. cit.
[15] K. Viëtor: *Goethes Anschauung vom Menschen*. Bern, 1952.
[16] W. A. Lampadius: *Felix Mendelssohn-Bartholdy*. Berlin, 1872.

for the benefit of inattentive pupils—as a teacher must do. But even
when Felix lost his temper, his pupils continued to feel the basic kindliness that lay behind his impatience.[17]

"It was good to be loved by Felix!" Eduard Devrient wrote decades
after his friend's death.[18] Devrient remembered how Felix's eyes would
light up when a friend entered the room; the way he raised his head from
his desk, stood up, smiled, fingered his cheek in that way he had. "Is it
really you? Welcome, welcome!" And the genuine curiosity of the
creative artist: "What have you brought?" A few moments later the
friend himself was the "centre of the world", the sole subject of talk and
questions. Felix put himself entirely into the background. All his concern
was for his friend.

It was good to be loved by Felix. From his childhood he had possessed
this talent for friendship. The earliest letter of his we possess—here reproduced in facsimile for the first time—is a mixture of playfulness and
friendliness such as we never look for in a child. The letter is addressed
to a boy of whom nothing is known, and bears the date 1st November
1819. Felix was ten, then. It reads:

> My dear Signore Rudolph,
>
> "I really do not know what to think of you"— You think I
> am a scoundrel, a good-for-nothing, and you, you rogue, what
> do you think you are??—" "—I write him twice but he doesn't
> answer shouldn't I get even? and reproaches! unworthy friend!
> Well! Pace! That was a joke. Well! Pace! Now comes the serious
> part. I still often think of [here follow three measures of music
> for the horn in F major, three-four time]. How the big rascal
> stood there and puffed on a horn twice as big as he was.
>
> But really, I didn't answer you because I've had so much to do
> these days that I myself was made of Latin and French and
> arithmetic. A double sonata I was composing added to all that,
> and so I was seldom done with work before half past eight.—Of
> course you've been having a good time at your uncle's!
>
> ...Le Cor et la paresse se disputent mon coeur. And believe
> me, if you had stayed here (and still been my friend) I would
> have come to you sometimes with a sheaf of work the way you
> came with a sheaf of work to me that time. I have just been read-
> ing over your letter and see that at the end of October you're

---

[17] H. Barbedette: *Felix Mendelssohn, sa Vie et ses Oeuvres.* Paris, 1868.
[18] E. Devrient: *Meine Erinnerungen an Felix Mendelssohn-Bartholdy.*
Leipzig, 1872.

Letter from Mendelssohn at the age of ten to an unknown friend. Hitherto unpublished autograph. Property of the International Felix Mendelssohn Society.

going to Kaiserslautern. I have already told you why I did not
write sooner; but I would be very sorry if you did not receive this
letter, then you would have reason to be angry with me. Our
little sofa is very well and sends you regards; so does Herr
Berger; he told me you would soon be travelling back to
Berlin again, so do write me whether that is settled. This letter is
being finished at seven o'clock in the evening, and I want to take
occasion to send regards to your father too. My Rudölphchen,
don't forget my kisses, which were maybe wet: here I am sending some drier ones, and remain very firmly

your friend

F. Mendelssohn.

It is an engaging letter, and a precursor of so many of the amusing
touches of the later overture to *A Midsummer Night's Dream*. It is all
there: horn music and laziness contesting for Felix's heart. The sofa, too,
is personified, and takes its bow along with Berger, the piano teacher.
But what the letter supremely reveals is Mendelssohn's affectionate nature
and his talent for friendship. The more serious his life became, the more
intense this talent for friendship grew. It became the dominant note in
his relationships with other human beings.

It was good to be loved by Felix. He radiated so much warmth that
many of his acquaintances inevitably thought of themselves as his friends,
and quite a few of them as his "best" friends. Was he hypocritical then?
There is no reason for us to think so. He had no reason to deceive, since
he never wanted anything of others. Rather, what emanated from him
was his natural friendliness. As a general rule men of genius in the
classical age had not been overgenerous with expressions of friendship.
The lives of Haydn, and particularly of Mozart, were too difficult for
them to have cultivated friendships. As for Beethoven, he was far too over-
bearing. It is true that because of his very gruffness, his friendships with
Wegeler or Oktavio von Breuning had a special weight. And when we
come across a letter written the week of his death, beginning, "My dear,
good Moscheles"—we are strangely moved by it.

There is a good·deal that might be said about Moscheles, who was
Mendelssohn's friend as well as Beethoven's. In fact, he too was one of
Mendelssohn's "best" friends, and in his memoirs he says the very thing
that Devrient said. But then so does Droysen, the great historian of
classical antiquity.

Johann Gustav Droysen was probably the person of the greatest stature,
after Goethe, whom Felix Mendelssohn knew. Like Goethe, he was a

perfect union of the scholar and the artist. His *History of Alexander the Great* (1833), his *History of Hellenism* (1836), were masterpieces of philosophic and political understanding, and Felix had the highest regard for them. And indeed this new approach to the writing of history seemed an inspired one.[19] Subsequently, only the works of Mommsen and Jacob Burckhardt and, in our own times, of Spengler and Toynbee have proved so seminal. Droysen had also made translations of Aeschylus (1832) which had deeply affected young Felix Mendelssohn. When he composed his choruses for Sophocles' *Antigone* in 1842, he was drawing upon memories of the resonance and rhythm of Droysen's versions of Greek tragedy.[20]

In the cordial atmosphere of the Mendelssohn household young Droÿsen was soon transformed from Felix's tutor to his friend. We have a wonderful letter from Droysen to his sister describing a little birthday celebration in his honour:

"I arrived and was met with loud congratulations from everybody. The two sisters had decked themselves out with my favourite flowers, white lilies and cornflowers; at my place at table stood, hidden under a napkin, a coffee-maker (!), the gift of Frau Mendelssohn...." Droysen was very fond of a new delicacy: anchovy-paste, and so there was an immense dish of this at dinner. "The painter Hensel had fashioned the paste into a dolphin; it had blue stock petals for eyes, and seemed to be spouting from its nostrils—the jets of water being represented by blades of grass. ... After the soup the ladies Fanny and Rebecca in solemn procession brought this masterpiece into the room."[21]

"He was the finest we had!" Droysen as a very old man said of Felix Mendelssohn. (These were almost the same words that Moritz von Schwind used of Franz Schubert.) The pianist Adolph Henselt likewise placed the highest value on his friendship with Felix. As late as 1876, when he received the Order of Vladimir and a patent of nobility from the Russian Tsar, he mentioned that his friendship with Mendelssohn forty years before had been as great an honour to him.[22] Heinrich Dorn, who in 1844 and 1847 directed the Lower Rhine Music Festival as Mendelssohn's deputy, had similar feelings. So did Stephen Heller. And there was not a foreigner who made a musical pilgrimage to Leipzig, the city which

---

[19] C. D. Pflaum: *J. G. Droysens Historik in ihrer Bedeutung für die moderne Geschichtswissenschaft* (*Lamprechts Untersuchungen*). Gotha, 1907.

[20] O. Hintze: *Johann Gustav Droysen*. Leipzig, 1903.

[21] J. G. Droysen: *Briefwechsel*, vol. I. Berlin, 1929.

[22] G. Krolop: *Adolph Henselt, nach seinen Erinnerungen gezeichnet*. Leipzig, no date.

had become the real centre of German musical life, who departed without feeling deeply and personally impressed by Mendelssohn. This was true for hosts of Englishmen, Americans, Swedes, Norwegians and Dutchmen. "He bowled me over," declared William Sterndale Bennett, who came to Leipzig for the first time in 1836. Thirty years later, when he assumed the directorship of the Academy in London, he referred to his compositions, which enjoyed a great success in England, as "works of a Mendelssohn pupil". There were Mendelssohn pupils in any number of important posts in Prague, Warsaw, Berlin, Frankfurt and Munich. Theodor Kullak and Julius Stern had Mendelssohn's example in mind when they founded their Berlin Conservatoire in 1850.

Yes, things were well run in Leipzig, and always with a warm concern for the individual musician—that Mendelssohnian warmth, that deep thoughtfulness and helpfulness. It must also be said that Mendelssohn's friendship and courtesy were amply reciprocated. Seldom have colleagues worked so harmoniously. Perhaps this was because Mendelssohn, Moscheles, David, Hiller, Devrient and most of the Leipzig circle were all happily married men. Where musicians are taken up with unhappy love affairs and women-chasing, there is small chance for friendships, shared experiences, humour.

Their humour was often strictly professional. "The whole of your D flat major piece is amusing", Mendelssohn wrote to Moscheles, "but when it modulates into D major toward the end, I laugh every time, and when the whole thing comes back in D major and then again in D flat major, and then that last measure *fff* is splendid; and the delicate étude in G major is wholly you; I feel as if I see and hear you talking or playing. My greatest favourite is the fairy-tale for children—so gracious and graceful, and especially when the bass repeats the melody deep down, like a fat bassoon or one of the other growling instruments; and the first transition to B flat major, and the return to E flat, and the final measures leggiero—all that is absolutely unforgettable...." Such was the letter Mendelssohn sent from Leipzig to London, and it comes as a bit of a surprise to us. Every history of music records the fact that Ignaz Moscheles was a very great pianist. But was he so great as a composer that a Felix Mendelssohn should go into transports over his études? A vain question. Mendelssohn did go into those transports—perhaps because he was carried away by friendship.

Felix Moscheles, to whom Mendelssohn had stood godfather, has described[23] how the friends would "sit down at the piano to improvise

[23] F. Mendelssohn-Bartholdy: *Briefe an Ignaz und Charlotte Moscheles.* Leipzig, 1888.

together as only the two of them could! Playing sometimes together, sometimes alternately, they showered one another with musical ideas. Like a
ball the theme would be tossed and caught, hurled boldly into the air or
delicately suspended by the one, recaptured by the other, artfully analysed,
didactically dissected, then perhaps to be carried triumphantly off into
other worlds in a new form by the four hands. Often it sounded like four
hands and one soul. If sometimes they stumbled, they would quickly
retrieve the situation. They reached in among and under each other's
fingers, or rather, their fingers contested, for one would wish to bring out
such and such a theme from the other's works and the other snatched it
away from him and by giving it an ingenious turn transformed it into a
melody from the friend's pen. I can see Mendelssohn's eyes shining with
high spirits one evening when he succeeded in defeating my father
melodically. But 'Stop', my father said after the next few chords, 'this
time you fell into the trap. Now I have you!' And so the contest went on
to the bravura close, which sounded as though it had been written and
engraved and was now being given a public performance by two masters."

That sort of entertainment reminds us of the well-known inscription on
the Gewandhaus in Leipzig: *Res severa verum gaudium*—seriousness
alone is true amusement.

THE QUARREL WITH MARX

Mendelssohn's charity came to an end, however, when he encountered
inadequacy—or what he felt to be that. Art was a serious matter; kindness
went so far and no further. There was, for example, the Buber case in
Leipzig, which took a most unhappy turn.

A singer named Franz Buber had called upon Gewandhaus Direktor
Mendelssohn for an audition; he hoped to sing in opera. Mendelssohn
was noted for being a kindly and encouraging examiner. But he candidly
told Buber that he feared his voice would be too small for the stage. Buber
seemed deeply upset at this verdict. Whereupon Mendelssohn wrote him
a letter. The date was 17th June 1840 and the text has so far never been
printed. It began: "My very dear Sir! In our recent interview it was not
my intention to deny your capacity for dramatic singing; if my remarks
seemed to imply any such thing, I did not mean them so. I believe on the
contrary that any matter that is undertaken in earnest and with true zeal
can be brought to a certain degree of perfection . . . provided there are no

mechanical or other insurmountable obstacles opposing it. . . ." Unfortunately, he went on, he did consider that there were such obstacles. Buber, he said in effect, would be ruining his life if he persisted in pursuing a career as a dramatic singer. However hard he worked he would never be able to do anything about the inadequacy of his larynx. "I have no choice but to tell you my frank opinion of your natural equipment, although it may run counter to what others have told you. I hope that I have done so for your good, and I trust that you will not find anything offensive in these remarks, but will see them only as expressions of sincere good will."[1]

Franz Buber's reply to this letter came three days later: he shot himself.

Yet what could Mendelssohn have done? Should he have encouraged something which his deepest convictions told him was not worth encouraging? A year before the Buber case Mendelssohn had offended Marx in a similar way. Marx was the friend of Mendelssohn's youth who had done more than anyone else to promote the fame of the young composer. He had published his *Berliner Musikzeitung* from 1824 to 1832, and in it had constantly proclaimed the genius of a somewhat ill-assorted trio, Beethoven, Mendelssohn, and Spontini, which did help to make Mendelssohn known. In 1830, partly on the recommendation of his grateful friend Felix, Marx became a professor of music at Berlin University. Thereafter the two friends developed in entirely different directions. Marx became one of the most respected musicologists of his time. In 1837 he published a four-volume text on composition, *Kompositionslehre*; in 1858 a biography, *Ludwig van Beethovens Leben und Wirken*; in 1862, *Gluck und die Oper*. He was also the author of one of the earliest manuals on how to play Beethoven's piano works; it is full of fascinating insights into Beethoven's method of building melodies and contains masterly analyses of the sonatas.[2]

One day, probably during the Munich music festival which both friends attended together, Marx told Mendelssohn that he wished to write an oratorio on Moses. Would his friend care to sketch out a text for it? Felix did so, but no doubt treated the matter too carelessly. Marx felt it would not do, and probably with justice. He rewrote the text himself, frequently hitting on ideas of astounding modernity. In his memoirs he speaks of the cursory way in which Scripture treats the great culture of the Egyptians. The ancient Hebrews, he says, could only see the Egyptians as their oppressors. But an oratorio, Marx thought, called for another

---

[1] Manuscript letter in the possession of the International Felix Mendelssohn Society, Basle.

[2] A. B. Marx: *Anleitung zum Vortrage Beethovenscher Klavierwerke.* Berlin, 1863.

attitude. He spent months at the Berlin Egyptian Museum, studying the paintings, sculpture and mummies of Ancient Egypt.[3] So overwhelmed was he by Egyptian art that for a time he wanted to abandon his project. The conflict nearly made him ill. For there was another problem that preyed upon him: Could any man living in the middle of the nineteenth century truly present things belonging to a past so far away and long ago? And then he had a strange experience, something that he took as proof of the "simultaneity of all events".

He was taking a stroll one day, with his recently wedded wife Thérèse, on the Kreuzberg, a small, sandy elevation in the south-west part of Berlin. He remarked to his wife, alluding to the problem on his mind: "This is sand all right, but it is far from being a desert." At that moment a man came out of a byway leading a large animal. The man was certainly not an Egyptian fellah; probably he was connected with the circus. And for the first time in his life Marx saw a camel. "I, who have always been a lover of strange animals, without thinking anything in particular went up to the peculiar creature. And it looked at me. It looked at me with its great, eternally tranquil brown eyes as though it were musing on the past and *remembering*. . . . And at that moment I *took possession* of the desert. I rushed home and began to write."[4]

As soon as Marx had finished his work, he set out for Leipzig to lay it before his old friend who was now director of the Gewandhaus. Who else would bring his work before the public, if not Felix Mendelssohn? The two men sat down at the piano, and Marx played and sang the first part ot the score. When he had finished, Mendelssohn rose, his face deathly pale. "Please don't take it amiss, but I cannot play this music," he said. That was his artistic conviction. And Marx was equally convinced that the reason was jealousy, and that Felix Mendelssohn was "the most ungrateful human being" he had ever met. Back in Berlin, his bitterness was so great that he took his store of Mendelssohn's letters to the Tiergarten and threw them into the lake—precious, irreplaceable letters, thirty or forty of them, perhaps more. Marx himself does not tell this story in his memoirs, but we know it from his wife Thérèse.[5]

Liszt, be it noted, was very much impressed by Marx's *Moses* and later sponsored its performance in Weimar where it had a great success.[6] Schumann, on the other hand, agreed with Mendelssohn and considered it a

[3] A. B. Marx: *Erinnerungen aus meinem Leben*. Berlin, 1865.
[4] Ibid.
[5] Th. Marx: *Adolf Bernhard Marx's Verhältnis zu Felix Mendelssohn-Bartholdy*. Leipzig, 1869.
[6] A. B. Marx: op. cit.

great shame that a theoretician who had sufficient claim to distinction in his own right should have attempted to foist a bad composition upon his friends.[7] Schumann was not entirely right, just as Mendelssohn was not entirely right in failing to take a second look at Marx's opus. At any rate, the two old friends parted ways on that day in Leipzig. We feel the sadness of it, even after the passage of a century. For at the core of the misunderstanding is the eternally unsolved question: What is great? As well as the other question, that of receptivity: Why are our minds at certain times quite closed to works of merit?

Marx outlived Felix Mendelssohn by almost two decades, but never forgot that blow to his feelings. A wife is supposed to share her husband's joys and sorrows—and Thérèse Marx sympathized completely with her husband's sense of injury at the rejection of *Moses*. Unfortunately she sympathized almost excessively, and where Marx treats the matter with great constraint in his own memoirs, she wrote a book on her husband's relations with Mendelssohn, in which she suggests that Felix, a "happy" man and above all wealthy—had no feeling for people who were born poor and had to make their way in the world by struggle.[8] Ferdinand Hiller later went out of his way to correct this unfair picture, though he tactfully refrained from mentioning the Marxes.[9] Hiller was totally lacking in envy, although he too had little luck with his oratorios (which were rediscovered at the beginning of the twentieth century by Max Reger). Hiller wrote a biography of Felix in which he took issue with such prejudices as that embodied in the proverb, *Le génie, c'est la faim*. Why should genius spring only out of privation? Was genius only a struggle with the outer world; was it not also a struggle with the inner self? And Hiller poked fun at the kind of satiated bourgeois who sat at his loaded table and *demanded* that his Schillers go hungry. . . . "Otherwise he would not develop into a genius—after all, we've seen in Goethe's case what wealth leads to."

Hiller might have added a good many other arguments. For example, he might have pointed out that Mendelssohn—except when travelling—preferred a rather modest style of life. Rich though he was, he worked incessantly, just as Mozart in his poverty had done. Felix was never really aware of his wealth—and consequently escaped the social dangers money brings in its train. It did affect him to the extent that several times, in employment and publishing contracts, he was inclined to dismiss the

[7] R. Schumann: *Gesammelte Schriften über Musik und Musiker*. Leipzig, 1891.

[8] Th. Marx: op. cit.

[9] F. Hiller: *Felix Mendelssohn-Bartholdy*. Cologne, 1878.

question of payment as unimportant. But his wise father forcefully intervened. If Felix Mendelssohn had waived his fees and freely given his
services as a conductor and director, it would have been what today is
called unfair competition, and he would have incurred the mortal hatred
of all artists who had to work for a living. This factor underlay the spite-
ful verdict of the Wagnerian period: "Well, of course he was a banker's
son." But the slur was completely undeserved. Even after his father died,
Felix was not financially independent. His affairs were governed by his
younger brother Paul.

THIS YEAR IS THE KING'S

Despite his youth Paul Mendelssohn was regarded as virtually the head
of the family, and in the autumn of 1840 the Prussian court applied to
him to ask whether the composer would be prepared to give up his work
in Leipzig and under certain conditions move to Berlin. The inquiry was
made in confidence, and the terms offered were magnificent. But there
was a certain vagueness about the actual details, although this did not at
first become apparent.[1]

The plan was approximately as follows, the existing Academy of the
Arts was to be divided into four schools: painting, sculpture, architecture
and music. Each school would be headed by a director, and these directors
would take turns to serve as general heads of the whole Academy. Felix
Mendelssohn would be director of the music department, and it was
expected that he would choose among the foremost teachers to set up a
conservatoire which, in conjunction with the Royal Theatre, would produce public concerts of spiritual and secular works.

It sounded splendid, and Paul Mendelssohn was keenly interested.
Fanny, who had never reconciled herself to having Felix off in Leipzig,
was delighted. Above all Leah Mendelssohn, who had greatly aged since
her husband's death, saw the prospect of her life's taking on new meaning
if her favourite son returned home. Paul offered to go to Leipzig at once
and lay the proposal before Felix. He also put some stress upon the
feelings of the family: everyone would be so delighted to have Felix in
Berlin.

Felix was by no means delighted. He temporized for many months

[1] S. Hensel: *Die Familie Mendelssohn 1729–1847*. Berlin, 1879.

before consenting. To Klingemann in London he wrote that he would probably have to "bite the sour apple".[2] He stressed that he had no intention of tying himself up for more than a year, and he did not give up his post in Leipzig; instead he appointed a deputy.

But the apple was not really so very sour.

How had this mysterious appointment come about? The old King of Prussia had passed away at last. He had been succeeded by Frederick William IV, who during his protracted period as Crown Prince had moved in circles in no way like the dignified royal milieu. The father had been sober, taciturn, and averse to dabbling in matters he might not understand. Frederick William IV, on the other hand was a great chatterbox and took wild delight in involving himself with people and subjects which required more from him than he might have anticipated. He was the sort of person who becomes intoxicated by his own words—as William II was to be.[3] In contrast to his father and to old Metternich in Vienna, he seemed initially to have no fear of the German democrats. Upon his accession he decreed an amnesty for political prisoners and even gave an audience to Georg Herwegh, the poet of freedom, the "iron lark" of the coming German revolution. His conservative advisers at court were horrified.[4]

In outward appearance, too, the new king was his father's very opposite. When Frederick William III was mounted, his long legs almost touched the ground. But Frederick William IV—like his younger brother, William I, founder of the German Empire—had short legs; in compensation the upper part of his body was exceedingly long, and his face was animated —the face of a rhetorician addicted to the gesture of casting his eyes heavenwards.

Nevertheless the new king began his reign in a thoroughly enlightened spirit. He had little patience with the bitter quarrels within the Protestant camp. Thus, he gave short shrift to the Magdeburg Dispute which was currently agitating many minds. In 1841 a painting had been exhibited in Magdeburg entitled *Christ Healing a Blind Man*. The tale was told that a blind woman had been cured of her affliction when led before this picture. The newspaper *Magdeburger Zeitung* published a poem hailing the miracle. A minister named Sintenis rushed into the fray, denouncing the newspaper's poet and calling the whole affair idolatry and Popish belief in miracles. Whereupon Draeseke, the Protestant Provincial Bishop,

[2] F. Mendelssohn-Bartholdy: *Briefwechsel mit Klingemann*. Wiesbaden, 1909.
[3] E. Friedell: *Kulturgeschichte der Neuzeit*, vol. III. Munich, 1931.
[4] *Briefe von und an Georg Herwegh*. n.p., 1896.

in turn denounced Sintenis, charged him with being a Judas and atheist, and called upon the Provincial Synod to expel him from the ministry.[5] When the King heard of this fracas, he expressed regret that he no longer possessed the absolute powers of Frederick the Great; if only he had, he said, he would consign preacher, Bishop and newspaper editor to the military prison of Küstrin. It is one of the tragedies of German history that this king later abandoned this kind of good sense and assumed the reactionary and hypocritical piety of his ministers, Eichhorn and Raumer. If he had only looked toward England (for he was very fond of Victoria and Albert[6]), he might have observed that Royalty's most pressing task at the moment was to protect the common folk who were being victimized by the spread of industry. But apparently Frederick William IV only knew of the workers' problems by hearsay.[7]

Yet the common people had looked forward so hopefully to this liberal monarch. It was something of a shock when he began revealing his true principles. He cherished a romantic belief in the Estates, that is, in a division of the populace that had ceased to exist with the French Revolution. He was strongly in favour of a medieval relationship between the Prince and the people; his far less imaginative father had prudently avoided touching on such matters. "Will you help me", he exhorted the Estates on 15th October 1840, when he demanded the oath of homage from them, "will you help me bring to their height those qualities which have enabled Prussia with her fourteen millions to join the Great Powers of this earth—the qualities of honour, loyalty, striving for light, justice and truth, progress toward the wisdom of age united with heroic youthful vigour?" The people—who had been waiting eagerly for a programme of social reform—felt such rhetoric as empty wind (though he meant something by it, after all). And when he finished one of his speeches with the grand flourish: "This I swear, and may God help me," Berlin cynics echoed him: "May God help me."

A book appeared to enlighten him. Bettina von Arnim, Brentano's sister, widow of the poet Achim von Arnim, was first and foremost a poet. Her books, often foolishly belaboured, such as her *Goethe's Correspondence with a Child*, hovered by choice between truth and fiction. In this they approached closer to reality than more documented works. For there is a reality that is not to be found in documents—and it is the business of seers and poets to capture it.... Bettina's book, entitled, *This*

---

[5] Barz und Macke: *Der Magdeburger Kirchenstreit*. Berlin, 1868.
[6] J. Cottrell: *Bunsen and the Court of St. James*. London, 1872.
[7] K. Kersten: *Die Deutsche Revolution 1848–49*. Frankfurt, 1955.

Book is the King's, begins in a thoroughly inept manner. The presiding genius is Goethe's wife, who is presented speaking Frankfurt dialect. The year is 1800 and the lady airs her mind concerning the injustices in the world. Then, with a wild leap, the book swings into the present, the early eighteen-forties, and lectures the King of Prussia about the present injustices within his realm. Bettina had been doing field work, investigating conditions within the workers' quarters just outside the gates of Berlin; she had also come to know a young Swiss student, Heinrich Grunholzer, who encouraged her in her researches.[8] The book concludes with a vivid account of her findings, and a strong appeal to the King to relieve the sufferings of the labouring classes.

It was published on 15th July 1843, at first anonymously. A copy was sent directly to the King with a personal letter. The King was evidently dismayed: he declared that he could make nothing of the book and had "no time to read it."[9] At this a member of the Young Germany movement, Adolf Stahr, wrote an essay summing up Bettina's main arguments. The essay attracted a great deal of attention, so much so that hundreds of thousands of people read such audacious sentences as: "But for Prussian indifference there would be no Prussian proletariat. When it is a matter of marching against the enemy, then, to be sure ... the state puts uniforms on the workers and lines them up in rank and file. When the father of the country wishes to win glory, then these serve splendidly as fodder for the enemy cannon. Those who return home and themselves cry out for fodder are regarded as scum of the people and are pressed back into the old mire. ... If they complain, it will be no problem to subdue them!" Though statements of this sort are commonplaces today, in those days they were proclamations of naked revolution. Stahr's book was instantly banned, and Bettina herself fell into disgrace.[10]

Felix Mendelssohn read Bettina's book. The Frankfurt tone, the poetic scapegrace quality of it, meant more to him than its politics. He interpreted the title in terms of his own life, grumbling: "This year is the King's"—although the comment was somewhat outdated.[11] For Felix's one year in the King's service had already become two.

In purely artistic matters the King was not at all reactionary. He felt that a king should surround himself with the choicest spirits, and in accordance with this monarchical ideal tried to assemble the most famous

[8] T. Koller: *Heinrich Grunholzer, Lebensbild eines Republikaners.* Zürich, 1878.

[9] B. v. Arnim: *Sämtliche Schriften.* Weimar, 1853.

[10] A. Stahr: *Aus der Jugendzeit. Lebenserinnerungen.* Schwerin, 1870.

[11] Krebs: *Antigone-Erinnerungen.* Berlin, no date.

artists and the most freethinking scholars in Berlin. Thus he summoned Alexander von Humboldt, Friedrich Rückert, the Grimm Brothers, and most emphatically of all, Ludwig Tieck. Mendelssohn was another obvious choice, as the Crown Prince, Frederick had known Felix well. He had attended Mendelssohn's splendid revival of Handel's *Israel in Egypt* at Düsseldorf, and had had a solemn conversation with the conductor about Old Testament subjects. (The psalms of David were Frederick William's favourite reading.)

For the enhancement of Prussian musical life, Frederick William IV wished to hold Meyerbeer and Mendelssohn permanently in Berlin. Why should these native composers live abroad at all—the master of opera in Paris, and the creator of the *St. Paul* in Leipzig? After all, both of them were bred-in-the-bone Berliners! And so flattering letters were sent out, inviting the two musicians to return. Meyerbeer came, and replaced Spontini, whose fall had long been impending. Meyerbeer turned himself into a super-Spontini.[12] Mendelssohn made less of a splash. It was gratifying to be so in the King's favour, but the plans for the Academy remained vague, and Felix did not quite know what he was supposed to be doing in Berlin. He was receiving the magnificent salary of three thousand talers a year, and his sense of honour insisted that he must earn it somehow. But how?

He was soon to find out. In tracing the story of the Academy appointment, earlier biographers invariably came upon the name of Bunsen. The diplomat and theologian Josias von Bunsen, Mendelssohn's friend from Rome and London, expected that the return of Mendelssohn to Berlin would quickly lead to remarkable things. After all, Berlin had been the cradle for the Bach cult, having given that enthusiastic reception to the revived *St. Matthew Passion*. True, the Bach festivals were now set in Leipzig, but they could easily be reinstated in Berlin. But Bunsen's ambitions went still further. Mendelssohn had been composing a good deal of religious music recently. On the strength of this Bunsen went to the King and suggested that Mendelssohn be put in charge of all Protestant church music in the realm. Alarmed, Mendelssohn declined the offer. Bunsen, taking the cue from the anti-Catholic English, was advising that Germany too should take measures against the claims of the Curia. During the protracted dispute between the Prussian State and the Archbishop of Cologne over the question of mixed marriages, Bunsen sided fully with the state.[13] But as a musician, Mendelssohn attempted to be neutral in

[12] J. Kapp: *Meyerbeer, Leben und Schaffen.* Stuttgart, 1924.
[13] Freiherr von Droste-Vischering: *Über Kirche und Staat.* Münster, 1838.

this religious struggle. Many of the things he wrote at the time—such as the 22nd Psalm, "My God, my God, why hast Thou forsaken me?" could have been taken for Catholic and Gregorian music.

But Protestant or Catholic—it would have been a great pity if Felix had been brought to Berlin to serve only as a church composer. Fortunately other forces were at play. As we now know, another of the King's intimates was behind the invitation to Berlin. This was the famous Hellenist August Böckh, who had some special plans in mind for Mendelssohn. Böckh was perhaps one of the longest-lived professors ever to hold an academic chair—he staggered his students on the occasion of a university jubilee by saying that he had lectured for one hundred and twenty terms without a break.[14] His intellect was enormous and wide-ranging, and he was well aware of this, for he signed the poems he at one time wrote for Arnim's *Einsiedlerzeitung* with the pseudonym "Polyhistor". His knowledge extended from astronomy to the political economy of Athens—a subject on which he published a brilliant book (*Staatshaushalt der Athener*) in 1817—and to systems of weights and measures in the economic life of the ancient world. But his greatest, most abiding interest was in the metrics of the Greek tragedians. He would spend whole nights at the piano hoping to deduce (as his study on *Antigone*—1824—reveals) how Sophocles wished his choruses sung and stressed. But he did not find out—and most of the musicians of the day could not have been of help. But what of Felix Mendelssohn, a musician with antiquarian inclinations? Perhaps he could be interested in the problem. While he was still a poor secondary-school teacher, Böckh had given private Greek lessons to a wealthy lady named Madame Levy, who had conceived the desire of reading Pindar in the original. In this lady's house Böckh had made the acquaintance of Abraham Mendelssohn. Subsequently Felix attended his lectures at the university, and Böckh became a frequent guest at the Mendelssohns'. When Bunsen spoke of bringing Mendelssohn back to Berlin for the honour and glory of the new monarch, Böckh lent his hearty support to the idea. He began persuading the King that the Royal Theatre must revive the Greek drama; that there must be performances of Sophocles's *Antigone* and *Oedipus at Colonus* and many other such works. They might also do a series of neo-classical dramas such as Racine's *Athalie*. And Mendelssohn would be the right man—or rather, he would be the only man—to write the music for these productions.

[14] Sachse: *Erinnerungen an August Böckh*. Berlin, 1868.

THE HERITAGE OF ANTIQUITY

Yet the theatre was a law unto itself. The King wondered whether Professor Böckh would be able to transmute his vast knowledge of things Greek into living theatre. Another man might do it better: Ludwig Tieck.

Tieck was almost seventy at this time. Born in 1773, he had displayed considerable histrionic gifts even as a child.[1] His love of the theatre showed itself in his work with August Wilhelm Schlegel at the task of translating Shakespeare into German. He also became the first of the great readers and dramatic monologists,[2] one who could play all parts at once without donning the comic or the tragic mask—a Hans Andersen or a Dickens.

In his youth Ludwig Tieck had been a great walker, and also a rider. At the age of thirty he was badly hurt by a fall from a horse and was forced to abandon the free life of the open air and remain confined to his room. His residence was in Dresden, and no distinguished person passed through the city without going to pay his respects to Wilhelm Tieck. He would entertain these visitors with his remarkable monologues. In his free time, he arranged and catalogued the sixteen thousand volumes of his precious library.[3]

We do not know how the King contrived to lure Tieck from Dresden to Berlin. At any rate, Frederick William IV set him up magnificently in Potsdam. A carriage was always at the disposal of the invalid writer so that he could be driven to the Royal Theatre for discussions of any problems that arose. Nothing was done at the theatre without Tieck's advice and approval.

Böckh was determined that the Greek revival should open with *Antigone*. All members of the theatre were convoked at the home of Count Redern to hear the play read by Tieck in person. Böckh and Mendelssohn sat in the first row. Probably Eduard Devrient, who was to play the role of Haemon, Antigone's betrothed, was also present. True to his reputation, Tieck read magnificently, differentiating the various characters by voice, facial expression and gestures, and giving tremendous

---

[1] M. Talmann: *Ludwig Tieck, der romantische Weltmann aus Berlin.* Berne, 1955.

[2] H. C. Andersen: *Das Märchen meines Lebens.* Leipzig, 1849.

[3] E. H. Zeydel: *Ludwig Tieck.* Princeton, 1935.

sonority to the great choral songs. It was for these that Felix Mendelssohn was to write the music. Felix was deeply moved. Devrient was not; he thought Tieck's histrionics superficial.[4]

The great sensation of the day, however, was Tieck's introduction. Speaking in a low and modest voice he posed the following propositions: "His Majesty the King has commanded the theatres to undertake the revival of Greek drama. Our first play shall be the *Antigone* because its emotions are *modern* and for that reason it is closest to us. Antigone is a Christian, a 'Christian martyr'. What she does may be likened to the act of the Blessed Virgin and Mary Magdalene when they took Jesus from the cross and 'tended him with spices'." It was true, Tieck continued, that Antigone's act was even more heroic—for in providing her brother's body with loving burial, she incurred the penalty of death. Incidentally, the character of Antigone displayed something of the "Christian harshness", the uncompromising spirit contained in those words of Jesus: "He who is not for me is against me." This became evident in her rejection of poor Ismene for advising moderation and questioning whether it was really worth while sacrificing happiness and even life itself for the sake of burying their dead brother.[5]

Mendelssohn was profoundly impressed by this exposition. Böckh was outraged. Himself a poor reader,[6] he seethed inwardly and swore "to pay back that pious hypocrite". He soon had an opportunity to do so. A few days later another meeting was held, for the further instruction of the actors, and this time Böckh was prepared for a scholarly disputation. He had brought Karl Behnsen with him, and the two now challenged Tieck. What was all this about Antigone's being a Christian? After all, Hegel had given the definitive interpretation of Antigone's act. In his *Philosophy of Religion* Hegel had asserted that Sophocles's heroine was "a servant of the gods of the dead", who by the essentially symbolic act of strewing earth over the dead man was "rendering to Hades what had been wrested from it, contrary to law, by the ban on burial".

Tieck paled. His round face began to quiver and his eyes to squint slightly. This was Berlin, after all, and it was no simple matter to run foul of disciples of Hegel. Of course Hegel had had his enemies, such as Otto Friedrich Gruppe, who in 1831 had written the witty and delightful satire: *The Winds, or a Completely Absolute Construction of World*

---

[4] E. Devrient: *Meine Erinnerungen an Felix Mendelssohn-Bartholdy*. Leipzig, 1872.

[5] W. Krägenbrink: *Tieck als Vorleser*. Königsberg, no date.

[6] F. G. Welcker: *Briefe an Droysen*, in *J. G. Droysens Briefwechsel*. Berlin, Leipzig, 1929.

History, by Absolutus von Hegelingen. People had laughed heartily over it; but Hegel was still something of a god in Berlin's intellectual circles. ... Within a few moments, however, Tieck had regained his composure. Hegel's exegesis was obviously wrong, he observed. For *the soul of a dead man always went to Hades,* whether the body drowned in the sea or mouldered on the battlefield. Of course Antigone's act was a "protest". But not on behalf of the "gods of the dead"; rather, it was a protest against the state's interference with a duty imposed by love and humanity, *"and therefore we call her a Christian"*.[7]

There was no humbling the man! In high dudgeon, Böckh and Behnsen took their leave and dragged Mendelssohn off with them, although Felix privately was much taken by Tieck. They drove—this episode took place in the late summer of 1841—to the Mendelssohn mansion where Böckh was staying as guest. The composer had broken up his household in Leipzig and had moved bag and baggage to Berlin, where his Cécile was most affectionately welcomed by Fanny and Leah. Böckh had been put up in the Mendelssohns' summerhouse so as to be always on hand to advise the composer in his work on the music.

At the moment, however, Mendelssohn was troubled by other matters more vital than the academic question of whether Antigone had been Christian or pagan, whether her deed had been a gesture of love or a religious rite. In reading the drama he had discovered what seemed a terrible dramatic flaw. Like Shakespeare's *Romeo and Juliet* and Gottfried von Strassburg's *Tristan und Isolde,* the play concluded as a tragedy of love—and yet there had not been a single love scene in the entire work. Haemon and Antigone never spoke to one another, never so much as stood together on the boards. Had Sophocles been so "poor a poet" that he had simply forgotten this? Mendelssohn wrote an anxious letter to Tieck, and received a detailed reply. (Both letters have unfortunately been lost.[8])

But how was this question to be settled? Anyone who is familiar with the books of Schadewaldt, Kerényi and Karl Reinhardt[9] knows that to this day—more than a century later—the aesthetics of the structure of the *Antigone* have not yet been clarified. Where in this exceedingly sober tragedy is the Dionysiac element which would justify the great bacchantic chorus of the Thebans?[10] Eberhard Schmausius has even offered the

---

[7] W. Krägenbrink: op. cit.
[8] *Letters of Tieck.* New York, 1937.
[9] K. Reinhardt: *Sophokles.* Frankfurt, 1933.
[10] K. Kerényi: *Sophokles und das Tragische in der Antigone.* Frankfurt, 1934.

hypothesis that the choruses in the *Antigone* are interpolations "from another play".

Whatever the answers, in a bare two weeks Mendelssohn had got the overture and the choruses on paper. He did not use the Hölderlin translation (there were good reasons for that), but Donner's translation as revised by Böckh. Musicologists have been amazed at this creative alacrity, but this is only because they have failed to reckon with Felix's strong intellectual interests. What works we might possess if Mozart, Weber or Schubert had attended a university and sat at the feet of men like Böckh, Droysen and Hegel! But the viciousness of the anti-Semites has quite obscured this aspect of Mendelssohn's nature.

No, Mendelssohn was as much drawn to the classics as he was to Biblical subjects. He had always, for instance, wanted to set Homer to music, so from the vast canvas of the Odyssey he singled out, as specially congenial, the episode of Odysseus and Nausicaa.

He had been fascinated by the world of the Greeks ever since he was introduced to it as a boy, by his tutor Karl Wilhelm Ludwig Heyse. Later he had read the books of Preller and Nitzsch on the Greek myths.[11] But the matter was taken up in earnest by Johann Gustav Droysen—for after the success of the *St. Paul* Droysen decided that he must write a Greek oratorio for the composer. Both men probably laughed at the designation "oratorio". The piece would have to be a choral poem, something like the *Walpurgis Night*, with many choruses, recitatives, and still more unmixed orchestral music. In a letter of October 1836, Droysen described the various effects he intended to incorporate in the oratorio. "You will have a great deal of the Odyssey before you once again! Graceful, bashful Nausicaa, who greets you with her *chaire xein*, her "Welcome, stranger". And certainly you will have wind and waves enough, and sunny vistas, and the smoke rising straight above the house of Ithaca. I really think that such strictly defined subjects as antiquity provides, with their clearly sketched characters and situations, present wonderful material for composition. . . ."[12]

The poem was written and Mendelssohn approved of most of it. He very much liked the descriptions of Odysseus emerging from the sea, skin burned red by the impact of the salt waves, holding a branch in his sinewy hand to cover his nakedness; of the King's daughter Nausicaa, her girl companions and her father Alcinous. But then the correspondence

---

[11] L. Preller: *Demeter und Persephone. Ein Zyklus mythologischer Untersuchungen*. Hamburg, 1837.

[12] "*J. G. Droysen und Felix Mendelssohn-Bartholdy*." *Deutsche Rundschau*. Berlin, April–June, 1902.

lapsed; his work in Leipzig interfered; and in addition there were the usual Mendelssohn doubts when confronted with a subject. The poet-scholar sensed the cooling-off of Felix's interest, and concluded that the project no longer appealed to him. It was now the composer's turn to re-assure his friend: "I keep thinking about Nausicaa: the storm, falling asleep, playing ball, finally the conducting of Odysseus over the sea..." he wrote in January 1838. "As for the very part you consider difficult, the ball-playing passage—the music will find itself...." Naturally, for the vignette of girls playing ball has in itself a Mozartian quality.

Nevertheless, Droysen released the composer from any obligation to himself. Let him use the material only to make another orchestral tone-poem out of it, as he had done with the "Hebrides" overture. "Deep-voiced Poseidon" would sound better instrumentally, he declared.[13]

Here was genius for friendship! Eduard Devrient would not have been able to hide his chagrin at having laboured in vain. But Droysen was free of such feelings. He would still remain the leader of Hellenism in Germany, despite the fact that Mendelssohn set aside his text of *Odysseus and Nausicaa*. When Droysen moved on to a chair at Kiel and Mendels-sohn was busy composing the music for *Antigone*, the scholar sent a shower of heartening letters to the composer in Berlin. "I believe that it would be a thing of great importance", he wrote in the autumn of 1841, "if the glory of antiquity could really take possession of you.... I have no idea what the relation of antiquity to your musical creations would be, and as yet no musician has attempted any such penetration. Or are you smiling? Of course I do not mean that you should translate from the Greek into music; Raphael did not do that either. But..." How clearly he saw the problem! Raphael painted like an Italian when he painted *The School of Athens*. And Mendelssohn would certainly have to com-pose like a modern when he composed the *Antigone*.[14]

He went at his task with a sure hand. "What is stage music?" Friedrich Nietzsche asked in his *The Birth of Tragedy*. And answered: "A *com-mentary* on the events on the stage." But commentary implies interpreta-tive explanation. The events on the stage may belong to remote antiquity, and the problems they present may be remote from us; but the comment-ing music must be contemporary. Mendelssohn knew that long before his admirer, Friedrich Nietzsche—and he also knew that archetypal events could be brought out musically only by romantic means. Ludwig Tieck had expressed it well: "I am now conscious of the transformation of mythology.... There is nothing bygone, nothing past ... everything still

[13] Ibid.   [14] Ibid.

is thus and must be thus. Everything that has been, history, poetry, nature, fixes upon me the gaze of a single eye like a bottomless pool, full of love but also full of terrifying meaning."[15] The continuance of everything that is, the presence of what has been, was one of the firmest principles in Mendelssohn's creed. And so he set to work with modern techniques to compose his "commentary" on Sophocles.

During the final weeks before the première he was almost the only one involved who did not lose his head or have the jitters. The actors, Devrient, even Tieck himself, feared that at the last moment the King might cancel the entire production—Frederick William IV was as unstable as King Ludwig II of Bavaria was to be, and for the same tragic reason. But Felix forged ahead with the work.[16] He also had to quell the doubts of August Böckh (who had warned him against making his music excessively modern). The rehearsals began, and from the first bars of the mighty prelude what Mendelssohn was aiming at became apparent:

The beginning is archaic. But at once the dissonances in the fourth, sixth and seventh measures produce those outcries of grief that are scarcely consonant with the measured pathos of classical drama.[17] On the other hand these were effects to which the audience responded powerfully—especially the passion and nervous force of the Allegro. Here was a timeless theme. It is significant that for Mendelssohn's funeral service in 1847

[15] L. Lüdeke: *Ludwig Tieck und die Brüder Schlegel*. Frankfurt, 1930.
[16] Krebs: *Antigone-Erinnerungen*. Berlin, no date.
[17] A. Reissmann: *Felix Mendelssohn-Bartholdy*. Berlin, 1867.

not his church music, but the introductory music to *Antigone* was played.[18]

Certainly August Böckh, who in his capacity as adviser on the classics had stood behind the whole enterprise, had never dreamed of any such approach—although he was musician enough to acclaim the music. The choruses, with strophe and antistrophe:

How they express Sophocles's amazement at man! The Athenians' favourite poet, the apostle of moderation, piety, civic virtue, remained awestruck at the dual nature of man:

> Many the forms of life, wondrous and strange to see, But nought than man appears more wondrous and more strange.... Earth, of all Gods, from ancient days the first, He ... wears ever year by year. The thoughtless tribe of birds, the beasts that roam the fields, the brood in sea-depths born, he takes them all in nets.... And speech, and thought as swift as wind, and tempered mood for the higher life of states, these he has learnt.... Only from death he fails to find escape.... So gifted with a wondrous might, above all fancy's dreams, with skill to plan, now unto evil, now to good he turns.[19]

It is so: man can do anything. Anything, for good or evil. He has tampered with the ways of nature to an extent undreamed of in the Age

---

[18] B. Bartels: *Felix Mendelssohn-Bartholdy*. Bremen, 1947.
[19] A. Hibbard, H. Frenz: *Writers of the Western World*. Boston, 1954.

of Pericles. The poet's fundamental amazement is as modern as ever. And so is Mendelssohn's music: the ancient Greek metres, the dactyls, anapests and spondees, hammer at the gates of our souls with such clarity and force that they seem newly fashioned. Mendelssohn was too fervent an admirer of the poets to depart from them in his accentuation. But his *instrumentation* was resolutely modern. He did not try to make his music sound Greek, for no one knew what Greek music may have been like. Instead, he worked with brass, flutes, clarinets, harp and strings, set his strophes and antistrophes differently, alternated choral songs with recitatives. Certain parts of the work were even composed as musical melodrama, and these turned out to be particularly effective.

Naturally a scholarly dispute immediately ensued. Was it "possible to compose music for an ancient Greek tragedy using instruments the Greeks had not known"? Of course it was possible. Rather, any other procedure was impossible. We may imagine Wagner's scorn had anyone tried to tell him that the bridal chorus in *Lohengrin* should be accompanied by instruments such as were used in the twelfth century, at the time of Henry the Lion. Or that he should use the ancient Germanic lyre for his *Ring of the Nibelungs*. Instead Wagner made use of the most modern musical means available: the orchestra of Beethoven and Weber. Mendelssohn did exactly the same.

Despite his private reservations on the matter, Böckh chivalrously came to the defence of the composer, in association with two other scholars who backed him up.[20] Droysen also published an article commending his friend highly for not having made a foolish attempt to write ancient Greek music, the character of which was more or less a mystery. Really? That was a bold statement to make, considering that August Böckh was something of an authority on all things Greek. And yet it was so. Felix Mendelssohn had instinctively made the right choice—as has become more evident today when we read the conclusions of a present-day specialist, himself a Greek: Thrasybulos Georgiades, Professor of Music in Munich.[21] He points out that we cannot imagine what Greek music really sounded like, for only a few pieces in Greek notation have come down to us, and we have no idea of how the musicians of the time brought this notation to life. The signs are mere ideographs, in no way parallel to modern musical notes. Only the ancient Greeks knew how these written characters were meant to sound.

[20] A. Böckh, E. H. Tölken, F. Förster: *Über die Antigone von Sophokles*. Berlin, 1842.

[21] T. Georgiades: *Musik und Rhythmus bei den Griechen*. Hamburg, 1958.

The première of *Antigone* took place on 28th November 1841 in the New Palace in Postdam. A classical stage-set had been designed, representing an arena in which semichoruses came forward at deliberate pace to meet one another.[22] The dazzling audience included the Royal Family, scholars and artists from all over Germany, and a sprinkling of distinguished Russian and English visitors. There was tremendous applause, and the audience was even more enthusiastic at the repeat performance given on 6th December. Although the play had so stark and alien a background, it came to life, thanks to Mendelssohn's musical commentary.

For us, the striking thing about the drama is its modernity—twentieth-century modernity. The protagonist of the work is not so much Antigone as her adversary Creon. Creon is an anti-hero, such as we might encounter on the modern stage, in the plays of Giraudoux or Sartre. It seems only a few steps from such un-Greek plays as *The Trojan War did not Take Place* or *The Flies* to Sophocles's *Antigone*. The Berlin actor Rott, who took the part of Creon, carried off the role masterfully.

At the court reception which took place after the première, Frederick William IV was overwhelmed with congratulations. Scholars and artists, officers and clergy, the high society of Berlin and Potsdam, guests from the rest of Germany and from abroad—all were wildly enthusiastic about the play. Overflowing with pride, Frederick William IV ordered that a medallion be struck in honour of this memorable day. The obverse showed the head of Sophocles, the reverse had the figure of Antigone and, in small circles, the profiles of Felix Mendelssohn and Ludwig Tieck, who had made the triumph possible. There was to be a further honour: in the spring of 1842 Mendelssohn was named Knight of the Order *Pour le Mérite*. That was the highest distinction the King could give to intellectuals.

Good-natured mockers had their say about the affair, too. The humorist Adolf Glassbrenner turned out a parody called *Antigone in Berlin, freely adapted from Sophocles*. Albert Lortzing followed (in Leipzig) with a comic opera, *Der Wildschütz*, in which a crazy countess appeared on the stage and rattled on in a silly monologue about Antigone and the revival of Hellenism.[23] The most amusing comment of all came from London, when the English première took place in 1845. In January of that year Tom Taylor, the editor of *Punch*, published a caricature on the subject. Mendelssohn admitted that he laughed for three days over the cartoon.[24]

[22] S. Hensel: *Die Familie Mendelssohn 1729–1847*. Berlin, 1879.
[23] E. Wolff: *Felix Mendelssohn-Bartholdy*. Berlin, 1909.
[24] G. A. Macfarren: *Addresses and Lectures*. London, 1888.

FAREWELL, BERLIN

For decades afterwards *Antigone* was often to be imitated but never matched. Yet in spite of this outstanding triumph, Felix was more discontented than he had ever been before in his life. What were the reasons?

His letters provide only misleading answers. They say, for one thing, that nothing but bad music was being produced in Berlin. Berlin was a city of music critics—for which reason alone the music made there could not be bad. In those days the critics of Berlin set the canons for the musical world. Ludwig Rellstab, Adolf Bernhard Marx—there was a whole phalanx of famous names which culminated in Adolf Weissmann, Oscar Bie, Hans Heinz Stuckenschmidt. Each one of these men was a stimulating musicologist with a strong penchant for experimentation. Thus Berlin became a city of experiments. But for that very reason, perhaps, Berlin was fickle. Experiments followed one another in rapid succession. Even the revival of the *St. Matthew Passion* had been fundamentally an experiment, and, moreover, an affair of the upper ten thousand. Thus the musical situation was not the same as it was in Vienna, where music was a popular art form. The violins of Johann Strauss père and Josef Lanner did not sing for the aristocracy alone.[1] The common people of Berlin, on the other hand, were not merely unmusical, but anti-musical.

Perhaps Mendelssohn had felt this antipathy—though his letters do not mention any. Nor do his letters mention something else which *must* have struck him: that is the Berliners' profound dislike of religious music, of religious art in general. Mendelssohn was a grandson of the Enlightenment, and remained linked to it all his life by uncommonly strong ties. Lessing's doctrine of the equal value of the religions of civilized man was deeply meaningful to him—and he felt that religious disputes were altogether odious. But the Berlin populace was anti-religious. More than that, it made mock of religion.[2] The author of the Enlightenment novel *Herr Lorenz Stark*, one Johann Jakob Engel, noted morosely that most Christians went to church only four times in their lives.[3] The first time

---

[1] H. E. Jacob: *Johann Strauss, Vater und Sohn.* Hamburg, 1953.
[2] *Düsseldorfer Künstlerbriefe.* Düsseldorf, 1858.
[3] J. J. Engel: *Herr Lorenz Stark.* Berlin, 1801.

they were carried there to be baptized; the second time they walked on their two legs to be confirmed; the third time to be united in marriage; and the fourth time they were carried again, in a coffin. Was there any sense in writing church music for such a public? Nor was hostility to religion confined to the common people. There was Alexander von Humboldt at the age of eighty-five, showing his collections to Karl August Varnhagen von Ense.[4] One of the specimens was a living chameleon. Humboldt commented: "I think this is the only animal which can direct one of its eyes upward and the other downward simultaneously—except for our parsons, who manage to keep one eye on heaven and the other on the goods and advantages of this world." The artists shared in the general cynicism. Friedrich Rückert, who was anything but a revolutionary, wrote the following verses:

> I used to be a Christian soul
>   And might have grown still more so.
> But nowadays I find the whole
>   Flock are inclined to bore so.

> I cannot stand your Christian glooms,
>   Your sighs and painful breathing.
> My heart still springs to gayer tunes,
>   So I've become a heathen.

> You may still catch me in that hour
>   When I'm at death's door lying,
>   But here on earth your doctrines sour
> Are only good for dying.

If this poem had been written by Heinrich Heine, there would have been nothing very remarkable about it. For Heine, in anticipation of Nietzsche, stood whole-heartedly for the spirit of sensuous Hellenism. But it was written by Friedrich Rückert, a quiet man, and anything but a mocker. No, this anti-religious attitude was not a purely intellectual fad. Rather, it was deeply rooted in the people, and expressed the general point of view. Any pro-church activity was regarded with suspicion. Religious themes in painting, poetry or music simply antagonized people who were steadily moving toward the revolutionary year of 1848.

Thus Felix Mendelssohn's compositions for the church met with a

---

[4] L. Assing: *Briefe von Alexander von Humboldt an Varnhagen von Ense aus den Jahren 1827–58*. Leipzig, 1860.

divided reception in Berlin. Either, people thought, they sprang from the excessive zeal of the convert, or else, and still worse, they were a form of toadying to the King and his ministers, the Bunsens, Eichhorns and so on. No one wanted to accept them as something else entirely, the "spiritual diary" of an extremely sincere man—just as the *Songs without Words* may be called his secular diary. Since the Jewish elements in Mendelssohn's personality always held his Christianity in equilibrium, there could be no question of his exhibiting a convert's zeal. The 95th Psalm had been written while he was still in Leipzig, and jubilantly cried his thanks to God for a life of fulfilment in his profession and his family: "O come, let us worship and bow down, let us kneel before the Lord, our Maker!"

But Berlin was a "Voltairean city", as Georg Brandes had called it,[5] and had no patience with prayers. Not that this was ever put bluntly to Mendelssohn; but his finely organized psyche nevertheless recognized it. He wanted to get away. Above all, he felt impelled to leave because of his relationship with the King, whom he felt had broken his word. The King had not given him what he had promised: the post of director of the public concerts which were to be performed by the musical personnel of the Royal Theatre. This assignment was to have recompensed him for the loss of his position in Leipzig, with its tremendous scope and influence. Instead, the composer sat waiting for commissions. But for the present, no second *Antigone* commission came along.

Twentieth-century readers will think of a Kafka novel: A man is called to a position which is just right for him; he can execute all its duties perfectly. Files are established and the bureaucracy begins to operate. But he is given no real work, and he cannot locate his employer. Finally the job and he himself are shattered.[6] How Mendelssohn chafed at it all emerges from a letter of Richard Wagner's. Wagner had also come to Berlin and asked in vain for an audience with the King. In May 1842 he wrote:

> In order to orient myself, I asked Mendelssohn, who received me with the utmost friendliness, to tell me about everything I should know. His report made sad hearing; significantly enough, he revealed that he himself would be leaving Berlin next winter because he was so angry at being kept there for absolutely nothing at all. His appointment, he said, was mere braggadocio on the part of the King, who takes pride in attracting celebrities

[5] G. Brandes: *Voltaire*. Berlin, 1923.
[6] M. Brod: *Franz Kafka*. New York, 1960.

Autograph of the 95th Psalm. Property of the International Felix
Mendelssohn Society.

to himself, without providing them with the kind of work and scope of activity which alone makes the appointment worthwhile. As he put it, neither he nor anyone else knows what he is really supposed to be doing in Berlin, since nothing has been said about the establishment of a conservatoire and since it is impossible for him to get anything whatsoever moving of its own accord. It is all fine words, he says, and in reality nothing is happening, nothing at all. . . .[7]

Of course Mendelssohn was constantly being asked for memoranda and proposals, all of which vanished into the files. Meanwhile the people of Leipzig were waiting for him. And he was waiting for the King. Things could not go on in this way—and so he called upon Herr von Massow, the King's chamberlain and adjutant, to arrange a farewell audience. The adjutant was terribly upset at the news. His Majesty would be deeply offended, he said; he would address only a few words to the composer and leave the room in a huff.[8] But just the opposite took place.

Frederick William IV, his face slightly swollen (his features had changed markedly of late), looked straight at Mendelssohn and said in a low voice that he appreciated the composer's patience. He was sorry, but with so many factors having to be co-ordinated at the ministry, at the office of the superintendent of the opera, it had not proved possible to proceed any faster with the establishment of the Academy. If Mendelssohn really wanted to leave, he could not hinder him, but (and his voice sounded troubled) his departure would make an irreparable rent in all the royal plans. "Why irreparable?" Mendelssohn asked in surprise. He pointed out that there were so many other good musicians who might fill the post.

"Could we not set up a small capella for you, Herr Doktor, a chorus of thirty singers, say, and a small orchestra of proven musicians, so that you could compose music for this body and conduct it?"

Mendelssohn was stunned. The directorship of the Academy was vanishing, and the idea of a conservatoire was vanishing also. But should he not *after all* . . . ? As he considered he remembered how his mother had taken the news that he would be returning to Leipzig. He had told her of his decision that very afternoon walking in the garden, and Mother Leah, after a long silence, had begun to cry. Fanny had joined them and attempted to comfort mother and brother; the two had wept. . . .[9]

[7] B. Bartels: *Felix Mendelssohn-Bartholdy*. Bremen, 1947.
[8] S. Hensel: *Die Familie Mendelssohn 1729–1847*. Berlin, 1879.
[9] Ibid.

He looked at the King, wondering whether he could trust him this time. "A musician must have an instrument with which to make music", the King said. "I realize that. I will create one for you, rely on me for that. But", he added with a faintly querulous note, "will you also be available for me? I know, I know, you love travelling. You are an eminent guest conductor. People love you in Leipzig, in Düsseldorf, in London. But don't forget that it was due to me that the *Antigone* ..." At this point the King launched into his usual rhetoric. Mendelssohn was in no way obliged to continue living in Berlin, he said. Let him go where he liked, for surely he could compose the things the King would ask of him wherever he was situated. *Oedipus at Colonus*, music for Racine's *Athalie*. And had he never thought of completing his magnificent overture to *A Midsummer Night's Dream* by composing music for the *entire* play?

Mendelssohn's head was reeling. What a variety of plans! In an abashed murmur he asked only that his salary be cut in half—fifteen hundred talers. The King was greatly moved at this request. Von Massow, equally astonished, showed Mendelssohn out. Now there was only the matter of writing a letter confirming all that had been discussed, and of having it out with the young head of the family, Paul, who would certainly not approve of his departure. Then he could take his wife and children back to Leipzig at once.

It is never given to us to know the future. Greek tragedy saw this clearly. How would Sophocles have depicted them, the two characters, king and composer? The King of Prussia, obeying hidden mechanisms which he could not control, and which in a few years would take full possession of him—the King was destined to become insane and to abdicate the throne in favour of his brother.[10] And the composer, Mendelssohn, at the peak of his energies, burning with a fever to work, would be felled by his own drive and vigour in another five years.

[10] C. Ledoux: *Les Rois insanes*. Paris, 1899.

BACK TO SHAKESPEARE!

"It was as though they had been waiting for me!" Felix Mendelssohn later told his English friend Lumley. "I came to a rehearsal at the Gewandhaus. The winds had pursed their lips, the strings raised their bows and my friend David the baton. When he saw me, he lowered it, picked up his violin, and stepped into the first row of the strings. . . ."[1]

It was magical, the sense they gave him of having only been waiting for him to return. And magical, too, the way he instantly plunged back into all the work awaiting him in Leipzig. He had so many persons to be grateful to—but above all his friend Ferdinand David, that eminent violinist. As early as 1835 he had promised David a violin concerto. Now, out of gratitude, he took up the task at once. The Violin Concerto in E minor (opus 64), completed on 16th September 1844 and given its first performance on 13th March 1845, by David, proved to be one of his principal works.[2]

The great composers had long known that it was possible to sing *jubilantly* in the minor. But the principle was most gloriously embodied in that passionate Allegro with which the Mendelssohn concerto begins:

After the theme has been sung to an end, the solo violin drops to low G: an organ-point lasting eight measures, before the woodwinds initiate the second theme:

[1] B. Lumley: *Reminiscences.* London, 1864.
[2] J. Eckardt: *Ferdinand David und die Familie Mendelssohn-Bartholdy.* Leipzig, 1888.

After the development comes a cadenza—something quite unheard-of previously, for the cadenza is ordinarily reserved for the close of a movement. But here it no sooner fades away than the first theme returns, and the concerto makes a fresh beginning. The joyous flutes, oboes and violins, interwoven with arpeggios of the solo violin, mount to a climax of rejoicing. Then follows the dreamy Andante. It is in three-part song form, in C major, and is perhaps a bit too long. But the third movement makes up for this. Although it is distinctly couched in sonata form, this finale, an E major vivace, hurls itself toward the end with tremendous strength. "You see", Schumann said to David, who was also a composer, "now you have played the concerto that you always wanted to write."

Innumerable violinists have played it since David—Joseph Joachim, Mendelssohn's own pupil, probably most frequently of all.[3] We still recall what that incomparable violinist said at a party given at his seventy-fifth birthday in 1906: "The Germans have four violin concertos. The greatest, the one that makes fewest concessions, is Beethoven's. The one by Brahms comes close to Beethoven's in its seriousness. Max Bruch wrote the richest

[3] A. Moser: *Joseph Joachim*. Berlin, 1908–10.

and most enchanting of the four. But the dearest of them all, the heart's jewel, is Mendelssohn's."

What about Berlin, meanwhile? Long before the first notes of the violin concerto reached that city, the King and his court were asking themselves what they had been about. How could they ever have let Felix Mendelssohn leave? Before long—in fact, on 4th December 1842—the King sent an official missive from Berlin appointing him Generalmusik-direktor. Mendelssohn was not hungry for titles. But if he were to hold his own alongside Meyerbeer in Berlin, he had to be given an imposing rank. Why had no one seen that before? Everything else he had desired was now granted, and a letter from Herr von Massow requested him to come to Berlin for two days on 17th December, in order to ratify all points of the agreement. He came earlier, to bury his mother. Leah's bitter tears at their parting may have sprung from the fear that she would never see her Felix again.

But now Berlin had become a city of mourning to Mendelssohn. And so he hurried back to Leipzig, seeking to lose his sorrow in his work. He kept his word to the King of Prussia, writing music for Racine's *Athalie* and the *Oedipus*. But he could no longer achieve the uniqueness of the *Antigone*. These compositions were duty-tasks; he had promised the King he would attend to them promptly. The King's requests from Berlin grew increasingly strange. Would he not like to undertake a musical setting of the *Eumenides* of Aeschylus? The choruses of a trilogy! Mendelssohn refused, of course. As he diplomatically explained it, he did not feel "equal to the sublimity of the subject".[4]

But he did take up once more the idea of music for *A Midsummer Night's Dream*, and here the miracle happened. Now older and more experienced he understood better the world of the fairies which can torment and bewitch lovers; the comic world of the rude mechanicals and the chivalrous world of Duke Theseus of Athens.[5]

The première in the New Palace in Potsdam surpassed all expectations. After the overture, the orchestra fell silent. Then, in the second act, the flutes began the Scherzo:

[4] S. Hensel: *Die Familie Mendelssohn 1729–1847*. Berlin, 1879.
[5] H. E. Jacob: "Die Dreiwelt in Shakespeares Sommernachtstraum." *Blätter des Deutschen Theaters*. Berlin, 1912.

Woods, night and a dream! Then the entr'acte with horn and bassoon, clarinets, oboe and flute at the end imitating the famous bumbling gait of the artisan-fools. Then the Nocturne, with the superb, slumbrous horn:

The Wedding March begins with an ordinary trumpet fanfare. But almost immediately an alien tonal world enfolds the procession.

The audience at the première rose to their feet and did not sit down again. It was as though they were the wedding guests invited by the Duke of Athens in person. But the climax of it all was the Bergomask Dance that brought the festivities to a triumphant close. The ass brayed again, and it ended on as mysterious a note as it had begun, with those four chords of seventeen years ago. . . .

"What a pity that Mother did not live to hear it. I kept thinking that all the time!" Fanny Hensel wrote to Rebecca Dirichlet, who was staying with her husband in Rome.[6] And she added: "Isn't it still another remarkable piece of good fortune on the part of this remarkable man that the youthful work which first established his reputation is now being

[6] S. Hensel: op. cit.

glorified anew, and in this new form will certainly make its way throughout Germany?" Everyone rejoiced: the Leipzig visitors; the musicians of
the Gewandhaus and the municipal authorities who had come to witness
their director's triumph; the Berliners who arrived in Potsdam by train;
and the Potsdamers, who a few days later rode to Berlin to see and hear
the same work in the Hoftheater. The applause simply would not stop.
Only one person was strangely out of humour. That was the composer.
He was annoyed that Tieck, instead of adhering to the time-tested division established by August Wilhelm Schlegel, had divided the play into
three acts in order not to interrupt the night in the forest, and this without
consulting the composer. The result was that the entr'acte music now
had to be played with the curtain up. He was also angry because the
costumes had been changed to seventeenth-century Spanish baroque—on
the grounds that Shakespeare's Theseus and his courtiers had not been
really Greeks. Even when Wagner, who was in Berlin for the production
of *The Flying Dutchman*, came up to offer his congratulations, Mendelssohn scarcely even murmured his thanks. Instead he asked rather abruptly
whether Wagner did not think that the Berlin comedian Gern, who
played Bottom, was not doing the part too broadly.[7]

Max Reinhardt had the same fears when he produced *A Midsummer
Night's Dream* with Mendelssohn's music sixty years later. He gave more
than one thousand performances in thirteen different versions, between
1904 and 1934, in German, Italian and English, in theatres, parks and
open-air arenas. The lovers laughed and wept, the rude mechanicals
shambled. Shakespeare's words became Mendelssohn's songs. Under how
many skies the words and music sounded: on Bavarian meadows, in
Klessheim Palace; in the Boboli Gardens of Florence, and in Oxford and
other English universities. And long after Mendelssohn and Reinhardt
had been expelled from Germany the play was produced, finally, in the
Hollywood Bowl. And when the glittering wedding procession walked
with stately tread to the music of Mendelssohn, with the mountains of
Southern California as a backdrop, a hundred thousand spectators burst
into applause....[8]

Frederick William IV, the King of Prussia, could not foresee such
triumphs. Nevertheless he promptly commissioned Mendelssohn to do
Shakespeare's *Tempest*.

[7] S. Hensel: op. cit.
[8] H. Herald: *Max Reinhardt, Bildnis eines Theatermannes.* Hamburg,
1953.

MELUSINA

We might assume on the strength of this, that Mendelssohn went ahead with music for *The Tempest*—certainly Lumley published an elaborate account in *The Times* of January 1847 which seemed to indicate that the work was practically finished. In reality Felix Mendelssohn never wrote a note for *The Tempest*.[1]

As a matter of fact, in 1847, the year of his death, he was completely taken up with fairy-tales. Grillparzer, who himself loved fairy-tales, once described the feeling they evoked: "A sense of the wonderful combined with *not wondering at wonders*—being at home in the world of wonders."[2] That had also been Mendelssohn's experience when at the age of twenty-five he had used an opera libretto of Grillparzer's for his early tone-poem, *Das Märchen von der schönen Melusine*.

It was the story of the beautiful woman who is under a spell and must become a nixie every seventh day. She has made her husband swear that he will not attempt to discover the reason for her disappearance on this seventh day. Under the proddings of his kinsfolk, the knight breaks his vow, whereupon his wife must take leave of husband and children and live forever as a water-nymph.

Schumann once remarked that Mendelssohn's admirers could be divided into Midsummer Night's Dreamers, Fingallers and Melusinans. He said he almost counted himself among the third group.[3] And Schumann's biographer Walter Dahms made this astounding comment on Mendelssohn's *Melusina*: "There has hardly been a more touching, more German work written in the realm of music."[4] But however this may be, the dreamy tranquillity, the passionless, contemplative, but also sorrowful quality of this work was never surpassed by either of the two friends. The tone-poem has three protagonists: water, Melusina with her human love, and the chivalrous husband. The interplay of these three scarcely has its match in music. There is the billowing figure at the beginning:

[1] *The Times*. London, January 1847.
[2] F. Grillparzer: *Sämtliche Werke*. Stuttgart, 1872.
[3] R. Schumann: *Gesammelte Schriften über Musik und Musiker*. Leipzig, 1891.
[4] W. Dahms: *Mendelssohn*. Berlin, no date.

and the other plaintive water-figure with its tiny intervals (how different water can be at different times!)

and then the most beautiful motif of the tone-poem, which shows that Melusina is truly a loving human woman:

Like Schumann, Mendelssohn spent a good part of his time in the nursery, telling his children stories. Sometimes the stories were based on solid fact. Thus, one winter in Zürich he had seen a hobbyhorse forgotten in a garden and half-covered with snow. To his regret he could not rescue it because it stood behind a fence.[5] He thereupon decided to write a "Requiem for a Hobbyhorse", together with Ferdinand Hiller, who was as fond of children as he was. Nothing came of the plan—but it is an indication of how readily he fell into the fairy-tale vein. The year of his death he conceived of an opera based on Geibel's *Loreley*.[6] Actually he composed the finale of one act, a vintners' chorus and an Ave Maria, which were published posthumously as opus 97. Before he came across Geibel's work, he had again been corresponding with Devrient on the subject for an opera. He insisted that it would have to be something "very German". "And likewise very noble and gay. It must *not* be Michael Kohlhaas and *not* Bluebeard or Andreas Hofer or the Loreley—but it might contain elements of all these!" Devrient thereupon proposed a subject from the Peasant Wars, to be called "Knight and Peasant". Mendelssohn was horrified. He was disturbed by the "intrusion of the themes of liberty, serfdom and social reform". Such elements could be used for

[5] Communication from Frank C. Slatter. New York, 1950.
[6] *Emanuel Geibels Gesammelte Werke.* Hamburg, 1861–69.

colouring he supposed, where necessary. "But where they are not necessary, then for God's sake let us not have them, for then it becomes the
worst sort of striving for effect, playing up to the masses."[7]

His words show that, unlike Wagner or Devrient, Mendelssohn would
have little sympathy for the revolutionaries.

THE CONDUCTOR AND THE TIMES

The forties were an unhappy decade. As early as 1839 there had been
riots and sabotage on the part of the workmen of Birmingham.[1] A few
years later the linen weavers in Prussian Silesia decided that they were not
going to continue weaving for their employer, Herr Zwanziger. The
factory-owner called on the military for help. At first the soldiers fired
over the heads of the workmen. But when the weavers advanced on them
with sticks and stones, they aimed lower. There were many dead, and
Heinrich Heine wrote:

> Germany!
> We weavers are weaving your winding sheet,
> With a triple curse woven in every pleat.
> We are weaving, weaving.
> We are weaving a curse for the rich man's king
> Who bears not and cares not for poverty's sting.
> We are weaving, weaving![2]

Everywhere in Europe people were talking about a social revolution. As
the prophets said, the coming revolution would be another thing altogether from the revolution of 1830—that change of regimes in France, a
carnival-like escapade of students, artists and bourgeois who were sick
and tired of the Bourbons.[3] Music was becoming increasingly popular.
Perhaps people went to concerts to forget the threat that hovered over
their heads. At any rate they listened to Mendelssohn's concerts with
enthusiasm. He conducted with vigour, but also with elegance—and the
musicians, to use Liszt's phrase, were not at all his "galley slaves". In

[7] E. Devrient: *Meine Erinnerungen an Felix Mendelssohn-Bartholdy.*
Leipzig, 1872.
[1] E. Friedell: *Kulturgeschichte der Neuzeit,* vol. III. Munich, 1931.
[2] H. Heine: *Gesammelte Werke.* Hamburg, 1861–69.
[3] M. Petit: *Histoire de la Révolution de 1830.* Paris, 1831.

those days it was by no means a matter of course that a conductor should be cultivated and sociable, a man of the world. Wagner, in his essay on conducting published in 1869, poked great fun at certain boors among orchestral conductors. Master Mendelssohn had, he was forced to admit, put an end to such loutishness. No doubt about it, the new type of conductor was an aristocrat who knew how to express himself and how to practise reticence. His conducting resembled in some ways the "art of conversation."[4]

But why, Wagner asked himself, did "Mendelssohn often conduct so fast, where speed was not at all in order." And he found a rather unpleasant answer to this rhetorical question. Mendelssohn had often talked candidly with Wagner. They sometimes attended rehearsals together and exchanged opinions. "Mendelssohn personally told me, as regards conducting, and he expressed this view several times, that a too slow tempo was more harmful than anything else, and that he would rather recommend taking a piece somewhat too fast; that a really good performance was a rarity at any time, but that it was possible to delude the audience so that a bad one would not be too much noticed, and that this was best done by not lingering too long on the piece, but passing rapidly over it."

Delude? The word was not chosen at random. Wagner was well aware of its implications, for he went on to say that he had never been able to teach "Mendelssohn who was always too fast" any feeling for Beethoven's Eighth, that Mendelssohn always botched the third movement of that symphony by neglecting to play it in the proper tempo.[5]

As it happens, it is possible to have widely divergent opinions about the eighty-one measures of that third movement. It is hardly a true minuet. Its rococo gracefulness is rather ironic. Moreover, the following Allegro vivace of the Finale, with its five hundred and two measures, is filled with such wild high spirits that we can very well understand how a modern conductor might also not take the previous movement altogether seriously, and might play the minuet as if it were an introduction to the Allegro vivace.[6] And everyone knows that "lingering too long" on an introduction is inartistic.

But Wagner's conclusions were devastating. Wagner found Mendelssohn's cardinal sin still cultivated in London after the conductor's death: "It flowed like water from a public fountain; any slowing down was unthinkable, and every Allegro inevitably ended as a Presto. . . ." Naturally

[4] R. Wagner: *Gesammelte Schriften und Dichtungen.* Leipzig, 1907.
[5] Ibid.
[6] K. Nef: *Die neun Sinfonien Beethovens.* Leipzig, 1928.

this procedure also ruined the dynamics: "The orchestra never played anything but mezzoforte; it no longer could play any real forte, as it never achieved any real piano...." the breed of "elegant composers" raised by Mendelssohn, Wagner snarled, lacked "faith in, hope for and love of a genuine Adagio", could not attain the "depth and length of a fermata" as Beethoven had composed it. They no longer trusted the redeeming force of their own music; they were always afraid of being *boring*.[7]

Why had Wagner written all this? Hatred as well as love can penetrate disguises. The brother to whom we have shown our most secret soul is more dangerous than any enemy. A speech teacher, whose name we do not know, had taught Felix that in order to overcome his stammer he must take the beginning of a sentence rapidly. On the other hand, he must moderate his pace at the climax of the sentence, lest he "sputter". Wagner, who could always scent out the secrets of his fellow-men, and who ruthlessly exploited his insights, knew about this speech impediment, and insinuated that it carried over into Mendelssohn's art, into his composing and his conducting. "The person afflicted with the natural defect of stammering or lisping will avoid all passion in utterance, in order not to fall into embarrassing stammering or sputtering. He must always be careful...." That, according to Wagner, was the reason for Mendelssohn's tranquillity and his avoidance of strong accents. That was the reason for his "mediocre dignity" in tempos and dynamics! But had Wagner no ears? When and where had Mendelssohn ever imposed his own style upon the works of other composers? When and where had he been careful in order to spare himself?[8]

Art was more important to him than life. What Wagner failed to see, or did not wish to see, was that Mendelssohn expended himself utterly, and that as conductor, educator and administrator he had long been living beyond his physical means. His sense of what music asked of him was too strong for him to trim his work to his own physical limitations.

[7] Wagner: op. cit.
[8] W. A. Lampadius: *Felix Mendelssohn*. Berlin, 1872.

THERE IS A REAPER, DEATH HIS NAME

On 13th April 1847 Mendelssohn suffered an attack of giddiness while standing on a bridge of the Thames looking across at Cecil's Tavern where he had dined with Charles Dickens five years before.[1] Suddenly he could no longer bear the mist rising from the river, and had to cling to the railing of the bridge. But he quickly recovered and went to Klingemann's house, where he was staying and where he had just left the sixteen-year-old violin prodigy, Joseph Joachim.[2]

Mendelssohn might well feel a little giddy. His programme was fantastically crowded. Concerts in London, Manchester, Birmingham, and London again. But above all he had been invited to call once more on the Queen and Prince Consort. He had to thank the Queen for accepting the "Scottish" Symphony, which he had dedicated to her, and to explain to Albert why he had once more revised (eternally unsatisfied with his work) the *Elijah*, which he had performed in England the year before.

At tea with the Royal couple, these and a hundred other matters were discussed. He was asked what had impressed him most on his first visit to England, at the age of twenty. That question was not hard for him to answer. He had been overwhelmed, he said, at having been commissioned to write a song for a festival that was to take place in Ceylon. *Ceylon*, of all places! The natives had won a measure of freedom there, and on the anniversary of this notable event Sir Alexander Johnston had asked him to set a poem to music. An extraordinary commission. For three days, he said, he had laughed over the incongruities involved—over the vastness of the globe, the greatness of England![3]

Then had come the last rehearsals of *Elijah*. There were four performances—the Queen and Prince Albert were present at the second. Albert was very moved. He wrote into his libretto a tribute such as few sovereigns had given to any composer:

> To the Noble Artist, who surrounded by the Baal-worship of
> debased art, has been able, by his genius and science, like another
> Elijah, faithfully to preserve the worship of true art, and once

[1] *The Times*. London, March 1861.
[2] A. Moser: *Joseph Joachim*. Berlin, 1908–10.
[3] S. Hensel: *Die Familie Mendelssohn 1729–1847*. Berlin, 1879.

more to accustom our ear, amid the whirl of empty frivolous sounds, to the pure tones of sympathetic feeling and legitimate harmony; to the Great Master who brings home to us the unity of his conception through the whole maze of his creation from the soft whispering to the mighty raging of the elements: Inscribed in grateful remembrance by

Albert[4]

Buckingham Palace
24 April 1847.

In the meantime Felix had also conducted the music for *A Midsummer Night's Dream*, the "Scottish" Symphony, and had appeared as soloist in Beethoven's G major Concerto at the Philharmonic concert. The conductor, Costa, thinking the long cadenza was at last over, raised his baton so that the orchestra could once again launch into the notes Beethoven had written.[5] But Mendelssohn put out his hand: "Not yet! Not yet!" And after the performance he confessed to William Bartholomew that he had been unable to stop because two such great women were in the audience: Queen Victoria and Jenny Lind. . . . Jenny Lind, the Swedish nightingale, for whom he had written the *Loreley*. He had already discussed the whole thing with the great lyric-dramatic singer, and played out for her some of her principal arias, which were already written.[6]

On the 1st May he lunched with the Bunsens at the Prussian Embassy. That afternoon he had another two hours of piano-playing with Victoria and Albert. On 4th and 5th May more concerts: Beethoven, and Bach fugues. On 6th May visits to picture galleries, and in the afternoon back at the Prussian Embassy once again for a concert in honour of Gladstone —then out of office—and Mrs. Gladstone. Suddenly Felix left the room; he did not even have the strength to bid the company good-bye.[7] Alarmed, Klingemann noticed that his friend's hair had become grey and that his face looked utterly worn as soon as he was no longer sustained by music and congenial banter. On 8th May he paid a farewell call on the Royal couple at Buckingham Palace, and boarded a train for Dover. Across the Channel to Ostend, and then straight on by rail again. At Herbesthal, on the Prussian border, he was suddenly stopped. An official asked him whether he was Dr. Mendelssohn, and when he assented, asked him to step out of the train. Yes, yes, his name was Mendelssohn, and he had

---

[4] Sir T. Martin: *Life of the Prince Consort*. London, 1920.
[5] E. Kuhe: *My Musical Recollections*. London, 1896.
[6] Holland and Rockstro: *Jenny Lind, the Artist*. London, 1891.
[7] A. J. C. Hare: *Freifrau von Bunsen, ein Lebensbild*. Gotha, 1881–83.

proper identification papers with him. What was his occupation? Composer. The officials shook their heads. He was led into a kind of guardroom. Was he not the Mendelssohn who was involved in the Hatzfeldt case?* That Dr. Mendelssohn, in whom the police were interested, was a friend of the politically notorious Ferdinand Lassalle. But who was Lassalle? Felix wanted to know. Varnhagen and Alexander von Humboldt might have told him that, among other things, Ferdinand Lassalle was writing a book on Heraclitus, the Greek philosopher, and that just by the by he was bringing a trial for high treason down upon his head. . . .[8]

The outraged Felix had to spend the whole morning and afternoon writing explanations of which Mendelssohn he himself was (it cost him as much time as it would have taken "to sketch out an overture").[9] Finally the officials released him, and he was allowed to travel on to Cologne and thence to Frankfurt, where he arrived half-dead from fatigue.

There he was, home at last, with Cécile and the children, when a message arrived from Berlin. He opened it and, with a cry, collapsed unconscious.

His beloved sister Fanny, his musical conscience, to whom he always submitted whatever he had written, Fanny was dead. She had been very busy. What a social whirl she had been in, especially since the death of her mother, who had always managed the household in her own magnificent fashion! Fanny Hensel did not have her mother's talent for this. She was a musician, nothing else. The grand concerts at the Mendelssohn mansion —which had become a Berlin institution—and the special concerts given in honour of Felix on his visits home—for he came every few months to conduct the cathedral choir—these concerts were exhausting affairs for Fanny. She had to receive in grand style. "When I tell you", she wrote to her sister Rebecca Dirichlet, "that twenty-two equipages waited in the court and that Liszt and eight princesses attended our Sunday musicale in the salon, you will forgive me if I do not describe in greater detail the magnificence of my hut. . . ."[10]

---

* Countess Sophie von Hatzfeldt, a friend of Ferdinand Lassalle, was involved in a sensational divorce case. During the trial a strong-box containing documents important to the countess's defence was stolen by a Dr. Mendelssohn, at Lassalle's instigation, so it was said. Lassalle later successfully defended himself against the charge of complicity in the theft. —*Translators' note.*

[8] G. Brandes: *Ferdinand Lassalle*. Berlin, 1900.
[9] Sir G. Grove: *Dictionary of Music and Musicians*. London, no date.
[10] S. Hensel: op. cit.

On Friday, 14th May 1847, she presided over another rehearsal of Felix's *Walpurgis Night*, which the chorus was to perform at the Mendelssohn house that Sunday afternoon. As she sat at the piano, her hands slackened, she could not speak, then she lost consciousness. Her sixteen-year-old son Sebastian was called from his drawing lesson, told that his mother had suddenly been taken ill and that he must run for the doctor. "I ran with all my might, and know that I kept saying to myself the whole while: 'It can't be anything serious, nothing bad can happen to us....' "[11] But the doctor diagnosed a cerebral haemorrhage, and by eleven o'clock at night all was over. Fanny had died as had her father, her mother, all the Mendelssohns....

Wilhelm Hensel nearly went out of his mind.

Felix was unable to come from Frankfurt; he was too ill. Instead, he wrote to Wilhelm:

> If my handwriting interferes with your weeping, put the letter aside, for there is probably nothing better we can do now than to weep until our eyes are dry. We were happy together; now life will be a grave, mournful affair. You made my sister very happy all through her life, as she deserved to be. I thank you for that today, and will as long as I breathe, and probably longer— not with mere words, but with bitter repentance that I did not do more for her happiness, that I did not see her more, was not with her more....[12]

In this crisis Cécile proved her worth as never before. She conspired with her brother-in-law, Paul, to arrange a visit to Switzerland, the land of glacial waters and glorious mountains, which had often been Felix's best physician in the past. Perhaps it would restore his health this time also.

A preliminary cure in Baden-Baden did him no good. He suffered acutely from insomnia. And so they travelled on. The only activity that would calm his mind was painting. From Schaffhausen he went to Neuhausen, and lived in a hotel above the Rhine Falls. There he painted the plunging waters with feelings such as Mörike has described:

> Restlessly thundering masses tossed upon thundering masses,
> Whither can ear and eye flee from such turbulence?

[11] P. Hensel: *Sebastian Hensel, ein Lebensbild aus Deutschlands Lehrjahren*. Berlin, 1904.
[12] S. Hensel: op. cit.

Soon they moved on to Lucerne, where Mendelssohn did more water-colours. Then they stayed in Thun for a while, and then in Interlaken, where the chestnut trees reminded him of Fanny.... He had been here with her as a child. It was hopeless. He could not go on with the painting. But he could compose again: the sorrowful F minor String Quartet (opus 80). It is a work of wild anguish. Now and then there comes a brief ray of light, like the A flat major theme in the first movement. The second movement goes into hammering syncopations until, in an anticipation of Brahms, the violins take up their lament above the basso ostinato. The Adagio in two-four time has the characteristic Mendelssohnian melan-choly. But then comes the harshly pounding Finale, which seems to declare with certainty: there is no comfort.

Perhaps painting might have distracted him. But he could no longer even try. He hastened toward the passes, toward the highest land, as though he could no longer breathe in the valley. Once on the heights, he strode ahead so fiercely that his wife and children could not keep up with him. Perhaps life in Leipzig would heal him—his work, the Conserva-toire. But he decided to go first to Berlin.[13]

He wandered through the garden of Fanny's house. Through her room, where everything remained untouched, just as she had left it. The Afghan on the sofa, the open piano.... He embraced Wilhelm, asked him about his work, and realized that with the loss of Fanny, Wilhelm Hensel had lost all will to work. Wilhelm talked wildly: perhaps the two of them should go off together, travel to the Orient, to Jerusalem, and try to fathom the mystery of ancient Christian art? He was collecting books and making notes on the Near East. Felix saw no sense in such projects. He pushed on to Leipzig. Somewhere, in the course of that summer, he had come across the deeply moving poem *Comitatus*, by Hoffmann von Fallersleben:

> Now at the end of day
> Since you must be on your way
> We will bear you company a while.[14]

Now he composed the music. For himself? For Fanny? His tears smeared the letters as he wrote: "Now in cloud, now in sun, our life's course is run," and the gentle ending: "Such is our lot upon this earth."

Back in Leipzig he found that he could no longer conduct. Gade

---

[13] P. Sutermeister: *Felix Mendelssohn-Bartholdy, Briefe einer Reise und Lebensbild*. Zürich, 1958.

[14] A. H. Hoffmann von Fallersleben: *Mein Leben. Aufzeichnungen und Erinnerungen*. Hanover, 1868.

directed the Gewandhaus concerts. Ignaz Moscheles headed the Conservatoire as his deputy. All he was now able to do was to compose. And so he
wrote his swan song, for his friend Konrad Schleinitz. Or rather, for all
his friends: the affecting and melancholy *Nachtlied*:[15]

> To mark the passing of the day,
> The church bells ring from far away.
>> Time forges on all through the night
>> And many, unwarned, will not see the light.

When all is said and done, how lonely is man:

> Where are they now, where pleasure's art,
> A friend's good cheer and faithful heart,
>> The sweetness in a woman's smile?
>> Will none be glad with me a while?

The poem is by Eichendorff—could have been written by no one else. It
is a poem that does not attempt to "persuade", to overwhelm by the
power of words. It does not attempt those verbal acrobatics that sometimes
leap so high that it takes a kind of diplomacy to fetch them back. In
short, it does without imagery. It is altogether plain, altogether unassuming. And was meant to be so, for Eichendorff practised a kind of voluntary
poverty in poetry.[16]

This "Franciscan poverty of words" was Eichendorff's secret. Schubert
had not known Eichendorff—but the composers to whom his poetry was
available, beginning with Mendelssohn and Schumann and continuing
but not ceasing with Brahms, Hugo Wolf, Pfitzner and Strauss, turned
back to him again and again. It would seem that the more plain and
sincere the flow of verse, the more profoundly it stirs the sources of
music. Fanny had drawn her last musical inspiration from Eichendorff's
"Wanderlied":

> Vom Berge Vöglein fliegen
>> und Wolken so geschwind,
> Gedanken überfliegen
>> die Vöglein und den Wind.

These words are just as "impoverished" as a Japanese woodcut. Always
the same Fujiyama—but when we look closer we observe the delicate

[15] M. F. Schneider und W. Reich: *Felix Mendelssohn-Bartholdy*. Basel,
1947.
[16] J. v. Eichendorff: *Gesammelte Werke*. Berlin, 1924.

variations of air and weather that the lines depict. Heard so often and forming the stock elements of poetry, Eichendorff's words are always entering into new combinations:

> Die Wolken ziehn hernieder
> Das Vöglein senkt sich gleich,
> Gedanken gehn und Lieder
> Fort bis ins Himmelreich.

And these last words were the ones destined to be inscribed on Fanny's gravestone: Thoughts and songs go on into the Kingdom of Heaven.

On 9th October Felix Mendelssohn sat with his friend Livia Gerhardt-Frege. Again and again he had her sing for him his last Eichendorff song: "Vergangen ist der lichte Tag". Ah yes, the day was truly passing. At twilight, Livia went to fetch a lamp for the room. She returned to find Felix collapsed on the sofa, shivering with violent chills, his hands cold, almost incapable of speech. There were terrible pains in his head. He was taken home in a carriage.[17]

On 28th October he ventured to take a walk with Cécile. He had to shuffle. They turned back. As they entered the house, he collapsed with a stroke. On 3rd November came another stroke. On 4th November 1847 the doctors declared that it was impossible to save him. His family and friends stood around his bed. He was unconscious but—as the dying Mozart had once done!—he pursed his lips and with wheezing breath began attempts at orchestra sounds....[18] Paul, summoned from Berlin, stood with hands clasped behind his back, motionless as a statue. Beside him was Cécile. She bent over her husband. At nine o'clock in the evening it was all over.

"People whispered in the streets as though a member of the royal house had died," an English student wrote home. Bulletins were posted on the street corners, and crowds stood silently around them. Demonstrations of mourning in Dresden. Mourning in Munich, too, where Ludwig I had always hoped to make Mendelssohn the court composer of Bavaria.

He was mourned in London, Milan and Vienna. In Leipzig thousands filed past the open coffin with bared heads. Then the coffin was closed, and a special train carried the mourners to Berlin. At night the train suddenly stopped in Dessau: Friedrich Schneider stood on the station platform leading a great chorus to pay homage to the dead composer.

---

[17] B. Bartels: *Felix Mendelssohn-Bartholdy*. Bremen, 1947.
[18] J. Eckardt: *Ferdinand David und die Familie Mendelssohn-Bartholdy*. Leipzig, 1888.

From that same city of Dessau his grandfather had set out, ragged and barefoot, to become a great man in Berlin. And now the grandson of the "son of Mendel of Dessau", covered with fame and honours, travelled the same way on a November night in 1847. At the Anhalter railroad station his coffin was received like that of a sovereign. Great crowds were there, and in the morning mist voices were singing: "Es ist bestimmt in Gottes Rat. . . ."[19]

A week after Mendelssohn's death Ferdinand Hiller came to Leipzig. "In the evening there was a concert in the Gewandhaus in memory of Felix. The saddest of all things, George Sand says somewhere, is the table-cloth that is laid on the table at the proper meal-time after the passing of a beloved person. . . . There stood the orchestra, there stood the chorus, there the audience who for years had been coming with such enthusiasm. They made music, they played and sang, and a few days before they had accompanied his body to the church. . . . Should it not have been utterly impossible to make music in the Gewandhaus now? But the tablecloth was laid again—and the orphaned family met once again for their accustomed musical meal. . . .

"And then again, a few years later, I came to my native city of Frankfurt am Main. Friends had told me the saddest news about the health of Felix Mendelssohn's widow; they feared the worst, they said. On 25th September 1853 I went to the home of Cécile's family and rang the familiar bell that I had rung so often in the past when I was looking forward to pleasant hours. After a few moments Mendelssohn's mother-in-law, Madame Jeanrenaud, came rushing to the door and flung it open. She had been expecting the arrival of Cécile's brother-in-law, Paul Mendelssohn. 'Oh, it is you, dear Herr Hiller,' she said without inflection, with that uncanny calmness that is so often the product of despair: '*I have just lost my daughter!*' "[20]

THE DARK GREEN TUNE

The untimely death of the composer was perhaps most strongly felt by the multitudinous members of the numerous glee clubs whose staple fare was songs of Mendelssohn's. In 1840, at the Lower Rhine Music Festival,

---

[19] E. Wolff: *Felix Mendelssohn*. Berlin, 1909.
[20] F. Hiller: *Felix Mendelssohn-Bartholdy*. Cologne, 1874.

a chorus of more than a thousand voices had sung his "Wer hat dich, du schöner Wald" for the first time.[1]

Felix Mendelssohn was well aware of the pleasure of choral singing, and provided for it with his *Lieder im Freien zu singen* (Songs to be sung out-of-doors), his male and mixed choruses, opus 50 and opus 59. "After all", he wrote to Klingemann in explanation of these songs, "the most natural music is produced when four people go walking together in the woods or sailing a boat, carrying music with themselves and in themselves. . . ."[2]

Scarcely any of the great German masters of the *lied* had concurred or were to concur with this opinion. Neither Schubert nor Schumann, neither Brahms nor Wolf. These other composers felt song as the expression of a powerful ego not at all disposed to merge into a collectivity. The songs of Wolf, Brahms, Schumann, Schubert are *vocal concertos*—that is the name for them. A dominant human voice holds its own against the instrumental storm, the onslaught of non-human voices. Franz Schubert, true, wrote male choruses—there is, for example, his magnificent setting of Goethe's "Gesang der Geister über den Wassern". But the sociability of the chorus was not really to his taste. Sometimes he paid choral tribute to Salieri, his teacher, sometimes to other friends; or he would write in homage to a deceased master like hard-drinking Michael Haydn, the composer of so many Salzburg rounds. But the more than six hundred *lieder* written by the *real* Schubert were unthinkable apart from the piano. The piano was the partner and antagonist in Schubert's songs.[3]

Why should glee clubs be taken to task for not singing Schubert? How could the German people have known Schubert before such great masters of the art of song as Julius Stockhausen, Johannes Messchaert and Lilli Lehmann performed him in the concert halls?[4] Could Müller's sad little love story in songs be translated into choral terms? "Ich hört ein Bächlein rauschen" is a lyric-dramatic solo in which (as in all the Müller songs) two extra-human voices mingle with the human voice, singing, growling, cajoling and laughing: the silvery brook and the old dark mill wheel. These entities are at odds with one another: the voice of the brook is different from that of the mill wheel, and they quarrel with one another in almost every song. And the man who sings listens to their dispute.

[1] W. Hauchecorne: *Blätter der Erinnerung an die Niederrheinischen Musikfeste*. Düsseldorf, 1868.

[2] *F. Mendelssohn-Bartholdys Briefwechsel mit Legationsrat Karl Klingemann*. Essen, 1909.

[3] F. Günther: *Schuberts Lied*. Stuttgart, 1928.

[4] J. Wirth-Stockhausen: *Julius Stockhausen, der Sänger des deutschen Liedes*. Frankfurt, 1927.

Either he hears the sorrow of his love in the sullen grinding of the mill, or sees his jealousy in the green colour of the water ("Was sucht denn der Jäger am Mühlbach hier? Bleib, trotziger Jäger, in deinem Revier!")—or, in the last song of the cycle, the mill wheel suddenly stands still, and out of the brook—which suddenly subdues its semiquavers to mournful quavers—rise the wish for death and the certainty of death. . . .[5]

Schubert had a "genius for solitude"; in almost all his songs—but especially in the *Winterreise* cycle—he wrung the utmost from the potentialities of suffering. Mendelssohn's talent was by no means so introspective. His wonderful choral songs were, curiously enough, offshoots of the Berlin style.[6] They sprang out of the works of Reichardt and J. A. P. Schulz.[7] Perhaps they would not have been possible but for Zelter's *Singakademie* and his rigid principles forbidding through-composition and insisting upon the strictly stanzaic song. They differed, however, in being infinitely more profound than the typical Berlin songs for social occasions. For behind such miracles of choral song as "O Täler weit, o Höhen" was not upper-class society, but the common people.

The people loved tartness as well as sweetness. We therefore have no right to criticize Friedrich Silcher (who set Heine's *Loreley*)[8] or Hans Georg Nägeli, the popular Swiss master, for sentimentality. The same criticism was made of Mendelssohn—totally without justice. That a song brings tears to the eyes is no proof of its being bad art. To be so on guard against sentimentality is an error of bogus masculinity or, we might say, a Wagnerian-German error. The people are not ashamed of their feelings, as a poet like Eichendorff well knew.

But whether the mood of his song was exultant or sorrowful, Mendelssohn was apt to cast every song as a chorus. So natural was this to him that he would not notice that the sentiment expressed by the text was a purely private one. His sister Fanny used to laugh heartily—and a good many of their friends joined in the laughter—because Felix Mendelssohn carelessly set the romanza from Eichendorff's *Taugenichts* as a duet:

Wohin ich geh und schaue
in Feld und Wald und Tal,
vom Berg hinab in die Aue:
viel schöne, hohe Fraue,
grüss ich dich tausendmal.

[5] A. Einstein: *Schubert*. Zürich, 1952.
[6] L. Leven: *Mendelssohn als Lyriker*. Krefeld, 1927.
[7] H. J. Moser: *Geschichte der deutschen Musik*, vol. III. Stuttgart–Berlin, 1930.
[8] *Liedersammlung des Schwäbischen Sängerbundes*. 1851–61, n.p.

And people shook their heads when he had Uhland's *Schäfers Sonntagslied*:

> Das ist der Tag des Herrn
> Ich bin allein auf weiter Flur;
> noch eine Morgenglocke nur,
> nun Stille nah und fern

sung by a men's chorus.[9] But there was something deeper involved, something that Fanny and their friends did not see: the immersion of the *I* in the *We*, of the self in the collectivity.

What is a folksong? Scholars have had a great deal to say on that theme; whole libraries have been written on it. Ever since Florentin von Zuccalmaglio published, between 1838 and 1840, his two volumes of *German Folksongs with their Original Melodies*, there had been intense interest in the subject.[10] As a very young man Rochus von Lilienkron went to Master Mendelssohn to ask him what he thought were the reasons why one song became a folksong and not another. What could Mendelssohn have answered? It was not only a question of a perfect accord between words and music. There appeared to be other, mysterious laws governing the process. "The folksong", Lenau once said, "lives like the Emperor Barbarossa in the Kyffhäuser mountain. It does not know that we, outside on the slope, are seeking it and calling it."[11] That was very handsomely put by the man whose *Schilflied* and *Primel* were set by Mendelssohn, but who never had the satisfaction of seeing his poems becoming folksongs.

But Eichendorff's songs did. We can only guess the reason. The genesis of a song such as, "Wer hat dich, du schöner Wald, aufgebaut so hoch da droben?" is really quite incomprehensible. Such miracles certainly cannot be explained in terms of "an intimate bond with landscape". If the definitive song of the German forest were to be written, we would imagine that Gluck should have been the composer to do it. Gluck was the son of a forester. He grew up as a genuine child of nature. It is said that in winter he often walked barefoot over the snow, accompanying his father on his rounds of the Bohemian forest.[12] But strangely enough, not a single tree is so much as mentioned in all of Gluck's operas. If we were

[9] S. Hensel: *Die Familie Mendelssohn 1729–1847*. Berlin, 1879.

[10] H. J. Moser: op. cit.

[11] E. J. Morehouse: *German Weltschmerz and French Romantisme*. New York, 1904.

[12] E. Preussner: *Musikgeschichte des Abendlandes*. Vienna, 1931.

to judge by the "milieu theory"—that rather simple-minded theory con-
cocted by the clever and subtle Hippolyte Taine—Gluck should have been
the right man to express the forest in music. What Taine and his followers
forgot, however, was that every genius has more than his proper share of
pride, of defiance, of the determination to move on beyond what ancestry
and environment have made him. The Spirit which, according to the
Gospel, "blows where it lists" also has a word to say. The German forest
did nothing for Gluck but freeze the urchin's feet. On the other hand
Mendelssohn, the banker's son whose home was not the woods at all,
wrote the most beautiful forest choruses in German music.

Manuscript of Mendelssohn's setting of Eichendorff's *Durch
schwankende Wipfel*. Property of the International Felix Mendelssohn Society.

And in truth, when he set "The Hunters' Parting" or that other
familiar forest song:

O Täler weit, o Höhen, / O schöner grüner Wald,
Du meiner Lust und Wehen / andächtger Aufenthalt!
Da draussen, stets betrogen, / saust die geschäftge Welt,
Schlag noch einmal die Bogen / um mich, du grünes Zelt!

—when he set these songs so that a hundred thousand singers instantly took them to their hearts—how could the milieu theory possibly explain that? The background of those texts was Eichendorff's Upper Silesia[13] where Felix Mendelssohn had never been: a landscape of medium-high mountains, nowhere stony, nowhere barren, where dark-green mixed forests succeed the lush grass of the lower slopes.

The air is heavy with water vapour, making distances deceptive. These are modest mountains scarcely more than hills:

Tief die Welt verworren schallt
oben einsam Rehe grasen,
Und wir ziehen fort und blasen
dass es tausendfach verhallt

Manuscript of Mendelssohn's setting of Eichendorff's *O Täler weit, o Höhen*. Property of the International Felix Mendelssohn Society.

[13] H. Taine: *Philosophie de l'Art*, 2 vols. Paris, 1881.

But where did Mendelssohn choose to set these lines? In Interlaken, Switzerland, where the forests form only a narrow band around the waist of towering naked crags.[14] He sketched out the music in the face of those ice-coated peaks. The Mönch, Jungfrau and Eiger gazed down in the flush of morning upon the man who thought so tenderly of the German forest hundreds of miles away:

> Banner, der so kühle wallt!
> Unter deinen grünen Wogen
> hast du treu uns auferzogen,
> frommer Sagen Aufenthalt!

Regionalism does not enter into the picture. Mendelssohn had never been in Ratibor and in Eichendorff's Lubowitz—but this choral song, with its tricky narrow pass through which the first and second voices must proceed, with the solemn upbeat, the triple upbeat to the fourth, the sixth and the octave—this song was couched in precisely the sort of organlike tone Eichendorff must have had in mind when he beheld the dark-green trunks of the trees as the pillars of a cathedral.

"The dark-green tune of Mendelssohn" was how Stephen Foster's friends referred to Mendelssohn's choral settings of those Eichendorff songs.[15] As early as 1844 there had been efforts to lure the composer to America; but like Johann Strauss the Elder, Felix had declined the invitation to attend a music festival in the New World. America was much too far! His music would have to go in his place.

Soon after Mendelssohn's death his setting of the Eichendorff hunting song, "Durch schwankende Wipfel schiesst goldener Strahl", was sung in Philadelphia and Boston. His music came to be known in many other cities, and by 1871, when Leopold Damrosch founded the New York *Männergesangverein*, Mendelssohn was its spiritual godfather. At any rate, for its first concert, Mendelssohn's great songs were chosen. During the second half of the nineteenth century, musical life in America was largely the affair of its German-speaking element, and was centred in the various glee clubs in New York and throughout the land. Such conductors as Damrosch, Karl Bergmann and Theodor Thomas established the Mendelssohn songs firmly in the repertory.[16] And during the shameful years

[14] A. E. Cherbuliez: *Die Schweiz in der deutschen Musikgeschichte*. Frauenfeld, 1932.

[15] E. F. Morneweck: *Chronicles of Stephen Foster's Family*. Pittsburgh, 1944.

[16] E. T. Rice: "Personal Recollections of Leopold Damrosch". *Musical Quarterly*. New York, July 1942.

of Hitlerism, when the word German carried sinister connotations to Americans, Mendelssohn's choral works were still sung, their dark-green tune a reminder of a better Germany.

Mendelssohn's songs for piano and voice may be questioned or partly forgotten. But his choral songs will never be. The German people took them to their hearts and cherished them when Mendelssohn's name was outlawed in the Fatherland.

THE SNIPER'S BULLET

In 1850 came the shot out of the darkness that struck at Mendelssohn's reputation. A pamphlet was published entitled *Judaism in Music*— slander tricked out with the trappings of psychology and bogus social science, and the more effective because the author was able to hide under the pseudonym of Karl Freigedank. It was many years before his real identity came to light. His thesis was that the penetration of the Jews into German musical life had done immense harm. He did not say how, or why—his statements were as categorical as those of the Nazis would later be. Hitler's henchmen did not have to invent their filthy balderdash about Mendelssohn; they could simply draw on the contents of that 1850 pamphlet.

When Robert Schumann, his strength failing, had to retire from the editorship of his *Neue Zeitschrift für die Musik*, he thought he could find no better person to take his place than his competent and cultivated assistant, Franz Brendel. True, Brendel was an adherent of the New German movement of Wagner and Liszt, but that should not count against him. His Leipzig lectures[1] had made it clear that he respected other schools of criticism and composition. Concerning Mendelssohn he had written that a man need not be a pioneer in order to be a first-rate composer: "Accomplishing the utmost in secular composition, and pre-eminently gifted for that task, a personality preponderantly inclined toward lyricism, he affords us the *edifying spectacle* of the extent to which it is possible for an artist to extend the limits of his own personality and also to fill the vast empty spaces of epic composition with oratorios." And this man, who shortly before had praised Mendelssohn's *Songs without Words* as "masterpieces of miniature art", and the "Hebrides" and

[1] F. Brendel: *Geschichte der Musik in Italien, Deutschland und Frank-reich. Fünfundzwanzig Vorlesungen.* Leipzig, 1852–55.

A Midsummer Night's Dream as "insurpassable", placed his magazine at the disposal of a man who turned out to be a kind of masked assassin, who was to introduce something altogether new into German musical life: *Anti-Semitism*.

Anti-Semitic writings had long existed. The German Enlightenment had laid great stress on equality for the Jews, and Napoleon, Hardenberg and Metternich had made that equality a fact. This was resented by many Germans—precisely because it came from above. The various German governments, moreover, were the sworn enemies of the students' corps, the *Burschenschaften*, and so the rift was widened, the government and the Jews on one side, the nationalistic students on the other. The students also had their spokesmen, and university professors such as the philosopher Jakob Friedrich Fries could publish an essay in the respected *Heidelberger Jahrbücher* entitled "How the Jews Endanger Germany's Prosperity".[2] The essay attempted to establish a connection between Jewish money and the tyranny wielded by the German princes over the people. Was there any such connection? It is doubtful. The reactionary excesses of 1819 which were euphemistically called the "persecution of the demagogues", had even included a pogrom, the last great German pogrom before Hitler. It is curious that the allegedly pro-Jewish governments permitted the rioting to go on and did not call out the army and police until the last moment—after fire had been set to a great many synagogues and houses. But perhaps this was not so curious if we accept the thesis of the American scholar Monkton Presley,[3] who contends that the anti-Semitic excesses may have been provoked from above in order to discredit the members of the German *Burschenschaften* throughout Europe. "The Germans", Ludwig Börne wrote clairvoyantly at the time, "should come to understand that certain people seduce them into the abuse of freedom in order to be able to say that they are unworthy of freedom."[4]

The great German popular uprising of 1848 found the Jews politically disunited. Among those who died in the March fighting and whose coffins were lined up in front of the Palace in Berlin, were more than fourteen Jews. On the other hand, the majority of Jews who were elected to the German parliament that sat in St. Paul's Church in Frankfurt in 1848–49 were conservatives who opposed any reduction in the power of

[2] J. F. Fries: *Über die Gefährdung des Wohlstands der Deutschen durch die Juden*. Heidelberg, no date.

[3] E. Sterling: *Er ist wie Du. Aus der Frühgeschichte des Antisemitismus in Deutschland* (1815–50). Munich, 1956.

[4] L. Börne: *Gesammelte Schriften*. Hamburg and Frankfurt, 1862.

the authoritarian state or any infringements upon property.[5] Neither they nor the Jewish Left had any inkling of the ghastly developments which would follow when the petty bourgeoisie struck up an alliance with the real powers in Germany, the landed proprietors and the industrialists.

A considerable body of pamphlets had already been written on the anthropological and spiritual differences between Jews and Germans. Karl Freigedank, an omnivorous reader, drew heavily upon them. But his accusation that the Jews were "ruining German music" was completely new. He ignored the fact that Beethoven had Jewish friends, he ignored the author who had written the song-cycle, *An die ferne Geliebte* for the master.[6] Did he know nothing of the vital friendship that linked E. T. A. Hoffmann, composer of *Undine*, with the Jewish lawyer Hitzig?[7] Was he oblivious of the innumerable Jewish musicians active in German orchestras? Had he forgotten the London performance of Weber's *Oberon*, in which the prototype of Christian chivalry, the hero, Huon of Bordeaux, was sung by a Jew—none other than Byron's friend John Abraham-Braham?[8]

Freigedank seemed unaware (or pretended to be) of the excellent and fruitful way in which Jewish and German artists had been working together for decades. For this is how he pictured the situation:

> Forthrightly repulsed in his efforts at contact with our people, at any rate wholly incapable of grasping the spirit of our race, the cultivated Jew sees himself forced back upon the roots of his own clan where ... understanding is more easily granted him. Willingly or unwillingly, he must draw upon this source; but he can only take method from it, not substance. The Jew has never had an art of his own—consequently has never possessed a life capable of having artistic content.

The Old Testament and the psalms, then, offer no evidence of artistic talent? Freigedank hypocritically concedes the point. But since the Jew knows nothing of the German folksong, the German art song and instrumental music, he remains entirely "dependent upon the melodic ornamentations and rhythms of synagogue singing". Such musical Hebraisms, Freigedank continues, might have been very beautiful in antiquity—but the present-day singers in the Jewish synagogues have made them into

[5] E. Sterling: op. cit.
[6] S. Kaznelson: *Beethovens Ferne und Unsterbliche Geliebte*. Zürich, 1955.
[7] W. Harich: *E. T. A. Hoffmann*. Berlin, 1921.
[8] A. Maurois: *Byron*. Paris, 1930.

repulsive caricatures. Moreover, even where a solemn divine service is in progress, one need only look at the faces of the worshippers to discover in what profane and indifferent spirit these people attend the synagogue. (Yet were the Christian congregations always so attentive?)

The Jew is different from the German, Freigedank continues as if he were writing an early edition of the *Völkischer Beobachter*. Whenever the Jew approaches German art, he does so "in an altogether superficial manner", able to reflect back only the chance elements in that art. Consequently, all Jewish music is bound to "strike a German as alien, cold, strange, indifferent, unnatural and distorted. Jewish musical works produce upon us the same sort of impression as would, for example, the recitation of a poem by Goethe in the Jewish jargon...." Julius Streicher could not have formulated that more pungently in his *Stürmer*.

And now comes a strange passage:

> What phenomenon can make all this clearer to us ... than the works of a composer of Jewish origin endowed by nature with a musical talent such as was possessed by few musicians before him? Everything that our study has laid bare concerning the antipathy between the Jewish character and the German character, all the contradictions of this character in itself and toward us ... combine to create a wholly tragic conflict in the nature, the life and the artistic works of the late and prematurely deceased Felix Mendelssohn-Bartholdy. He has shown us that a Jew can possess the richest abundance of specific talent, the finest and broadest culture, the most intense and sensitive sense of honour, without ever being able once to produce upon us a profound influence, an effect that moves the heart and soul ... such as we have felt innumerable times as soon as a stalwart of our own art ... merely opens his mouth to address us....

It is all put so elegantly, so obliquely with such deceptive good manners! This balanced tone and these refined arguments were used to damn not only Mendelssohn but also Gustav Mahler and numerous other Jewish composers who came later.[9] For what was Freigedank actually saying but: "Try your hardest—it's no use, for you're a Jew." A Jewish musician, he continued, could entertain us by novelties and acrobatic tricks. That was what Mendelssohn had done when "he catered to our amusement-hungry imagination, presenting us with a series or a pattern of the subtlest, smoothest figures, as in a kaleidoscope", ever-changing impressions of colours and forms. But these conceits could never arouse deep feelings in

[9] D. Newlin: *Bruckner, Mahler, Schönberg*. New York, 1947.

the human heart. "Only where the oppressive sense of this incapacity seizes upon the composer and drives him to the expression of weak and melancholic resignation, does Mendelssohn present his characteristic mood. ... This is, as we have said, a tragic trait.... And if in the field of art we were to lavish our sympathy upon personality pure and simple, we would not be able to withhold it from Mendelssohn."

In other words, the sadness, the profound melancholy so often expressed in Mendelssohn's oratorios, but also in his German folksongs, could be ascribed only to his being "a Jew who could not truly feel himself a German".

Distortion could scarcely go further! And though people with any reasonable degree of insight saw through these sophisms, the assertion was nevertheless deadly.

Karl Freigedank succeeded only too well with his cowardly shot from ambush at a deceased composer. And then, having disposed of Mendelssohn, he exhibited even greater cowardice. He turned upon Meyerbeer, likewise a Jewish composer, but without mentioning his name—for Meyerbeer was alive and extremely powerful. Freigedank set forth all the bad qualities of Meyerbeer as a composer, his facility, his love for glitter and cheap effects, his trivial melodies, and explained them by Meyerbeer's being a Jew. In doing this Freigedank involved himself in a ridiculous inconsistency—for if Mendelssohn's qualities were specifically Jewish, how could Meyerbeer, worlds apart from Mendelssohn, likewise be unequivocally Jewish? But Freigedank found a specious answer to this question: the lack of feeling in Meyerbeer, the absence of really truthful emotions, was also typical of Mendelssohn, who, however, compensated for this lack by exaggerated feeling, by "Jewish sentimentality". Sentimentality, then, was un-German despite its obvious presence in many of the songs of Schubert.

And now, at the end, the pseudonymous author turned—inevitably— upon Heinrich Heine, himself a pamphleteer. First Freigedank made use of Heine's jokes about Mendelssohn and Meyerbeer to support his dastardly thesis. Then Heine himself was tarred with the same brush. "No counterfeits deceived Heine; he was restlessly driven on by the inexorable demon of denial to negate everything that seemed worth negating, was propelled through all the illusions of modern self-deception to the point where he lied himself into the ranks of the poets and in recompense had his versified lies set to music by our composers."

That was an insult to Schubert and Schumann. It was also an insult to the composer Richard Wagner, who while in Paris had set to music the French translation of Heine's *Die beiden Grenadiere.*

CAN SUCH THINGS BE?

At this point one imagines that Wagner would be likely to enter the fray himself.

He was deeply interested in all the controversial questions of his time. An essay such as *Judaism in Music* could not escape his attention. Moreover, during his Paris days—in those trying years around 1840—he had associated with Jews a great deal and had formed close friendships with Jews. Why was he so attracted to them? Perhaps because they had certain characteristics which he believed himself deficient in. At an age when most other young men had long since decided who and what they were, Wagner was not sure whether he should be a painter, actor, poet or musician. "His youth", Nietzsche later wrote, "was that of a versatile dilettante who seemed to be going nowhere in particular."[1] The remarkable sureness with which his Jewish friends set about their life's tasks—whether in art, scholarship or business—must have impressed Wagner. No doubt his curious "overestimation of Judaism" dates from that period. To Wagner it seemed that the Jews "succeeded in everything". Had his judgment been somewhat clearer, he would have seen that that was not so; and that where it did happen to be so, the reason probably was that these people, disciplined by suffering, were temperate in their habits of life and exceedingly hard-working. They were self-controlled, and avoided any excesses which might "endanger their life-work".[2]

That sort of thing had no appeal at all for Wagner. He liked to be flamboyant. (Paul Bekker has pointed out that an element of histrionics entered into his excesses and enmities.[3]) For a while he made Paris his home. He railed at the Parisians, denounced their superficiality, their soullessness, their worship of success—but he stayed. His poverty, his idealism, his harmlessly melodramatic temperament, his love of animals, his devotion to his extremely pretty wife, his naïve way of running up debts, and his perennial optimism—all these traits were rather endearing.[4] There was no one who disliked him.

While in Paris, Wagner encountered the Young Germany movement.

[1] F. Nietzsche: *Unzeitgemässe Betrachtungen*. Leipzig, 1930.
[2] K. Rosenkranz: *Aus einem Tagebuch*. Leipzig, 1854.
[3] P. Bekker: *Wagner, das Leben im Werk*. Berlin–Leipzig, 1924.
[4] K. Gutzkow: *Briefe aus Paris*. Leipzig, 1842.

He sympathized with its ideas of socialistic liberation; he was attracted to
Heine and learned the technique of pamphlet-writing from him. He
thereupon became the Paris correspondent for the *Dresdner Abendzei-
tung*, contributing a series of articles that somehow fell short of the proper
tone for this sort of journalism.[5] He was not very good at light, witty,
sharp-minded commentary. But he had borrowed the legend of *The
Flying Dutchman*—from Heine's *Salon*—and thereafter he was almost
irrationally grateful to Heine. After all, Heine had done nothing except
give him his leave to use the Dutchman legend for operatic material—a
very small matter in a world where everyone plagiarized everyone else.
But from that moment, Richard Wagner was ready to go through thick
and thin with Heinrich Heine. Other Germans in Paris might wonder if
Heine's private escapades were not in dubious taste; Wagner was up in
arms if he heard as much as a word against his friend Heine. Even in the
sensational dispute that raged around Ludwig Börne after Börne's death,
Wagner ranged himself on Heine's side. Heine, he maintained, was "the
true pride of the German Fatherland in Paris". If he was now flat on his
back at a spa in the Pyrenees, it was because the malice of his countrymen
had made him ill. It was to be hoped that his sense of honour and his
sensitive spirit would survive these blows!

Wagner aired these and similar opinions in his newspaper articles. That
he fervently admired not only Heine's prose, but also and chiefly Heine's
lyrical poetry, shows that he was no especial judge of the latter. But as a
music critic he had no peer. He discovered the Jewish composer Halévy,
praising his *The Jewess* and later *The Queen of Cyprus*.[6] In view of the
kind of music he himself was to create, we may wonder at his enthusiasm
for Meyerbeer. There is, for example, the paean unearthed by Julius Kapp
in 1912 and to the consternation of all Wagnerians reprinted in the
magazine *Die Musik*. It is an essay on *The Huguenots*, three thousand
words in length; and carefully chosen words they are, clear and direct
in spite of the typical Wagnerian bombast centring around the word
"German".

> Meyerbeer wrote world history, history of hearts and feelings;
> he smashed the barriers of national prejudices, annihilated the
> confining limits of idioms. He wrote deeds in music—music such
> as Handel, Gluck and Mozart had written before him. Those
> men were Germans, and Meyerbeer is a German. And we ask, by
> what miracle has this German managed not to be entrapped in

[5] R. Sternfeld: *Aus Richard Wagners Pariser Zeit*. Berlin, no date.
[6] C. de Lorbas: *Fromental Halévy*. Paris, 1862.

the emotions of this or that assumed national mode, not to become lost in these modes after brief flashes of brilliance, and so not to become the slave of foreign influences.

He has preserved his German heritage, the naïveté of emotion, the chastity of invention. These virginally pure aspects of a profound sensibility constitute the poesy, the genius of Meyerbeer; he has preserved an unstained consciousness, an integrity that shines with a chaste glow behind the tremendous productions of an often highly subtle inventiveness, and that modesty reveals itself as the deep well from which all those impressive billows of the royal ocean were drawn.

. . . And is not that almost excessively vehement impulse toward religious statement in Meyerbeer's works a striking demonstration of the profoundly sincere intentions of the composer? And is that not precisely the trait that so movingly calls to mind his German birth?[7]

Meyerbeer deeply religious! And in *The Huguenots*, of all works! How could Wagner believe such nonsense? Here was the composer of *Rienzi* prostrating himself before the phenomenon of Meyerbeer in a manner which is altogether incomprehensible.

The Wagnerians, who could not but be embarrassed by all this, later asserted that Wagner had been forced to write in such excessive terms lest he lose the sponsorship of Meyerbeer in Berlin and Dresden. That statement was far from the truth. Meyerbeer was a Grand Seigneur—like Paganini and Liszt—who knew how to give without receiving. He was always well disposed towards Wagner and did everything in his power for both *The Flying Dutchman* and *Rienzi*.

But whether that paean to Meyerbeer was or was not dictated by opportunism, Wagner had taken his position, and when the scurrilous pamphlet *Judaism in Music* appeared, he should have come out and protested—if not on behalf of the late Mendelssohn, toward whom his relationship had never been really cordial (though also never chilly), at least on behalf of Meyerbeer and Heine.

But he said nothing. Was his silence due to his own personal and political difficulties in 1850? He had been forced to flee from Dresden because he had taken part in the uprising of May, 1849, had stood on the barricades and called upon the troops not to fire on the rebels. A warrant for his arrest had been issued. With the courageous and unselfish assistance of Franz Liszt, who was no revolutionary, Wagner had fled to

[7] J. Kapp: *Richard Wagners ausgewählte Schriften*. Berlin, 1914.

Zürich, where he found a generous patron in the Swiss-American silk magnate Wesendonck and his wife Mathilde.[8]

Unrebutted, the pamphlet smouldered and smoked in the German mind. Wilhelm von Lenz, the Beethoven scholar, accepted Freigedank's theses as if they were axiomatic, and in 1852 unburdened himself of the following thoughts in his *Beethoven and his Three Styles*:

> We believe that the Hebraic element detectable in the ideas of Mendelssohn stands in the way of his work's universal acceptance. The Hebraic nature, once fertile and powerful, is today a substance worn out by history.... The Jews often attain first rank where it is a question of developing mechanical adroitness or of applying knowledge intelligently.... That may be sufficient for a scholar.... But the real artist, the composer, is not derivative; it is his own nature which he must express. Yet the Hebrew mode of thinking has its own peculiar stamp. The music of Mendelssohn echoes the psalmodic chants of the synagogue, just as the Jewish spirit plays a part in his thinking.[9]

It is scarcely possible that a musicologist of that time did not know what every novice knows today: that the "chants of the synagogue" had been incorporated centuries before by the Church into Gregorian chant.[10] Lenz was therefore sliding over this fact. No one had ever found fault with Mendelssohn's "Jewish spirit", while he was alive, but now the venom quickly spread. Soon people were talking about the late composer's "un-Germanism" as if that were a settled point. From that it was only a step to asking whether he had not "long been overestimated". His delicate, classic-romantic tone.... The Biedermeier age was over, people wanted stronger, more revolutionary fare. When all was said and done, weren't the *Songs without Words* insipid stuff? Which way the wind was blowing could be seen in a poem of the nineties by Detlev von Lilienkron —a poem, moreover, which he called "Purification":

> The tall lieutenant with the decoration
> Sings a song by Felix Mendelmaier.
> The spinster hatches riddles, pokes the fire,
> Prepares the tea and breathes an incantation.
> "O Isis!" the basso roars like a town crier.

[8] R. Wagner: *Briefe an Otto Wesendonck, 1852–70*. Berlin, 1905.
[9] W. v. Lenz: *Beethoven*. Kassel, 1855.
[10] E. Nikel: *Geschichte des Gregorianischen Chorals*. Breslau, 1908.

How slowly goes the clock's perambulation.
It's over. God be thanked. My sole desire
Is Bach and Handel now, for purification.[11]

Lilienkron was no anti-Semite. But why the caricature "Mendelmaier"? And why did he not know that but for Mendelssohn's activities, the *St. Matthew Passion* might have been lost to music-lovers of the future?

But Wagner had no part in these later developments, for he had long been resting in his Valhalla. His great time was the fifties and the sixties, decades in which his restless genius had laboured on a mighty scale to create a new music-drama. Every work was a new experiment; the *Dutch-man, Tannhäuser, Lohengrin* were each unique in their own way. And then came the full plunge down untrodden paths, the period in which he wrote *Tristan*, the *Ring* and the *Meistersinger*. These works did not evolve successively, but side by side, frequently interesecting. Wagner's greatness lay not in the invention of the leitmotiv—for it had been used long before him—but in the genius with which he applied this principle. As Alfred Lorenz has shown in his studies,[12] the tensile forces in the ten-act vault of the *Ring* produced something that went beyond the "excess of sound" and the "simple pleasure in going on and on" which marred the work for certain critics. A wholly new type of harmony had been created and a melodic line "that brings out the full brilliance of this Wagnerian harmony."[13] Together these resulted in opera so deep and powerful and overwhelming that nothing like it had heretofore been known. Neither Gluck nor Monteverdi, however boldly those older musical dramatists had addressed their own times, had been as bold as this.[14] Wagner never achieved the same popular success as his old patron Meyerbeer, as was shown in 1861 by the demonstration of the influential Paris Jockey Club against those "wearisome pilgrim scenes" in *Tannhäuser*.[15] But did such trivialities really count? The more advanced Frenchmen, Gautier, Baudelaire, Mallarmé,[16] had long since affirmed their sympathy with the original and brooding qualities of Wagnerian music.

[11] D. v. Lilienkron: *Kämpfe und Ziele. Gesammelte Gedichte*, vol. II. Berlin, 1901.

[12] A. O. Lorenz: *Das Geheimnis der Form bei Richard Wagner*. Berlin, 1924–33.

[13] Ibid.

[14] H. Prunières: *La Vie et l'Œuvre de Claudio Monteverdi*. Paris, 1926.

[15] C. Servières: *Le Tannhäuser à l'Opéra 1861*. Paris, 1895.

[16] A. Liess: *Deutsche und französische Musik in der Geistesgeschichte des XIX. Jahrhunderts*. Vaduz, 1950.

In 1864 Meyerbeer died. And four years later, in 1868, with Meyerbeer dead, "Freigedank" lifted his mask, had his Jew-baiting pamphlet re-printed in a large edition, and gave his real name: Richard Wagner.

Can such things be! After eighteen years, Wagner acknowledged this pamphlet. He did not dismiss it as a youthful mistake, a piece of student brashness, an excess of which he was now ashamed. On the contrary, he gave it the sanction of his name—and in the intervening years the name of Richard Wagner had become known throughout the world, for his music-dramas were winning recognition such as none of his contempor-aries enjoyed. . . .

Can the inexplicable be explained? Various people have tried; they have constructed a kind of "theory of revenge". Primitive communities are vengeful, to be sure. But can a great artist like Wagner be considered primitive? And what had Mendelssohn ever done to Wagner to make him vengeful? Had Wagner taken offence when Mendelssohn conducted the *Tannhäuser* overture in Leipzig? True, the performance had revealed a basic lack of comprehension on the part of Mendelssohn, but any artist must realize that no one is compelled to understand his work. Mendels-sohn had treated the piece of music in a somewhat routine manner. As events proved, he would have been wiser never to have attempted it. But can such lack of true enthusiasm be represented as an underhand assault upon Wagner's art? From Minna Wagner's illegitimate daughter, Natalie Bilz-Planer, we learn the nasty fable current among people in Wagner's circle: that Mendelssohn, the slick, slippery Jew, had had the vileness de-liberately to mutilate and debase the score of the *Tannhäuser* overture so that the work was howled down at the London performance (to Natalie, Leipzig was the same as London) and could not be played through to the end.[17] Nevertheless, the malignant lie was believed. Wagner's own jealousy toward his great predecessor, and his guilty conscience at his own underhand act of malice, had to be justified retroactively.

But what about the hostile reception *Tannhäuser* had received in Munich, where it was performed under Court Conductor Lachner? The overture had been interrupted by shouts of protest and whistling. Was the late Mendelssohn also behind that foolish affront? Or when Swiss philistines were scandalized at *The Flying Dutchman* because Daland sold his daughter to a stranger for money and she broke her vow to her fiancé—was that likewise Mendelssohn's doing?

Or was Meyerbeer possibly the culprit? What was the real situation

[17] R. Wagner: *Briefe der Sammlung Burrell (1835–65)*. Frankfurt, 1953.

with Meyerbeer? Had he ever shown any animosity toward Wagner? Or rather, had he not helped wherever he could, and opened all doors to the younger man?[18] (Karl Friedrich Glasenapp's story that Meyerbeer wrote to the publisher Maurice Schlesinger, "Débarrassez vous de ce fou!" has long since been scotched by Ernest Newman.[19])

So there was nothing, nothing that justified Wagner's vicious act—unless it was his paranoia. It happens that anti-Semitism is one of those views which border on paranoia.

Group suspicion and group hatred are always madness. It is not easy to explain the genesis of Wagner's anti-Semitic feelings. There were actually few Jews among Wagner's opponents, and none who was influential—except, perhaps, for Paul Lindau who paid a visit to Bayreuth when the Wagner festivals were already a flourishing institution and wrote some unimportant anti-Wagnerian pamphlets.[20] But the famous critic Hanslick, the leading enemy of Wagner's music in Vienna, and a man of high integrity, was not Jewish; he was of Czech peasant origin.

Shall we then say that hatred of the Jews was not based on any special grievances but was simply part of Wagner's *Weltanschauung*? Perhaps that was it. But Wagner's work was always the supreme thing for him, far more important to him than his *Weltanschauung*. And his work sometimes entailed things that were not at all in accord with his general views on life.

We know that anti-Semites sometimes have good Jewish friends. That means little. Yet it remains curious that Wagner should have associated so closely with Jews, should have had them in his immediate following and even in his family. A Hitler or a Goebbels could not have done that.

Has anyone ever heard of Wagner refusing to have Jewish singers in his music dramas? Or expelling Jewish musicians from his orchestra—as he should have done, had he believed his own thesis as expressed in *Judaism in Music*? With hundreds of people looking on, he embraced Julius Lieban, who had sung the part of Mime. And what about his other intimates? There was Karl Tausig, the pianist, who made brilliant piano arrangements of the early Wagner operas, notably the *Meistersinger*—a fantastically complicated undertaking. When Tausig was suddenly carried off by typhus in Leipzig, a young man of barely thirty, he was mourned by the whole Wagner family. And there was Heinrich Porgres, the publicist and assistant director at Bayreuth. There was Angelo Neumann,

---

[18] J. Kapp: *Meyerbeer*. Stuttgart–Berlin, 1924.
[19] E. Newman: *The Life of Richard Wagner*. New York, 1933–46.
[20] P. Lindau: *Nüchterne Briefe aus Bayreuth*. Breslau, 1876.

who from sheer enthusiasm for the Master conceived the seemingly mad plan of founding a Richard Wagner Theatre and taking the whole *Ring* cycle on tour through all of Europe.[21] Through these tours North Germany and South Germany, England, Holland, Belgium, Austria, Italy and Russia were conquered for this difficult tetralogy, despite its complicated librettos. Angelo Neumann was a theatrical impresario of the highest rank. His close associate, Hermann Levi, was the greatest opera conductor of his time.[22] And Levi, the conductor of *Parsifal*, was the son of a German rabbi. Wagner had in fact innumerable Jewish allies; their loyalty and hard work were precious to him.[23]

Why then did not the ageing Wagner, with the struggle for recognition far behind him, do the one dignified, natural, human thing: repudiate the scurrilous pamphlet and *forbid* its further publication? But the author of *Parsifal* could not summon up the spiritual magnanimity to do so. For if his old anathema upon Jewish *composers* were lifted, then Mendelssohn and Meyerbeer would be restored to honour and popularity. And that must not be—for they were his rivals. What horrible frankness prompted him to say to Cosima, his second wife, about Mendelssohn: "Such a shadow does not grow. It can only vanish!"[24] Mendelssohn must remain in Hades, a suffering shade with bloodless face—as Thackeray had envisioned him back in the forties, when the world still called him *felicissimus*.

When Hiller and Eduard Devrient, two thoroughly modest and harmless persons, published their memoirs of the friend of their youth, Wagner fell upon them with a wolfish rage. Not, of course, that he revealed his true motive: his frenzied feeling that no one must even think about Mendelssohn. The violent attacks that Wagner published against Schumann, Brahms and Joachim—those pure and glorious musicians—were also based on the fact that they had been friends of Mendelssohn and had continued to honour his memory. Mendelssohn had to be extinguished. That was Wagner's resolve.

Several decades ago we had a conversation with Benedetto Croce. His remarks were full of remarkable insights concerning Wagner's inner nature. It was a mistake, he said, to consider Wagner as a nineteenth-century figure. What resemblance did he have to Beethoven or Schiller, with their moral idealism? Rather, Wagner was a Renaissance character, a contemporary of Leonardo da Vinci and Michelangelo—but above all of

---

[21] A. Neumann: *Erinnerungen an Richard Wagner*. Leipzig, 1907.

[22] T. W. Adorno: *Versuch über Wagner*. Berlin and Frankfurt, 1952.

[23] C. v. Westernhagen: *Richard Wagner. Sein Werk, sein Wesen, seine Welt*. Zürich, 1956.

[24] R. du Moulin Eckhart: *Cosima Wagner*. Munich–Berlin, 1929.

Benvenuto Cellini. Croce pointed out the parallels between Wagner and the brash, boastful character of Cellini as revealed in the latter's auto-biography. Cellini quotes a pope as saying: "Artists like Benvenuto Cellini are so extraordinary that they cannot be bound by the laws of the rest of humanity." In the name of his art, Cellini disdained neither slander nor murder. Even Goethe, who translated the *Autobiography* into Ger-man, had certain grave reservations about its hero: "This irascibility had the most unfortunate results. Excited to implacable rage by the most trivial cause, Cellini left city after city ... and the slightest offence to his property and his honour—*even when it was imaginary*—brought in its train bloody revenge. . . ."[25]

Envy, jealousy, paranoia. Even the *Rienzi* music—another Italian has written—music which is in many respects magnificent, has a demagogic quality. There is an element of violence in it, a disturbing revelation of Wagner's amorality, his Renaissance ruthlessness; in fact it points the way of Fascism.[26]

That may well be. Without a doubt Wagner's writings on culture fore-shadowed the ideology of National Socialism. The question has been deeply explored by a lover of Wagner's music, the French-Canadian critic André Hémois, and these are his conclusions:

> What damage Wagner's writings on culture have, incidentally, done his works of art. . . . What a barbarous jungle of concepts, of ideas ... knock their heads together within the confined space of one of his works? What did Schopenhauer's quietism, his Platonism, his pessimism, his comprehensive doctrine of suffer-ing, have to do with Feuerbach's materialism? What did both have to do with the theories of Bakunin, the Russian nihilist and Dresden revolutionary? Was not Schopenhauer's Nothing-ness something altogether different from Bakunin's? All these ideas assassinate one another, and the jungle is filled with the foetid odour of decay, as the corpses of ideas swell up and putrefy. How can all this be resolved into a unity, such as is basic to a humane, classically valid work of art? What an ego-obsessed muddlehead this man is! Only a few years ago—or were they months, or weeks?—Wagner opposes the nobility and contends that landed property is the most immoral power in the world; with revolutionary fervour he proclaims that the feudalism of the

[25] *Das Leben des Benvenuto Cellini.* Translated and edited by Goethe. Tübingen, 1803.
[26] G. Volpe: *Italia Moderna.* Florence, 1946–51.

Middle Ages was a crime. Immediately afterwards he pillories—
with considerable justice—the new powers of his age, money and
industry. Then he swings his whole life around, begins to grab
at money, cannot live without luxury, basks in the protection of
princes, while in his writings he goes to great lengths to explain
that he is in no way changed. One lie chokes off another. A new
jungle of treatises on art. The year 1870 arrives. He hurls a tasteless lampoon at the defeated French, a sneering comedy. He now
has a new craze: the Reich as it has just been established by
Bismarck. This, he decides, is to be a "redemption of the Germans". But Bismarck himself regarded it as nothing more than
a political fact whose permanence was highly dubious. Wagner,
however, hailed it as a "popular-religious miracle". Essay follows
essay. There is no subject on which he does not air his opinion.
... Why should the world be interested in his private opinions on
vegetarianism, art and climate, politics and race? Had he not
spent year after year on this windy philosophizing, he might
possibly have given us three or four more such glories as *Tristan*.
That alone is what concerns us today. That is the reason for our
shame and our sorrow—and that no one told him he was being
foolish, because he was the great Richard Wagner! As though a
sculptor, say, must also insist on being a botanist. As though a
mathematician could not reduce an empire to ruin by his rule.
This insane notion of a "pansophia" which would yield the
right answer in every given case. In this Wagner was a forerunner of Hitler. . . .[27]

Some of this sounds extreme—but Hémois was defending Wagner's
music, which he respected, against Wagner's worse self—against the dog-
matist who even in his own time aroused prophetic horror in such great
humanists as Gottfried Keller and Jakob Burckhardt. And a humanist
of our own day, Thomas Mann, has pointed out how often Hitler was
unfortunately able to appeal to the works of Wagner the writer.[28]

Littera scripta manet. The written word lives on. Alas, how durable is
the printed word! "Is not every word a seed that can generate a thousand
deeds? Hence an evil word is worse than an evil deed," the Chinese sage
has said.[29] How is it possible that Wagner's vicious essay on *Judaism in*

[27] A. Hémois: *Les Coupables.* Montreal, 1946.
[28] Thomas Mann: "Bruder Hitler" in *Altes und Neues.* Frankfurt,
1953.
[29] R. Wilhelm: *Chinesische Lebensweisheit.* Tübingen, 1950.

Music is still allowed to do its evil work, as if nothing had happened in the meanwhile? That it remains a part of his *Collected Writings*, and is reprinted without comment? That it can address a new generation as if it were part of the established canon of criticism? Can such things be? This is indeed incomprehensible.

Music, as history has shown, is by no means immortal. But it is the deepest expression of every age, and like the age itself, it has a right to a *natural death*. Felix Mendelssohn's music did not die a natural death. It was murdered. It must be resurrected. And until it too passes away—as will the music of his enemy Wagner, ultimately—may it give joy by its "halcyon beauty", its serenity, its gravity.

INDEX